Perspectives on Korean Dance

PERSPECTIVES ON KOREAN DANCE

Judy Van Zile

WESLEYAN UNIVERSITY PRESS

MIDDLETOWN, CONNECTICUT

Published by Wesleyan University Press, Middletown, CT 06459

Copyright © 2001 by Judy Van Zile

Printed in the United States of America

5   4   3   2   1

Library of Congress Cataloging-in-Publication Data

Van Zile, Judy
    Perspectives on Korean dance / Judy Van Zile.
        p.   cm.
    Includes bibliographical references.
    ISBN 0-8195-6493-1 (cloth : alk. paper) — ISBN 0-8195-6494-X (pbk.)
    1. Dance—Korea—History. 2. Folk dancing, Korean. I. Title.
GV1703.K7 V36 2001
793.3'19519—dc21   2001002709

Without the willingness of my late parents to allow me to pursue
what often seemed like strange and exotic undertakings,
the continual "why not" attitude of my husband and his unbelievable
support and patience in reading virtually everything I have ever written,
and the often unanticipated humor of our daughter,
my involvement with Korean dance would have been short-lived.
It is to my family that I dedicate this volume.

Contents

Illustrations

Plates (following page 168)

Preface

Romanization

The McCune-Reischauer system of romanization is used for Korean words and names, with several exceptions. (See Anonymous 1961.) "Shi" and "sshi" are used in lieu of "si" and "ssi" to more closely approximate the sounds represented by these Korean spellings. "Seoul" is used instead of "Sŏul," and "Ewha" instead of "Iwha" (for Ewha Woman's University), since these have become the standard spellings for the name of this city and institution. The common spelling of Park Chung Hee has been retained in the name of one of Korea's presidents, in lieu of Pak Chŏng-hŭi, and "Yi" is used in lieu of "I" for this common family name. For Korean authors who have published in English and used alternate romanizations for their names, the spelling used in the original publication is retained. In these instances, McCune-Reischauer spellings are provided in parentheses in the list of references cited. When such authors have published in both Korean and English, the McCune-Reischauer spelling is used for Korean language publications, and citations are cross-referenced so readers may locate all materials by a single author. A name list of individuals discussed in the text, but not including authors cited, is also provided. When individuals discussed in the text have become known by alternate spellings, these alternate spellings are included in the name list. Japanese romanization follows the Hepburn system, and Chinese the Pinyin.

Korean and Japanese Names

Korean and Japanese names are cited in the traditional manner—family name first and given name last, except for individuals who have taken English-language names. For Korean given names containing two syllables, the syllables are hyphenated. Because many Korean authors referred to share a common family name, both family and given names are used in in-text citations to avoid confusion.

Content

Several chapters are based on previous publications, in most instances with significant modification and updating. Acknowledgment is made to the following sources for permission to republish, or publish in modified form, portions of the text contained herein:

Chapter 1—Perseus Books Group ("The Many Faces of Korean Dance," in Donald N. Clark, editor. *Korea Briefing, 1993. Festival of Korea*. Boulder: Westview Press, in cooperation with the Asia Society, pp. 99–119)

Chapters 1, 4, and 9—Korean Cultural Center of the Consulate General, Los Angeles ("Dance in Contemporary Korea," *Korean Culture* (Fall 1991), "*Ch'ŏyongmu*: An Ancient Dance Survives," *Korean Culture* (Summer 1987), and "Halla Pai Huhm. Portrait of a Korean-American," *Korean Culture* [Fall 1993])

Chapters 1 and 5—Gordon and Breach Publishers ("For Men or Women: The Case of *Chinju Kommu*, a Sword Dance from South Korea," *Choreography and Dance*, Vol. 5, Part 1, pp. 53–70) and "New Trends in Korea," in Ruth and John Solomon, editors. *East Meets West in Dance. Voices in the Cross Cultural Dialogue*. Switzerland: Harwood Academic Publishers, pp. 239–252)

Chapters 6 and 7—Royal Asiatic Society, Korea Branch ("Movement in Shamanic Contexts: An Inquiry," in Keith Howard, editor, *Korean Shamanism. Revivals, Survivals, and Change*, Korea: Royal Asiatic Society, Korea Branch, 1998, and "Kim Ch'ŏn-hŭng: Portrait of a Performing Artist, *Transactions of the Royal Asiatic Society, Korea Branch*, Vol. 66, 1991)

Ch'ŏyongga (Song of Ch'ŏyong), which appears on page 21 of the 1981 volume *Anthology of Korean Literature From Early Times to the Nineteenth Century*, edited by Peter Lee, is reproduced here by permission of University of Hawai'i Press.

March 2001   J.V.Z.

Introduction

Lift your kaleidoscope to the light and gently turn it. When you stop, the jumble of colors and shapes transforms into a meaningful image from a particular time and place. Your eye transforms the pools of bright colors into attractive young women who float slowly through crisp geometric shapes in a large palace hall. The king sits on a dais with his visiting dignitaries, enjoying spicy meats and wine as the entertainers abruptly, yet delicately, flick their wrists to propel long sleeves upward. As the rich silk fabric falls gracefully to their sides, the dancers bend their knees and humbly lower their gaze. The evening's entertainment concludes with a danced game in which the brightly clad women attempt to throw small pincushion-like balls through a hole in a tall wooden gate in the center of the performing area. Those who succeed are rewarded with a flower; those who fail receive a stripe of black ink on the cheek.

Turn the kaleidoscope a notch and as the shapes become fixed in a new pattern discover four solemn Buddhist monks in gray robes with red capes draped over one shoulder. They each hold a large pair of gleaming metal cymbals. While reciting ancient Sanskrit chants they alternately bend and straighten their knees and noisily clang the instruments in their hands. When the chant ends they yield the space to two monks with elaborate chimney-shaped hats and long white sleeves that reach to the ground. As the monks gently wave their extended arms, their sleeves flutter like butterfly wings.

Another turn of the kaleidoscope reveals cartoonlike characters jauntily strutting about an open field, their faces covered with masks that provide caricatures of an old woman, a young coquette, and a sly, but flirtatious, old man. They cajole each other with risqué dialogue and mime that make you want to remove this sector of the kaleidoscope so children cannot find it.

Another turn and a large group of smiling women in long, flowing gowns abruptly snap their fans open and shut. They raise them overhead and lower them around their bodies in a constantly moving splash of color. They then group themselves in a tight circle and, while turning, spread their fans to touch the edges of those of their neighbors. In a carefully coordinated choreography they raise and lower the fans slowly to create a ripple that passes around the circle.

A final turn transports you to a video arcade where a teenager jumps from one spot to another on an electronic pad, trying to respond to rapidly changing arrows on a computer screen that guide him through movements of the latest popular dance craze.

The next turn of the kaleidoscope discloses four men and two women in tattered T-shirts and skintight blue jeans. Colored lights flash blindingly from one spot on the stage to another in counterpoint to head-throbbing sounds that challenge your notion of the difference between music and noise.

Although it may appear that each sector of the kaleidoscope transported you to a different part of the globe, this is not the case. Your feet have stayed firmly planted on South Korean soil, and despite the fact that there is no longer a king, the variety of dances performed today in Korea is, indeed, as myriad as the combinations and permutations of color and pattern created by the bits of metal or glass lying inside the kaleidoscope.

*   *   *

My first exposure to Korean dance occurred in 1971, the year I moved to an island in the middle of the Pacific Ocean to become a member of the dance faculty at the University of Hawai'i. I began taking lessons in Korean dance, a style of movement vastly different from the ballet, modern, Japanese, East Indian, and Indonesian dance forms I studied previously. Eight years later I visited Korea and began a journey that introduced me to some of South Korea's finest dance masters, political history that was the bane of my existence in high school and college, and old paintings documenting an ephemeral art form. I discovered that my first teacher was the daughter of one of Korea's most treasured dance personages. Later I had opportunities to study with her father, and many other important dancers and scholars, as I pursued my research.

During four periods of residence in Korea and numerous short visits, I found a fascinating array of dance styles that beckoned me to dig deeply to understand them. Along the way I encountered many challenges. No dance form can be separated from its cultural milieu: the events with which it is associated, the people who do it, the institutions that support it, the music, literature, and belief systems that contribute to its manifestation. I quickly came to discover the incredible intricacies of Korea's past: its intimate ties with China and Japan, the ravages it suffered during numerous wars, its embracing and rejecting of religious and philosophical practices as seemingly diverse as shamanism, Confucianism, Buddhism, and Christianity. I also discovered the significance of not only the Korean language, but of Chinese and Japanese, in attempting to disentangle an intriguing web of cross-cultural interconnections.

As I sought to make sense of my studies I wanted to pass on insights I gained, but periodically abandoned my efforts. It would require a historian-linguist-folklorist-musicologist-dance ethnologist-literary specialist-art historian-religion scholar, to name only *some* of the relevant modifiers, to present a complete picture of Korean dance. Rather than attempt a definitive text, therefore, I set out to present a series of diverse perspectives.

Perspectives stimulated by my own experiences, by conference themes that sparked my thinking, and by trying to read, increasingly, in many disciplines beyond my own, dance. Perspectives that would create an informative and provocative text. A text that in some ways would be incomplete or unsatisfactory in providing the full historical background of a single dance for the dance historian, in completely contextualizing a dance or dance event for the social or political historian, or in providing the deepest meaning of all components of a dance for the semiotician. I chose, instead, to present perspectives of a dance researcher who, with each perspective, could inform, suggest avenues for deeper investigation, and indicate the interrelatedness of cultural manifestations.

Despite the diversity of perspectives presented in the chapters that follow, there is a unifying theme. The thread running throughout is identity. Identity of dance styles and genres, of individual people, of an ethnic group, and of a country. This theme winds its way through periods of preservation and change in the nature of the dances performed, and through political, religious, and economic changes in a country whose transformation escalated exponentially at the end of the twentieth century. As changes of many kinds took place throughout the country, dance was sometimes recontextualized from the palace to the common people, from the sacred realm to the secular. A government policy focusing on globalization brought with it increased concerns with individual identity, and contributed to the emergence of a tension between modernizing and remaining unique. A tension that led to both preservation, or perpetuation, and change in dance.

The perspectives presented here highlight this tension. They provide an overview of the varieties of dance forms in Korea at the beginning of the twenty-first century and a conceptual examination of selected issues relating to terminology, history and historical documentation of dance, gender, the creation of new ritual systems, cross-cultural influences, immigrant traditions, and ownership of traditional art forms. Making links to important historical events, the fine arts, and changing cultural constructs, I explore the changes that have occurred in a number of important facets of dance in Korea, and show that dance cannot be separated from other events and structures in society.

Because I am concerned with understanding dance in its broad cultural context, it is necessary to move back and forth between dance as a movement event and the sociocultural events and beliefs of the society in which it is embedded. But as a *dance* researcher, my *entrée* is always dance. I am concerned, for example, not just with the historical events that have impacted dance, but with how those events have impacted the movements used in dance and the people who perform and observe dance.

In Part I, I provide three perspectives that give a broad overview of dance in Korea today. In Chapter 1, I present the diverse manifestations of dance, emphasizing their nature and touching briefly on historical background. Rather than provide a chronology of dance genres or an exhaustive history, the overview focuses on a sampling of the visual images created by dance in South Korea at the beginning of the twenty-first century, and one way of categorizing these genres. The categorization scheme launches the issue of identity by raising the question of precisely what constitutes Korean dance. The overview creates a backdrop against which to understand subsequent more theoretical discussions. I learned to do some of the dances described, and thus the discussion is informed not only by conventional modes of intellectual inquiry, but by kinesthetic modes as well.

In Chapter 2 I examine some of the terminology used by Koreans in talking about their dance. Historical and political events contributing to changes in this terminology are described, and meanings are related to the categorization scheme of Chapter 1. I am not concerned here with an exhaustive examination of terminology, but with suggesting the influence of politics on words, the challenge of sorting out some of the contributions to the contemporary dance scene, and the changing identity of Korean dance as exemplified in terminology.

In Chapter 3 I describe a Korean-government system for perpetuating what is considered to be the heritage of the past, a system for officially recognizing important dances and dancers. The establishment of this system following the Japanese occupation of Korea is described, together with the role it plays at the beginning of the twenty-first century. By examining the system from the perspective of ritual, the issue of identity again emerges in relation to the way the system fixes the nature of dances to which it accords recognition and facilitates the passing on of standardized choreography.

I then move on, in Part II, to a closer look at several aspects of Korean dance. In Chapters 4 and 5 I focus on Ch'ŏyongmu and Chinju Kŏmmu, two dances the government has selected for official recognition to assure their preservation for succeeding generations. Both developed from ancient roots, and both have ties to court and village traditions. While both display features clearly identifying them as Korean dances, each is unique in some of the movements used and in the way it evolved. The discussion documents the dances as they are performed today and attempts to piece together events leading to their present manifestations. I trace the historical backgrounds and gradual transformations in both form and function, analyze iconographic documentation of one of the dances, analyze movement characteristics of one in relation to gender, and describe, in detail, how space is used in each of the dances. In the end, a variety of contributors to the identity of each of the dances emerges. For both dances, because I learned to perform them, the discussion is informed by my kinesthetic understandings.

In Chapter 6 I examine the use of movement in several contexts intended to suggest shamanism and shaman rituals. The concern here is not with any specific shaman ritual, nor with the complex layers of symbolism involved in ritual contexts, but with how shamanism is represented in

nonshamanic contexts. I emphasize the importance of looking at movement to see precisely how it is used as functions of dance change and
issues of identity continue.

In Chapter 7 I examine selected facets of the life of Kim Ch'ŏn-hŭng,
a former court dancer and senior figure in the Korean dance world who
has lived through extraordinary changes in Korean society and dance.
The intent here is not to provide a definitive biography, but rather to let
the personal story of selected life experiences elucidate the complex interactions between daily activities and dance—interactions contributing
to how one individual chooses to identify himself and his role in the
dance world.

With the shrinking of the globe, Korean dance has spread beyond the
shores of the Korean peninsula. Korean dancers have performed abroad,
and dancers from other countries have performed and taught in Korea.
As Koreans emigrated to other countries, they took with them aspects of
their heritage and perpetuated, in new lands, what they chose to retain.
These cross-cultural enterprises contribute to a need to reassess the identity of Korean dance. What is retained? What is put forward as an identity marker in a new locale? What is affected by influences from dancers
and dances of other countries? What role does dance play in making the
statement, "This is Korean," or "I am Korean"?

In Part III I look at two situations involving Korean dance beyond the
shores of South Korea. In Chapter 8 I examine the American reception of
Ch'oe Sŭng-hŭi, a highly political figure who performed under her Japanese name of Sai Shoki in the United States just prior to the start of World
War II. Ch'oe brought to the United States a changing style of Korean
dance, one influenced by a Japanese colonial presence in Korea as well
as by contemporary developments in the western dance world. But her
American audiences were likely unaware of precisely what they were seeing, and read into her performances their own vision of Korean dance. As
Ch'oe responded to audience reaction, she modified her repertoire. When
she returned to Korea, this repertoire had a significant impact on developments there. In this instance the identity of Korean dance changed as it
was affected by a complex web of cross-cultural and personal influences.

In Chapter 9 I explore the role of Korean dance in one American community. In Hawai'i Korean dance serves as an identity marker, a function
that raises issues regarding which dances are performed, the individuals
who perform them, and the individuals who teach them. Korean dancers
in Hawai'i have maintained close links with some dancers in Korea, but
they have often retained older styles of dance while those in Korea have
moved on. Largely perpetuated in Hawai'i by a woman of Korean heritage and her students, the continuation of her studio, upon her death, by
a non-Korean poses intriguing questions about cultural ownership. In
this case, the identity of the dance as well as those who do it and pass it on
are brought into question. As in several other chapters, the content here is
based on participant-observation: I studied at the studio for several years,

participated in studio activities, and continue to observe studio classes and public events.

I conclude, in the Afterword, by emphasizing the importance of looking at Korean dance from many perspectives, and the necessity of examining dance in relation to the larger culture of which it is a part. Because dance is always changing, future research that adds to the diverse perspectives presented here will continue to enhance the understanding of the changing identity of Korean dance.

A few of the chapters, or portions of them, particularly those relating to movement analysis and Korean terminology, are, of necessity, rather technical. I hope they are presented in a sufficiently accessible manner so that, with a bit of perseverance, they will be appreciated by a broad readership. In addition, the introductory and concluding remarks in these chapters should be understandable independent of the more technical analyses that support them. While each chapter may be read and understood independently and in any sequence, understanding will be deepened by reading the volume in the order presented.

The focus throughout is on information obtainable and the situation of dance in the Republic of Korea, commonly referred to today as South Korea. While some historical information relates to Korea in the days when it was unified, the inaccessibility of information on dance in North Korea (Democratic Peoples Republic of Korea) requires the emphasis taken here.

* * *

Few texts result from the efforts of a single person. With apologies in advance to individuals or organizations inadvertently overlooked, I wish to acknowledge those who have contributed in important ways to the research and writing resulting in this volume. I am grateful to Daniel Cole, Alan Heyman, Chu Yŏn-hŭi, Kim Sŭng-ja, Yi Chun-hae, Yi Yŏng-nan, Gary Rector, Yu Ran, Sohn Ho-min, Ŭm Hae-gyŏng, Alexander Vovin, and the late Tim Warnberg, all of whom provided valuable translation assistance during research; to the countless Korean dancers and scholars who answered unending questions, particularly Kim Ch'ŏn-hŭng, Chung-won Meyer (Kim Chŏng-wŏn), the late Halla Pai Huhm, Chŏng P'il-sun, Sŏng Kye-ok, the late Chang Sa-hun, Mary Jo Freshley, Han Man-yŏng, and Yi Hye-gu; to Gary Rector and Brian Barry for friendship, inspiration, and knowledge of Korean ways; to Edward Shultz for a reading of the manuscript with the eyes of a Korean historian; to Barbara B. Smith and members of my writing groups, who provided comments on early drafts of various chapters; to friends and colleagues at the Bellagio Study and Conference Center for inspiration; and to Mary Sweeney and Lucy Venable, who helped check the dance notation scores upon which much of the movement analysis contained herein is based. I am grateful to Choi Haeree (Ch'oe Hae-ri) and Kim Ŭn-hŭi for research and translation assistance, and for stimulating conversations during and after their graduate work at the University of Hawai'i; to Gary Rector, Kim Ŭn-hŭi and Pak In-kyu, for assistance in romanization and in compiling the name and terminology lists; and to Brian Barry for detective work and assistance in obtaining permission to reproduce some of the photographs. Portions of some chapters were originally presented at conferences or were published in earlier versions. I am grateful for questions and comments from publishers and audiences that, in many instances, contributed to the refinement of ideas. While the information and insights offered by these people were invaluable, I am solely responsible for the content of this volume.

I am also grateful to the Korean Culture and Arts Foundation (Han'guk Yesul Munhwa Chinhŭngwŏn), Academy for Korean Studies (Han'guk Chŏngshin Munhwa Yŏn'guwŏn), Korean-American Educational Foundation (Fulbright Program), International Cultural Society of Korea (Han'guk Kukche Munhwa Hyŏphoe), and the University of Hawai'i at Mānoa's Center for Korean Studies, without whose financial assistance my travels to Korea would not have been possible; to the Rockefeller Foundation, for providing a residency at their Study and Conference Center in Italy that enabled significant progress on selected chapters; and to the University of Hawai'i, whose several offices provided travel funding to present selected material in this volume to a broad range of conference audiences. Acknowledgment is also made to the Hawai'i Council for the Humanities, an affiliate of the National Endowment for the Humanities, and the Korea Foundation (Seoul), for funding assistance that facilitated the inclusion of the large number of illustrative materials. Research was carried out in Korea during four extended periods of residence from 1979 to 1990, and during numerous shorter stays since 1990. It is based heavily on *in situ* participant-observation and direct interaction with contemporary practitioners, scholars, historians, and individuals involved with dance in various ways.

Part One

A BROAD VIEW

I

The Many Faces of Korean Dance

On October 16, 1990, I sat in the Munye Theater watching a performance that was part of the twelfth Seoul Dance Festival. Initially I was struck by the stage set—a backdrop of three-dimensional, quite realistic trees. At first they swayed gently; then they became agitated, as if rustling in a winter storm; the lighting changed to red while crackling sounds contributed to the effect of a forest fire; finally, all became calm again.

A lone male dancer, clad in pants and jacket clearly inspired by the attire of aristocrats of former times (*yangban*), appeared to wander through a forest. His movements could have come from anywhere—England, the United States, Japan. But in a moment I was very definitely in Korea; the meandering stopped as the dancer placed both feet together, torso tilted forward a bit, and knees slightly bent. As he faced the corner of the stage he straightened one knee and lifted the other forward, ankle bent and toes turned up. With one arm he delicately grasped the edge of his jacket and pulled it back just a little. The other arm reached forward creating a counterpoint to the lifted leg that forced the torso to twist. The movement was held in animated suspension. Amidst the contemporary, realistic stage set, and movements that could have emanated from almost any geographic locale, I was suddenly in the heart of older Korean dances—watching a movement that can be seen again and again in sŭngmu, often referred to in English as the monk's drum dance, and salp'uri, a type of dance believed by many to be rooted in shaman ritual.

As the dance continued I was transported alternately between a kind of geographic any-man's-land and Korea. Just when I had settled comfortably into a forest that could have been near my hometown in the United States, I was suddenly taken back to Korea, seeing isolated moments of dances that are usually identified by Koreans as traditional dance (*chŏnt'ong muyong*). An arm lifted to descend lightly with the hand almost caressing the back of the head, an inwardly turned arm lifted sideward at shoulder height with the wrist relaxed so the hand trailed slightly behind, or a movement stopped with a suspension, as if the dancer inhaled quickly, to be followed by a release as the movement relaxed downward. This piece that seemed to keep shifting geographic locales was called Bamboo (Tae). It was choreographed by Min Chun-gi, a member of the Myŏngji University dance faculty.

Later in the week I attended another festival performance. In the first piece a lone male in a costume of a design derived from the attire of Korean Buddhist monks executed prayerlike gestures. Then a group of similarly clad women entered, performing the same gesture walking *en pointe* as in classical ballet. Throughout the piece there were shifts between prayerful movements and *pointe* work and the long, lean lines of ballet, with the occasional interjection of the rounded, suspended movements of traditional Korean dance.

The second piece opened with a tableau of male and female dancers in varied relationships, the men in tights, snug-fitting bolero jackets, and ballet slippers, the women in dresses of various lengths and *pointe* shoes. There was no fluctuation in dance style. I could have been at a ballet theater anywhere in the world. My Korean colleague said both dances were part of an afternoon of ballet.

The next day I braved the crowded Seoul subway to go to Chamshil, south of the Han River, for an afternoon at the Seoul Nori Madang. This delightful outdoor amphitheater comes alive in the afternoon with performances, usually masked dance-dramas, that have popular appeal.

I watched as the musicians and dancers of Kosŏng Ogwangdae danced around the periphery of the circle in an opening processional. This dance-drama form originated in the city of Kosŏng, near the southeastern tip of the Korean peninsula. Primarily through satire it tells of contempt for the privileged upper class, an apostate monk, and the triangular relationship of a husband, wife, and concubine.

As the drum rhythms became more accentuated and the dancers each took a turn in an introductory solo, my gaze shifted to the audience. There was a sharp contrast to the viewers I had seen at the Munye Theater. There the audience members were mostly young girls, probably college age, with a sprinkling of young men. The few older people were identified by colleagues as primarily dance teachers. At the Nori Madang the audience seemed to be a random sampling plucked from the streets, subways, and buses. Or perhaps not quite so random; this time the scales were weighted with older people, particularly men. A surprising number of cameras was poised to bring home memories of the masks and story. And there were many faces darkened from outdoor lives and creased with the lines of age. Although western-style dress predominated, the audience was dotted with men and women in traditional Korean attire (*hanbok*).

What initially pulled my eyes away from the central performing space, however, was not the composition of the audience, but dance. As the drum rhythms became more incessant, some of the older audience members were drawn to move. In time to the drum beat they began to lift and lower their shoulders, a movement that is one of the most prevalent features of much Korean dance, and that is described by Koreans as the "shoulder dance," *ŏkkae ch'um*. Gradually the dancers lifted their arms sideward, wrists relaxed and hands softly pointing downward. One woman took out a handkerchief and gently manipulated it in a manner reminiscent of the long flowing scarf used in *salp'uri*. Some people left their seats and ventured into the formal performing space. An elderly gentleman braced himself momentarily and then lifted one knee—a novice's attempt at the same movement performed by a trained dancer at the Munye Theater.

A *hanbok*-clad grandfather (*haraboji*) who had become a dancer walked back toward his seat, but not to sit down. Instead, he cajoled his companion, trying to lure another dancer into the arena.

Ten years later I saw a similar array of performances during a one-week stay in Seoul. As I headed back one evening to the dormitory where I was staying, I stopped at the open door of a dimly lit room where the latest popular music blared deafeningly. Alongside teenagers manipulating buttons and levers to play video games were youngsters frantically jumping in hopscotch-like patterns. Each stood on a small platform with footprints placed on a grid. And each watched a computerized screen positioned at eye level as arrows pointing in different directions rolled past. The mission? To respond in time to the music and, according to the directions, to learn the latest in techno-dance. This was DDR, Dance Dance Revolution, the latest dance import from Japan.

*   *   *

If you wish to see dance in Korea you have to make choices. Should you visit one of the theaters of the National Center for Korean Traditional Performing Arts (Kungnip Kugagwŏn) for a sampling of older forms of music and dance from the court and the villages? Go to the outdoor arena of the Nori Madang and watch masked performers relate, through speech and movement, a traditional story about a supposedly celibate Buddhist monk and his cavortings with a young maiden? Sit in the plush red seats of the Little Angels Theater to see a traditional Korean story performed by lithe female dancers wearing *pointe* shoes and muscular male dancers in tights and tunics? Purchase tickets for a performance at the Munye Theater in the trendy student section of Taehangno to observe the latest creations of a young Korean dancer nursed on traditional Korean dance forms, reared on modern dance at an American institution, and set loose to express deep-seated emotions and current concerns? Or don whatever youthful attire you can muster and join the latest dance craze?

Dances performed today in Korea range from those that have a distinctively Korean identity to those that do not, with clusters centering around specific categories named by Koreans themselves. These categories may be placed on a continuum, with one extreme containing "traditional dance" (*chŏnt'ong muyong*) and the other western-style ballet, modern dance, and popular trends.[1] Dances falling between these two categories are not as easily labeled. In fact, there has been considerable debate among Koreans over some of the most appropriate terminology for dances that fall within this "middle ground." (The terms and debate are described in Chapter 2.) For convenience, I discuss the dances in this middle ground under three groupings. The first I identify as "derived dances" because of their origins in older dances. The second I identify, like most Koreans, as "creative dance" (*ch'angjak muyong*), which is actually a unique kind of derivative dance. And the third, "social dance," is mentioned only briefly to identify a kind of dance that, until very recently, has not become as prevalent in Korea as it has in other parts of the world. This terminology should only be considered a convenience, however, for establishing both shared and distinctive features of Korea's dance landscape at the beginning of the twenty-first century.

In addition to describing sample dances, the overview here includes a bit of historical background to contextualize their development. The purpose is not to offer a definitive history of dance in Korea, but rather to show the variety of kinds of dances still performed. This serves as a backdrop against which to view the theoretical issues presented in later chapters. Korean-language terminology is minimized here in an effort to emphasize the dances themselves. English-language glosses are used wherever possible, with Korean terms placed in parentheses. Terminology is dealt with at greater length in Chapter 2, and details of selected dances and issues are discussed in subsequent chapters.

The Heritage of the Past: Traditional Dance

The variety of dances classified by Koreans as traditional dance (*chŏnt'ong muyong*) differ in both the contexts and manner in which they were originally performed. What unifies them in the minds of Koreans is the belief that most have been passed on over a long period of time and that they reflect the uniqueness of Korean culture. One key to former support for many of these kinds of dances was the royal court, which, at different times, nurtured some dances for entertainment and others for ritual purposes. In the context of entertainment, dances were performed for the pleasure of local and visiting dignitaries. Elaborate palace banquets included grand spectacles that not only entertained but also demonstrated wealth and power. Extant paintings and written texts portray large numbers of dancers clad in rich, colorful costumes moving through precise geometric formations to the accompaniment of music played on diverse and elaborate instruments. During some periods the dancers portrayed are men, but more frequently they are women.[2]

Court entertainment dances are generally classified into those said to have originated in China (*tangak chŏngjae*—the name taken from China's T'ang dynasty, 618–907) and those said to have originated in Korea (*hyangak chŏngjae*). This classification is a reminder of early political interactions between China and Korea, which included a visit by a group of Korean performers sent to China during the Unified Shilla period (668–935) who returned with musical instruments, dance properties, and costumes. Later, in 1116, a complete music and dance ensemble from the Chinese court visited Korea. Although such interchanges might suggest substantive differences in the two kinds of dance, documents such as the 1493 Guide to the Study of Music (*Akhak kwebŏm*; music was assumed to include dance), which contains detailed dance descriptions, and the manner in which the dances are performed today, attest to a difference in overall format but little difference in the movements themselves. In the dances of Chinese origin, a formal procession by individuals holding various kinds of standards precedes and follows the dance, the dance name is announced, and the dance is interrupted for a brief song sung in Chinese by the dancers; in the dances of Korean origin, the dancers begin with a bow to the king and brief song sung in Korean praying for his happiness, and end with a bow to the king, but there are no standard bearers or processions. Any early movement differences between the dances of Chinese origin and those originating in Korea no longer exist.

Most of the court dances performed today involve large numbers of dancers moving elegantly through circle, square, and line formations (Plate 1). They generally wear colorful costumes in the bright hues reserved, in the past, for royalty. The long sleeves of stiff, multicolored silk, which reach almost to the ground, are considered by some to be related to the long sleeves used in Chinese opera forms. With arms frequently extended sideward, the dancers walk, almost as if floating, while gently bending and extending their knees. They punctuate their movements with flicks of the wrist that gently propel their sleeves upward and outward. The ensemble that provides accompaniment for court dances is comprised of traditional wind, string, and percussion instruments. (Although many instruments used in the court originated in China, they became so integral to Korean music that they are often considered Korean.) The conductor plays the *pak*, an instrument with six slats of wood fastened at one end with a leather thong (Plate 2). He contributes to the visual picture, standing motionless at the side of the performing space, and moving only when necessary to signal the beginning and ending of a piece and transitions between sections by spreading the slats apart and then snapping them shut to provide a loud clap.

The movements of some court dances are literal, as in Beautiful Women Picking Peonies (Kain Chŏnmoktan) (Plate 1). Said to depict the pastimes of court women, the dancers move around a large vase containing flowers that they eventually pick and hold while dancing. Another court activity is depicted in The Ball Playing Dance (P'ogurak). This time the dancers try to throw small, pincushion-like balls through a hole in a simulated gate. Those who succeed are rewarded with a flower; those who fail receive a black stripe painted on the cheek.

Many court dances are more abstract. The Nightingale in Springtime (Ch'unaengjŏn), one of only two extant solo court dances, suggests the quality of a nightingale through its delicate movements; the gentle, sometimes wavelike motions of the arms, often extended sideward, are birdlike, but there are no movements that mime the flapping of wings or the soaring of a bird (Plate 3).

Two of the court dances performed today are quite distinctive because the dancers wear masks. The Crane Dance (Hangmu) is believed to have ritualistic origins. For Koreans, the crane is a symbol of longevity that figures prominently in paintings and embroidery. In the version of this dance performed today, two dancers in realistic crane costumes that extend over their heads to form a kind of headdress, concealing the entire torso, arms, and head, execute pantomimic movements of flying, roaming through fields, and pecking at food (Plate 4). Historical sources indicate The Dance of Ch'ŏyong (Ch'ŏyongmu) was also once part of rituals to expel evil spirits at New Year, and that it was performed out-of-doors (Plate 5). Five dancers said to represent the directions (north, south, east, west, and center) wear large masks suggestive of Ch'ŏyong, a son of the Dragon of the Eastern Sea. At some time The Dance of Ch'ŏyong was brought into the court, where it was transformed into a dance done purely for entertainment and became part of a suite of dances that included The Crane Dance. (Ch'ŏyongmu is discussed more fully in Chapter 4.)

The dances previously performed in the court are done today in concert settings in theaters, where they are perpetuated primarily by dancers and staff members of the National Center for Korean Traditional Performing Arts (until 1988 known in English as the National Classical Music Institute, and then the Korean Traditional Performing Arts Center). The Center traces its roots to the end of the fourth century via a royal music institute in the palace. The institute moved several times when the government was relocated, but in 1955 it became independent and was established in Seoul. The Center's original goals were to preserve and transmit court dance and music, but in the late twentieth century they were broadened to include the fostering of all forms of traditional dance and music as well as new creations. The Center is best known, however, for its court repertoire. The original court dances are believed to have been quite long, and full performances are rarely given today. Every Saturday throughout most of the year the Center presents a ninety-minute program of excerpts from the traditional dance and music repertoire, each being approximately ten to twenty minutes long. It is only here that one can regularly see the slow, stately movements of brightly attired women in dances reconstructed from old documents describing court festivities.

Court dance repertoire is also taught at universities that offer a dance curriculum. As part of ongoing activities, students occasionally perform selections from the extant repertoire. Adaptations, some more extreme than others, of what are believed to be the most historically accurate versions of court dances are performed by many companies purporting to do traditional Korean dance.[3]

Besides dances for entertainment, the royal court also supported dances that continue, today, to serve ritual purposes associated with Confucianism—again a reminder of influences from China. Although Confucianism entered Korea from China as early as the fourth century A.D., it did not become official orthodoxy until the Chosŏn dynasty (1392–1910), when it replaced Buddhism as the state's main philosophical tenet. Although Confucian dances are sometimes categorized as ritual dances because of the occasions on which they are performed, many Koreans prefer to identify them as court dances because of their early sponsorship (see Chapter 2). Confucian dances were originally performed several times a year at memorial services. Today these dances take place three times a year: twice (in the second and eighth months of the lunar calendar) to honor Confucius, and once (in May) to honor the spirits of Chosŏn dynasty rulers (Plate 6). They are perpetuated primarily at shrines in central Seoul, and are performed by students of the National High School of the Performing Arts (Kungnip Kugak Kodŭng Hakkyo) and descendants of the royal Chosŏn lineage.[4]

Despite the slightly different reasons for which these dances were traditionally done, there is little difference in their performance today. Dancers are large groups of older men or, in the case of performances by students of the performing arts school, young boys and girls. They perform in a square formation of precise rows and columns, today usually eight rows and eight columns, or sixty-four performers in all. The number of performers originally depended on the rank of the individual in the audience for whom the dances were performed: sixty-four dancers for an emperor, thirty-six (six rows and six columns) for a feudal lord or baron, four (two rows and two columns) for a ranking government official or lesser aristocrat. The dancers execute simple arm movements and bows to a slow, consistent tempo. The stark movement simplicity and ponderous tempo contribute to a meditative and highly ritualistic atmosphere. The performers hold symbolic implements: For dances classified as "civil" (*munmu*), a stick with a dragon's head and pheasant feathers in one hand and a flute in the other symbolize peace and prosperity; for dances classified as "military" (*mumu*), an ax and mallet or wood sword and spear symbolize war.

Masked dance-dramas (*t'alch'um*) were at one time associated with the court, but originated in conjunction with village shaman rituals and eventually became largely an entertainment form for commoners. They evolved to cleanse houses and villages, afford protection from calamities, and assure good crops. Their support from the court varied. During the Koryŏ dynasty (918–1392), the court maintained an Office of Masked Dance-Drama (Sandae Togam) and some dances were performed at royal banquets; during the Chosŏn dynasty, probably because of the new importance of Confucian values, the office was abolished. Despite former occasional affiliations with the court and frequent performances today in large cities, masked dance-dramas are still closely associated with villages. There are many regional variants, but most revolve around humorous themes that allowed the people of former times the opportunity to poke fun at things they would normally not discuss in public: liberties taken by ostensibly serious, wholesome monks; frivolous rompings of upper-class noblemen; and bawdy activities of matchmakers (Plates 7 and 8). As performed today, masked dance-dramas perpetuate the traditional satirical stories of the past but also occasionally incorporate references to important contemporary individuals or events. Performers serve as caricatures who strut and dance as they sing and engage in sometimes risqué dialogue that creates a lively atmosphere in which audience members shout their delight at peak moments.

Although masked dance-dramas are most frequently performed today in formal settings by government-recognized master performers and their students, they are a popular activity among university students, who sometimes perform them on campuses. This interest originated with the student nationalism of the 1980s, one aspect of which was a movement to heighten Korean cultural consciousness and revive or strengthen the performance of traditional dance forms. Masked dance-dramas are also sometimes used to make political statements during times of unrest.[5]

Farmers' band dance and music (nongak)[6] is another traditional form with strong connections to villages (Plates 9 and 10). Believed by some to be the oldest form of dance in Korea and to have shamanic origins, this is a loud, extremely vigorous performing tradition originally engaged in by farmers in conjunction with agricultural events. Performers paraded through villages, then stopped in large open areas to perform, while playing wind instruments, drums, and gongs that created a piercing cacophony as they danced. In farmers' band dance and music, as in many Korean dance forms, the interplay between dance and music, and dancers and musicians, is particularly important: Dancers play musical instruments and musicians perform highly stylized movements. Dancers play several varieties of drums, ranging from a small handheld drum (sogo) to a large hourglass-shaped drum (changgo), the latter fastened to their bodies with sashes around the waist and shoulder. A musician playing a harsh sounding brass gong (kkwaenggwari) skips and leaps at the head of the group as the ensemble's conductor. A highlight of farmer's band dance and music is the performance of dancers wearing a tightly secured hat with a small flexible rod (sangmo) in the top that can revolve. Affixed to the rod is a long streamer. With continuous, small, strong, abrupt movements the dancers rapidly tilt their heads forward, to one side, backward, and then the other side, causing the streamers to whip through the air as they trace large circular designs in space. They may also play the small handheld drum and fly through the air in gymnastic aerial turns, all simultaneously.

Today farmers' band dance and music, like masked dance-dramas, is performed by government-recognized masters and their students, by groups of villagers who gather for entertainment and to maintain community spirit, and by students from elementary through university levels. It has also been used for political purposes by labor unions and campaigning politicians.

The shamanism that contributed to the development of masked dance-drama and farmers' band dance and music also gave rise to dance and stylized movement that remain a part of shamanic rituals. Although not always looked on favorably by the government, shamanism has never disappeared and is practiced today in both villages and large cities. "Clients" who enlist the services of a shaman to heal the ill, appease the spirits of the deceased, or thwart other negative forces, participate in elaborate rituals including food and monetary offerings, singing, and dancing (Plate 11). Singing is generally done by the shaman, who in most regions is female, and who also engages in various forms of structured movement.[7] Stylized movements are often used when the invoked spirits descend and speak through the shaman, or when the shaman approaches clients while holding out a fan to solicit monetary offerings. At climactic moments the shaman will insist that the client don special clothing, execute movements similar to those of other traditional dance forms, and jump up and down. As in masked dance-dramas, regional variants of the rituals and movements used in shamanic activities abound. Shaman dances are still performed by practicing shamans in the context of rituals. Even though the values of a highly modernized society tend to reject shamanistic practices, at the beginning of the twenty-first century women wearing the highest fashions of Europe, and businessmen in sleek western suits, consult shamans. Many Koreans believe shaman movement has had the most pervasive impact on all types of traditional Korean dance, a view likely rooted in nationalistic perspectives emphasizing the uniqueness of Korean shamanism as a way to separate Korea culturally from Japan (Janelli in Yang Jong-sung 1994:25.)

Formalized movements are also found in the traditional dances of Buddhist rituals. Buddhism was introduced from India via China in the fourth century A.D. It became the official national religion during the Unified Shilla period. Buddhist dances were originally performed by monks, usually in large open courtyards at shrines, to the accompaniment of ritual chant and recitation (*pŏmp'ae*), and originated in India, Buddhism's homeland. Only four Buddhist dances are performed today. The Butterfly Dance (Nabich'um) is believed by some to be symbolic of the spreading of the Buddha's will in all directions. Performing either solo or as a duet, the dancers wear white cloaks with extremely long sleeves. They move slowly, bending and extending their knees as their lifted arms sweep gently forward and backward like the wings of a butterfly in slow motion. The Cymbal Dance (Parach'um) is also said to spread the word of the Buddha (Plate 12). This dance is most often performed by four dancers who, as in farmers' band dance and music, function as musicians, in this case each manipulating a pair of large cymbals. While playing the cymbals, the dancers turn in various directions, bend and extend their knees, and rotate their arms overhead so that the cymbals contribute to the overall visual design as well as produce sound. The Monk's Drum Dance (Pŏpkoch'um) is a solo, and the dancer again functions as a musician. He performs highly stylized movements as he plays a drum mounted in a tall wooden frame, often described as symbolically beating out temptation. (Originally, the drum was extremely large; nowadays, it is often small to facilitate transporting it to performance locations.) In The Dance of the Eightfold Path (T'aju), an octagonal box with inscriptions on each side, representing the eightfold way of the Buddha, is placed on the ground between two dancers. Each holds a long, thin stick, and gently taps the top of the box as he moves around it.

Buddhist dances are performed today primarily by male monks, but in the last part of the twentieth century nuns began receiving training in the dances and performing them. The dances are most often done at Pongwŏn Temple in central Seoul on traditional religious occasions, but occasionally at other temples and for other events. In 1990, for example, they were performed in a temple courtyard as part of activities to celebrate the raising of the roof beam for a new temple building, and on a small stage along the banks of the Han River for thousands of Buddhist devotees and religious leaders attending the Seventeenth General Conference of the World Fellowship of Buddhists. By 1998 the dances were performed for paying visitors, who also received a meal, every Saturday and Sunday as part of a re-enactment of the Yŏngsanjae, a ceremony praying for the attainment of nirvana. But by the year 2000 this practice was abolished when it did not generate sufficient funds.

Characteristics of Traditional Dance

No discussion of traditional Korean dance would be complete without mention of *mŏt* and *hŭng*. Among the more difficult Korean words to translate, these terms refer, respectively, to an inner spiritual quality of charm or grace and a feeling of lively animation or enthusiasm, both of which lead to an almost irrepressible joy or giddiness. This is described by Koreans as the ultimate quality the Korean dancer strives to achieve in folk dance, and specific movement characteristics either contribute to achieving this desired state or are the physical manifestation of its having been achieved. (See Chapter 2 for a discussion of the term "folk dance.") *Mŏt* and *hŭng* are not usually used to describe court dance because of the influence of Confucianism on these dances. Confucian ideals of femininity would not allow for the kind of frivolity suggested by *mŏt* and *hŭng*, and since court dancers were most often women, these qualities would have been inappropriate. (For further discussion of gender issues see Chapter 5.) Such behavior was also likely inappropriate for men in the context of official court ceremonies, which called for dignity and propriety. Many of the movement characteristics contributing to the qualities to which *mŏt* and *hŭng* refer are, however, present in all traditional dances of Korea; their dynamics are simply modified to make them appropriate for particular kinds of dance.[8]

One of these movement features is an emphasis on verticality. Throughout most traditional Korean dance there is a persistent alternation between up and down actions. In the slower forms, such as the court and Buddhist dances, the dancers regularly alternate between bending and extending their knees. Hence, the whole body lifts and lowers. In the faster, more vigorous dances, such as the farmers' band dance and music and the masked dance-dramas, the bending of the knees serves as a preparatory push that propels the body into a jump, enlarging the up and down action. This is also prevalent in shaman dancing when the spirits take over the shaman's body, which results in vigorous jumping.

The upward-downward action is also emphasized in a smaller, but very important, way in the "shoulder dance." Movement is initiated in the chest area with what appears to be a quick inhalation of the breath that causes the spine to lengthen upward and eventually forces the shoulders to rise. This movement is then released as the shoulders and spine relax, creating a visual "sigh of relief." In court dances this movement is extremely subtle, but in such genres as the farmers' band dance and music and the masked dance-dramas, it can become a very obvious, exaggerated shoulder shrug. What is important in this movement, however, is that it emanates from an internal feeling generally manifest in the flow of the breath rather than from a conscious, mechanical action of the shoulders.

Another distinguishing feature that pervades many forms of traditional dance is a feeling of suspension. The dancer begins a movement that rises, in some fashion, and then appears to stop abruptly. The dancer briefly remains poised, as if deciding whether to lift even higher or to move on to something else. As the contained energy verges on explosion, the performer quickly rises just a bit higher, almost like a small hiccup, before releasing everything into a gentle downward movement. This moment of suspension, a delicate hovering, provides a strong, dynamic tension for the viewer and contributes to the visual sigh of relief created by the shoulder dance.

Yet another distinctive feature of traditional dance is a particular way of using the foot. Koreans are quick to point out that their dance is characterized by walks in which the dancer steps first on the heel rather than the toe or the ball of the foot. But what is unique in this movement is the way in which dancers seem to caress the floor with their feet, curling their toes upward before placing the heel on the floor and then gently rolling the entire foot down. This action is enhanced by the tight-fitting padded "socks" with upturned toes (*pŏsŏn*) that most dancers wear. Whether done slowly or quickly, the overall effect is as if the dancer is walking on something quite delicate, which contributes to the feelings of *mŏt* and *hŭng*.

In many Korean dances the arms frequently extend sideward at shoulder height. They are turned inward so the thumb surface of the hand is directed forward, and the wrist is relaxed, allowing the fingertips to point gently downward. There are many movements in which the wrist is flicked to manipulate a long sleeve or scarf, and then the sleeve or scarf and fingertips all finish pointing downward. This same movement is also done when there is no sleeve or scarf to manipulate. Additionally, the arm often rotates outward and then inward, concluding with a relaxation of the wrist that returns the fingertips to their downward orientation.

All of these elements contribute to an emphasis on motion rather than isolated positions or posturing. In fact, Koreans sometimes describe their dance as "motion in stillness" (*chŏng-jung-dong*).[9] One Korean writer (Chung Byung Ho 1997a:105) relates this three-part term to movement that demonstrates a tensing of emotion, a pacification of emotion, and a release of the emotion—what I have described as a visual sigh of relief. The fluid, ongoing movements that appear to stop are, in reality, simply collecting energy that ultimately gently explodes, or runs over, into the next series of fluid actions. Korean dancers move *through* positions rather than arriving *at* them, creating curvilinear shapes as well as a rounded, ongoing quality of energy use.

The skillful manipulation of costume components or hand-held implements and the playing of musical instruments are also features of many traditional Korean dances. In court dances and masked dance-dramas performers manipulate long sleeves that are a part of their costumes; in Buddhist dances musical instruments are manipulated; and in many kinds of dance the performers play one or more of a wide variety of drums.

One final feature prevalent in many traditional dances is an emphasis on compound meters. Movement phrases are choreographed in three-beat units, and underlying musical pulses are typically further subdivided into units of three. This triple-meter emphasis frequently ties in with the emphasis on verticality and suspension: the rising action that leads to a brief suspension on the first two pulses and a slight accent at the end of the second pulse just before the downward release on the third pulse.

Derived Dance Forms

The various dances described thus far, whether originally supported by religious institutions or the former court, whether done for entertainment or as part of ritual, and whether performed by highly trained specialists or village farmers, are considered by Koreans to be traditional dances, and are readily identifiable as being Korean. Although many are said to trace their roots to earlier eras, as performed today the dances are believed to be akin to those performed during the Chosŏn dynasty. But as the country once known as the Hermit Kingdom opened its doors to the rest of the world in the late nineteenth century, and as various kinds of interactions, both peaceful and otherwise, developed with close geographic neighbors and countries considerably farther away, significant changes began to occur in dance.[10] In some instances choreographers looked to their traditional heritage as a source of inspiration for new creations that retained strong ties to the past. In other instances a conscious effort was made to merge features of traditional dances with those of dance forms introduced from other cultures. In some instances the newly created dances were still recognizable as emanating from Korea; in others, the departure was sufficiently great to raise questions regarding a specific cultural tie. Several of the new dances with clear roots in older dance forms eventually became so significantly representative of Korea that Koreans added them to their traditional category, even though they evolved in more recent times than others in this grouping. Some dances led to the development of new categories and ways of conceptualizing Korean dance.

It is often difficult to draw clear boundaries between the kinds of dances that began to develop. Western-style ballet and modern dance (discussed shortly) are performed in Korea today, and they are frequently easy to differentiate from other kinds of dance. In various ways ballet and modern dance contributed to other kinds of dances. But the dances that are not traditional and that are not distinctly ballet or modern dance can contribute to terminological complexity. Yet, these dances form an important part of the Korean dance landscape of the recent past and of the start of the twenty-first century. Terminology is dealt with at greater length in the next chapter, as is further explanation of precisely how some of these new dance forms evolved. Here, however, I cluster together several different kinds of dance under the heading of "derived forms" (a term not commonly used by Koreans), and then discuss separately "creative dance" (an important term used by Koreans), one particular type of derived dance. Because of the inspiration and movement characteristics drawn from older Korean dances, I believe many of the new dances can be described most easily as "derived dances": Their movements and overriding qualities clearly emanate from those of the more distant past. Choreographers also adapted older dance movements for performance on a western, proscenium-arch stage, rather than in a royal palace, temple courtyard, or outdoor setting, and in a context of theatrical entertainment, rather than entertainment at a royal banquet or as part of a ritual occasion. During their early development, some of the derived dances were performed in the more intimate settings of restaurants or bars to entertain.[11]

There are many complications preventing an entirely clear elucidation of the visual manifestation of some of the early derived dances. Because of political circumstances and the lack, until very recently, of good dance documentation, little remains of some developments beyond vague verbal descriptions. Contributors to what led to the changes creating these dances, however, *are* clear. First, Korea became a colony of Japan in

1910. From that time until independence in 1945, there were periods in which Japan made every effort to obliterate traditional Korean culture and times when the prevailing government authorities allowed Koreans to assert their identity in specific contexts. With independence came the division of the Korean peninsula into two political entities that have had minimal interaction ever since, and this was followed quickly by the Korean War (1950–1953). Thus, political upheavals contributed to fluctuating opportunities for dance to occur and fluctuating amounts and nature of support for it.

Second, with the colonization of Korea by Japan came the end of the royal court. Around the same time, western-style theaters began to appear in Seoul.[12] The tradition of female court entertainers was transformed as dancers began to perform in restaurants and for parties among the common people and in the newly built theaters. Thus, new contexts and physical environments in which dance occurred contributed to changes.

Third, Korea's increasing contact with other cultures brought increasing contact with different kinds of dance, some of which contributed to conscious changes and some of which contributed to a gradual "filtering in" of outside influences.

Some of the derived dances, together with the older traditional dance forms, have become symbols of Korea. They are used to represent the country at official international events, to adorn posters intended for tourists, and in television commercials advertising such things as the wares of a traditional medicine manufacturer.[13] One such dance, generally described as representing the epitome of Korean dance features, is salp'uri.[14] There are many versions of this dance performed today, but certain elements characterize most of them. Salp'uri is a solo dance, generally performed by a woman, but occasionally by a man (Plate 13). It starts very slowly, sometimes with the performer facing away from the audience. When performed by a woman the dancer wears the traditional female Korean garment, which includes a floor-length full skirt that billows out from just below the breast area and a short jacket-type top with sleeves extending to the wrist in a soft, full curve under the arm. When performed by a man the dancer typically wears traditional baggy pants and either a vest or long, lightweight coat. The garment is most often white or a very muted color. In most salp'uri the dancer carries a long white scarf, made of a very lightweight silk, in one hand.

As the dance progresses the performer traces circular pathways, turns around herself, and manipulates the scarf so that it, too, flows in graceful curves. The movement characteristics of traditional dances described earlier are highlighted, with many alternations between moments of suspended action and a kind of hurrying as the dancer resolves the suspension into a series of rapid steps. At one moment the dancer gently throws the scarf and it wafts to the ground. She lowers herself to a kneel and hovers over it, almost caressing it before retrieving it and returning to her standing dance.

Although dancers and dance teachers today consistently point out that the roots of salp'uri lie in shamanism, the basis of the concert form of the dance seen today is generally attributed to Han Sŏng-jun (1874–1942), who is said to have choreographed it in Seoul in the mid-1930s, and to have named it after a rhythm and dance used in shaman rituals in South Chŏlla Province (Loken-Kim and Crump 1993:14, Ku Hee-seo 1997:156, and Kim Kyoung-ae 1997:178).[15] Other theories attribute the dance to female entertainers of the twentieth century, claiming that the only tie to shamanism is the dance's name, which is usually described as meaning "to expel evil spirits." (Salp'uri's possible relationship to shamanism is discussed further in Chapter 6.)

Salp'uri is still very popular and, despite the relative newness of its origin as a concert dance form, the quality of a traditional dancer today is often determined by how well she can perform this dance. Many say that salp'uri embraces the essence of *han*—a term translated variously as sorrow, bitterness, or unsatisfied desire.[16] Salp'uri's close movement ties to older Korean dances clearly show its derivative nature.

Another popular derived dance is sŭngmu, which, like salp'uri, has many variations. Although sŭngmu is usually identified in English as the monk's dance or the monk's drum dance, this gloss leads to confusion since it is the same name given to a traditional Buddhist dance. It is the Korean terms, Pŏpkoch'um for the Buddhist dance and sŭngmu for the derived dance, that clarify which dance is being described. Recall that the original Buddhist dance (Pŏpkoch'um) was performed as a solo by a monk in conjunction with temple ritual. During the dance the monk plays some relatively simple patterns on an extremely large double-headed drum suspended in a standing frame. Sometimes a second monk plays a steady pulse on the opposite side of the drum. Early in the twentieth century, choreographers elaborated on this dance and created an adaptation of it for performance in a concert setting. Sŭngmu, as the adaptation and any of its variants is known, generally begins with a lengthy, slow introduction that does not involve playing the drum but rather the manipulation of extremely long sleeves (Plate 14). This is followed by a section in which the dancer pulls his or her arms through openings in the long sleeves near the base of the arm and, using drumsticks originally concealed inside the sleeves, executes intricate rhythmic patterns on the surface of the drum (which is generally smaller than that originally used in Buddhist rituals), on the wooden frame of the drum, and by beating the drumsticks themselves together. Stories attribute the origin of this dance to a monk trying to drive out the temptation of a young woman or exuding the ecstasy experienced during enlightenment. Both the stories and the playing of a drum in a standing frame during the dance reflect its derivative nature. Much of the movement, particularly in the danced portion preceding the drum-playing, constitutes a considerable departure from the original Buddhist dance.

There were many other drum dances created in the early- and mid-twentieth century that are also derivative in nature. Borrowing the hourglass-shaped drum tied to the dancer's body in the farmers' dances, virtuosic dances known as changgoch'um (*changgo* dance) were choreographed. The traditional Buddhist drum dance (Pŏpkoch'um) was adapted beyond sŭngmu to incorporate three, five, seven, and occasionally as many as nine drums. One small drum in a standing frame was placed upstage, parallel to the audience. One or more drums were then placed perpendicular to it and extending toward the audience to form a kind of alleyway in which the dancer performed. She progressed up and down the alleyway as she played on various parts of the drums, sometimes facing one drum but bending backward to play on the surface of the opposite drum. Several such drum formations might be placed on the stage at once, with a group of dancers creating a dynamic dancing percussion ensemble. Again, movements derived from older traditional dances fueled the imaginations of choreographers to create new works intended to entertain.

Similar derivative entertainment dances were created based on shaman rituals. The jumping performed by shamans when they were taken over by spirits became codified and choreographed into theatrical depictions on concert stages of shamans. Carrying fans (Plates 15 and 16), bell trees, scarves, and other implements typically manipulated by shamans, professional dancers created dances *representing* shamanism rather than trying to depict actual rituals on stage. (Aspects of such representations are discussed more fully in Chapter 6.)

In derived dances choreographers both look back to their traditional heritage and forward to creating new works based on that heritage. While new versions of these dances continue to be choreographed, the creativity employed remains within the boundaries of the models established for these dances in the early and mid-twentieth century. The aesthetic of these derived dances is based on presenting the beauty of the dancers' movements by rearranging, in a homogeneous fashion, many of the movement patterns of older dances.

Creative Dance

For Koreans, the term "creative dance" (*ch'angjak ch'um* or *ch'angjak muyong*) refers to a type of dance in which individual movements relate to traditional dance, but themes and choreographic structure are new and reflect either stories or ideas considered to be uniquely Korean or issues relevant to contemporary Korean society. Thus, creative dances are also derived dances. In the derived dances discussed in the previous section, the movement vocabulary is drawn from that of traditional dances and is essentially elaborated or rearranged to create dances intended to be enjoyed for their visual interest. While some are meant to create virtuosic display, such as those in which the dancer or dancers play multiple drums, and others are intended to create a deep-seated emotional quality, such as salp'uri, visual entertainment is the predominant goal. In creative dances, however, while movements are also based on those used in traditional dances, there is considerably greater adaptation of these movements as well as a conscious intent to use movement to make a particular statement. Dances may be narrative in nature (i.e., use movement to tell a story), or they may, in a more abstract way, relate some facet of traditional Korean society or provide socio-political comment. One creative dance choreographer describes this form as a creative succession of tradition that does not simply revive the past, but modifies and transforms it to suit contemporary lives (Kim Mae-ja 1990:107). Thus, creative dances are a distinctive type of derived dance.

There are two primary contributors to the development of creative dance: the introduction, and reintroduction, of western-style modern dance, and a political movement among intellectuals and university students to rediscover traditional culture and create a modern identity. In 1926 a Japanese dancer performed German expressionist-style modern dance in Korea.[17] Several years later, two Koreans who studied with him began to perform in Korea. Although the type of dance performed by these three individuals was not initially well-received among the broad Korean community, the emphasis on creativity and individuality began to influence dancers in Korea. Later, when western-style modern dance was reintroduced in the mid-1960s, the climate was more receptive. And when dance was introduced as an independent discipline in higher education in 1963 at Ewha Woman's University, course offerings were structured around the concept of creativity, further instilling ideas of individuality and creativity in young dancers. Thus, the seeds planted in the 1920s matured in the 1960s and contributed to new ways of thinking about what dance might be, ultimately influencing the development of what is now known as creative dance. In addition, political repercussions of the Japanese occupation, the Korean War, and the influx of western culture that accompanied a push for modernization led to a movement to reestablish a distinctive national identity. This contributed to a rediscovery of tradition in order to use the distinctiveness of older forms as a basis for fashioning a modern identity. Thus, considerable creativity developed in consciously establishing new forms.

Three dances, one from the early days of the development of creative dance and two from 1990, exemplify the merging of traditional dance movements with creativity that typify this distinctive type of derived dance. The Silk Road (Pidan Kil) was choreographed in 1977 by Kim Mae-ja. The music to which it is performed is a modern composition by a Korean composer (Hwang Pyŏng-gi) for the Korean *kayagŭm*. The piece is described by the choreographer as having been "created to represent the famous Silk Road" (in Choi Haeree 1995:74–75), a route through China, East India, and the Arab world that brought Eastern and Western cultures in contact with each other. The choreographer interpreted the music as symbolizing the Silk Road, which she, and many others, identify as "the

Figure 1. Dancers at the National Center for Korean Traditional Performing Arts in Pyŏ (Rice Plant), choreographed by Mun Il-chi. Photo by I Yong. Courtesy of Kungnip Kŭgagwŏn.

womb of Korean culture" because so many things brought to Korea by travelers on the Silk Road had a significant impact on Korea (ibid.:75).

The costume in this dance is a slight modification of the traditional attire worn by Korean women (the same type described earlier as commonly used in the dance salp'uri), with the skirt greatly enlarged for the central figure at the beginning of the dance, creating a kind of womb from which other dancers emerge. Many of the movements are identical to those used in traditional dances: shoulder actions initiated in the chest area with the breath, arm movements initiated in the upper arm that leave the hand trailing slightly behind and that culminate with a flick of the wrist, and steps in which the heel is planted on the ground first and the dancer then rolls carefully through the whole foot to lower the toes. But the overall choreographic structure of the dance (i.e., the way it progresses from beginning to end), the exaggerated use of the costume, the role of lighting to enhance the choreography, and the departure from movements used in older dances are different from both traditional dance and the derived dances described previously.

Mun Il-chi, a former choreographer at the National Center for Korean Traditional Performing Arts, premiered an evening-length work titled

Rice Plant (Pyŏ) in October, 1990 (Figure 1). Based on a poem of the same name by Yi Sŏng-bu, Mun stated that in the dance she tried to capture the spirit of life among the Koreans of former times: "The scene of paddies standing against each other in the rice field brought up the image of ancient Koreans who lived leaning against each other in closely-associated communal societies" (in Anonymous 1990). The costumes incorporate elements of traditional Korean attire. Although the movements replicate, or are based on, those found in traditional dance, they are drawn from a variety of forms rather than adhering to a single dance style (as in other derived dances). In this case, the incorporation of movements from various traditional dance styles, the use of costumes based on traditional attire, and the use of a story reflect both the derivative and creative nature of the dance.

Kuk Su-ho's The Myth of Mount Paektu (Paektusan Shin'gok), premiered in 1990, was described in the printed program for the performance as an "epic spectacle" and was compared to Beijing opera and Japanese kabuki (Figure 2). The script, by philosopher Kim Yong-ok, is based on the legend of the founding of the Korean nation. A she-bear and a tigress seek the help of the son of the divine creator in enabling them to become human. They are each given a bunch of mugworts and twenty bulbs of garlic to eat, and then are told to stay out of the sunlight for 100 days. Only the she-bear is able to complete the task and ultimately emerge as a woman. She subsequently gives birth to Tan'gun, who is said to have descended from heaven to the highest point in Korea (believed to be

Figure 2. Paektusan Shin'gok (Myth of Mount Paektu), choreographed by Kuk Su-ho. Photo by Cho Tae-hyŏng. Courtesy of Kuk Su-ho, Didim Dance Company of Korea.

Mount Paektu, near the Manchurian border in what is now North Korea). In 2333 B.C. Tan'gun founds the Korean nation.

In The Myth of Mount Paektu a cast of almost 200 actor-dancers, accompanied by a fifty-member live orchestra, combines traditional dance movements with movements that have no relationship to any traditional Korean dances. In one section the stage is almost entirely filled with performers who sit or kneel. A small drum on the floor in front of each performer is struck using stylized movements in a manner that produces a powerful and dynamically varied rhythmic interlude as well as a visually spectacular dance. As pointed out earlier, the beating of drums by dancers in a way that emphasizes both sound and movement is an integral part of many traditional and derived Korean dances. In another section, however, performers crawl, writhe, and extend their arms as they work their way over a hill created on the stage in a symbolic dance of the birth of the Korean people. Movements in this section have no relationship to any traditional dance forms. In this case the choreographer used many traditional movements as well as purely creative ones to tell a traditional story. He also used elaborate group formations, a feature typical of traditional court dances, but in new ways.

Clearly these three dances are diverse in nature. What binds them together as creative dance is that, although they are not considered traditional by Koreans, they do bear a distinctively Korean stamp. And although derivative in the sense that they draw on the movement vocabulary of traditional dances, they modify this vocabulary in innovative ways, they have a textual theme, and they are part of a kind of dance that is actively practiced and still being developed. This differentiates them from the derived dances described in the previous section, some of which are no longer developing and others of which are created anew, but still within quite narrow boundaries.

Modern Dance

Some of the dancers who choose to move beyond traditional Korean dance and derived forms become involved in dances rooted in movement techniques that originated in other cultures and that, at least to the non-Korean, often bear little resemblance to anything uniquely Korean. They pursue either ballet or modern dance. First introduced to Korea in 1926 by the Japanese dancer Ishii Baku, modern dance did not really take hold in Korea until the 1960s and 1970s. In the 1950s there was some modern dance taught at Ewha Woman's University. Pak Oe-sŏn, who began her dance studies with some of the derived dances described earlier, went to Japan to study ballet and modern dance. In 1953 she began teaching ballet, modern dance, and Korean dance (Choi Haeree 1995:172). But it was one of her students who had the greatest impact on the modern dance movement in Korea. Following early studies with Pak, Yuk Wan-sun, later a chairwoman of the Ewha Woman's University dance program and head of the modern dance area, went to the United States in 1961. There she studied modern dance at the University of Illinois, and eventually moved on to New York City, where she studied at the studio of Martha Graham, one of the founders of the American modern dance movement and one of the most widely known modern dance choreographers, as well as at the José Limón and Alvin Ailey studios (Raher 1986:24). Yuk returned to Korea in 1963 and solidly established the Graham technique in the dance curriculum at Ewha.[18] The program subsequently became the source for many modern dance activities in Korea, and the Graham technique was the standard for modern dance until well into the 1990s, when some young choreographers tried to go beyond the established mold. They include individuals who studied in university dance programs in diverse locations in the United States, a few who studied in Europe, and several who, despite their Ewha training, made conscious efforts to break away from the Graham style fostered at Ewha.

The term "modern dance," or "contemporary dance," as used most often in Europe, refers to a vast array of movement styles. The diversity of movement is the result of modern dance's underlying premise: Say what you want to say, and devise a movement style or vocabulary suited to your idea. Modern dance originated in the late nineteenth and early twentieth centuries in Europe and the United States, and is often associated with the emphasis, in these geographical areas, placed on individuality. Modern dance continues to evolve in Europe and the United States. Unlike traditional and derived Korean dance, modern dance in Korea strives to make either a broad universal or an intensely personal statement, rather than a clearly identifiable Korean statement. While movements used in traditional dance sometimes influence those of modern dance, there is seldom a *conscious* effort to use the movement vocabulary of former times. While the traditional and derived dances performed today seem to consciously speak of the past, intentionally use movement vocabulary of the past, and make the statement, "This is Korea," a modern piece such as Nam Chŏng-ho's Hey, Children, What's Beyond the Mountain (Aiya, Chŏ San Nŏmŏe Muŏshi) tries to make a more universal statement—in costume, movement, and idea. Following her dance studies at Ewha University, Nam pursued training in France. She became a member of the dance faculty at Kyŏngsŏng University and then moved on to head the choreography department of the dance school of the Korean National University of the Arts (Han'guk Yesul Chonghap Hakkyo). According to one modern dancer, Nam is famous in Korea because her work is "different," meaning that it departs from the Graham style. In the first section of Hey, Children, one of her early works choreographed in 1990, a group of uniformed children go through the rigorous disciplines of a school day. An austere teacher "calls them to order" through movement, and they mechanically perform their classroom routines. But the moment the teacher leaves or turns her back, the children become playful

Figure 3. Mannam (Meeting), choreographed by An Ae-sun. Courtesy of An Ae-sun.

and mischievous. The dance movements are not literal or pantomimic, nor do they incorporate the movement vocabulary found in many of the traditional dances. Rather, they are abstractions of regimentation and repetition interspersed with spontaneity and enthusiasm. Both the theme and movements of the dance make a universal statement that could as easily have come from a German, British, or American choreographer, and that could as easily be construed as representing the youthful days of children in Frankfurt, London, or New York City. The dance's tie to Korea lies in the fact that although its theme is potentially universal, it is relevant to contemporary Korea.

Another dance with a universal statement is Meeting (Mannam). Choreographed by An Ae-sun as an abstract portrayal of various encounters, this work won the Grand Prize at the 1990 Seoul Dance Festival (Figure 3). Although the theme is universal, the stage set and its use of movable components are clearly reminiscent of the work of American choreographer Alwin Nikolais. With set pieces that create dynamic shapes and long pieces of elastic stretched across the stage, against which the dancers press and twist to alter the straight lines, any American dancer would say, "Aha, the stamp of Nikolais." A member of the dance faculty at Ewha University when she choreographed the dance, An received virtually all of her dance training in Korea, taking only a few classes with American dancer-choreographer Jennifer Muller during a brief performance tour to the United States in 1987. Although Nikolais's New York–based company has never performed in Korea, Shin Sŏn-hŭi, An's set designer, studied in New York for fifteen years.

Traditional dances and derived dances are primarily concerned with making a Korean statement—a statement that says, "This is *Korea*," or, "I am *Korean*." Creative dances strive to say, "I am Korean, but I am also very modern." Modern dance, in contrast, is more concerned with making either a more personal or a more universal statement—"This is *I*," or, "This is one facet of *world society*." This attitude is reflected in a *Korea Times* statement attributed to the 1992 choreographers of Flying (Pihaeng).[19] The dance is described as symbolically exposing social evils, and the choreographers believe that now is the time for Korean dancers to "get out of the pattern [of] sticking to traditional image[s] of beauty and emotion" (Anonymous 1992). In other words, the theme is potentially universal, but particularly relevant to Korea at a specific time. Interestingly, this attitude is also reflected in the symbolic use of traditional and derived dances done in new contexts as vehicles for protest. In 1987, for example, Yi Ae-ju, a dance professor at Seoul National University, used traditional dances as inspiration for a dance of mourning that she performed in the streets of Seoul at a public funeral service for Yi Han-yŏl, a university student killed by a tear-gas bomb during the June 1987 democracy demonstrations.[20] Korean writers and critics describe the subject matter of Korean literature in the late 1990s as shifting to such topics as gender, the generation gap, the inner self, the information society, the environment, multimedia, popular culture, and sex (in Kim Youngna 2000:109, 111); the same shift exists in dance.

Ballet

Although first presented in Korea by a Russian girl, remembered only as Helen, prior to the introduction of modern dance (around 1917—Pak Yong-gu in Choi Haeree 1995:12), ballet did not become well established until 1954. Im Sŏng-nam, a former director of The National Ballet Troupe (Kungnip Palledan), studied ballet in Japan from 1950 to 1954. Upon his return to Korea in that year, he began to train many subsequent Korean performers of ballet. Rooted in an imported dance style, ballet in Korea continues to manifest its classical European sources, as well as Korean influence. Classical and new repertoire items from Russia and the West, such as Giselle and Nutcracker, are staged by local or visiting choreographers; perhaps the only thing that makes them remotely Korean is that they are performed by dancers who are from Korea. A piece such as one in which Buddhist-inspired costumes, prayerlike gestures, and *pointe* shoes are combined (The Road of Birth and Death Is Right Here—Saengsaronan Ye Isyamae, choreographed by To Chŏng-nim), reflects a mixing of Korean and non-Korean components that could place it in my "derived" category. However, when asked why she classified this dance as ballet, a Korean replied that the use of *pointe* shoes and ballet movements placed it in this category, despite the acknowledged Korean theme and Korean-inspired costumes and movements.

Another "mixture" identified as ballet is a work titled Shim Ch'ŏng, premiered by the Universal Ballet Company in 1986. Choreographed by American Adrienne Dellas, founder of the company and its first artistic director, the ballet tells the traditional Korean story of a faithful daughter, Shim Ch'ŏng, and her blind father. With its wicked sailors, mythical underwater scene, trials and tribulations of a poor country girl who eventually marries a king, and grand palace celebration, the story lends itself perfectly to the fairy-tale tradition of nineteenth-century European ballet. Although the designs of many of the costumes are based on traditional Korean attire, the performers are easily recognizable as a poor country girl, fairy-tale underwater creatures, or members of royalty—Korean or otherwise.

The movement in this dance, on the other hand, is drawn almost entirely from the codified vocabulary of ballet. Shim Ch'ŏng dances her concerns and joys using the long, outwardly projected lines of ballet and *pointe* shoes, the wicked sailors perform an athletic display of strength using the elevation and intricate footwork of male ballet *allegro*, and Shim Ch'ŏng and her lover express their feelings toward each other in a typical ballet *pas de deux* (duet). In only two brief sections is there a conscious attempt to incorporate Korean dance movements: Five dancers attired in costumes and executing movements taken from one particular style of masked dance-drama (the Pongsan style) provide entertainment in the court of the story's king, and the village blind men to whom sight has been restored perform a dance of joy using movements traditionally found in dances portraying young male aristocrats.

Members of the cast were both Korean and non-Korean. (The Universal Ballet seems to try to live up to its name and includes dancers from a broad spectrum of ethnic and national backgrounds.) With a Korean story as its basis, an American choreographer, performers of varied ethnic backgrounds, Korean-inspired costumes, and movements drawn almost entirely from classical ballet, Shim Ch'ŏng is described as "ballet with a Korean story."

In the early 1990s, ballet became quite popular in Korea. Increased activities of two professional companies, The National Ballet Troupe (then directed by Kim Hye-shik) and the Universal Ballet Company (then directed by Mun Hun-suk), both contributed to and were the result of this popularity. In addition, two well-known ballerinas, Kang Su-jin and Kang Ye-na, received top awards at world-famous competitions (the Swiss Laussanne Ballet Competition and the Paris International Dance Competition), bringing ballet to the foreground in popular news. The presence, in 1995, of Kang Su-jin as prima ballerina at the Stuttgart Ballet

Company in Germany and Kang Ye-na in key roles with the Kirov Ballet in Russia, also contributed to this increased popularity (Choi Haeree 1995:12).

Social Dance

Korea does not have a history of couple dancing for social purposes, such as the western tradition of ballroom dancing, nor any sort of codified social dance, such as some early European village dances. Perhaps because of long-standing Buddhist and Confucian principles, public interactions between men and women, particularly of a sexual and/or physical nature, were minimal. Instead, at parties or picnics dance was an impromptu event, often participated in by individuals under the influence of alcohol (see, e.g., Loken-Kim 1989:14). People might stand and move spontaneously and as individuals rather than couples, like the older man described at the Nori Madang performance at the beginning of this chapter. In doing so, rough attempts might be made to replicate movements typical of traditional dances, based on the performer's memory of past events.

The notion of couple dancing was apparently introduced in the late nineteenth century as significant western influences began in Korea. But the physically close connections between a man and a woman typical of ballroom dance were generally confined to bars at which female hostesses entertained men, or to the limited few who chose, in usually discrete contexts, to break from conventional decorum.[21] As modernization escalated at the end of the twentieth century, however, even these restrictions began to loosen, and the same broad array of dances found in nightclubs and discotheques in Europe and the United States are seen in similar contexts in Korea.

Major Contributors to Dance in Korea Today

Although dance has played an integral role in various facets of Korean society for centuries, and has been supported by the court and religious institutions to greater and lesser extents at different times, there has been a phenomenal dance boom since the 1970s. This boom is manifest in both the variety and quantity of dance activities. Dance offerings in higher education have increased, dance studios have been established throughout the country, dance students and performers have gone abroad to perform and to study, and professional dance organizations have been created. During the ten years from 1980 to 1990, the number of dance performances per year increased from forty to 400, and in 1994 there were almost 1,000 dance performances in Korea and abroad; in 1989 twenty dance theory books were published, approximately seven times the previous average of three books per year; in 1990 alone, six new dance companies were formed (Kim Seong-kon 1991:113; Kim T'ae-wǒn 1997:151; *Korea Annual 1990* 1990:280; and *Korea Annual 1991* 1991:296). By 1997 twenty-eight universities and eight junior colleges had established dance departments, with most retaining four to seven full-time professors and three to eight part-time instructors (Kim T'ae-wǒn 1997:150). And in 1998 there were forty-five dance departments in universities and more than 150 dance companies (Kim Kyoung-ae 1998).

I believe four forces contributed significantly to this growth: the Dance Department at Ewha Woman's University, the Korea branch of the American Dance Festival, increased financial support in the form of grants from government agencies and private corporations, and Korea's National Treasure System.

Originally begun as part of the physical education program in the 1950s (a genesis parallel to the beginnings of dance in higher education in the United States), in 1963 Ewha Woman's University became the first four-year university in Korea to establish an independent dance department (again following a pattern common in the United States) (Kim Kyunghee 1993:42). At the end of the twentieth century the curriculum offered both bachelor's and master's degrees in one of three emphases: Korean dance, ballet, and modern dance. Graduates have contributed to virtually every facet of dance in Korea—founding their own companies, establishing dance programs in other universities and colleges, opening studios, going abroad to further their education, and participating in festivals.

A reflection of the growth of dance in academic institutions in Korea is the Ministry of Culture and Sports's 1992 establishment of the Korean National University of the Arts, the first Korean university arts program emphasizing a conservatory approach. The institution-wide focus is on performance and professional training. The School of Dance opened in 1996, and includes performance, choreography, and dance studies (theory) departments. The performance department maintains the Korean dance, ballet, and modern dance sectional model initiated by Ewha. It will take some time before the impact of this program is felt, but the fact that it is governmentally supported reflects a significant national contribution to dance.

A second important influence on dance was the establishment of a Korea branch of the American Dance Festival. The festival, a United States–based administrative body that facilitates the creativity of modern dance choreographers and fosters the appreciation and awareness of dance, began in the United States in 1934.[22] Its goals are achieved through intensive summer classes, workshops, and performing opportunities for faculty and students. The success among Americans of festival-sponsored activities in the United States eventually led to participation by foreigners, and subsequently to the establishment, by festival administrators, of branch programs abroad. In 1980 Yuk Wan-sun, modern dance teacher formerly affiliated with Ewha University and the woman largely responsible for the beginnings of modern dance in Korea, brought forty

Korean students to the festival in the United States. The participation of Korean dance students continued, and Yuk was ultimately instrumental in the establishment, in 1990, of the Korea branch of the festival. From July 30 to August 11 of that year, 487 students in Seoul participated in classes taught by visiting American modern dance instructors as well as several Korean instructors. The event continues to be extremely popular and contributes substantially to the awareness in young dancers of what is being done in modern dance in other parts of the world. The long-range impact of the American Dance Festival in Seoul on the development of modern dance in Korea remains to be seen, but it has clearly contributed to training and motivating young modern dancers.

The third major impact is the increased financial support for dance. Impetus came from the government's Culture and Arts Promotion Act, which led to the establishment of the Korean Culture and Arts Foundation in 1974. Initially supported by tax revenues on movie tickets and broadcasting advertisements, the government eventually contributed direct appropriations (Yŏ Sŏk-ki 1997:53). Prizes awarded by the Ministry of Culture at dance competitions and outright grants from government and nongovernment agencies afford dancers the means to pay for costumes and to rent performing spaces, and offer individuals financial support while they develop skills and rehearse. So substantial have both the number of dance activities and the nature of support for them become that the government declared 1992 the Year of Dance, and featured performances, workshops, and symposia. In 1996 the government was reported to have paid 530,000,000 *wŏn* (almost $628,000 U.S., based on the average exchange rate for the year) for international exchange through dance performances, and in 1997 an equal amount was spent for the cultural promotion of dance (Kim T'ae-wŏn 1997:151).

The fourth contributor to dance in Korea today is the government's National Treasure System. A formalized procedure for identifying important dances and dance masters (discussed further in Chapter 3), the system provides for the preservation of distinctive traditional dances by supporting research, documentation, and teaching and performing opportunities.

Serious financial changes in Korea at the end of 1997 created a nationwide crisis. In November of that year the economy plunged, businesses declared bankruptcy, and countless individuals lost their jobs. In times of financial constraints the arts are typically among the earliest, and most profoundly, affected in negative ways. But the dance boom of the 1970s established sufficient momentum to carry the art form through to the twenty-first century. One of the early statements of Kim Dae-jung, inaugurated as president in February of 1998, indicated that "he and his administration would support cultural activities even as the economy contracted" (Kim Youngna 2000:103). Young students continue to go abroad to study, performances of all kinds abound, the number of dance periodicals has increased, and new dance books are published regularly. Dance continues to be a vital ingredient in modern-day Korea.

2

Korean Dance Terminology
The Politics of Words

Dance terminology in Korea has changed over time, sometimes in response to changes in what is being danced, and sometimes in response to external forces.[1] In this chapter I examine selected dance terminology used by Koreans to describe their dances. I briefly mention terminology from the past, but focus on contemporary terminology, and on both denotative and connotative meanings. Developments in dance terminology are juxtaposed against important societal events, and reveal the contributions of politics and issues of power to both the development of dance in Korea and to how it is identified.

Background

Korean dance terminology has been greatly influenced by the Chinese language and writing system. The Korean language was originally written in a complex system using Chinese characters for both their phonetic and semantic values. In addition, many Chinese words were borrowed, given a Korean pronunciation, and used in both the spoken and written language. It was not until 1443 (during the reign of King Sejong, r. 1418–1450) that the development of the Korean alphabet, known as *han'gŭl*, was completed, and 1446 when it was officially adopted by royal decree. In spite of court decree, however, the Chinese script remained the primary written mode of communication for official business and much scholarship until the end of the nineteenth century (Kim Yersu 1976:31). Even as *han'gŭl* became increasingly used, however, many Chinese-derived words continued to be written with Chinese characters.[2] Among Korean dance writers today, some continue to write Chinese-derived dance terms with Chinese characters, others write them using the Korean script, and still others use a mixture of the two. Regardless of the script, Chinese characters serve as the basis for the meanings of much Korean dance terminology now in use. Such words are referred to as Sino-Korean words, in contrast to those identified as pure-Korean words.

The English language has also influenced some Korean dance terminology. As Korea opened its doors to the West in the late nineteenth century, English words (pronounced in a Korean way) came to be used for some things previously not found in Korean culture (such as "eye-sa cream" for ice cream), but also instead of, or in addition to, existing Korean words (such as "ttaen-su" for dance and "ri-dum" for rhythm).

The Japanese language began to influence Korean dance terminology in the first half of the twentieth century when the Japanese occupied Korea (1910–1945) and the government implemented procedures to prevent Koreans from using their own language. A generation of Koreans grew up with Japanese as their first language of instruction in school. Japanese and Japanese-derived words, including many that were, in turn, derived from Chinese words, found their way into usage in Korea.

A German dance influence in Japan in the early twentieth century was passed on to Korea, possibly influencing some terminology, and the importation of ballet brought with it the French-derived term for this genre.

Early Terminology

It is difficult to determine the precise nature and meaning of the earliest dance terminology. Because of the challenges of capturing movement details in words, even when words assumed to mean "dance" are found, little is known about the characteristics of the movements to which such words referred. Therefore, this brief discussion of early terminology is intended only to provide a tentative context against which to place terminology used today.

In many of the oldest documents relating to the performing arts in Korea, the Chinese character "*wu*," pronounced "*mu*" in Korean and literally translated today in both Chinese and Korean as "dance," is used for what are assumed to be various kinds of dance. (See the glossary for Chinese characters and *han'gŭl* spellings.) But without an indigenous writing system until the fifteenth century, we do not know if Koreans were using this character to write a word that existed in their own language, or were borrowing the Chinese word itself. Because there is no Chinese character approximating the pronunciation of the pure-Korean "*ch'um*," a word used today, Koreans long ago might have written the Chinese character "*wu*" for "dance," but pronounced it "*ch'um*" when speaking (Gary Rector, personal communication 30 Dec. 1997). It is possible, therefore, that the oldest term was the indigenous word *ch'um*, and that *mu*, based on the Chinese *wu*, was used only from the mid-fifth century after Chinese characters became the basis for writing the Korean language.

It is also possible that a separate term for dance was not used in some contexts because of an assumed relationship between dance and music. In the past there was a prevailing attitude, which still exists in many contexts today, that dance and music went hand in hand: When there was dance, there was also music. Therefore, a term translated as, or literally meaning, "music" was understood to include "dance."[3] This concept probably contributed to different terms for individual kinds of dance, but none referring generically to dance. For example, the term *aak* (see page 270, note 3, and pages 270–271, note 12) might broadly have referred to "the whole coordinated music/dance event at a sacrificial rite," but when used more narrowly to refer to individual components of the rite, "*aak* meant the music only, and *mumu/munmu/ilmu* the dance only" (Robert Provine, personal communication 3 Jan. 1998).

Thus, although the Sino-Korean *mu* may be among the earliest generic terms for dance in written text, *ch'um* may have existed earlier in spoken discourse. Regardless of whether an indigenous or Sino-Korean word was originally used for "dance" in the past, the Sino-Korean *mu* is the basis for two terms used today.

General Terms for "Dance" in the Twentieth Century

Among the terms used in Korea at the beginning of the twentieth century for "dance" are *mudo, ttaensŭ,*[4] and *ch'um* (Pak Yong-gu in Choi Haeree 1995:9). *Mudo* is the Korean pronunciation of the Chinese *wudao, wu* meaning "to dance" and *dao* "to step." *Ttaensŭ* is the Korean pronunciation of the English "dance." In the early twentieth century both *mudo* and *ttaensŭ* were used to refer to western-style ballroom dance and to dancelike fitness exercises. *Ch'um* is a pure-Korean word referring broadly to all kinds of dance that existed since ancient times, including, for example, dances performed for entertainment in the palace and those performed in religious contexts (all of which are described below).

During the Japanese occupation, a new Chinese-derived term, *muyong*, was introduced in a 1914 newspaper article (*Maeil Shinbo* — Daily Newspaper) (Pak Yong-gu in Choi Haeree 1995:9). The term originated in Japan, where it was invented in 1904 or 1905 by Tsubouchi Shōyō, a scholar of English literature.[5] Because existing Japanese terminology included only separate terms for specific kinds of dance, Tsubouchi sought a synonym for "dance" as it was used broadly in other languages, such as *tanz* in German and *danse* in French.[6] He chose the character *wu*, from *wudao*, that was a component of the earlier Korean *mudo*, but translated it as "to circulate or turn the arms" rather than "to dance," and *yong* (pronounced approximately the same in both Chinese and Korean), the Chinese character meaning "to leap" or "to jump." When combined and given their Japanese pronunciation, this produced *buyō*.[7] With the Japanese colonial push to transform Korean culture, including the language, the Chinese-derived Japanese term *buyō*, which had been introduced through a Korean newspaper article, was given its Korean pronunciation —*muyong*—and gained common usage. The terms *ch'um*, *mudo*, and *ttaensŭ* were then reserved to designate nontheatrical (such as village) or recreational (such as ballroom) dances. These dances were considered inferior, and the terms declined in usage. Rather than *muyong* serving as a general term for all types of dance, as Tsubouchi advocated with the term *buyō* in Japan, Korean dancers preferred to use this Chinese-derived but imported-through-Japan term to refer specifically to theatrical dances performed in concert halls (Yi Song in Choi Haeree 1995:9). Thus, with the introduction of the term *muyong* there was still no term for identifying "dance" generically, and the political authority of Japan added yet another term to those that already existed.

Following the end of the Japanese occupation (1945) and the Korean War (1953), a strong nationalistic movement evolved, reaching a peak in the 1970s. This brought an increasing effort to use pure-Korean terms, and the pure-Korean term *ch'um* was revived in Korean dance circles. However, this created confusion over the meanings of *ch'um* and *muyong*, which were sometimes used in the same contexts; were they intended to identify different kinds of dance or to be synonyms for a generic concept of dance? For example, *ch'angjak ch'um* and *ch'angjak muyong* (discussed below) were both used in reference to a dance genre evolving in the 1970s. A little later, in the middle of the 1980s, dancers became increasingly aware of this conflicting terminology. Some dance scholars and critics advocated abandoning the Sino-Korean *muyong* altogether and using only the Korean *ch'um* to refer broadly to all kinds of dance, a choice clearly in line with nationalistic sentiment. For example, dance critic Kim Ch'ae-hyŏn, in his 1989 book *Ch'um kwa sam ŭi munhwa* (Culture of Dance and Life), asserted that Korean dancers should replace the foreign-derived *muyong* with the pure-Korean *ch'um*, and gave three reasons for doing so, all related to the search for a distinctive Korean identity (in Choi Haeree 1995:171–172). First, because of the nationalistic trend to use pure-Korean words, members of the younger generation who grew up after the Japanese occupation were more familiar with pure-Korean terms than with the older Sino-Korean words. Second, with the 1976 publication of the inaugural issue of *Ch'um*, which was the first Korean dance magazine and which had a profound influence in Korean dance circles, the term *ch'um* had become more familiar to dancers. Third, the government emphasis on pure-Korean words was intended to influence all aspects of culture. Nationalistic interests became so pervasive that dancers created many new pure-Korean words, such as *ch'umkkun*, meaning "dancer"; *ch'umt'ŏ*, "dance theater"; *ch'ump'ae*, "dance group"; and *ch'ump'an*, "dance performance." In their writings, scholars and critics began to avoid using *muyong*, except in such terms as *muyongkwa*, "dance department," and *Han'guk muyong*, "Korean dance." Koreans do not seem bothered by words of mixed origin, and the half Sino-Korean/half pure-Korean *"Han'guk ch'um"* was also used for "Korean dance."

Twenty-first Century Terminology
for Specific Kinds of Dance

At the beginning of the twenty-first century, some dancers and writers use only *muyong*, others use only *ch'um*, and still others use both. For some scholars the choice to use the Sino-Korean *muyong* is based on the long-established tradition of Chinese being the language of the scholarly and the elite, regardless of the Japanese route through which the term came to Korea. For others, the nationalistic advocacy of "things Korean" mandates using the pure-Korean *ch'um*. Regardless of the choice, however, these terms now refer broadly to all types of dance. For example, in advertisements in the magazine *Ch'um*, *ch'um* and *muyong* are found in the titles of ballet, jazz, and modern dance companies as well as those that perform only traditional Korean dance.

In examining the origins and meanings of additional terms, it is easier to move through the terminology categorically rather than chronologically. Although the overriding categorical scheme used here is my own, it intersects at many points with indigenous Korean schemes. It is provided here as a means to help sort out the complex terminology rather than to argue for particular categories. Figure 4 organizes, in a way that facilitates tracking the relationship between the terms and the types of dance they identify, most of the terms discussed.

The Sino-Korean word *Han'guk*, meaning Korea, is sometimes added to either *muyong* or *ch'um* to create *Han'guk muyong* and *Han'guk ch'um*.[8] Although the literal translation of *"Han'guk muyong"* is "Korean dance," the term is used by Koreans with two applications of different scope. In its broad application, *Han'guk muyong* embraces all dances performed in Korea, including dances of western origin (ballet, modern dance, and social dance). In its narrow application it refers only to traditional dances of Korea and dances that evolved from, but maintain close links with, them (identified as "derived" dances in Chapter 1). In this narrow usage, Koreans place *Han'guk muyong* in opposition to the Sino-Korean *sŏgu muyong*, literally "western dance," or *oeguk muyong*, also Sino-Korean, meaning "foreign dance." These latter two terms refer to types of dance introduced from outside Korea in the early twentieth century.

Today, the Sino-Korean *Han'guk muyong* and the half-Sino-Korean/half-pure-Korean *Han'guk ch'um* are often used interchangeably by Koreans, many using them in only the narrow sense: traditional Korean dance and its close derivatives. To avoid confusion, and for the sake of consistency, except when quoting others who specifically use *ch'um* or in composite terms where only *ch'um* is used, *muyong* rather than *ch'um* is used hereafter, and *Han'guk muyong* is used in its narrow application.

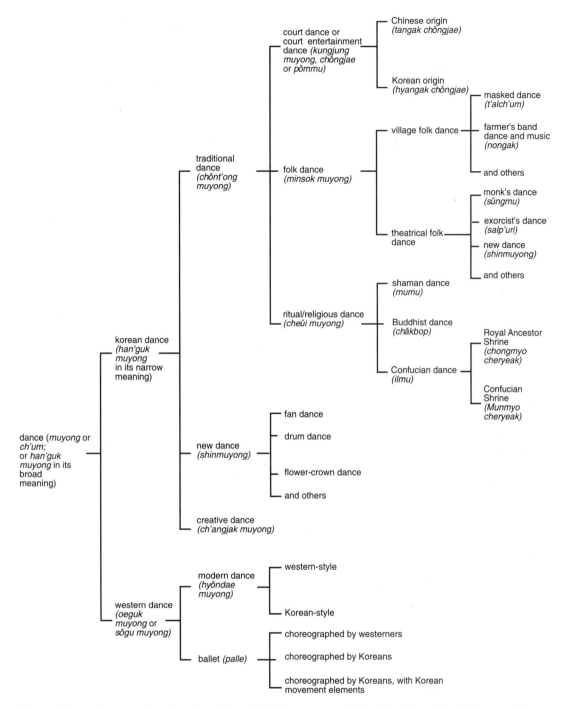

Figure 4. Korean dance terminology (adapted from Choi Haeree 1995:27). This chart is intended to facilitate tracking the complexities of terminology in current use and the interrelationships between some of the terms, but not as a definitive classification scheme.

Koreans today generally divide *Han'guk muyong*, Korean dance, into three categories: "traditional dance" (*chŏnt'ong muyong*), "new dance" (*shinmuyong*), and "creative dance" (*ch'angjak muyong* or *ch'angjak ch'um*, the latter another half-Sino-Korean/half-pure-Korean term).[9]

The word *chŏnt'ong* is derived from two Chinese characters, one meaning "to transmit" or "to pass from," as in "passing from one place to another," and the other signifying "to gather," "to govern," or "to unite." Thus, the implication is that dances identified as *chŏnt'ong muyong* have been passed down over time, corresponding to the usual connotation of the English "tradition," with emphasis here on a continuing heritage.[10]

Korean dancers and scholars generally agree on two subcategories within the traditional category of Korean dance, categories glossed in English as "court dance" and "folk dance." Court dance, sometimes referred to as "court entertainment dance," was originally performed in the palace for entertainment at court banquets. This subcategory is identified in Korean by one of two terms, *kungjung muyong* or *chŏngjae*. The Sino-Korean *kungjung muyong*, from characters meaning "palace" and "center," hence "dance within the palace" or "dance at the center," describes dances in terms of the physical environment in which they were originally performed. *Chŏngjae*, a Sino-Korean word from characters meaning to "present" or "submit," and implying from an inferior person to a superior person, and "talent," hence "showing talent to a superior," emphasizes the act of performing and the hierarchical social rank of the performer and the audience. *Chŏngjae* is generally glossed in English as "entertainment."[11]

By the middle of the fifteenth century (during the reign of King Sŏngjong, r. 1470–1494), court entertainment dances were officially further subclassified into two types.[12] The term *chŏngjae*, showing talent to a superior, was used in conjunction with two other Sino-Korean words, *hyangak* and *tangak*, designating the country of origin of the dances and the music to which they were performed. *Hyang* means "the countryside" or "one's native place," in this case, Korea, and *ak* means "music." When combined with *chŏngjae*, the term refers to dance, and *hyangak chŏngjae* identifies indigenous dances that present talent. The term *tangak* is based on *T'ang*, from the T'ang dynasty of China (618–907). Thus, *tangak chŏngjae* refers to dances originating in China that present talent.[13] Noteworthy here is the acknowledgment of geographic origin of the individual dances and the fact that dances originating in China are now considered traditional Korean dances, or *Han'guk muyong* in its narrow usage.[14]

In addition to court entertainment dances, Korean dancers and scholars identify a second type of traditional dance as *minsok muyong* or *minsok ch'um* (depending on whether the Sino-Korean or pure-Korean word for "dance" is used). *Minsok* is based on the Chinese characters for "people" and "custom," which, when combined, refer to the "common people." Therefore, *minsok muyong* means "dance of the common people," and is generally translated as "folk dance." This English-language gloss, however, can be confusing. First, what is meant by "folk dance" among native English-language speakers is not at all clear. To some, the term conjures up images of European villagers performing simple repetitive movement patterns in a circle on festive occasions. European and American dance scholars have debated varying definitions in their efforts to arrive at concensus on what the term means, but no common definition has emerged and many avoid using the term.[15] Second, the Korean term identifies dances with quite different characteristics and that are done in quite different contexts, suggesting two distinctive subcategories. To facilitate the discussion here, I retain the Korean grouping of "folk dance" at the same time I distinguish between subcategories I refer to as "village folk dance" and "theatrical folk dance." My terminology for these subcategories is based on the original settings in which the dances were, and in some instances still are, performed.

Village folk dances generally originated in rituals of the commoners or village people. They were, and sometimes still are, done as part of daily life and work, such as masked dance-dramas (*t'alch'um*) and farmers' dances (*nongak*) that are part of agricultural celebrations performed on ritualistic occasions. Origins of these dances are generally attributed to a distant past, and most frequently these dances were performed by itinerant performers or individuals who earned their livelihood through other occupations (such as farming), focused on themes relating to village concerns (such as harvesting crops), and used movements based on those found in daily activities (such as planting rice, walking across bridges, or household activities). Theatrical folk dances are danced by professional performers who learn through formal training and present their performances in theatrical settings. These dances generally have no specific story line, and use movements derived from older court dances or the village folk dances. They were created primarily early in the twentieth century, and are essentially adaptations choreographed for performance on a western-style proscenium-arch stage.[16] These include sŭngmu, a dance based on a Buddhist dance, salp'uri, a dance most commonly described as being rooted in shamanistic ritual dances, and many dances at one time identified as *shinmuyong* (see discussion below). These are the dances referred to in Chapter 1 as derived dances. Note that in the terminology chart in Figure 4 *shinmuyong* appears as a subcategory of theatrical folk dance as well as a subcategory of Korean dance. This reflects the derivative nature of many dances in this grouping, the importance of this category, and the confusion (discussed below) in sorting out some of the currently used terminology.

The premise underlying the Korean grouping of these seemingly diverse dances into the single category of folk dance lies in the fact that they were all originally intended for the common people. Although rooted in dances originally done for royalty in the courts and for aristocrats, the theatrical folk dances originated during the Japanese occupation, when the court no longer existed, and they were intended for common people rather than an aristocracy. In other words, the "folk" label as distinguished from the "court" label reflects the audience for whom the dances were intended as well as a traditional Korean concern with social class differentiation. In this case dances performed within the court were juxtaposed against those performed outside the court, regardless of the nature of the dances, the training of the performers, or the performance venue, and reinforced both location and social hierarchy.

In addition to folk dance (*minsok muyong*) and court dance (*chŏngjae* or *kungjung muyong*), a third category of traditional dance identified by some Korean dancers and scholars is ritual or religious dance. Dances that are part of shaman, Buddhist, or Confucian practices are identified in Korean as *cheŭi muyong*, from the Chinese characters meaning "sacrifice" and "appearance," "ceremony, rite," "presentation, gift," or "apparatus, instrument (tool)." Hence, *cheŭi muyong* is glossed as "ritual dance" or "religious dance." In this case the term describes the functional contexts of the dances.

In the past, shaman ritual dance was referred to as *mumu*, a Sino-Korean word from the Chinese characters literally meaning "shaman dance." In more recent times, it has come to be referred to as *musok ch'um*. *Musok* is from the Chinese *wu*, meaning shaman (a different character than the *wu* meaning "dance"), and *sok*, meaning "village." Thus, the term refers to the location in which the dance usually occurred as well as to who danced it, and the inclusion of "village" in the term carries with it a connotation of lower class. Although some people do not consider the type of movement included in shaman rituals to be dance, because there is a structure to it and because there is a movement component in the training of shamans (see, for example, Kendall and Lee:1991), it is included in the dance classification system presented here. (The issue of dance versus structured movement in shaman contexts is discussed more fully in Chapter 6.) Structured movement is performed by shamans during a ritual (*kut*), with the most significant movement, or dancing, occurring when the shaman is taken over by the spirits invoked during the ceremony. At moments of ritualistic climax those for whom the ritual is being performed move in ways similar to shamans, and the term "shaman dance" emphasizes the importance of the movements done by the shaman or in the context of a shaman ritual.

Buddhist ritual dance, an integral part of many ceremonies at temples, is known as *chakpŏp*, from the Chinese characters meaning "to do" or "to make" and "method" or "law." The Chinese word for method or law (*fa*, pronounced *bŏp* in Korean) often refers specifically to Buddhist law (*dharma*), hence its Korean use to identify Buddhist dance. Besides its reference to Buddhism, the term *chakpŏp* may have been used to identify this type of dance because of its extremely methodical movements, which follow a particular method or law. In this case the term refers to either the function of the dance or its characteristics.

Confucian dances, performed on ceremonial occasions at shrines, are known as *ilmu*, from the Chinese characters referring to an ancient music and dance formation described in the Confucian Analects. Use of the term in Korea undoubtedly originated from the direct importation of these dances from China, and from the arrangement of the dancers during performance; they stand primarily in one spot in rows and columns. These dances are classified as *munmyo cheryak*, again Sino-Korean, from the Chinese characters meaning "Confucian temple sacrificial ritual music," and referring in Korea to Confucian Shrine Dance and Music, or Chongmyo cheryak, also Sino-Korean, from the Chinese characters meaning "ancestral temple sacrificial ritual music," and referring to Royal Ancestors' Shrine Dance and Music. The terminology for this classification identifies both the function and context in which the dances are done. This is also an instance in which terms literally meaning "music" are assumed to include dance.

Confucian Shrine Dance is further classified as *munmu*, from the Chinese for "civil dance," or *mumu*, from the Chinese for "military dance." (The *mu* used in *mumu* meaning shaman dances and the *mu* used in the term here for a kind of Confucian dance are written with different Chinese characters. Hence, the meaning is different.) The "civil" and "military" terminology relate to the intended symbolism of the dances, which today is seen only in implements held by the dancers rather than in the movements (see Chapter 1).

Some Korean dancers and writers classify Confucian dance as a sub-category within court dance because of its original sponsorship: Since Confucianism was at one time the official government ideology, associated activities received government support. When this type of categorization is used, the larger category of "court dance" is subcategorized as court entertainment dance or Confucian dance. Labelling Confucian dance as either court dance or ritual/religious dance depends on whether function or sponsorship is emphasized.

The second major category within the narrowly defined term "Korean dance" (*Han'guk muyong*) is *shinmuyong*, a word and concept influenced by Japan and, indirectly, Germany. In the early twentieth century the western world had a strong influence on virtually every aspect of Japanese life. A new kind of dance introduced into Japan at this time was based on a trend in Germany known as *neue tanz*, literally "new dance," known in English as German expressionist dance, which is one type of western dance identified as "modern dance" or "contemporary dance" (see Note 17, Chapter 1). Just as many other elements of western culture were introduced to Korea through Japan, this German dance style was brought to Korea when Japanese dancer Ishii Baku performed it in Seoul in 1926. According to one theory, Ishii billed his dance as *shinmuyong*, which he described as a translation of the German *neue tanz*[17] (Choi Haeree 1995:19). The Chinese character *shin* (pronounced essentially the same in Chinese, Japanese, and Korean), meaning "new," combined with the Japanese *buyō*, meaning dance, to produce *shin buyō*. When pronounced in Korean, the term becomes *shinmuyong*. Although Ishii's style was never really adopted by dancers in Korea (a different style of modern dance was introduced later), he may have been responsible for introducing the term *shinmuyong*.

A second explanation for the introduction of the term *shinmuyong*, or "new dance," relates to other developments occurring in Japan at the same time. Based on western ideas, Tsubouchi Shōyō, the Japanese literary scholar referred to previously, advocated the reform of *kabuki*, a traditional Japanese theater genre, and *nihon buyō* (literally "Japanese dance"), the *kabuki*-derived dance genre (Pronko 1985:112). The specific reforms proposed by Tsubouchi greatly influenced some *kabuki* actors, and *nihon buyō* dancers also adopted many of his recommended revisions. A new kind of dance emerged that became known as *shin buyō*. Thus, Japanese dances choreographed since the 1920s, which in general are based on classical themes, are simply identified as "new dance" (Ito 1979:267). It is possible that as Koreans began, concurrently, to develop their own dances in new ways, they used the term common in Japan to describe their evolving trend.

A third explanation for the introduction of the term *shinmuyong* is proposed by Korean dance scholar An Che-sung. An takes a nationalistic stance, stating that the term *shinmuyong* came into use *after* Ishii's performance, that it was coined by Koreans themselves, and that it referred to a style that grew from the seeds planted by Ishii but that was strongly rooted in traditional Korean dances (in Choi Haeree 1995:19). Thus, the "new" related to a kind of stylistic development in dance that was based on the past, rather than on something imported from another country, and that simply paralleled dance developments in Japan rather than emanated from them. If this was, indeed, the case, the terminology may have been inspired by other terminology Koreans began using in the 1920s. With the importation of western ideas via Japan, and Korea's interest in modernizing, new developments occurred and terms were created to describe—and emphasize—these innovations. Koreans began to talk about new poetry (*shinshi*), new education (*shin'gyoyuk*), new theater (*shin'gŭk*), and even new women (*shinnyŏsŏng*). As dances developed in different ways from those of the past, people began to use a term that paralleled that used in Japan, rather than consciously importing the term.

Further contributing to—and confusing—the terminology of this period is *kŭndae muyong*, another Sino-Korean term that probably predates *shinmuyong*. *Kŭndae* is from the Chinese characters meaning "near generation" or "near era." In China these characters are used by people to identify the recent past when they are looking back, and therefore the specific period to which the term refers is always changing (Daniel Cole, personal communication 22 Oct. 1997).[18] Although of Chinese origin, Koreans borrowed the term *kŭndae* from Japan, some time in the late nineteenth or early twentieth century (Alexander Vovin, personal communication 16 Dec. 1997), to refer to the new, or modern, era. Thus, the literal meanings of *shin* and *kŭndae* are quite close. In the early twenty-first century, Korean historians tend to use *kŭndae* to refer to a specific time period—the late Chosŏn dynasty (1392–1910) through the end of the Japanese annexation (the late nineteenth century through the early twentieth century) in order to identify an era of extreme modernization strongly influenced by the western world and brought to Korea largely through Japan.[19] Since *kŭndae* refers to a particular time period, *kŭndae muyong* was at first applied to all dance in Korea that originated in this period and that was considered to contribute to modernization. Hence, it embraced new dance (*shinmuyong*) as well as ballet and western-style modern dance, the latter two also introduced at this time. This again contributed to confusion (as with the earlier use of both *muyong* and *ch'um*), with *kŭndae muyong* and *shinmuyong* sometimes used synonymously. Korean dancers and scholars today prefer to differentiate between dances sharing many characteristics and disparate dance styles that simply developed during a common time period. Thus, they use *kŭndae muyong* as a broad category referring to dances of the *kŭndae* period, which includes ballet, western-style modern dance, theatrical folk dance, and *shinmuyong*, reserving *shinmuyong* to specifically identify dances created primarily during the Japanese occupation that merged movements and themes of traditional Korean dance with a modern western aesthetic imported through Japan.[20]

By the late 1970s dances identified as *shinmuyong* (new dance), declined in popularity because of the nationalistic trend; despite their movement and thematic ties to traditional Korean dance, new dance was too closely associated with the period of Japanese occupation. Koreans involved with the nationalistic movement of the 1970s believed cultural manifestations influenced by or adapted from Japan should be discarded and replaced by Korean forms. They also began to consider words incorporating *shin*, including *shinmuyong*, to identify past events or out-of-date styles. Today many of these dances have been revived. They are used as stereotypically representative of "Korean dance," are sometimes identified as "folk dance," and would fall into the category I have identified as "theatrical folk dance." In scholarly contexts, however, the term *shinmuyong* is still used to identify a particular type of dance from a particular time period, and *shinmuyong* is considered a bridge between the older forms, the traditional dances (*chŏnt'ong muyong*), and the more recent development, "creative dance" (*ch'angjak ch'um* or *ch'angjak muyong*), which constitutes a third category of Korean dance (*Han'guk muyong* in its narrow meaning).

Ch'angjak is the Korean pronunciation of the Chinese word meaning "to create." Hence, *ch'angjak muyong* means "creative dance." (*Ch'angjak muyong* and *ch'angjak ch'um* are both used today, depending on the user's preference for the Sino-Korean or pure-Korean word for dance. For the sake of consistency, except in direct quotations I will continue to use *ch'angjak muyong* here.) All newly choreographed works, including theatrical folk dance and new dance, both being creative works derived from older traditional dances, could be considered *ch'angjak muyong*, but the term has a special meaning for Korean dancers and dance scholars. Unlike the term "new dance," ultimately applied to dances maintaining elements of traditional Korean dance in both movement and basic theme, *ch'angjak muyong* refers to Korean dances in which some individual movements are derived from traditional dance (*chŏnt'ong muyong*), but themes, which reflect contemporary society, and choreographic structure are new. The retention of traditional movements in both new dance and creative dance was rooted in the nationalistic spirit of the period in which each developed, a rediscovery of tradition used to express national identity. But the way in which traditional movements were used in each of these dance genres differed. Dance critic Yi Sang-il notes that "all dance that seeks the creative succession of traditions can be called *ch'angjak ch'um*" (in Choi Haeree 1995:21), and it is the "*creative* succession of tradition" that is the hallmark of *ch'angjak muyong* choreographers. But they have gone further with creativity than the choreographers of new dance. Choreographers who work in the creative dance style use a process that combines an impulse toward individual expression and creativity with movements based on those found in traditional dance; they try to create modern theatrical dance forms based on the distinctive movements and qualities of traditional Korean dance, but use them in innovative ways. And these movements and qualities serve as the basis for making statements about contemporary life.[21]

Because both new dance and creative dance use movements based on those of traditional dance, it is not always easy to distinguish between them. In general, the movements in new dance more strongly resemble those of traditional dances; some movements in creative dance *suggest* those in traditional dances, but are seldom exact replications. Movements in creative dance are often *inspired* by those in traditional dance, while movements in new dance are *variations* of those in traditional dance. Korean dance critic Kim T'ae-wŏn describes new dance as "romantic" and creative dance as characterized by principles of opposition—knotting and unknotting, enlarging and shrinking, and stopping and shifting; possessing "an internal tension and a keen lineal beauty while still having the curvaceousness intrinsic to the traditional movements of Korean dance" (1997:136–137). Additionally, new dance was generally intended to entertain without making a social or political statement, while creative dance most often comments on contemporary life. One pioneer of the creative dance style describes it as not simply reviving tradition, but modifying and transforming it to suit contemporary life (Kim Mae-ja in Choi Haeree 1995:23). Some Korean dance writers describe the differences by stating that new dance choreographers adopted many surface elements of traditional dance forms without acknowledging their roots or incorporating the feelings of *mŏt* and *hŭng* considered to be so important in traditional dances.[22] They argue that new dance spoiled the nature and spirit of Korean dance by simply displaying beauty and coquetry, and by emphasizing an entertainment function (see, for example, Kim T'ae-wŏn 1992:63). While the difference between creative dance and new dance is more readily distinguishable in recent creative dance choreographies, as the genre of creative dance continues to develop, distinctions between creative dance and what is identified as modern dance (*hyŏndae muyong*) become less clear. (See discussion of *hyŏndae muyong* below.)

The term *ch'angjak muyong* did not come into use until after the emergence of the dance style that it describes, and there are several possible explanations for its introduction. As western forms of modern dance were introduced to Korea (initially as early as the late 1920s with Ishii Baku's performance of German expressionist modern dance, and subsequently with their reintroduction in the 1960s, discussed shortly), their emphasis on creativity and individuality began to influence dancers in Korea. Young students were directly exposed to these new ideas in dance programs at universities, and some sought different choreographic methods from those used in new dance (*shinmuyong*). With the establishment of a dance major in 1963 and the strong presence of dance in higher education through its program, Ewha Woman's University began to structure its course offerings around the concept of creativity, or *ch'angjaksŏng*. Students were required to include creativity in dances they presented in annual and graduation concerts. They called these events *ch'angjak muyong palp'yohoe*, "creative dance concert," and referred to their creative works as *ch'angjak muyong* (Kim T'ae-wŏn in Choi Haeree 1995:24–25). Thus, one explanation for the introduction of the term *ch'angjak muyong* is the emphasis on creativity among university students and the inclusion of dances based on this concept in their course requirements.

A second explanation lies in the use of the term *ch'angjak muyong* by a dance company instrumental in the development of this genre. In 1976, Kim Mae-ja, then a professor of dance at Ewha Woman's University, established a company known as Ch'angmuhoe. The company's name is based on the Chinese "*ch'ang*" of "*ch'angjak*," and means "creative dance company." The focus of this company was on re-creating tradition and modernizing Korean dance, which implied creating a modern Korean idiom that reflected contemporary times but was rooted in the past (Choi Haeree 1995:25–26).[23]

A third explanation goes back, again, to developments in Japan and Japanese influence in Korea. Following World War II, developments in Japanese dance moved in a slightly different direction from those that had produced *shin buyō*, or new dance (comparable to the Korean *shinmuyong*). The Japanese began using the term *sosakubuyō*, derived from the same Chinese characters meaning "creative dance" that produced the Korean pronunciation *ch'angjak muyong*. The Japanese *sosakubuyō*, or creative dances, were further modified from their traditional sources than were *shin buyō*, and consciously sought international appeal (Pronko 1985:114). According to one theory, when the genre that came to be known as *ch'angjak muyong* began to fully develop in Korea in the 1980s, Japanese-educated dance critic Pak Yong-gu introduced the Japanese term *sosakubuyō*, which was then given its Korean pronunciation of *ch'angjak muyong*, and was used to describe the newly developing creative style (Pak Yong-gu in Choi Haeree 1995:25).

Until the 1980s, and before the term *ch'angjak muyong* was widely used, people had been as creative in trying to devise new terms as in dance itself, leading to some rather unusual terminology. "Contemporary Korean dance" (*hyŏndae Han'guk muyong*), "new-new dance" (*shin-shinmuyong*), "new traditional dance" (*shin chŏnt'ong muyong*), and "creative Korean dance" (*ch'angjak Han'guk muyong*) were all inconsistently used to identify this new genre. Korean dance writers contributed to unifying terminology. Beginning with Pak Yong-gu in the late 1980s and then Kim T'ae-wŏn, dance critics consistently began to use the term *ch'angjak muyong* in their writings (Kim T'ae-wŏn in Choi Haeree 1995:24). In this instance the creativity involved in seeking appropriate terminology clearly reflects an effort to determine which ingredients in this newly evolved type of dance were most important. The resolution explicitly reflects the emphasis on creativity within the dance style.

Despite its emphasis on innovation, creative dance is still considered by most Koreans to be distinctively Korean. Therefore, it is only in reference to dance styles that were imported in a more holistic fashion that the term "western dance" is applied. The concept of western dance (*sŏgu muyong*, literally "western dance," or *oeguk muyong*, literally "foreign dance," both Sino-Korean), as distinguished from Korean dance (*Han'guk muyong*) in its narrow meaning, is subdivided by Koreans into *hyŏndae muyong*, literally "modern dance," but conceptually "western-style modern dance," and *palle*, the Korean pronunciation for "ballet." The Sino-Korean, Japanese-derived term *muyong* has been reinstated here in conjunction with *hyŏndae* rather than the pure-Korean term *ch'um*, although *hyŏndae ch'um* is occasionally used today.

Hyŏndae muyong, *hyŏndae* from the Chinese "present era," is comparable to what is most often known in the United States as "modern dance" and in Europe as "contemporary dance." This style of dance was initially introduced to Korea in 1926 by the Japanese performer Ishii Baku, but was not successful at that time, contributing instead to the more indigenously based style that came to be known as new dance (*shin-muyong*). Modern dance (*hyŏndae muyong*) was reintroduced to Korea in a stylistically different form than that of Ishii Baku by Yuk Wan-sun, a former Ewha Woman's University professor and colleague of Kim Mae-ja, one of the leaders in the development of creative dance.[24]

Toward the end of the twentieth century, some modern dancers (*hyŏndae muyong* performers) of Korea again began to incorporate traditional dance forms (*chŏnt'ong muyong*) into their works. This led to the separation, by some Koreans, of modern dance into western-style modern dance (*oeguk hyŏndae muyong*) and Korean-style modern dance (*Han'guk hyŏndae muyong*). This, in turn, contributed to confusion in delineating creative dance (*ch'angjak muyong*) from Korean-style modern dance. Both creative dance and Korean-style modern dance could be considered modern dance, since both are quite recent developments. But creative dance performers generally do not identify their work as Korean-style modern dance; they prefer to maintain what they perceive as a stronger Korean identity and to use the label "creative dance." Often the major distinction between Korean-style modern dance and creative dance lies in the training of the dancers and choreographers: Creative dance performers and choreographers typically are trained primarily in traditional Korean dance, while Korean-style modern dancers and choreographers typically are trained primarily in western-style modern dance. This may result in unintended qualitative differences in the dancers' movements resulting from the very different physical technique involved in each of these styles. This attempt to identify individual kinds of modern dance parallels earlier debates about the most appropriate term for what is now known as creative dance. Clarity will undoubtedly come over time.

The second major subcategory of western dance is ballet, which became significant via a Japanese route[25] (see Chapter 1). In this case, however, there were no attempts to find a Korean term to identify it.

Korean dancers generally acknowledge three kinds of ballet, although they do not use specific terminology to refer to each. They distinguish between works created by western choreographers, such as *Nutcracker*, *Giselle*, and *Swan Lake*; works choreographed by Koreans in a classical ballet style; and works choreographed by Koreans that mix Korean-inspired elements, such as selected traditional dance movements, costumes, and stories, with conventional ballet movement vocabulary and *pointe* shoes.[26]

Terminology Summary

In summary, all dances performed today in Korea can be identified as Korean dance, using the term broadly. To be more precise, dances are categorized into two groups: Korean dance more narrowly defined and western or foreign dance. In its narrow definition Korean dance includes several types of traditional dance as well as new dance and creative dance, the latter two rooted in traditional dance. Western, or foreign, dance includes modern dance, referring to foreign-influenced modern dance and a Korean style of the foreign-influenced modern dance, and ballet, strongly based on its western counterpart. These classifications are reinforced by dance curricula in Korean universities in which students major in Korean dance, modern dance, or ballet. In addition, dancers in Korea precisely identify themselves as Korean dancers, modern dancers, or ballet dancers. But this three-pronged emphasis cuts across two "levels" of the overriding classification scheme presented here: All of the various subtypes of

Korean dance are clustered together, but the two subtypes of western or foreign dance—ballet and modern dance—maintain their identities.

The Korean terms for all of the classifications and subclassifications are based on Sino-Korean, pure-Korean, English, French, and possibly German words. Some of the Sino-Korean words, as well as those from other languages, were introduced via their Japanese usages. Both the terms and the dances to which they are applied have changed over time, sometimes prompted by Koreans themselves and sometimes by non-Koreans.

Analysis

These complex terminological developments result from several things. First, the scholarly study of dance in Korea by dance researchers is quite recent. It has only been toward the end of the twentieth century, with the explosion of dance activities in the 1970s and 1980s, that individuals became seriously interested in theoretical issues relating to dance, and that some people have been specifically trained in dance research. Earlier in this century writings about dance were most often produced by people trained in folklore, music, or aesthetics. For example, Chang Sa-hun was a musicologist, Yi Tu-hyŏn was trained in literature and folklore, Chŏng Pyŏng-ho specialized in folklore studies,[27] Kim T'ae-wŏn studied theater and film, and Ch'ae Hŭi-wan and Kim Ch'ae-hyŏn studied aesthetics. Even dance critics came from diverse fields of study. Quite naturally, the ideas and dance writings of these people, who have been extremely influential in proposing, advocating, and establishing trends in dance terminology, are influenced by the perspective of disciplines other than dance. Thus, the power these individuals hold through the impact of their writings and the concepts and ways of thinking emanating from the disciplines in which they were trained have an important influence on dance terminology.[28]

Second, it is often difficult to name and classify contemporaneous phenomena. Developments in dance in Korea occurred rapidly from the beginning of the twentieth century, gaining momentum as the century drew to its end. Because people are so close to what is happening, and in many cases are directly involved in it, they have difficulty sorting out the complexities that would facilitate delineating boundaries between classifications.[29]

Despite these problems the direct causes of some of the terminological changes can be identified. The strongest influence on Korean dance terminology is the Chinese language, which, with the exception of "*ch'um*" and "*palle*," is the source for virtually all of the key terminology used today. (Although *muyong* and *ch'um* are both frequently used, I have retained *muyong* throughout most of the discussion in an attempt to avoid further complicating an already complex issue.[30] Some terms came directly from China before Korea had its own written script, some came from China via Japan, and some were appropriated by the Koreans even after they had their own writing system. As people sought new words they often continued the Confucian tradition of the Chinese language and script being that of the scholar and upper class. Other terms came from English, French, and possibly German, but were influential in only three specific contexts: an early way to describe western-imported ballroom dances and dancelike exercises (*ttaensŭ*), a term for a kind of theatrical dance that maintained its clear western technique and form (*palle* for ballet), and possibly the translation of the German words for new dance (*neue tanz*) into a Chinese-derived Japanese word (*shin buyō*) that was then given a Korean pronunciation (*shinmuyong*).

In many instances terminology was invented by the Koreans (such as *Han'guk hyŏndae muyong*). In others, terminology was advocated—or imposed—by non-Koreans as, for example, with *muyong*, which was propagated by the Japanese during the colonial period as part of their effort to eliminate the Korean language. This effort, however, eventually led to a backlash. When Koreans gained their independence and established strong nationalistic priorities to re-establish their own identity, they rejected as relics of a negative past the Japanese-imposed terminology (substituting, for example, the pure-Korean *ch'um* for the Chinese-derived Japanese word that produced *muyong*) as well as Japanese terms they may have more willingly adopted (such as *shinmuyong*, according to one explanation of its evolution). Even dance styles that developed during the colonial period (such as *shinmuyong*) were subsequently either rejected, or at least looked down on, by many Koreans.[31] In the case of *muyong*, however, the term was subsequently revived. Some fluctuations in the use of the Sino-Korean *muyong* and the pure-Korean *ch'um* undoubtedly reflect vacillating government policies toward using Chinese-derived words and the Chinese writing system. From the end of the Japanese occupation in 1945 through 1977, the government enacted numerous laws restricting, then eliminating, and then reinstating the use of Chinese words and writing in schools and for official purposes (Hannas 1997:69–72).

In some instances, terminology paralleling that used in Japan may simply have resulted from parallel developments and both countries resorting to Chinese-derived terms to identify these developments (as may have been the case with *shinmuyong*, according to one explanation for the evolution of this term).

As the Koreans developed their own terminology, their choices were based on various criteria. At different times terms reflected the geographic origin of dances (such as the court entertainment dances of Chinese versus Korean origin and Korean versus foreign dance), the time of origin (such as initial meanings of the two terms for new dance: *hyŏndae muyong* and *kŭndae muyong*), the function the dance served (such as court entertainment versus ritual/religious), the source of support (court dance), the class of people for whom the dance was intended (court dance versus folk dance), or the movements in the dances (such as creative dance).

Underlying many of the changes and criteria used to establish terms are issues of power. The imposition of dance terminology from Japan reflected the colonizer's power, whereas its subsequent rejection reflected Korea's nationalistic sentiments and a newly established political freedom. Governmental politics, both external and internal, affected developments in dance terminology.

But governmental politics contributed to another kind of power. Government priorities and policies also affected new directions in aesthetic choices and development. Although initiated by the government, the power of aesthetic imperatives sometimes took charge. In at least one case, a terminological choice was made based solely on aesthetic criteria. During the 1970s, creativity as a form of modernization became a governmental driving force, and a new dance style developed that emphasized creativity. Instead of identifying this style with a term for modern (such as *hyŏndae muyong*) it was identified by a term focusing on creativity (*ch'angjak muyong*). Thus, it was the aesthetic emphasis in the dance form rather than when it was created that contributed to terminology. That this dance style reflected government priorities is apparent in statements by one of the dance style's pioneers. Kim Mae-ja, an early contributor to the development of creative dance, described the purpose of her company, Changmuhoe, and of creative dance in general, as being not simply to revive tradition but to modify and transform it to create a dance style reflecting contemporary life.[32] This statement is remarkably similar to a 1971 message of Park Chung Hee, following his inauguration as president for a third term, in which he said that his long-term development plan included promotion of culture and arts, and that the objective of the plan was " 'to create a new national culture based on the indigenous national philosophy and the consciousness of identity, a new national culture that would continue and further develop the cultural and artistic inheritance' "[33] (in Kim Yersu 1976:18). In 1973 this objective was incorporated into an official five-year plan (ibid.:19). In the case of creative dance, government policy led to a backlash that influenced aesthetic choices, ultimately contributing to the development of a new dance style and possibly to the term for that style as well. The emphasis on creativity may also relate to increasing concerns at this time regarding Korea's Intangible Cultural Asset system. In an attempt to preserve traditional culture, this government-sponsored program established fixed choreographies of what were considered to be traditional dances as the "correct" versions of them (see Chapter 3). Many objected to this rigidity and a term that emphasized creativity would have been most appealing. (For a discussion of these attitudes see Yang Jong-sung 1988 and 1994.)

One term is unique in the classification scheme used by Koreans— *tangak chŏngjae*, the court entertainment dances originating in China. The term is unique because it acknowledges an indigenized type of dance. Sanskrit chants accompanying Buddhist dances are a reminder of the Indian origin of this religious practice, and many scholars believe the

Confucian dances performed today retain their original Chinese manifestations. And while Buddhist dance, Confucian dance, and court entertainment dances of Chinese origin are all identified, by Koreans, as traditional dance (*chŏnt'ong muyong*), which is labeled Korean dance (*Han'guk muyong*), it is only the court dances that are identified by terms acknowledging their external geographic source. Although the dances to which the term *tangak chŏngjae* refers are believed to have undergone change, the term and type of dance it identifies now constitute one component of what is considered by Koreans to be part of a uniquely Korean identity.

There are several possible explanations for the retention of the term *tangak chŏngjae* and the dances to which it refers. First, the distinction between dances of Chinese origin and those of Korean origin was made long ago (at least by the fifteenth century). The ingrained respect accorded age, based on long-standing Confucian ideology, would make it more palatable to retain this terminology and to classify the type of dance it identifies as traditional Korean dance.

Second, as performed today, there is little difference between the court dances of Chinese origin and those of Korean origin. (See Chapter 1 and note 14 here. It is not clear whether the similarity in the dances is the result of conscious choice or natural evolution.) Thus, Koreans may not be concerned with the use of two terms.

Third, many Korean writers are disturbed that the Japanese distorted their history, showing it to be more significantly subservient to China than it really was, and devaluing whatever was intrinsically Korean[34] (see, for example, Kim Yersu 1976:10). By maintaining two distinctive categories of court dance Koreans could suggest greater equality in the contributions of each country to dance in Korea.

The politics of place reflected in terms identifying Chinese or Korean origin of court dances is also evident in recent times. Ballet and modern dance were both imported and are identified by broad geographic terms meaning western dance or foreign dance. The further division of modern dance into western-style modern dance and Korean-style modern dance also reflects recent concerns with asserting a uniquely Korean identity—this time in the midst of also asserting a modern, often associated with western, identity.

Some Korean dance terminology reflects an evolutionary pattern. New words are introduced, confusion develops between the new words and existing words, and then a sorting out takes place. This happened, for example, with the two terms that literally relate to time periods—*kŭndae muyong* and *shinmuyong*, meaning "modern dance" and "new dance." In this case, also, politics and power came into play. Until very recently it was primarily critics, other writers, and government officials not specifically trained in dance who, from their positions of power, provided impetus for the decisions.

Dance and its terminology are not immune to political tides and power structures. The examples of Korean dance terminology reflect issues of importance in the kinds of dance to which they refer, as well as in events and attitudes of the times in which the labels were used or during which they evolved. The power and politics of words have contributed in lasting ways to both the development of dance in Korea and to the terms used to identify dance.

3
Dance and Korea's National Treasure System

A Contemporary Ritual System for Preserving and Constructing Identity

A frog is liable to forget that it once was a tadpole, observes an old Korean saying. As a man is freed from his daily preoccupation with subsistence, he begins to look forward to the future. If he is a wise man, he will not only try to remember his own past, he will also attempt to chart his future on the basis of his past. So it is with a nation.

— ANONYMOUS 1979A:316

Background

T he preservation of material artifacts in museums is a common practice. Training programs in how to restore and care for physical objects created in the past that are considered to have special artistic merit provide instruction in what has become a highly developed science. But what of the preservation of intangible aspects of culture, things that are passed on orally or visually, things that exist primarily in a living, performative act? Various kinds of notation systems capable of recording dance in order to preserve it have evolved over time.[1] Until the twentieth century, however, most were associated with specific kinds of dance and served primarily to jog the memory of those who already knew the dances or dance style rather than to communicate clear information about movement to individuals who may never have seen the original. These notation systems seek to provide a tangible product that conveys information about this ephemeral art form.

In Korea, many historical documents sought to record dance through verbal descriptions and pictorial representations of dance performances, and they continue to serve as the basis for attempts to reconstruct dances of the past. (This is discussed further in Chapter 4.) But in the twentieth century, the Korean government made a concerted effort, in a different way, to formalize a procedure for assuring the continuation of intangible aspects of culture.

In 1962 the government of South Korea passed the Law on the Protection of Cultural Properties (Munhwajae Pohopŏp), a law intended to aid in preserving and promoting important facets of Korea's cultural heritage. This law related to both tangible and intangible things, and was rooted in Japanese practices that began in 1871. At that time a Japanese proclamation was issued to foster saving art objects from destruction that was brought on by an anti-Buddhist movement. This was followed by Japanese laws in 1897 and 1929 that sought to preserve primarily temple and shrine architecture and art objects, and to prevent their removal from the country, and in 1950 by the Cultural Properties Protection Law (Bunkazai Hogohō), which added legislation to preserve intangible cultural manifestations as well[2] (Tomoaki 1996:9, 55 and Ogawa 1968:xx–xi).

Prior to Japan's implementation of a law embracing intangible manifestations, and during the first year of colonial occupation of Korea, the Japanese government began to survey physical objects, similar to those considered for preservation in Japan, in the Korean peninsula: "In 1911, the governor-general of Korea's occupying force, Japan, passed a Temple Act . . . which required an inventory to be made of all movable and immovable properties in Buddhist sites considered worthy of preservation" (Howard 1996:92). Although much of the inventory legislation originated by the Japanese colonial authorities was left intact after liberation in 1945, and efforts to preserve tangible objects continued, Korea's 1962 law rescinded the previous legislation, replacing it with a law designed by Korean authorities (although still strongly resembling the existing Japanese model) (ibid.). With the nationalistic fervor following the end of the occupation and the Korean War, a push to simultaneously re-establish a distinctive Korean identity and modernize emerged. Asserting a Korean identity, a task explicitly mentioned in Korea's 1962 law, was addressed by advocating a re-examination and revival of the past. According to Howard, Pares, and English:

> In a series of articles in the *Han'guk Ilbo* (Korean Daily News), written between 1958 and 1962, the journalist Ye Yonghae sought to document what he regarded as dying traditions and introduced the idea of *In'gan munhwajae* (Human Cultural Assets), people who preserved old Korean arts and crafts. Ye lamented that most *In'gan munhwajae* were old, and nobody younger knew the traditions they had kept. In essence, he had taken on the mantle of 1920s cultural nationalists [see Robertson 1979]. . . . [I]n 1962, the incoming government of Park Chung Hee passed a law, the *Munhwajae pohobŏp* [sic] (Cultural Asset Preservation Law), arguing that people must identify with their heritage if they were to retain any self-esteem and national pride as Koreans. (1996:119–120)

Korea's 1962 law, similar to the 1950 law in Japan, established two categories of cultural properties for recognition, tangible items and intangible items. Artistic and historic objects and sites, scenic places, and natural resources considered to have outstanding merit are classified as Important Tangible Cultural Assets (Chungyo Yuhyŏng Munhwajae), and include such things as temple areas, mountains, and flora and fauna. Outstanding talents, arts, and techniques are classified as Important Intangible Cultural Assets (Chungyo Muhyŏng Munhwajae), and include such things as handicrafts, drama, music, and dance.

The government also recognized that Intangible Cultural Assets can only exist through people, and hence established a system for recognizing individuals who are outstanding bearers of the assets. Thus, recognition is given to specific dances and musical works as well as to individuals who are particularly adept in performing them. Over the years amendments strengthened the original law, enhancing recognition of these people, mandating that they teach and perform, and requiring research to find old traditions and offer preservation strategies (Howard 1996:93).

In recent years discussions have debated, often heatedly, the pros and cons of Korea's asset system. Rather than add yet another voice to that discourse, I will examine the system from a different perspective—that of ritual. Such an examination reveals that in the process of attempting to preserve things from Korea's past, the 1962 law and its amendments contributed to:

1. The development of a secular ritual system that involves identifying cultural manifestations to receive recognition;
2. Establishing masters and potential future masters of the cultural manifestations; and
3. Recontextualizing the presentation of performing arts, standardizing their presentation, and mandating repeated performances of them.

The system has also inadvertently contributed to an economic situation that encourages monetary exchange in a manner considered problematic by many. In addition, at the same time this ritual system has contributed to perpetuation, it has both inhibited and, inadvertently, encouraged creativity. Examining the system from the perspective of ritual reveals that dance is used both as an identity marker of a real or imagined past and as a cultural manifestation contributing to a contemporary Korean identity.

My examination of the National Treasure System as a ritual system is based on a secular definition of ritual emphasizing behaviors that are stereotyped, predictable, and prescribed (Guthrie 1976:336).

Structure of the National Treasure System

Korea's Ministry of Culture and Information (Munhwa Kongbobu), in consultation with the Committee on Cultural Properties (Munhwajae Wiwŏnhoe) of the Cultural Property Preservation Bureau (Munhwajae Kwalliguk), is responsible for administering what is often referred to in

English as the National Treasure System. According to the law establishing this system, its purpose is "'to strive for the cultural progress of the Korean people as well as to the development of human culture by preserving cultural properties and their utilization'" (in Yang Jong-sung 1994:51). Since 1964 the Ministry's program has focused on:

1. Recording the description, nature, and operational methods of each asset;
2. Training individuals in the skills of the assets;
3. Providing financial and other government support to individuals designated as possessors of the relevant artistic abilities; and
4. Providing opportunities for public exhibitions and performances. (Anonymous 1979a:320)

A government-appointed committee of scholars and artists accepts proposals for new items to be designated National Treasures. Research is conducted and a formal report is prepared to facilitate decisions.

A specific item, such as a particular dance, that is designated an Intangible Cultural Asset is known in Korean as a *muhyŏng munhwajae*—literally "intangible cultural asset." A hierarchy of knowledgeable individuals was established to insure the continuation of each asset. Individuals who are the most knowledgeable and expert performers of particular dances are referred to by one of three Korean terms: *poyuja*, "one who possesses or holds knowledge"; *in'gan munhwajae*, "human cultural asset";[3] or *muhyŏng munhwajae poyuja*, "an individual who possesses knowledge of an intangible cultural asset." Thus, an individual may, for example, be designated a Ch'ŏyongmu *poyuja*, and be responsible for carrying on the tradition of the dance known as Ch'ŏyongmu by performing it and by passing on knowledge and skill in that dance to other individuals. *Poyuja* are often identified in English as National Living Treasures, and they teach classes in the cultural asset for which they have received recognition.

A student who completes a course of study from a National Living Treasure is referred to as a *chŏnsuja*, "one who is instructed in or initiated into something." From among the *chŏnsuja* the National Living Treasures, together with a group of people from the Committee on Cultural Properties, select those most adept as potential successors to the National Living Treasures; an individual so selected is known as an *isuja*, "one who has completed a course of study." When a National Living Treasure dies, a successor is selected from among the *isuja*. Occasionally special students are provided scholarships to study a particular cultural asset, and they are known as *chŏnsu changhaksaeng*, "scholarship students." Hence, a hierarchy is established to insure the perpetuation of each cultural asset, with the government providing official titles to all and financial assistance to the highest ranking individuals to assist them in practicing their art form and teaching it.

Regional government offices may designate local outstanding cultural assets in a similar fashion. Regional and central government recognition may be for the same or different items.

Since 1969 the Cultural Property Preservation Bureau has sponsored annual performances of each of the Intangible Cultural Assets that are performing arts. At these performances individuals who are prepared are evaluated for potential promotion to a higher rank. These performances are often attended by tourists seeking a taste of the "real" Korea (which seems to mean a taste of the Korea of the past) as well as by Koreans. In addition, dances designated National Treasures are given privileged places in performances intended to speak of a national Korean identity. They are presented at special concerts showcasing "Korean heritage" and on formal government occasions intended to make a specifically Korean statement.[4]

Determining the precise number of dances chosen for recognition depends on how "dance" is defined. The Cultural Property Preservation Law includes, in several different categories, items that, in other contexts, are identified as "dance." For example, dance is included in Chongmyo cheryak, rituals performed at the Royal Ancestors' Shrine, which is officially classified as "music"; is a part of Kanggangsullae, which is commonly described as a dance but according to the Cultural Property Preservation Law is classified as a "play" or "ceremony"; and is integral to masked dance-dramas (t'alch'um), which are classified as "drama"[5] (Yang Jong-sung 1994:188–193). As of 1993, there were only seven items in the separate category for dance, but many more items that include dance are categorized under different headings.[6]

Group dances that have been identified as National Treasures are most often taught at official government-supported schools and performed by members of these institutions.[7] Solo dances, on the other hand, are most frequently taught in the private studios of individuals designated as title-bearers. These individuals participate in officially sponsored performances, but also present the solo dances in independently sponsored concerts. Government institutions maintain formal admissions procedures and staff members teach a prescribed repertoire of dances; title-bearers for solo dances are free to establish whatever procedures they choose for determining who they will teach and train as potential successors in the hierarchical structure. But it is the official government committee that selects successors from among those who have been trained.

The Law in Action

In early 1998, the monthly government stipend for National Living Treasures was 900,000 *wŏn*, approximately $500 U.S.[8] In addition to the monthly stipend, the government also provides family health insurance. This compensation is not intended to provide full support, but rather, according to one second-ranking title holder, "[i]t is meant as a symbolic manifestation of the nation caring for national performers by means of the taxpayer's money" (Yang Jong-sung 1994:106).

The greatest source of income for National Living Treasures, particularly those who are recognized for solo traditions, is not their government stipend. As might be anticipated, business laws of prestige, competition, and supply and demand enter the picture. There is a great deal of stature associated with the highest rank of National Living Treasure. Yang Jong-sung, a second-ranking title holder (*isuja*) for one type of masked dance-drama (Kangnyŏng T'alch'um), states that the highest ranking individuals "are seen as national heroes, national cultural educators, and national cultural promoters" (1994:5), and that recognition has created "a new level of elite among performing artists and in Korean society as a whole" [9] (ibid.:101). This is antithetical to the traditional status of performing artists, in which dancing women were among the lowest class of people, together with individuals involved in polluting activities, such as butchers (Sorensen 1989:165). In the National Treasure system, dancers may achieve the highest rank within the system and, as such, are given public stature as well. They therefore become sought-after teachers who can command sizable teaching fees. An individual interested in becoming the title-bearer for a particular dance pays large sums of money to study with a National Living Treasure in order to gain both knowledge and favor that may eventually allow him or her to move up the ranks and, in turn, collect money from others in order that they may eventually gain knowledge and rank. In the mid-1990s, one National Living Treasure charged an initial fee of 4,000,000 *wŏn*, approximately $5,000 U.S. at that time, *in addition to* monthly teaching fees, to learn one solo dance.[10] Although partial monetary support from the government is an official part of the National Treasure System, the large-scale "teaching economy" that has evolved outside of the system was never intended.

Prestige is also attached to being a student of the highest ranking individuals, as is the possibility of being elevated to a higher rank. According to the system, promotion to a higher rank initially occurs through an evaluation during one of the annual government-sponsored performances. But the highest rank is usually achieved only after substantial demonstration of ability as well as "waiting for one's turn"—promotion to the top rank is not allowed for individuals under the age of fifty, and must generally await the death of those already holding the title. This limits the number of National Living Treasures, and therefore contributes further to creating a hierarchical elite that can charge substantial teaching fees. Thus, procedures relating to skill and knowledge as well as to time and money are the prescribed way to ritualistically climb the ladder to National Living Treasure status.[11]

My description of advancing through the hierarchical ranks as "ritualistically climbing a ladder" and my characterization of the entire National Treasure System as a ritual system are based on anthropologist Stewart Guthrie's definition of ritual that "implies a category or an aspect of behavior which is stereotyped, predictable, prescribed. . . . It is prescribed in that its performance does not depend solely on the whim of an individual but is expected by others under specific circumstances and in a specific manner" (1976:336). This definition emphasizes the form or structure involved in ritual behavior, does not limit the subject matter to religious ties, and implies the repetition of behaviors.[12]

Although the National Treasure System has created a ritual hierarchy of personnel, and individuals within this hierarchy have become important in and of themselves, the system was originally established not to recognize individuals, but to insure the perpetuation of important art forms. Through the hierarchical structure that has been established, however, the government has defined prescribed ways of entering and advancing through its ranked system. These predictable procedures, or behaviors, are repeated again and again as succeeding generations enter the system. But additional procedures, ones that have become established by individuals with ranked titles and those who would like to obtain titles, have also been created. These official and unofficial procedures for awarding recognition to individuals have contributed to the ritual identification of masters and ritually based monetary exchange.[13]

Some of the procedures arising outside of the government law that relate to monetary matters have been the subject of veiled gossip as well as harsh public criticism. While doing research in Korea in 1990, I heard rumors that a well-known dance teacher paid a visit—and a large sum of money—to an elderly and ill National Living Treasure who had been hospitalized. The purported reason? To obtain a recommendation for an official second-ranking title, and hence be in line for the top-ranking title when the individual then holding the position died.[14]

Money became a very public issue with a 1994 Korean magazine article in which Byun Eun-mi proclaimed, " 'Human Cultural Asset System' Struck by Corruption, Scandal, Stagnation. Efforts to preserve tradition may be killing it off." In addition to commenting on the exchange of money outside procedures described in the government law, Byun expressed his belief that National Living Treasures were being excluded from deliberations in choosing their potential successors. According to Byun, "public outrage" centered on the process by which individuals are selected for ranks within the hierarchy. The government organization that maintains the National Treasure System includes a panel of ten judges who are artists, scholars, or government personnel. At least half of this panel must be present at selection sessions and unanimous approval of those present is required to "win" official status. While at one time the National Living Treasures held considerable sway in the selection process, according to Byun some people now claim that the voice of money paid to judges is louder than the voice of those who possess the knowledge (1994:30). According to Yang Jong-sung, such political maneuvering is not limited to high-ranking artists and the judging panel; it also occurs among students, who vie for attention from their teachers at times when nominations for higher ranking titles are being proposed (1994: 111). These practices occurred despite the Cultural Property Preservation Bureau's 1992 implementation of a code of conduct for National Living Treasures that was meant to prevent such unfavorable practices (ibid.: 112–113). In short, people ignore—or perhaps reshape—the ritual procedures established by government law.

The article describing monetary corruption also points to contemporary criticism focusing on aesthetic elements relating to issues of preservation and creativity, which, in turn, contributes to the ritual nature of the system. The author cites a Korean monthly classical music journal that faults the National Treasure System for rewarding individuals who "duplicate the skills of their mentors" by "mimicking" their performances. This is assumed to disregard "interpretive individuality," which the author considers to be "the most important quality in an artist" (Byun Eun-mi 1994: 30–31). Regardless of the greater importance of either preservation or creativity, this criticism ignores the fact that the Cultural Property Preservation Law itself emphasizes the perpetuation of a fixed, designated form of individual dances.[15] The fixing of choreography in the National Treasure report that serves as the basis for selecting dances, and the government mandate to adhere to this choreography, discourage creativity. Official policies relating to intangible cultural properties specifically state an objective of preserving an "original form and version" (wŏnhyŏng) (Chung Ki-young 1996:129). It is important to remember, however, that the National Treasure System did not begin until the mid-1960s. The ephemeral nature of dance and difficulties, particularly in former times, of documenting human movement (despite early attempts to do so), make it impossible to ascertain just how closely today's dance treasures represent what was performed in former times. And the likelihood of changes occurring is particularly great when taking into account political circumstances that, on several occasions, contributed to breaks in the continuity of performing traditional dances. (This is discussed more fully in Chapter 4.)

As part of the research done when considering a dance for recognition, authors of the report try to ascertain the original version of the dance. This then becomes the official version that must be strictly perpetuated.[16] But isuja Yang Jong-sung describes what he considers to be the almost arbitrary way in which this authentic or original version is often determined[17] (1994:77–86). He also points out that some "re-shaping" of tradition has occurred out of necessity, describing the designation of females to continue a tradition originally performed by men when no qualified men are available (1994:93–94). Government officials reiterate the need for some changes in dance by pointing out that time constraints of contemporary performance in nontraditional contexts generally require choreographic editing of lengthy original versions (Yim Dawn-hee and Im Jang-hyuk 1996:215). Thus, despite claims of authenticity, it is likely some changes occurred to "original" versions when determining the one that would be designated as the "official" version.

Officials of the Office of Cultural Properties counter public concerns of identifying a single correct version for preservation (or as one of them puts it, "creating a taxidermy out of a cultural heritage") by stating that fixing a particular version "is the only way to preserve what may quickly dissipate in a rapidly transforming society" (Yim Dawn-hee and Im Jang-hyuk 1996:214). They also point out that both tangible and intangible items are products of a particular time in history. Once tangible items are displayed in a museum, "later generations derive different inspirations from them;" similarly, they say, intangible items should be considered in light of a particular time in history (ibid.:215). Thus, the government stance is that creating a standardized version is not problematic if the dance is looked at from the perspective of a particular period in time, and it is, in fact, *necessary* to create a standardized version for preservation. Regardless of the validity of either standardization or creativity, standardization leads to ritualistic repetition of a single version of a dance, hence contributing to the ritualistic nature of the entire National Treasure System.

In addition to monetary and standardization issues contributing to the ritual nature of the system, there are also issues relating to the creation of entirely new dances that are claimed to have originated in the past. Accusations are made today by nongovernmental people that individuals who wish to obtain recognition for either themselves or their home towns actually create dances that they attribute to the past. Recall that the law firmly establishing the National Treasure System was passed at a time when Korea was striving to reassert its distinctive identity following the Japanese occupation and the Korean War. As a period of extreme nationalism when people were searching for a uniquely Korean identity, the temptation to elaborate on, or even create, things from the "past" would be great. As modernization (which often contributes to homogenization) continues at an astronomical pace at the start of the twenty-first century, the need to maintain a distinctive identity escalates, and "historical" traditions serve as the basis for this unique identity. Thus, in some instances the National Treasure System contributes, inadvertently, to "creating" things of the past, and hence serves both to mark an actual identity of the past as well as to provide the rationale for constructing an imagined or desired past.[18]

The concern expressed by the irate magazine article author with the stagnation of Korea's ritual system for preserving the past, together with the concerns over creating a past, may have been predicted by Richard Rutt, a longtime resident of Korea. In 1964, just two years after the Law on the Protection of Cultural Properties was passed, he lamented the lack of knowledge of Koreans in the roots of their "traditional customs." But he also questioned whether such practices might be reduced

to tourist attractions and curiosities for folklorists to collect and preserve artificially[.] Doubtless, like much else of the culture of old

Korea, they are bound to sink further into the subconscious mind of the nation. As they pass away there will be a sentimental pang; yet artificial efforts to restore culture are as disastrous as artificial efforts to change it. Both are liable to be more concerned with activities in themselves than with their compelling forces. (Rutt 1964:90)

While Rutt focused on the demise of tradition, had he foreseen the potential for creating "old" dances that never really existed, he surely would have added this type of creativity to his concerns. Certainly dances designated as National Treasures are showcased to tourists who are interested in seeing "typically Korean things," and folklorists contribute to the research and documentation of items and people being considered for National Treasure and National Living Treasure status. It is Rutt's statement regarding "activities themselves" versus "compelling forces," however, that is most significant here. Regardless of whether today's "dances of the past" represent an actual former reality or an imagined reality, they are important contributors to a rejuvenated and constructed contemporary identity. While there is certainly a "compelling force" driving this constructed identity, it is a conscious force that is quite different from the forces that propel the organic evolution of many cultural manifestations.[19]

Analysis

Despite the National Treasure System's basis in a similar system in Japan, and despite the initial concern with consciously rejecting things Japanese, the system was not disbanded altogether—perhaps because regardless of the country of its origin, it contributed to maintaining the heritage of Korea's past.[20] The role this ritual system plays in the construction of a distinctively Korean identity is more significant than the foreign roots of the system. In dance, this has given rise to a three-pronged dance presence today. In one prong are dances described as perpetuating forms of the past or as being a revival of the past. In another prong are ballet, imported from the west, and very contemporary forms that often bear little, if any, relationship to anything identifiably Korean. In the third prong we find a conscious attempt to blend movements from older dances with new ideas and choreography that reflect contemporary society—dances that attempt a "creative succession of tradition" rather than a revival.[21]

Dances in the first prong are based on things that were common before the country known as the Hermit Kingdom opened its doors to western cultures in the late nineteenth century. These are the dances formally recognized through the National Treasure System as being distinctively Korean. These same dances are performed today as they are believed to have been done in the past, but their movements also serve as the basis for creative new works—works that do not attempt to preserve or replicate the past, but that demonstrate very clear sources in the past, as well as being more modern.

The National Treasure System established by the Korean government has clearly succeeded in continuing and/or constructing an identity of Korea's past. In doing so, the tradition of national support for certain kinds of dance, established long ago in the royal court, has also continued. At the same time, however, the system itself has become a ritual and it has contributed to creating possibly new dances.[22] Dances originally supported by the country as part of spiritual rituals and subsequently for entertainment, are now part of a nationally supported ritual system in which the performing context has changed and the dances have become standardized. Performance accuracy, or ritual re-enactment, is important as a conscious construction of an identity of former times.[23] And that same identity is a part of the construction of a contemporary identity.

Identity is an ongoing process. Individuals and groups are constantly defining and redefining who they are. Rituals are also ongoing processes. They involve active agents carrying out prescribed, anticipated activities —activities that create a kind of rhythm through repeated sequences of behaviors.[24] The system has created its own community with a hierarchical structure, rewards, and fixed procedures. Perhaps it is *because* Korea's National Treasure System has become a kind of ritual—an active process for continuing a vision of the past—that the past has become an integral part of the construction of a contemporary identity. The continuing presence of dances of the past also makes it possible to create new dance forms that are based on old ones and that become a part of the same contemporary identity.

Some scholars claim that rapidly modernizing (particularly westernizing) societies tend to revive old rituals and customs "as a way of asserting their national identity and expressing their nationalistic feelings" (M. Bloch, Anthony Smith, and David Lan in Hogarth 1994:18). With the rapid pace of development and change in all cultural arenas in Korea, looking to the past establishes a base—a kind of anchor—from which it is possible to move ahead. By maintaining that anchor, it is also possible to measure how far one has advanced from it.

Anthropologist Hyun-key Kim Hogarth believes such revivals of former practices in Korea serve as a kind of "protest and protection against cultural 'colonialism' by the West, particularly America, and a reaction against pan-global cultural homogenization" (Hogarth 1994:19). Performer Yang Jong-sung asserts that "reshaped" revivals are used "for political and nationalistic purposes by both government policy makers and cultural movement leaders" (1994:128ff). But the "reshaping" occurs primarily in performance *contexts*, since every effort is made to retain the *form*, at least as it is believed to have existed in at least one early performance.

Ethnomusicologist Tamara Livingston (1999:66) ties revivals to modernization and commodification. She believes the ideologies on which they are based stem from "middle class people in consumer-capitalist and socialist societies" that privilege "exchange value over use value, the objectification, commodification and rationalization of various aspects of life, participation in the 'cult of consumerism,' an ideology of modernity, and the imagined community of the nation." All of these descriptors relate to the development of Korea's National Treasure System and the ritualistic nature it has taken on in modern times.

Folklore scholar Dan Ben-Amos asserts that tradition "is in a constant state of disarray, about to disintegrate under the pressures of change; and members of the society strive to restore and maintain it in new rituals, displays, and diverse forms of entertainment—constructed and if necessary invented—or the revival of old ones" (in Bausinger 1990:vii–viii). Korea's National Treasure System has contributed to both the revival and construction of tradition as well as to the creation of a new ritual system.

There is no question about the interest the National Treasure System has sparked in dance. Village people try to revive, or create, traditions from the past; annual "folk festivals," attended by thousands of Koreans as well as visitors from abroad, are held, in which performers compete to receive government recognition and monetary prizes; concerts, also attended by Koreans and visitors, are staged to showcase performances by acknowledged masters and their students; and publications are written to document historical and performance details of the various traditions. Together with other art forms, the National Treasure System "authenticates, stabilizes and promotes the preservation" of dance (Sorensen 1989:161). Hence, whether dances selected for recognition are actual activities from the past or recent constructions of a romanticized past, they nonetheless contribute to an important contemporary living tradition. Yang argues that through governmental use of the performing arts "Korean tradition has been transformed into *symbols* of the nation's cultural heritage, rather than serving as expressions of that culture" (emphasis in original) (1994:129). I propose that in Korea, the past is actively used as a way to create a present national identity. As the world becomes increasingly homogenous, people are increasingly concerned with finding ways to assert their distinctiveness. Invoking the past at the same time that progress and modernization accelerate can help retain distinctiveness. Even *isuja* Yang Jong-sung suggests that doing so can provide "support to those whose world is so quickly changing" (1988:33). Dance is an important visible manifestation of a newly constructed identity—a composite identity made possible by Korea's National Treasure System that creates contemporary identity symbols. Through the formalization of this system for maintaining these symbols, with prescribed procedures all along the way, a new ritual system has been created.

Part II

A CLOSER LOOK

4

Ch'ŏyongmu

Prologue

Five figures wearing brightly colored tunics, baggy pants, and soft slippers enter in a single file, laboriously bending and straightening their knees in a stylized walk. Their large, identical, dark-colored masks—resembling caricatures rather than real-life creatures—seem to weigh down their entire beings.

They arrive in a straight line extending across the width of the stage and sing a brief song. This completed, they bow to the audience and to each other, and then continue their heavy walk. As they advance directly toward the audience, they thrust their long sleeves upward and outward, emphasizing their almost continual rising and sinking movements.

They form a square, with one dancer in the center, and then regroup several times to form a circle, a straight line, and a diamond. One dancer performs a brief solo, and then is joined, in turn, by each of the other four. The upward thrusting of the long sleeves becomes a sideward swishing as the dancers circle the performing space, form a straight line, and retreat upstage. They cease their dancing briefly to sing again, and resume their walk—which has now become a bit lighter and quicker—as they advance, retreat, and trace one final circular path before exiting in a single file.

These five beings have told no story. They have created a mood, perhaps suggested mythological creatures, or simply left an impression of strength and deliberateness as they executed their choreographed movements.

Legendary Origin

Although classified as a court dance (*kungjung muyong*), Ch'ŏyongmu stands out in marked contrast to other court dances performed today. It is the only one in which the performers wear masks; it is performed by men rather than women; and its movements are comparatively strong and vigorous. Movements in other court dances are soft and subdued.

Ch'ŏyongmu was performed in royal courts at one time, but its roots lie outside the royal setting, and its origin and development undoubtedly contributed to its distinctive nature. The most frequently cited story of the origin of Ch'ŏyongmu is first presented in the *Samguk yusa* (Memorabilia of the Three Kingdoms). Compiled by the Buddhist monk Iryŏn (1206–1289), this document was completed in the late thirteenth century, and contains a sometimes indistinguishable mixture of history, anecdote, folk tale, and legend. Although the text deals with the Three Kingdoms period (57 B.C.–A.D. 935, and comprising the kingdoms of Koguryŏ, Paekche, and Shilla), its content focuses largely on the Shilla Kingdom (57 B.C.–A.D. 935). This work dates the origin of Ch'ŏyongmu to the last century of the Shilla dynasty.

The *Samguk yusa* states that performances of Ch'ŏyongmu began during the reign of King Hŏn'gang (r. 875–886), forty-ninth ruler of the Shilla dynasty, and relates the following story. One day the king ventured into the woods, and while resting by the seashore a heavy fog set in. Concerned for the safe return of himself and his entourage, he consulted his astrologer, who advised the king that the Dragon of the Eastern Sea was unhappy and had caused the fog; if the king would do something to please the dragon, the fog would lift. The king instructed his followers to build a temple, whereupon the fog immediately cleared. The Dragon of the Eastern Sea was so pleased that he and his seven sons appeared before the king and sang and danced.

The king then invited one of the sons, whom he later named Ch'ŏyong, to return with him to the court. Ch'ŏyong became a faithful official and was given a court woman to be his wife. The woman was so beautiful that she attracted the attention of the spirit of the plague, who came to see her. One night when Ch'ŏyong returned home he discovered that things were not as they should be. Instead of becoming angry, as most mortal men would, he sang a song and danced. The song is known today as Ch'ŏyongga (Song of Ch'ŏyong).

> Having caroused far into the night
> In the moonlit capital,
> I return home and in my bed,
> Behold, four legs.
>
> Two were mine;
> Whose are the other two?
> Two were mine;
> No, no, they are taken.
>
> (Peter Lee 1981:21)

Figure 5. Cheung, straw
image used to dispel evil
spirits at New Year. From
*Chosŏn shitae sajin-ŭro
ponŭn. Yi-Dynasty
through Pictures*. Vol. II.
Seoul: Somun Dang,
1988, p. 146. Courtesy
Somun Dang.

Ch'ŏyong then turned to leave. The spirit of the plague was quite taken
with Ch'ŏyong's lack of anger. He told Ch'ŏyong that if he saw a picture
of Ch'ŏyong's face at the entrance he would never again visit the house.
From that time on people began hanging masks of Ch'ŏyong on their
gates and door lintels as protection against the spirit of the plague.

The *Tongguk seshigi* (Account of Korean Seasonal Customs), an 1849
collection of descriptions of Korean customs associated with specific times
of the year (written by Hong Sŏng-mo), says that "Ch'ŏyong" is the same
as "*cheung*," *cheung* being a straw effigy used at New Year time (Figure 5).
Each person pushed small coins into the straw, the amount depending on
the individual's age. The straw doll was then thrown into the street and
burned to keep away evil spirits. Thus the *cheung* and the Ch'ŏyong
masks placed on door lintels functioned similarly in warding off evil spirits, and the straw doll may simply have been another manifestation of the
Ch'ŏyong story. Both the Ch'ŏyong masks on door lintels and the straw
dolls are still seen today.

The *Samguk yusa*'s story of Ch'ŏyong and the dance he performed upon discovering the spirit of the plague with his wife are considered legendary. References to actual performances of dances that undoubtedly were predecessors of the present-day Ch'ŏyongmu ("*mu*" from the Sino-Korean "*muyong*," meaning "dance," is frequently appended to the titles of dances, hence, The Dance of Ch'ŏyong) are found in documentation of religious rituals.

History

RELIGIOUS ROOTS

Historical documents mention a Ch'ŏyong dance in connection with three religious festivals—a Buddhist festival known as P'algwanhoe (Festival of the Eight Vows), to honor various spirits; a Buddhist lantern festival known as Yŏndŭnghoe, to honor the Buddha; and a New Year celebration known as Narye, to rid the country of evil spirits.

The P'algwanhoe dates from the Shilla period, possibly from the reign of King Chinhŭng (r. 540–576) (Rutt 1961:54), and was held under royal patronage in midwinter during the full-moon day of the eleventh lunar month. Its original purpose in the sixth century was to honor those who died in battle. Soon, however, it became an occasion to honor the spirits of heaven, the five major hills, famous mountains, large rivers, and traditional gods (Henthorn 1971:71). Such an event was believed to bring peace and tranquillity to the nation and the royal household (Lee Ki-baek 1984:133). The P'algwanhoe was celebrated for two days and was so grandiose in scope—two five-foot-tall stages were erected on the ball-playing field at the palace to accommodate performances of plays, singing, and dancing (Anonymous 1959:288–289)—that two government offices (*P'algwanbo* and *P'algwansa*) were established to manage the operation of the festival and its finances.

Performers were a distinctive feature of the P'algwanhoe celebrations at the court during the Koryŏ dynasty (918–1392) (Rutt 1961:54), and among their presentations were masked dance plays and a Ch'ŏyong dance (Song Bang-song 1974:17).

The Yŏndŭnghoe (lantern festival) originated during the Koryŏ period and was held on the full-moon day of the first lunar month. It was originally a temple festival to honor Buddha, and a time when festival participants constructed lanterns to decorate the temple. In a manner similar to the P'algwanhoe, the Yŏndŭnghoe became rather substantial in scope, and large sums of money were spent on performances of music, dance, acrobatics, and juggling, again in hopes of bringing peace to the nation (Lee Ki-baek 1984:133).

During the Three Kingdoms period and the Koryŏ period the government assumed the responsibility for much of the support of Buddhism.

Since both the P'algwanhoe and Yŏndŭnghoe were Buddhist festivals, they apparently thrived and developed into lavish spectacles. But in the Chosŏn dynasty (1392–1910) support for Buddhism declined. Confucianism, originating in China, became the favored ideology, and a festival to rid the country of evil spirits, known as the Narye, replaced the P'algwanhoe and Yŏndŭnghoe as an annual, government-sponsored event.[1]

The Narye was an all-night festival held at the palace on the last day of the lunar year. Pictures of evil spirits were drawn in hopes of preventing their appearance during the coming year, and a Ch'ŏyong dance was performed (Chang Sa-hun, personal communication 25 Nov. 1981). The drawing of pictures to dispel evil spirits is potentially a direct link to the Ch'ŏyong legend, with its description of replicas of Ch'ŏyong's countenance placed on door lintels.

SECULARIZATION OF THE RELIGIOUS FESTIVALS

Although all three festivals were originally associated with major religious and philosophical beliefs, each eventually became secularized or incorporated a secular component. The extent of the secularization of the P'algwanhoe is reflected in King Sŏngjong's (r. 981–997) order that "'unorthodox and disturbing' games and shows accompanying the ceremony be prohibited" (Peter Lee, trans. 1969:65). Apparently Sŏngjong's efforts to abolish the celebration were not successful, and it continued into the twelfth century (Pihl 1991:3).

The original Narye festival was solely religious or ritualistic in nature, much like its predecessors. During the Koryŏ dynasty, however, a secular, entertainment component was added at the conclusion of the festival.

RECONSTRUCTIONS

There are two known disruptions to the continuity of performances of a Ch'ŏyong dance, at least one of which is attributed to political circumstances. These are indicated by the absence of references to a Ch'ŏyong dance during certain periods, and by references to two reconstructions.

Scholars describe the first performance of a reconstructed version of Ch'ŏyongmu as occurring in 1828 (Kim Ki-su, personal communication 4 Jan. 1982 and Han Ok-hŭi, personal communication 6 Nov. 1981), following an absence of it from the court repertoire from some time in the late 1700s. (The last reference to a Ch'ŏyong dance prior to 1828 appears to be an indication in the *Chosŏn wangjo shillok* to a 1795 performance (Pak Chŏng-hye, personal communication, 16 June 1998).) The performance was at a special feast sponsored by Prince Hyomyŏng (Crown Prince during the reign of King Sunjo—r. 1800–1834, posthumously given the title King Ikchong). The evening's entertainment featured performances of many dances that had been reconstructed after a period of inactivity, as well as dances with choreography attributed, today, to Hyomyŏng himself. Ch'ŏyongmu is said to have been reconstructed at this time by

Kim Chang-ha, a court musician, supposedly based on previous records of the dance (Han Ok-hŭi, personal communication 6 Nov. 1981).

Once reconstructed, Ch'ŏyongmu continued to be performed for about forty years. But although there are nine important records of court events (*ŭigwe*) from 1868 to 1902, none mentions Ch'ŏyongmu (Park Jeong-hye 1997:142). With the move toward Japanese colonization and the abolition of the court, there are no court documents after 1902, and, at the beginning of the Japanese occupation, traditional Korean activities were suppressed. But as time went on Japanese policies changed and some Korean activities were allowed to resume. Hence, following another performance hiatus, in 1923, Ch'ŏyongmu was again reconstructed, this time as part of celebrations for the fiftieth birthday of former King Sunjong (r. 1907–1910; d. 1926), last ruler of the Chosŏn dynasty. This reconstruction is also said to have been based on earlier records.

The 1923 reconstruction was done by Kim Yŏng-je (1883–1954), fourth director of the court music academy (Yiwangjik Aakpu) and grandson of Kim Ch'ang-ha (said to have been responsible for the 1828 reconstruction); Ham Hwa-jin (1883–1948), fifth director of the court music academy; and Yi Su-gyŏng (1882–1955), a court singer. Although none of these men was a dancer, they attempted to revive the dance and teach it to five young male music students at Yiwangjik Aakpu, the court music academy set up outside the palace during the Japanese occupation that eventually became the National Center for Korean Traditional Performing Arts. The boys were specifically recruited to revive court dances so they could perform them at Sunjong's birthday celebration.[2]

The birthday festivities lasted two days, and Ch'ŏyongmu was one of at least ten dances performed. The dancers were highly praised, and it seems the Japanese allowed occasional dance performances—including those of Ch'ŏyongmu—throughout the remainder of their occupation of Korea. Following independence in 1945, performances of Ch'ŏyongmu became more frequent.

FROM PAST TO PRESENT

Although performances of Ch'ŏyongmu began as part of a community religious festival, primary sponsorship was taken over by the court and Ch'ŏyongmu was performed for both entertainment and ritual purposes. At some time during the Chosŏn dynasty (at least by 1828—the year of the feast sponsored by Crown Prince Hyomyŏng) Ch'ŏyongmu began to be performed in the court solely for secular purposes and no longer in conjunction with ritualistic religious festivities. It was also occasionally performed during the Koryŏ and Chosŏn dynasties as entertainment at the residences of high-ranking government officials and upper-class aristocrats (*yangban*) (Lee Du-hyon 1970:185).

In 1971 the Korean government gave formal recognition to Ch'ŏyongmu by designating it Intangible Cultural Asset number thirty-nine. This recognition brought with it the writing of an official report about the dance, the designation of five individuals as National Living Treasures (*poyuja*) for Ch'ŏyongmu, and an official annual performance in a concert environment. In subsequent years other individuals were designated to assist in its preservation, and they were given ranked titles that placed them in line for eventually becoming National Living Treasures.[3]

Ch'ŏyongmu is most frequently taught today at the National Center for Korean Traditional Performing Arts. It is also occasionally taught to university dance students, most of whom are female, and to students of the National High School of the Performing Arts (Kungnip Kugak Kodŭng Hakkyo). Both groups learn the dance as part of their school curriculum, but seldom, if ever, perform it.

Today Ch'ŏyongmu is performed annually at a concert specifically intended to showcase music and dance pieces that are Intangible Cultural Assets. Until 1980, the dancers in these performances were the National Living Treasures. Because of their advanced age, however, the dance is now performed primarily by those who hold second- or third-level designations in the National Treasure System.

Besides the official annual performance, Ch'ŏyongmu is also seen at concerts of classical music and dance presented at various times during the year, and occasionally at festivals.

Less frequently, Ch'ŏyongmu is considerably modified and incorporated into performances of modern style Korean dance. Interestingly, prior to its designation as an Intangible Cultural Asset, National Living Treasure Kim Ch'ŏn-hŭng choreographed a three-act dance-drama, titled Ch'ŏyongnang, based on the Ch'ŏyong legend. (Music for the performance was composed by Ch'ŏyongmu National Living Treasure Kim Ki-su.) This dance-drama was performed in 1959 and received an award from the government of the city of Seoul in 1960, but has never been performed again, remaining only in the memories of those who performed in it or saw its presentation.

THE NATURE OF EARLY PERFORMANCES

Passing references and poetic descriptions by writers provide only brief impressionistic glimpses of early performances of Ch'ŏyongmu. The first description of the dance that attempts a full documentation is found in the 1493 document, the *Akhak kwebŏm* (Treatise on Music and Dance). Location of the performers in the performance area is indicated by placing the word for "dancer" or "musician" in the corresponding spot on the page, providing a kind of diagram of the overall formation (Figure 6). Movement sequences are named, and in some instances an attempt is made to describe the nature of these sequences. Unfortunately, however, a description such as "[he] raises his right hand first and then repeats this again" provides only a faint suggestion of what the writer saw.

The *Akhak kwebŏm* does, however, refer to two different Ch'ŏyong dances: a "former," known as Chŏndo Ch'ŏyongmu, and a "latter," known as Hudo Ch'ŏyongmu. Chŏndo Ch'ŏyongmu was done as part

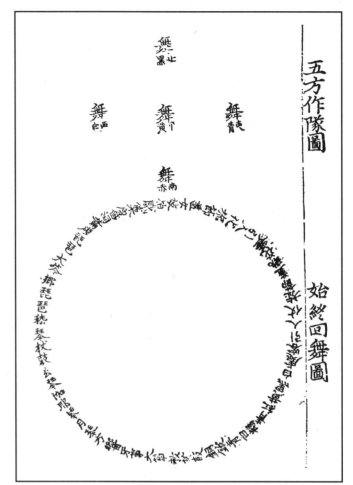

五方作隊圖

始終回舞圖

Figure 6. Akhak kwebŏm excerpt showing five-direction formation and procession, including Ch'ŏyongmu (1493). Courtesy of Kyujanggak, Seoul National University.

of a ritual, and is described as being elegant; Hudo Ch'ŏyongmu was done for entertainment, and is described as being lively.

The version of the dance performed for entertainment was part of a suite comprising three dances—Hangmu (Crane Dance), Yŏnhwadaemu (Lotus Pavilion Dance), and Ch'ŏyongmu. The name of the suite—Hak Yŏnhwadae Ch'ŏyongmu Hapsŏl (Crane, Lotus Pavilion, Ch'ŏyong Dance Suite)—is derived from the names of the three dances.

In Hangmu (Crane Dance, Plate 4) two dancers attired in realistic crane costumes performed movements resembling those of birds. Toward the end of the dance they approached two large artificial lotus flowers and pecked at them. One young girl emerged from each flower and together the girls performed Yŏnhwadaemu (Lotus Pavilion Dance), during which they shook golden bells (Chang Sa-hun 1978:15, 24). Illustrations also show the young girls on the backs of the crane dancers, a position in which all exited (Figure 7). This was then followed by a performance of Ch'ŏyongmu.

The suite of dances preceded the singing of three Buddhist songs: Mit'a

Ch'an, Kwanŭm Ch'an, and Ponsa Ch'an, all sung by female court entertainers (Chang Sa-hun, personal communication 25 Nov. 1981). It is possible these songs are remnants of earlier performances held in conjunction with the Buddhist P'algwanhoe and Yŏndŭnghoe celebrations.[4] Pratt (1987:207) indicates the emergence of the young girls from the lotus flowers symbolizes "the rebirth of souls in the Amitabha paradise," an interpretation that further links the dance to Buddhist ritual.

It is the livelier version of Ch'ŏyongmu from the three-dance suite that was reconstructed in 1923 and performed at Sunjong's birthday celebration, but the other two dances were not reconstructed at that time. (They were, however, reconstructed some time in the 1960s (Kim Ch'ŏn-hŭng, personal communication, 9 June 1998).) It is the livelier version as passed on since 1923 and as standardized in the 1971 Intangible Cultural Asset report that is performed today.

KOREAN DANCE OR CHINESE DANCE?

At least by the time of the 1493 *Akhak kwebŏm*, Koreans classified court entertainment dances on the basis of their origin in either China or Korea. How does Ch'ŏyongmu fit into this classification system?

Both the P'algwanhoe and Yŏndŭnghoe are considered indigenous Korean celebrations. The Narye, however, is believed to have originated in China and to have been introduced to Korea during the reign of King Chŏngjong (r. 1035–1046). So there are three possibilities regarding the geographic origin of Ch'ŏyongmu. First, it may have originated in Korea in dances performed as part of the P'algwanhoe and Yŏndŭnghoe. Second, it may have originated in China and have been brought to Korea together with the Narye festival. Third, it may have been added to the

Figure 7. Kyobang kayo illustration of Hangmu (Crane Dance) (1872). Courtesy of National Library of Korea.

Narye—based on Korean dances originally performed at the P'algwan-hoe and Yŏndŭnghoe—after the Narye reached Korea.

Two ideas support the contemporary belief that Ch'ŏyongmu is of Korean origin. First, according to Korean musicologist Chang Sa-hun (1978:25) the suite of dances referred to in the *Akhak kwebŏm* may have originated as early as the tenth century, during the time of King Sŏngjong (r. 981–997). If this is accurate, then Ch'ŏyongmu was performed in Korea prior to the Chosŏn dynasty importation of the Narye festival from China (some time after the fourteenth century), and it was, indeed, originally a Korean dance.

Second, Korean musicologist Yi Hye-gu (Lee Hye-ku 1981:7–8) states that in performances at court banquets dance and music selections of Chinese origin and those of Korean origin alternated. The middle piece in the Hak Yŏnhwadae Ch'ŏyongmu Hapsŏl suite—Yŏnhwadaemu—is considered to be of Chinese origin. If the notion of alternation is correct, then the beginning piece—Hangmu—and the concluding piece—Ch'ŏyongmu—would both be of Korean origin.

HOW MANY DANCERS?

Today Ch'ŏyongmu is performed by five dancers, but this was not always the case. Based on the *Samguk yusa* legend of the dance of Ch'ŏyong when he discovered the god of the plague with his wife, it is reasonable to assume that the dance was originally performed by only one dancer. Such a solo version is described in at least three historical documents—the *Koryŏsa* (History of the Koryŏ Dynasty), written in 1451; the *Yongjae ch'onghwa* (Collected Writings of Yongjae [sobriquet for Sŏng Hyŏn, 1439–1504]), compiled in the mid- to late-fifteenth century; and the *Tonggyŏng chapki* (Capital Miscellany—miscellaneous notes on Kyŏngju, capital of the Shilla dynasty), collected and edited in 1669. The *Yongjae ch'onghwa* indicates that the solo dance was performed during the Shilla period, but goes on to state that there were five dancers in the fifteenth century during the reign of Sejong (r. 1418–1450).

A fourth document contradicts the notion of a solo dance, indicating a performance by two dancers. A text collected between 1469 and 1490, known as *Shiyong hyangakpo* (Record of Korean Songs Based on Poems), contains a poem describing "the double Ch'ŏyong dancing in the moonlight." It is difficult, however, to know if this was an indication of how the dance was actually performed at the time the document was written, or if the poet created a second dancer for literary effect.

A number of documents from the nineteenth century contain detailed accounts of royal banquets and include descriptions of dances performed. While most show five dancers (for example, Figure 8), several show nine. In some illustrations with nine people the additional four dancers appear to be female, do not wear masks, and are interspersed between masked male dancers in a circle formation. In others (for example, Figure 9), the

Figure 8. Ch'ŏyongmu
illustration from
*Hŏnjong mushin
chinch'an ŭigwe*
(1848). Courtesy of
Kyujanggak, Seoul
National University.

additional dancers appear to be male, but they are dressed in costumes
different from the usual five masked dancers, and they do not wear
masks. (This is discussed more fully below.) Thus, it is possible the dance
began as a solo, evolved into a duet, a dance for five, and a dance for nine,
and eventually settled into its current version for five performers.

FIVE-DIRECTION SYMBOLISM

In some historical documents Ch'ŏyongmu is referred to as Obang Chaktae, "the dance of the five directions." Throughout history the number
five has been symbolic in Korean life (as also in China). Among the various symbolisms with which the number is associated is the five directions,
each of which is represented by a color: north—black, south—red, east
—blue, west—white, and center—yellow. Today, the predominant color
of the costume of each of the five Ch'ŏyongmu dancers is one of the five
colors associated with the directions, and in the version of the dance performed today, several of the group formations involve geometric placement of the dancers as if symbolizing the five directions.

Although the symbolism of the five directions is usually believed to have
been assigned to Ch'ŏyongmu in the nineteenth century, and the origin of

Figure 9. Ch'ŏyongmu illustration from *Sunjo muja chinjak ŭigwe* (1828). Courtesy of Kyujanggak, Seoul National University.

a Ch'ŏyong dance is attributed to the ninth century, it is interesting to note that the stage on which P'algwanhoe performances were done during the reign of King Chinhŭng (r. 540–576)—as early as the sixth century—was decorated with a brocade of five colors (Lee Du-hyon 1970: 184). It is possible, therefore, that a five-direction symbolism was originally a part of the P'algwanhoe festival, that a Ch'ŏyong dance was added to the festival, and that a five-direction symbolism was incorporated into the festival dance. If this is the case, performance of the dance by five dancers may have occurred considerably earlier than the nineteenth century and may have been started to accommodate this symbolism.[5]

The possibility that a five-direction symbolism was associated with a Ch'ŏyong dance prior to the nineteenth century is supported in two historical documents. Recall that the *Yongjae ch'onghwa* of the late fifteenth century indicates that the Ch'ŏyong dance was changed to a dance for five people during the reign of King Sejong, in the fifteenth century. The 1493 dance and music treatise, *Akhak kwebŏm*, contains both verbal and pictorial indications of five dancers. Hence these sources place the use of five dancers in Ch'ŏyongmu in the fifteenth century—after the sixth century stage decorated with a multicolored cloth, but prior to the usual notion of the nineteenth century.

Today Ch'ŏyongmu is seldom referred to as Obang Chaktae, and few audience members are aware of any symbolism. But the dancers continue to wear the colors associated with each of the five directions. The primary symbolism of Ch'ŏyongmu today is as a representation of Korea's past and, as such, it is a contributor to contemporary identity.[6]

FOR MEN OR WOMEN?

Several National Living Treasures for Ch'ŏyongmu alive at the end of the twentieth century consider the strong movements of the dance more suited to male than to female performers, and it is generally believed that Ch'ŏyongmu was originally performed by men. This notion is supported by several Chosŏn dynasty paintings, as well as by line drawings contained in written documents. However, it is possible the dance was also performed by women. This is suggested in several Chosŏn dynasty paintings, one of which appears to be women wearing the usual Ch'ŏyong masks (Plate 17) and one of which shows women interspersed with what appear to be the regular five male, masked Ch'ŏyong dancers.

It is generally said that only men performed at "outer" (*oeyŏn*) formal court banquets (held for the king and government officials) and women at "inner" (*naeyŏn*) formal court banquets (held for the queen mother or court women of official rank, and wives of officials). Segregation of the sexes is suggested in a 1724 painting (Plate 18) that shows a Ch'ŏyongmu performance in which male musicians accompany the dancers in an area screened off from the view of women. But this was not always the case. During the Chosŏn dynasty, female court entertainers (*kisaeng*) performed in both settings. Criticism of this practice led to a prohibition of female entertainers. This did not last long, however, and a 1706 resolution led to young boys (*mudong*) dancing at outer banquets and young women (*kisaeng*) at inner banquets (Park Jeong-hye 1997:128), while both young men and young women performed outside the court.

Segregation of the sexes poses an interesting question regarding the illustrations that include both male and female performers. In the illustration with additional female performers beyond the usual five masked male performers, it is possible the dancers behind the masks were women wearing pantaloons more likely to have been worn by men; in the illustration with additional male performers (Figure 9), it is possible the dancers behind the masks were men. If this is correct, then Ch'ŏyongmu may, indeed, have been performed by both men and women—but not at the same time. The selection of performers would have been based on the gender of the observers in order to satisfy Chosŏn dynasty principles of morality. If, however, all of the dancers behind the masks were men, then the illustrations suggesting both male and female performers offer reason to question the government's reinforcement of the moral code of the time.

More recent records indicate that women did, indeed, perform Ch'ŏyongmu—at least by the early twentieth century. When celebrations were held in the central court, female entertainers from outlying districts were often invited to participate together with local entertainers. Among the things the visiting entertainers did was to learn and participate in dances. Upon returning to their home districts the entertainers are said to have taught the newly learned dances to local dancers. *Han'guk pulgyo t'ongsa* (Treatise on Korean Buddhism), a book written at the time of liberation from Japan, tells of Kim Yŏng-wŏl, an entertainer from Kyŏngju who lived at the end of the Chosŏn dynasty, who performed Ch'ŏyongmu (Kim Ch'ŏn-hŭng, personal communication 14 Dec. 1981).

Not knowing whether the performers were men or women leads to questions regarding the dance movements used in Ch'ŏyongmu: It is possible they would have been different if the dance was done by performers of different sexes.

Today Ch'ŏyongmu is performed most often by men who are on the staff of the National Center for Korean Traditional Performing Arts. Because the Center's dancers are primarily women, and because the movements of Ch'ŏyongmu are considered more appropriate for men than women, the dance is usually performed by male musicians of the Center who are selected for their movement abilities and are trained to perform this one dance—an interesting duplication of the selection procedures and background of performers for the 1923 reconstruction. Occasionally, when members of the Center perform away from their home in Seoul and cannot bring a full compliment of performers, Ch'ŏyongmu is performed by some of the Center's female dancers.

The Dance Today

Since its 1971 designation as an Intangible Cultural Asset, Ch'ŏyongmu is generally performed in precisely the same manner. (Modifications relate to shortening the performance time. See Appendix 2 for a description of these modifications.) An effort to assure its precise continued performance, as stipulated in the Law on the Protection of Cultural Properties, was made by the National Center for Korean Traditional Performing Arts in 1986. At that time the Center published the first in a series of annual volumes documenting their dance repertoire. The dance selected for documentation was Ch'ŏyongmu (see Kim Ch'ŏn-hŭng and Sŏng Kyŏng-nin 1986). The volume contains a very brief historical introduction; the text of Ŏllak and Up'yŏn, portions of the musical accompaniment; information regarding the dance's designation as an Intangible Cultural Asset; a brief description of the costume and mask (including a facsimile reproduction of relevant pages from the *Akhak kwebŏm*); musical scores (in western notation) for Ŏllak and Up'yŏn; and a form of stick figure notation for all of the dance movements. A major advantage of the dance notation over descriptions contained in older documents is that the stick figures representing movement are directly aligned with the accompanying music notation (Figure 10). Despite the fact that the line drawings

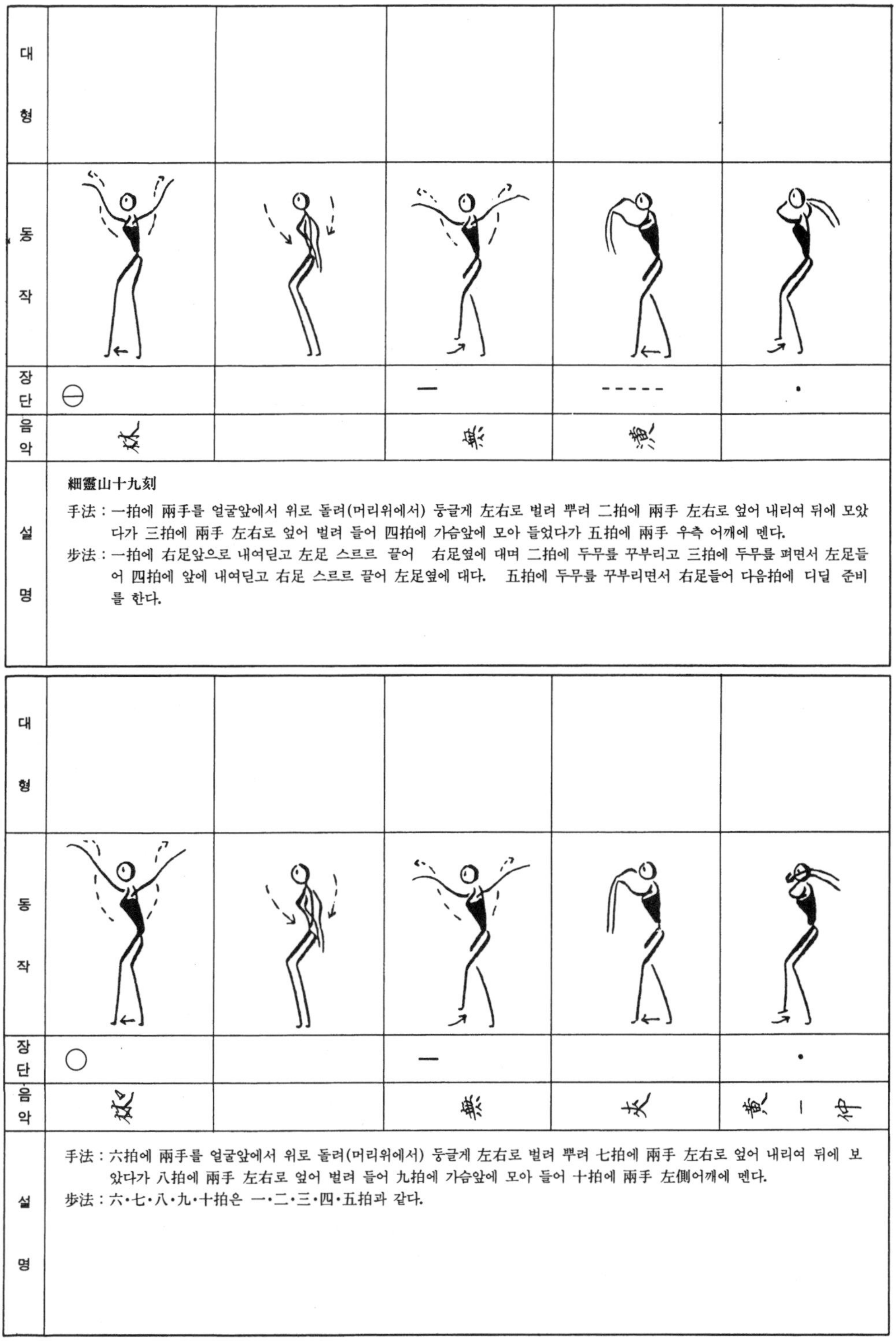

대형
동작
장단
음악
설명
細靈山十九刻
手法 : 一拍에 兩手를 얼굴앞에서 위로 돌려(머리위에서) 둥글게 左右로 벌려 뿌려 二拍에 兩手 左右로 엎어 내리여 뒤에 모았다가 三拍에 兩手 左右로 엎어 벌려 들어 四拍에 가슴앞에 모아 들었다가 五拍에 兩手 우측 어깨에 멘다.
步法 : 一拍에 右足앞으로 내여딛고 左足 스르르 끌어 右足옆에 대며 二拍에 두무릎 꾸부리고 三拍에 두무릎 펴면서 左足들어 四拍에 앞에 내여딛고 右足 스르르 끌어 左足옆에 대다. 五拍에 두무릎 꾸부리면서 右足들어 다음拍에 디딜 준비를 한다.
대형
동작
장단
음악
설명
手法 : 六拍에 兩手를 얼굴앞에서 위로 돌려(머리위에서) 둥글게 左右로 벌려 뿌려 七拍에 兩手 左右로 엎어 내리여 뒤에 보았다가 八拍에 兩手 左右로 엎어 벌려 들어 九拍에 가슴앞에 모아 들어 十拍에 兩手 左側어깨에 멘다.
步法 : 六·七·八·九·十拍은 一·二·三·四·五拍과 같다.

Figure 10. National Center for Traditional Korean Performing Arts notation of Ch'ŏyongmu. From Kim Ch'ŏn-hŭng and Sŏng Kyŏng-nin 1986:60. Courtesy of Kungnip Kugagwŏn.

suggest the overall flow of the movement, however, they lack sufficient detail to fully communicate the movement to someone who does not already know the dance.

COSTUME

> The old man Ch'ŏyong it was rumored came
> out of the blue sea.
> He sang of the moonlight
> with his shell-like teeth and reddish lips,
> And danced in the spring breeze,
> fluttering his wide scarlet sleeves
> like an eagle's wings.

(Yi Che-hyŏn in Song Kyong-rin 1963:7)

This song from the end of the thirteenth or beginning of the fourteenth century describes two elements that constitute significant features of the attire of Ch'ŏyong dancers today; long sleeves, although the color used is different from that described by Yi Che-hyŏn, and the "shell-like teeth," which are permanently fixed in the masks worn by contemporary dancers.

The masks (Plate 19) are said to have originally been made of lightweight wood. In the recent past they were constructed of a combination of clay and *papier mâché*. Today they are usually only *papier mâché*. The face has a large, protruding chin; bushy eyebrows; long mustache; very short beard emanating from just below the lower lip; and large, circular, wooden, gold-painted earrings. The mouth is slightly open in a small smile. There is speculation that the dark color of the mask, the earrings, and the structure of the nose suggest Central Asian (Indian, Iranian, or Arabic) influence. Attached to the top of the mask is a piece of black fabric that hangs down over the back of the dancer's head, reaching to approximately shoulder height. Thus, the performer's head is completely covered.

The masks of all five dancers are identical, and today are a dark, earthy, reddish-brown color. It is possible, however, that in former times each was a different color, corresponding to the predominant color of the individual dancer's costume. This is how they are shown in pictures from Kangwangdo, on Korea's east coast (Kim Ch'ŏn-hŭng, personal communication 14 Dec. 1981), and in a late eighteenth-/early nineteenth-century painting (Plate 17).

It is possible the Ch'ŏyong mask was modeled after religious images, and that it originally had a white beard. The *Samguk yusa* describes a "White Bearded Mask belonging to the reign of King Hŏn'gang (875–885) [*sic*], which was supposed to have been the image of Namsan deity." It also refers to a "footnote to Shilla Akjo [akcho], in which the Ch'ŏyong dance was described as having another name of the 'White-Bearded Dance'" (in Lee Du-hyon 1968:5).

Affixed as part of the mask is a black hat, with a rectangular piece with rounded corners protruding horizontally from each side—the style of hat formerly worn by court officials. Atop the hat is the branch of a peach tree, complete with leaves, peach blossoms, and a peach: "[T]here are five kinds of evil spirits corresponding to the north, south, east, west and middle. Each of these kinds can be exorcised by a particular kind of wood or fruit. The east spirits are exorcised by the peach . . . (Hulbert 1902:344). Since Korea was considered the "East Country" (in relation to China, which, in former times, was considered the center of the universe), it is appropriate that spirits of the east be exorcised, and hence the use of the branch of a peach tree. Further explanation for using the branch of a peach tree in the costume lies in the fact that shamans frequently hold the branch of a peach tree during rituals. Since the Ch'ŏyong dance was done to dispel evil spirits, and perhaps also since the king in the original Ch'ŏyong story erected a temple to appease the dragon spirit of the Eastern Sea, rationale for this symbolism is reinforced. This costume component has been retained despite the fact that the dance is no longer done in ritual contexts.

Following the Japanese occupation, none of the early Ch'ŏyong masks remained. New ones were constructed, based on descriptions in the *Akhak kwebŏm*, at the time of the 1923 reconstruction of the dance. Masks used today are all uniform in size and, as is shown in many old illustrations, are considerably larger than an average face: approximately twenty inches in height (from the tip of the chin to the top of the hat), approximately twelve inches at the broadest part (from ear to ear). They weigh approximately two-and-one-half pounds. Before putting on the mask the dancer ties a thickly padded band (*imatpaji*) to his forehead to prevent bruising.

The costume is rather bulky and consists of several layers of heavily brocaded silk (Plate 20). Baggy pants form the costume's foundation. These are topped by a Korean-style man's jacket, a tunic with sleeves, a loose-fitting belt (of the type previously worn by court officials), and several sashes.

In many Korean dance forms a separate pair of long sleeves (known as *hansam*), affixed to the wrists by means of drawstrings or elastic, are worn in addition to the sleeves that are part of the upper garment. In Ch'ŏyongmu the sleeves of the upper garment are simply lengthened, rather than being a separate costume element. They are entirely white, unlike the rainbow-colored sleeves of most court dances, and are of a very soft silk, unlike the stiff silk of court dance sleeves. These differences may relate to the fact that although Ch'ŏyongmu is classified as a court dance today, it originated outside the court.

The sleeves are approximately thirty inches in circumference, and their length varies with the height of the dancer; with the arms extended sideward at shoulder height, thumb-side facing forward and hands relaxed, the sleeves should drop to within four to twelve inches of the floor.

The dancers wear silk embroidered shoes resembling soft-soled slippers, each sporting a fringed pom-pom on top of the toes. In some old illustrations the dancers wore boots.

Today the outer tunic provides the most prominent color of the costume, and each dancer's tunic is of a different color. The colors relate to much of Korean symbology, including directions, elements, and seasons. Because Ch'ŏyongmu was also known as the dance of the five directions, however, it is the direction symbology that is most frequently referred to when explaining the reason for the different colors, and it is likely the colorful costumes originated at the time the dance was performed by five dancers and acquired the symbolism of "the dance of the five directions." Colors of the pants vary, also, but their color is based on complimentarity to the tunic color rather than to any symbolism.[7]

MUSIC

Contemporary performances of Ch'ŏyongmu are accompanied by both instrumental and vocal music. Instrumental music is based on that played in the past in the court and on formal religious and state occasions. It is provided by a traditional Korean ensemble of drums and string and wind instruments.[8] The text of vocal music is based on several old poems about the Ch'ŏyong legend, but the melody was composed in the twentieth century. Vocal music is most often provided by a separate group of vocalists, and occasionally by the dancers themselves.

The instrumental ensemble typically contributes to the visual image of the dance by virtue of its placement on stage. The male musicians wear bright pink robes, black hats, and black boots—attire worn by Chosŏn dynasty court musicians. If a sufficient number of male musicians is not available, females don male clothing and perform with the group. The musicians sit tailor fashion (legs crossed) and are aligned in a single row across the back of the stage on a raised platform or on the stage floor, forming a kind of backdrop for the dancers, or are in a small cluster at the side of the stage. If the dancers do not sing the vocal music, vocalists perform from a position offstage.

Instrumental court music is typically sectional in nature, and makes rather abrupt changes in tempo, melodic contour, and dynamics. It is not unusual, therefore, to find musical excerpts that are quite different in nature constituting the accompaniment for a single dance. This is the nature of the instrumental accompaniment for Ch'ŏyongmu, which is comprised of excerpts from five traditional court music compositions: Sujech'ŏn, Hyangdang Kyoju, Hŏnch'ŏnsu, Suyŏnjang Chigok, and Yŏngsan Hoesang (specifically the sections known as Sang Yŏngsan Hoesang, Karak Tŏri, and Yŏmbul Todŭri). The diversity of the origin and nature of these pieces may mirror the many changes in form and function Ch'ŏyongmu has undergone. For example, Sujech'ŏn, dating from the seventh century, was originally used for court banquets and royal processions and is said to have been influenced by Confucian ideals; it is slow, has long melodic phrases with many sustained tones, and has very subtle changes in dynamics. Yŏngsan Hoesang, on the other hand, was originally a Buddhist chant that eventually became *chŏngak* ("correct music")—music played by the literati during the Chosŏn dynasty—and it has sections that are a bit livelier than those of Sujech'ŏn.

The conductor of this traditional instrumental ensemble also contributes to the sound accompaniment. Because of his position and the way in which he creates sound, he is a more conspicuous part of the overall visual picture than the musicians. The conductor wears the same attire as the musicians, but often in a light blue color, and he generally stands at the side of the stage, close to the audience—even if the musicians are offstage. Each time a change occurs he "announces" it by one or more beats of the *pak*, an instrument made of six slabs of wood fastened together at one end with a deerskin cord (Plate 2). He holds the *pak* by grasping one of the free ends of each of the outermost wood slabs in each hand. Keeping his left hand stationary, he uses his right to spread the free ends of the slabs apart and then quickly snaps them shut so they make a percussive sound. Striking it once indicates the beginning of the music and dance or a change in the rhythmic structure; striking it three times indicates the conclusion of a major section and a transition to something different (Kim Ch'ŏn-hŭng, personal communication 6 Jan. 1982). The abrupt movements used to play the *pak* and the resulting sharp sound stand in clear contrast to the dance movements and music.

As is typical of many court dances performed today, the overall tempo increases as the dance progresses (from approximately forty pulses per minute in the first section to ninety-eight in the last two sections). This increase is abrupt and occurs at sectional changes. Another interesting musical feature is the change in phrase length: During the first three sections the musical phrases are ten beats long, and in the last three sections they are six beats long.

Throughout the performance the dancer's movements directly relate to the structure of the accompanying music. As the tempo increases so does the speed of the dance movements. The movements also adhere closely to the underlying metrical pulse and, except for one section, the movement and musical phrases are identical in length. In the section in which music and movement phrases differ, the music phrase length is ten beats, while the dance phrase length is fifteen beats. The fifteen-beat movement phrase is performed four times and the ten-beat music phrase six times. Thus, the movement and music phrases align halfway through the section and at the completion of the section.

Twice during the performance the dancers pause, place their hands on their hips, and an unaccompanied song is sung. (The *pak* is struck three times just before each song.) Although the singing was originally done by the dancers, it is more frequently done today by a separate group of vocalists. The only movement during the song is a slight sideways or forward-backward bouncing of the dancers' heads; this movement is small and is not choreographed, each dancer performing it in his own manner. The intended impression created by this subtle movement is that the dancers are actually doing the singing.

The text of the song has changed several times. During the Shilla dynasty it was very short, consisting of only three to four sentences, and the text was taken from the Ch'ŏyong legend (possibly the Ch'ŏyongga referred to earlier). During the Koryŏ dynasty the text was lengthened, and from that time on took the form of a "long poem," or *changga*.

The text used today is recorded in the 1493 *Akhak kwebŏm*. It is comprised of two parts—Ŏllak and Up'yŏn—that describe the beneficial, exorcistic powers of Ch'ŏyong.[9] The text is summarized by *poyuja* Kim Ki-su as follows (personal communication 8 Jan. 1982).

Ŏllak

The great peace, the golden era of Shilla, is due to
    Ch'ŏyong's protection.
Ch'ŏyong has rid us of the three calamities and the
    eight difficulties.

Up'yŏn

The size of the country and the scenic beauty;
The sun and moon rise and shine on the palace.
The common people thrive.

Although the *Akhak kwebŏm* documents the Ŏllak and Up'yŏn texts, it does not include any indication of the music or instrumental accompaniment, nor do subsequent texts describe the music. During the late 1920s Ha Kyu-il, who was primarily a musician but who knew a bit about dance, was asked to compose music for the two parts of the song (Kim Ch'ŏnhŭng, personal communication 20 Nov. 1990). Therefore, although the text used today was composed at least 400 years ago, the melody, which is sung without instrumental accompaniment, was created in the twentieth century.[10] This contrasts with the melodies of the instrumental music, which are quite old.

Although Ŏllak and Up'yŏn are transcribed in western music notation in 16/4 and 10/4 meters, respectively, because there is no instrumental accompaniment for them and the singing is relatively unaccented, the overriding impression is simply of a steady pulse progressing at a comfortable speed (typically approximately seventy-two pulses per minute).

Ŏllak is sung after the first instrumental section, and Up'yŏn just before the last instrumental section.

MOVEMENT CHARACTERISTICS

Because dances are movement events meant to be taken in visually or through participation, a great deal is lost when they are described verbally.

A detailed verbal description is provided in Appendix 1 for the reader interested in more closely examining how the dance progresses. Here I will describe predominant movement characteristics, analyze the use of space to suggest the dynamics of the dance, and explore a new perspective on the choreography of today's Ch'ŏyongmu. As described earlier, the history of Ch'ŏyongmu ties the dance to both the common people and the courtly elite. Movement characteristics of the dance as it is performed today reflect a similar duality, and display features that are both similar to other traditional Korean dances and unique to Ch'ŏyongmu.

None of the movements in Ch'ŏyongmu is pantomimic; the dance does not, in any literal or stylized fashion, attempt to portray, in movement narrative, the story of Ch'ŏyong. Only two movements are sometimes described as being "suggestive." Near the beginning of the dance the performers bend forward from the waist as they all face the audience, and then repeat the bending as they turn to face the dancer on one side and then the other. To the audience the dancers appear to be bowing—both to the audience and then to each other—and this is how the movement is described by contemporary performers. The other movement described as being suggestive of a specific action appears at the end of the dance. At this time the dancers begin with both hands near one shoulder and, with a strong and abrupt movement, "throw" their arms forward and upward, propelling the sleeves in the same direction (Plate 21). This is followed by a more legato movement in which the arms lower and are then placed near the other shoulder, so that the action can be repeated. Several dancers suggest this may be a literal movement translation of "throwing out evil spirits"—a reflection of the dance's origin and use at New Year festivals. Because sleeve manipulation is prevalent in so many other court dances and in some folk dances, it is difficult to know if the meaning gave rise to the movement or if the symbolic meaning was simply attributed to the movement as a result of the legendary origin and early function of the dance.

Sleeve Manipulation. One of the most distinctive characteristics of many Korean dances—whether folk or court—is the manipulation of long sleeves. As pointed out earlier, the sleeves used in court dances performed today are of a fairly stiff fabric, are multicolored, and are somewhat shorter than those used in Ch'ŏyongmu. The soft white fabric and length of the sleeves used in Ch'ŏyongmu are closer to those of many of Korea's masked dance-drama forms of the folk tradition. Their manipulation in Ch'ŏyongmu is also closer to that found in the folk forms. In the court tradition the sleeve is gently "flicked" by means of a preparatory folding action at the wrist followed by a small but abrupt unfolding, a movement sometimes enhanced by a rotary action in the forearm. In Ch'ŏyongmu the arms thrust and swish in order to propel the sleeves. This action is done by enlarging the folding activity of the wrist not only by turning the forearm, but also by extending the arm from a preparatory bent state, and often by quickly lifting the arm from a low position at the same time. In short, the whole arm, not just the forearm and wrist, contributes to a vigorous manipulation of the sleeves.

In most court dances the arm and sleeve movements occur primarily in the lateral plane (sideward from the dancer's body).[11] In Ch'ŏyongmu many of the arm and sleeve movements emphasize the sagittal plane: instead of moving directly to the side of the dancer's body they move slightly forward toward the diagonals, and in several sections they occur in a pure forward direction. Sagittal movements tend to be more confrontational than lateral movements, and in Ch'ŏyongmu they contribute to the overall feeling of strength in the dance.

Torso. Arm activity enhances the manipulation of the sleeves; so, too, does torso activity. As preparatory arm and wrist actions occur the torso often tilts forward. It then returns to its upright position as the sleeves are thrust upward and outward. In the later, more vigorous sections of the dance the torso twists slightly to the side as it tilts and untilts, so that the sleeves are propelled in a large upward arc rather than simply being thrust straight upward. Thus, the sleeve activity is supported by both the arms and the torso.

Tilting and twisting of the torso are relatively uncommon in court dances. Although the torso tilts to accommodate a bow at the beginning and end of many dances, the movement is very small and does not occur at other times. However, torso involvement is more common in supporting sleeve manipulation in folk dance forms.

Rising and Sinking. Besides support from the arms and torso, sleeve manipulation is also enhanced by the continual bending and extending of the knees. Prior to the thrusting of a sleeve the wrist folds, the arm may bend and lower, the torso tilts, and the knees bend. Concurrent with the thrusting of the sleeve the wrist unfolds, the arm extends and lifts, the torso lifts to its upright position, and one or both knees extend. In most instances only one knee extends while the other lifts high enough that the thigh is parallel to the floor (Plate 5). In short, the entire body goes from a preparatory sinking to a rising as it supports and enables the thrusting of the sleeves. This activity can also be looked at as going from a folding or shrinking inwardly directed configuration to an unfolding or expanding outwardly directed configuration.

Because of the natural activity of the body in the breathing process—the expanding and contracting of the rib cage and chest area, the lifting and sinking of the torso—this overall rising-sinking/folding-unfolding activity replicates the breathing process. The tempo of the dance makes it possible to breathe along with the flow of the movement—the slow tempo at the beginning in a fairly relaxed manner, and the quicker tempo at the end in a more agitated or excited manner.

Lifting the knee so the thigh is parallel to the ground during the rising phase of the movement is a frequent occurrence in the more vigorous folk dance forms, but is not at all typical of court dances. The majority of court dances are performed today by women, and the rising phase of the locomotor process involves only a subtle release of the foot from the floor and a slight lifting of the knee. Harking back to Chosŏn dynasty Confucian morality and decorum, it would be quite unladylike to lift a leg very high. In fact, the high leg lift together with the overall vigor of movements throughout the dance make it questionable as to whether Ch'ŏyongmu was originally intended to be performed by women. One National Living Treasure describes the laborious entrance walk as being "like the dragon coming out of the sea"; he feels that movements throughout the dance are "worthy of a dragon—heroic" (Kim Ki-su, personal communication 4 Jan. 1982). These kinds of movements would certainly be inappropriate for a Chosŏn dynasty woman.

Weight. There is a feeling of weightiness in Ch'ŏyongmu that is not found in other court dances. The viewer can almost sense a cycle of gravity pulling down on the pelvic area, the dancer working to lift up against this pull, and then a repetition of the cycle. This feeling results, in part, from the continual rising and sinking—which is typical of many types of Korean dance—but in Ch'ŏyongmu it is done in a manner that contributes to an overall feeling of strength not present in most court dances.

Use of Time. The full performance of Ch'ŏyongmu as prescribed at the time it was designated an Important Intangible Cultural Asset takes approximately twenty minutes. Occasionally, shorter versions of the dance are performed. At these times the overall choreographic structure is retained and the shortening is achieved by eliminating some repetition in both the movement and music. (See Appendix 2 and comments on repetition below.)

The overall tempo of Ch'ŏyongmu is quite slow—clearly in keeping with the nature of court dances. Even though the tempo increases during the dance, the culminating speed is relative, and could be identified as "*moderato*" in western music parlance.

As described earlier, with only one exception there is a direct relationship between music and movement. Dancers and musicians always maintain a common underlying pulse; there is never any syncopated relationship between the two. The only variation of this otherwise tight relationship is in the section in which movement and music phrases are of slightly different lengths.

An element contributing to a false impression of speed is the density of the movement.[12] At the beginning of the dance only a small number of movement events occur on each musical beat; the knees bend, or one knee extends while the other lifts, or one foot slides to meet the other, and so on. As the dance progresses multiple activities occur simultaneously; for example, the torso returns to an upright position at the same time it twists and the arms thrust upward and outward, all while the dancer steps forward. This creates figures that look "busy," and as more and more movements occur simultaneously the overall impression is that things are happening faster, even if, in fact, there has been no increase in the tempo of the accompanying music and the rate at which movements happen.

Repetition. There is a great deal of repetition in Ch'ŏyongmu. Once a pattern is executed it is most often repeated numerous times. In many instances the pattern is then slightly varied, and the variation is repeated.

The most repetitive component of the dance is the footwork pattern. Except for one brief section near the beginning of the dance (when the dancers are in a square formation), the footwork throughout the entire twenty-minute dance is a step-close-sink-lift pattern.[13] Variations of this pattern are achieved by changing the direction of the step, adding small pivoting actions to the step, and making minor modifications to the duration of the components that constitute the pattern.

One other particularly interesting modification in the footwork pattern is the timing of the stepping portion. During approximately the first half of the dance the step takes place on the second beat of the musical phrase; during the last half of the dance it takes place on the first beat of the musical phrase. There is no explanation for this shift in timing.

The potential monotony of the highly repetitive footwork is alleviated by variety that comes from arm movements, changes in tempo, increases in movement density, and the use of space.

USE OF SPACE

To facilitate the more detailed discussion of the use of space, Labanotation examples are provided for readers familiar with this system of recording movement.[14] However, it is not necessary to read these examples to understand the verbal comments that follow. The reader is referred back to the several paragraphs at the beginning of this chapter for a broad description of how the dance progresses, and to Appendix 1 for a more detailed description of the entire dance.

Floor Patterns. Figure 11 shows floor plans for the dance: an aerial view of the performing space, with the audience situated at the bottom of the page. They reveal the dancers' overall orientation to space via precise geometric formations, and their orientation to each other and to the audience via facings of each of the performers. (The "pins" placed on the area indicating the stage space represent the dancers, with the "pointer" of the pin pointing to the direction the dancer faces. Numbers at the bottom of each stage area indicate the measure numbers of the dance to which the floor pattern coincides. Subscript numbers indicate counts within measures. In the descriptions that follow, "M." means "measure." These descriptions can be meaningfully read without reference to the floor plan indications, or the floor plans may be followed to aid in visualizing the verbal descrip-

tions. Readers may wish to scan the floor plans before reading the detailed comments, and then only refer to them when desired.)

The dance begins with simple straight-line formations (M. 1–17). It
then becomes more complex as the dancers move through shapes that
change from a square with one flat side parallel to the audience (M. 20–
29) to a circle with one dancer in the center (M. 30–38), a brief transitional return to a line parallel to the audience (M. 39–40), a diamond
with one dancer in the center and one corner directed toward the audience (M. 42–74; I refer to this shape as a diamond rather than a square
because of its orientation to the audience), and a circle (M. 75–90). The
dancers then return to their line parallel to the audience (M. 95), advance
and retreat several times (M. 95–107), turn to face stage right so they are
in a line behind one another (M. 108), and one dancer leads the group in
a large curve to exit upstage left in a diagonal line (M. 108–end).

As the dancers move through these pathways they are sometimes oriented toward each other in pairs (e.g., as in M. 21), sometimes away from
each other (e.g., as in M. 26), sometimes toward the audience (e.g., as in
M. 11), and sometimes to the geometric shape (e.g., as in M. 30).

As described earlier, the formations may relate to those in shaman ritual ceremonies and the dance was once symbolically associated with the
five directions. In the version of the dance performed today, the placement
of the dancers in several of the geometric formations coincides with notions of direction. For example, the yellow dancer (center) is generally
in the center of the group—in the straight line formations, the square,
the circles, and the diamond. (Colors are reflected in the floor plans by the
first letter of the relevant color being placed near the pin representing the
respective dancer.) When the dancers face each other in the square formation, dancers representing opposing directions face each other—Red
(south) faces Black (north), and Blue (east) faces White (west). In the diamond formation the dancers are arranged as the directions on a compass—Black (north) closest to the audience, and then moving clockwise
around the compass to Blue (east), Red (south), and White (west).

An interesting observation regarding the diamond formation has been
made by a senior National Living Treasure for the dance (Kim Ch'ŏn-
hŭng, personal communication 28 Oct. 1981). All Korean palaces had a
gate in the south, and the king's official seat was in the north, facing the
gate. Since for many years the dance was done in the court, today's audience may represent the king. Hence, the dancer representing north (Black)
is closest to the audience and the audience, like the king, faces south.

The Legs. While the pathways traced in the performing area emphasize
precise geometric shapes, individual movements of the dancers emphasize
verticality. Figure 12, Example A shows the footwork pattern that serves
as the foundation of the dance (the step-close-sink-lift pattern referred to
earlier and described in Note 13). Figure 12, Example B shows a pattern
that includes three ways in which this basic sequence is spatially modified

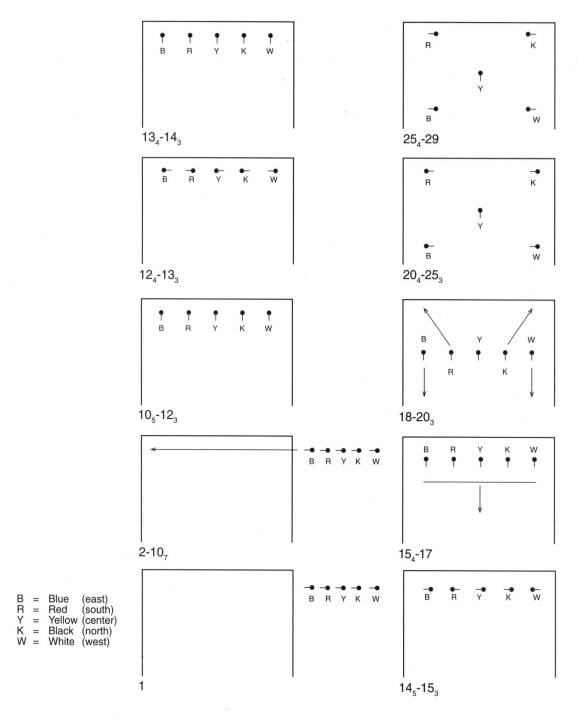

Figure 11. Floor plans, from the perspective of the audience, showing the spatial pathways of dancers in Ch'ŏyongmu.

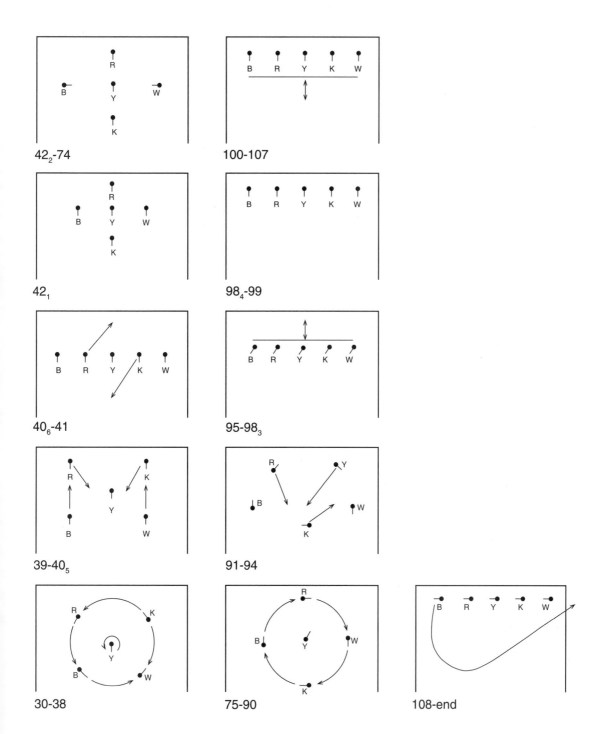

42₂-74

100-107

42₁

98₄-99

40₆-41

95-98₃

39-40₅

91-94

30-38

75-90

108-end

Figure 11 (cont.)

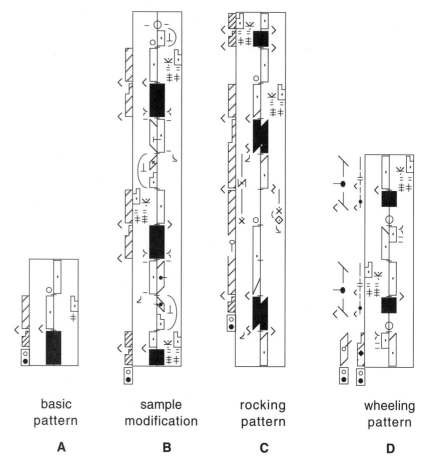

Figure 12. Labanotation scores of movement phrases from Ch'ŏ-yongmu. Notation by Judy Van Zile.

basic pattern	sample modification	rocking pattern	wheeling pattern
A	**B**	**C**	**D**

in variants that occur throughout the dance: by adding a directional step prior to drawing the feet together in middle level (counts 2 and 6); by adding a pivot to change the dancer's overall facing prior to or during the directional step (also counts 2 and 6), or during the drawing of the feet together (counts 3 and 7); and by adding a rise to the balls of the feet prior to the sinking at the beginning of the pattern (counts 3, 6, and 10).

The repeated lifting of one knee and bending and extending emphasize the linear vertical dimension. Although taking a directional step contributes a brief moment of another dimension (the sagittal), and pivoting changes the dancer's overall orientation to space, these modifications are sufficiently brief that the linear up-down emphasis is retained. And rising to the balls of the feet simply augments the established verticality. Hence, the continual repetition of the basic pattern establishes the vertical as a constant, on top of which modifications are layered.

Figure 12, Example C shows the pattern that serves as the foundation for the only major departure from the basic footwork pattern (this occurs in M. 21–24 and 26–29). In this sequence a forward-backward rocking movement is done simultaneously with the continuing rising and sinking. This combination results in the entire body tracing over- and under-curves that cycle through the sagittal plane, a sequence that briefly shifts the emphasis from linear to planar movement.

The Torso. Torso actions shown in Figure 12, Examples A and B, reiterate the vertical dimension established by the legs. In the basic, repeated pattern (Figure 12, Example A) the torso tilts to forward high and then returns to an upright position. Because this movement coincides with bending and extending the legs (tilting when the legs bend and returning to upright when they extend), it reinforces the verticality of the leg movements rather than creating a sagittal emphasis. The same torso action, which relates to leg actions in the same manner, is found in the variants of the basic pattern (Figure 12, Example B).

In the rocking pattern (Figure 12, Example C) the forward and slight backward tilts contribute to the sagittal planar movement, and once again we see the torso supporting the spatial emphasis established by the legs.

Figure 12, Example D shows the most complex change in torso action, which begins a little less than halfway through the dance (in M. 43). Here, the tilting is enhanced by a turning that results in wheeling (a simultaneous tilting and turning). But the continuing sinking and rising in the legs and the lowering and lifting of the torso also reinforce the initially established vertical dimension. The result here is a *dual* emphasis: the vertical, as well as three-dimensional spiralling (which is the product of an essentially planar motion occurring concurrently with the vertical).

Thus, the predominant overall emphasis at the beginning of the dance is on linearity: straight-line pathways and formations of the dancers as a group, and vertical dimensional movements of the individual dancers. As the dance progresses, however, it becomes increasingly complex spatially while maintaining the vertical rising and sinking.

The Arms. Although the vocabulary of leg and torso movements is limited, there is greater variety in arm movements. It is primarily the arms that, together with the overall pathways through the performing space, contribute to increasing spatial dynamics throughout the dance.

The use of long sleeves extends the dancer's kinesphere (the imaginary spatial "bubble" that surrounds the dancer and includes all the space he or she could reach with any body part without stepping through space). Because the sleeves are manipulated only in a way that thrusts them upward, or upward and outward, however, it is only the upper portion of the kinesphere that is emphasized. The repeated upward thrusting reiterates, in the arms, the verticality established in the legs and supported by the torso. And, as with the legs, other uses of space are layered onto this vertical constant.

Figure 13 shows the complete rocking pattern (based on the outline given in Figure 12, Example C). Verticality is seen in the continual rising and sinking of the legs, the repeated tilting and returning to upright of the torso, and the thrusting of the sleeves (the latter at the beginning and middle of M. 21 and M. 22 and at the beginning of M. 23). Despite the

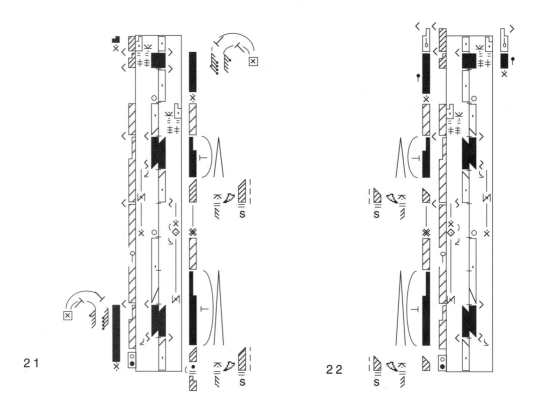

21   22

Figure 13. Labanotation score of rocking pattern from Ch'ŏyongmu. Notation by Judy Van Zile.

minor deviations in the arm directions, the interrelationship between the leg, torso, and arm activities makes the arms reiterate the sagittal cycling with over- and under-curves.

In addition to the verticality and planar sagittal emphases, the arm movements layer on a repeated opening and closing. This happens in measures 21–23 as first one arm, then the other, and then both move from close to the body to away from the body. But their circular movement is primarily in the sagittal plane, emphasizing the sagittal focus of the legs and torso. At the conclusion of the sequence (M. 24), verticality, opening, and closing remain, but this time the arms move in a spatially more complex way as they begin to enter the lateral plane and then progress three-dimensionally as they close, open out, and close again.

There are several variations of this simultaneous verticality, opening and closing, and three-dimensionality as the dance continues, but they reach their dynamic peak as the dancers exit. Figure 14 shows the phrase repeated throughout the concluding sequence. This exit is accomplished as the dancers start in a straight line across the back of the stage facing stage right (see the last floor plan in Figure 11), follow one behind the other as one dancer leads them in a large arc toward the downstage-right corner, and then move in a straight diagonal line so they exit upstage-left.

As the straight line progresses, the dancers return to a leg movement that is a simple variant of the basic pattern shown in Figure 12, Example A, but by this time the tempo has considerably accelerated. And this time

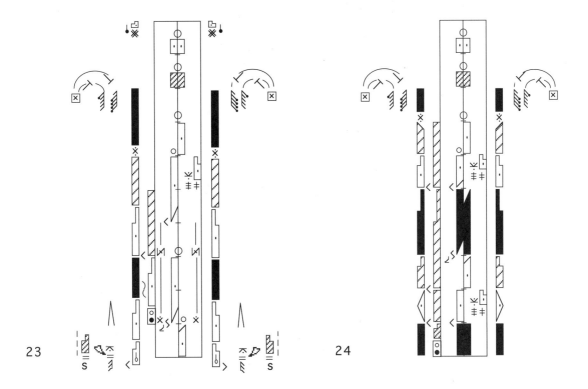

23   24

Figure 13 (cont.)

the continuing verticality has been layered with the torso wheeling and
a spiraling, three-dimensional arm movement, all of which are repeated
almost incessantly. The overriding total impact this time is a *triple* emphasis: linearity in progression through the performing area together with
verticality *and* three-dimensionality in the movements of the individual
dancers.

Spatial Variety. Spatial variety is achieved in a number of ways. There
are alternations between angular or linear movements and circular movements. This is seen in group formations and use of space as well as in each
individual dancer's use of space. The group formation changes from a
straight line to a square, a circle, a straight line, a diamond, a circle, and
a straight line, and ends with a sweeping arc that culminates in a straight
line as the group exits.

Individually the dancers perform quite flat, planar movements, such as
when they are in the square formation with one foot forward of the other
and rock back and forth as they tilt forward and backward. The flat sagittal plane is emphasized by an arm movement that starts low and close to
the body, thrusts forward and upward, circles to forward and downward,
and then reverses direction to return close to the body. Although the feet
and arm pass through the diagonal directions, the overall impact of this
sequence is as if fully traversing the sagittal plane.

This flat movement is contrasted with circular and spiraling movement. For example, during the second circle formation the dancers vigor-

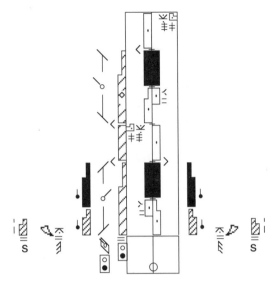

Figure 14. Labanotation of walking-with-wheeling pattern from Ch'ŏyongmu. Notation by Judy Van Zile.

ously thrust their arms upward and outward and then lower them and almost wrap them around their bodies as their torsos tilt and trace broad arcs to support the arm thrusts. This sequence creates the impression of broad swishing movements.

SUMMARY OF MOVEMENT CHARACTERISTICS

In summary, the size of the movement vocabulary used in Ch'ŏyongmu is not extensive: A limited number of patterns is established and then varied, with many repetitions of the basic patterns and variants. This repetition, in terms of movement pattern as well as continual vertical spatial emphasis, could become extremely monotonous. But the layering on of increased spatial complexity contributes to movement density and a vitality that literally keeps the dance moving.

The cumulative way in which space is used is what leads to my identification of modifications as "layering." The dance begins with an emphasis on simple dimensionality and linear floor patterns; dimensionality is retained as planar movements and geometric floor patterns are layered on; and the dance concludes with geometric shapes that move through space at the same time three-dimensional movements are added to the continuing dimensionality. Concurrently, however, the regularity and symmetry of the geometric shapes and the repetition of movement patterns give the dance a feeling of solidity and stability.

Noteworthy from a theatrical point of view is that rather than displaying the conventional western notion of a rise in activity to a climax and then a diminishing resolution, Ch'ŏyongmu displays a rise, a brief and somewhat abrupt "drop" or pause, and then a conclusion that continues to build, leaving the dynamic peak for the end. A dance that begins methodically and sedately concludes in a dynamic flurry of swishing sleeves that is supported by various forms of rising and sinking, and a major contributor to the dynamic build is the way in which space is used.

There are four ways in which performances of Ch'ŏyongmu may vary today. The most common way to vary what is considered the traditional version is to shorten it from the twenty-minute dance designated an Intangible Cultural Asset and documented in the Cultural Property Preservation Bureau report. Abridgment is achieved primarily by eliminating some repetition; occasionally, an entire pattern is eliminated. When the dance is shortened, no variation occurs in the sequence of movement patterns, and the dance takes between ten and fifteen minutes to perform. This type of variation is intentional, and involves only the length of the dance. (Appendix 2 provides a description of one abridged version.)

Minor movement variations are sometimes performed by individual dancers. These can be attributed to the impossibility of exact replication of the movement of another person (or oneself), to differing interpretations of movement descriptions contained in historical documents, or to the fact that movement is passed on primarily orally or kinesthetically (rather than via a consistent form of written documentation—despite the documentation provided in the official government report and publications of the National Center for Korean Traditional Performing Arts), and in the process runs the risk of subconsciously incorporating small variations. These individual variations are unintentional, and occur in the way movements are executed. Examples of such variations include differing amounts of twisting in the torso, differing heights of the leg lift, and differing uses of amounts of energy and when energy punctuation occurs. During a performance, such minor variations are usually perceptible to only the highly skilled observer.

Movement variations become more noticeable when a particular dance director provides a different interpretation than that of a previous director. For example, in a November 1990 performance of a new version several thrusting arm movements were performed to a sideward and upward direction rather than a forward diagonal and upward direction, several torso tilting sequences were performed to a single direction rather than in a circular fashion, and the quality of the lowering of the arms in several sequences was a deliberate punch rather than a simple relaxed drop. Because these changes could be clearly observed in all five dancers, they may be attributed to instructions they were given rather than to individual performing idiosyncrasies.[15]

Occasionally, choreographers will consciously choose to create a new Ch'ŏyong dance. In these instances five dancers attired in traditional costumes and masks perform, accompaniment comprises excerpts from the traditional music, the overall dance is shortened to usually less than five minutes, and movements are creative adaptations based—to varying degrees—on traditional ones. This type of variation is intentional, and involves both the way movements are done and the length of the dance. Contemporary choreographies are relatively rare, but one such creative performance was given by the Seoul City Dance Company in the early 1980s—complete with elaborate stage sets and a cloudy haze created by a smoke machine.

Who Choreographed Today's Ch'ŏyongmu

Ch'ŏyongmu was performed in royal courts at one time, but history traces its origin to a legend, and then documents transitions to religious contexts outside the royal setting, entertainment at banquets in the royal palace and for aristocrats, and finally to its contemporary theatrical concert setting. Documentation of the dance winds its way through historical sources dating from the late-thirteenth through the twentieth century, providing bits and pieces of information about the dance that suggest the contexts in which it was performed, transitions from one to two and ultimately five performers, the nature of costumes and masks worn, and hints of movements used in the dance on the occasions documented. Today's dance is said to replicate the version reconstructed in 1923.

Pictorial records are an important form of documentation in Korea: "Following the establishment of the Confucian state, much importance was given to the painter's function as a visual historian, and a great many documentary paintings on ceremonial occasions such as gatherings of scholars and palace events began to be produced" (Chung Hyung-min 1997:63). It is important, therefore, to examine such images when seeking to piece together history. Here I will explore the potential relationship between some of these images and the choreography of today's Ch'ŏyongmu.[16]

Pictorial images may take forms other than paintings, and I begin the discussion with images predating paintings of Confucian society with representations of Ch'ŏyongmu in the *Akhak kwebŏm*, the 1493 treatise considered to be one of the most important documents on court dance and music. Although this source contains detailed representations of Ch'ŏyongmu in both pictorial and textual form, I focus here on pictorial representations.

In the example shown from the *Akhak kwebŏm* in Figure 6 we see, in the top half, Chinese characters placed on the page in a manner suggesting the location of individuals at a particular moment. There are five identical Chinese characters, each being the word "dancer." Underneath each are additional characters for five directions and five colors—north and black at the top, south and red at the bottom, east and blue at the right, west and white at the left, and center and yellow in the middle. If we assume the dancers are in some way relating to the king (as they would in a court performance), and that the king is either at the top or bottom of the page, the dancers are positioned in the formation referred to previously as the "diamond formation," which is seen in performances of the dance today, and the colors coincide with the predominant color of the tunic worn by the corresponding dancers in the formation.

The circle at the bottom half of the page contains Chinese characters for the names of individual musical instruments, various kinds of ceremonial banners used at royal events, and dancers for several different dances. Based on the way in which they are read, the characters suggest a clockwise progression around the circle.

I consider this image (and several others) pictorial because it shows words carefully arranged on the page to suggest more than just what is conveyed in the words themselves. I thus use the concept of "pictorial representation" to refer broadly to a variety of kinds of representations distinguishable from "textual representations." The latter refers to narratives or poetry comprised of strings of words arranged on the page in the same manner as when they are intended to be read simply as connected text.

Textual descriptions in the *Akhak kwebŏm* indicate that large processionals of the sort suggested in the bottom half of this image were part of major court events. According to Ch'ŏyongmu National Living Treasure Kim Ch'ŏn-hŭng (personal communication 21 April 1995), the circle is a processional that was part of a New Year ritual (Narye) in which the dancers and musicians went through different parts of the palace to dispel evil spirits. This is potentially corroborated in this image by the Chinese characters in the top half of the page, to the right of the depiction of the diamond formation, that say Diagram of Five Directions Formation (Obang Chaktaedo). It is most likely, therefore, that this image shows a moment from the dance's ritualistic presentation to expel evil spirits, a moment from the elegant version of the dance performed as part of New Year rituals (Chŏndo Ch'ŏyongmu). The Chinese characters in the bottom half of the page to the right of the circle say Diagram of Beginning and Ending Turning Dance (Shiyong Hoemudo). If this portion of the image is assumed to be part of the presentation of the Dance of the Five Directions, it suggests that the procession occurred both before and after the performance of the dance. If, on the other hand, the bottom half of the page is intended as separate from the top half, "before" and "after" would suggest that a procession was part of both versions of Ch'ŏyongmu —the version done for ritual as well as the version done for entertainment. Performances today include only a Ch'ŏyong dance—there is no processional component. Since today's performances have been shortened from what are believed to have been the original versions, and since there are seldom as many personnel available as suggested in the illustration, it is difficult to substantiate either interpretation based on contemporary practice. But the formation shown at the top is used in today's Ch'ŏyongmu.

In this documentation from the *Akhak kwebŏm*, single words and their pictorial arrangement on the page combine to convey information. Regardless of interpretation details, including the ambiguity of the relationship between the two components of the illustration, part of what is communicated correlates with current performance practice and part does not.

The next pictorial representation (Figure 15), also from the *Akhak kwebŏm*, is similar in both content and method of communication. At the

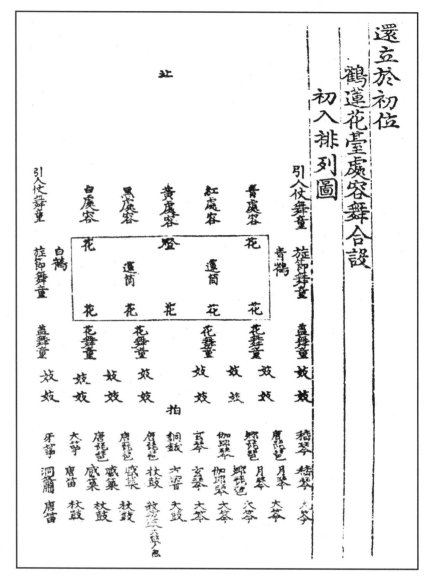

Figure 15. Ch'oip paeyŏlto (Diagram of the Arrangement upon Entering), for Hak Yonhwadae Ch'ŏyongmu Hapsŏl (Crane, Flower-Crown, Dance of Ch'ŏyong Suite), from *Akhak kwebŏm* (1493). Courtesy of Kyujanggak, Seoul National University.

top of the page is the Chinese character meaning "north." Because the king traditionally sat in the north, it is likely the character for north is placed here to indicate how the entire configuration orients to the royal personage.

The rectangle marks off an area described in narrative text, and shown in other pictorial representations (Figure 16), as a raised platform. Outside of the platform, at the northern edge, arranged from left to right as we view the illustration, are Chinese characters for the five Ch'ŏyong dancers. On the platform at the outer edges of the northern side and also along what would be the southern edge, are characters designating individuals holding flowers, in the center at the northern edge is a character for "lamp," and in the center of the platform are two characters for lotus flowers. Outside of the platform on the southern edge are characters for dancers holding flowers, behind them are indications for two rows of female singers, a single character for the musical instrument that serves as the "conductor" of the ensemble (*pak*), and behind that indications for thirty-five musical instruments. Immediately adjacent to the left and right sides of the platform are characters for a "white crane" and a "blue crane," and outside of these are characters for six standard bearers.

As mentioned previously, the *Akhak kwebŏm* describes two versions of a Ch'ŏyong dance. The lively version was performed for entertainment and was part of a suite comprised of three dances, The Crane Dance, The Lotus Pavilion Dance, and Ch'ŏyongmu. Since the illustration contains indications of cranes, lotus flowers, and Ch'ŏyong dancers, we can assume this is a representation of a moment from the entertainment version of the dance. And since the Chinese characters outside the right margin of the illustration say Diagram of the Arrangement upon Entering (Ch'oip paeyŏlto), this undoubtedly represents the opening formation of the suite.

Textual descriptions of The Crane Dance state that two performers attired in realistic crane costumes performed movements resembling those of birds. Toward the end of the dance they approached two large artificial lotus flowers on a platform and pecked at them (Figure 16). One young

Figure 16. Illustration of Hangmu (Crane Dance), from *Kojong imin chinyŏn ŭigwe* (1902). Courtesy of Kyujanggak, Seoul National University.

girl emerged from each flower and together the girls performed The Lotus Pavilion Dance (Chang Sa-hun 1978:15, 24).

Figures 7 and 16, both line drawings from later documents, show the cranes approaching the lotus flowers on the platform and the young girls, who have emerged from the flowers, on the cranes' backs. Both of these moments are described in narrative text in the *Akhak kwebŏm*. This was then followed by a performance of Ch'ŏyongmu.

Figure 15 shows what narrative textual documentations describe as the opening configuration of the three-dance suite. Although performances of Ch'ŏyongmu today are said to be the livelier version that was part of the suite performed for entertainment, the dance is performed now independently of the other two dances of the original suite. The Crane Dance is occasionally performed, but it, too, is performed as an independent dance, and although the cranes may peck at lotus flowers, no dancers emerge to exit atop the cranes. The Lotus Pavilion Dance is seldom done today. Apparently the only exception to the independent performance of the dances was the 1983 staging referred to previously and described more fully below.

Once again we find a combination of isolated words and their pictorial arrangement on the page combining to convey information. In this case what appears to be communicated does not correlate with current performance practice.

The final example presented here from the *Akhak kwebŏm* is a line drawing of the Ch'ŏyong mask, which includes an elaborately ornamented hat affixed to it (Figure 17). (Other illustrations in the *Akhak kwebŏm* include similar drawings of costume components.) Today all of the performers wear identical masks that follow quite closely the *Akhak kwebŏm* depiction. This example, unlike the previous two from the *Akhak kwebŏm*, shows a literal pictorial representation that is identical to what is seen today. It is interesting to note that the only pictorial representations of Ch'ŏyongmu in the *Akhak kwebŏm* are line drawings of the costume and mask and the pictorial arrangement of Chinese characters suggesting the placement of individuals in a performing space; there are no pictorial representations of actual movements or dancers in motion.

Let us now turn to another kind of pictorial representation and look at several genre paintings (*p'ungsokhwa*) that are part of a series said to have been completed in 1720.[17] In the first painting (Plate 22 and enlargement in Plate 23), we see a royal celebration to honor elderly high-ranking ministers and the longevity of the king (in this case, King Sukchong (r. 1674–1720)). The king is under the canopy, out of our view. Lining the open space in the center (outside the canopy) are the honored ministers—six on the left and four on the right. At the far sides are ceremonial standard bearers, and at the bottom and in the center are dancers and musicians. All of the individuals portrayed appear to be men. In the center are two dancers in red costumes. Immediately flanking the open space at the bottom are eleven figures. Based on their hats and garments,

Figure 17. Ch'ŏyongmu
mask illustration from
Akhak kwebŏm (1493).
Courtesy of Kyujanggak,
Seoul National University.

the outermost figures on either side appear to be musicians (as are the
figures in the two lines behind them). The inner nine figures, in costumes
of various colors, all appear to be dancers awaiting their turn to perform.
In the lower right-hand corner, approaching the performing space, are
five Ch'ŏyong figures.

Note the animation in the Ch'ŏyongmu dancers. (See enlargement in
Plate 23.) In many such paintings people who appear to be walking generally look rather static. In this case each dancer's torso is tilted slightly
forward. The first three dancers each appear to have the forward leg lifted
or, as with the last two dancers, have their legs spread rather widely,
with both the front and back legs considerably bent. (The precise position
is difficult to determine because of distortion in the two-dimensional
image.) I suggest the animation is more related to the animation of the

two figures in the center of the performing space than to the static figures in the rest of the painting. It would be speculative, at best, to suggest that the Ch'ŏyong dancers are actually dancing or "rushing" to the performance space, but there is a clear indication of energy and motion that is only present in the rest of this painting in the two center dancing figures.

Although admittedly tentative, I propose, in relation to contemporary performances of Ch'ŏyongmu, a qualitative similarity. There are movements in today's dance in which the knee is lifted in a manner resembling the position suggested here, and despite the fact that today's dance begins very slowly, as it progresses there is a decided increase in animation. It is also logical that the version of Ch'ŏyongmu performed in this context is the livelier version described in the *Akhak kwebŏm* as being performed for entertainment.

Another painting from the same series is described as portraying the somewhat inebriated ministers returning from their celebrations at the king's banquet.[18] At the far right are five Ch'ŏyong dancers, each in a separate row of figures and each preceded by either other dancers or ceremonial attendants and followed by musicians. (Plate 24 shows only three Ch'ŏyong dancers in a detail of the full image.) This is surely not intended to show dancing, but there is one interesting costume feature to note. In addition to the long colored sleeves that are part of the outer-garment, each dancer also has a set of even longer white sleeves that appear to be part of an under-garment. This is identical to the long white sleeves in most pictorial representations of Ch'ŏyongmu as well as to the sleeves used in contemporary performances.

In the third example from this series (Plates 25 and 26) a Ch'ŏyong dance is performed at the members' private party the day after the King's banquet. Again long sleeves extend from the outer-garment as well as from an inner garment, but interesting movement features are suggested. In an enlargement (Plate 26) we see a moment that is both similar to and different from a moment in today's dance. At one point in contemporary performances the dancers place themselves in the diamond formation, as described earlier, with one dancer in the center. The center dancer then faces and dances with the dancer in the black tunic, beginning a canon in which the remaining dancers each join in turn (starting with the dancer in the blue tunic, followed by the one in red, and lastly the one in white). The moment suggested here could easily be a canon, with the dancer in red awaiting his turn to finally join the others, but the order in which the dancers appear to join the canon is different from the order followed in today's performances. (The white and black dancers both appear to be dancing while the yellow dancer faces and dances with the blue dancer. Only the red dancer appears to be static.) And, as in Plates 22 and 23, there is a clear sense of animation (to all except the one dancer awaiting his turn). (There is a significant musical difference between this depiction and today's performance as well: The large drum at the bottom of the illustration is not used in contemporary performances.)

Another difference between this painting and contemporary performances is the way the dancers' movements relate to each other. In contemporary performances, once the dancers have joined the canon, they all perform exactly the same movement. While the yellow- and blue-clad dancers seem to be doing identical movements here, the black- and white-attired dancers, although animated and apparently dancing, appear to be doing something different—they do not have one leg lifted so high nor do they have one arm thrust upward.

In this case the formation shown and the suggestion of a movement canon parallel movements in contemporary performances. Details of the canon suggested here, however, both in terms of the order in which dancers join the canon and the relationship between their movements, are different from those in performances of the canon today.

We find another interesting feature in a painting generally attributed to Kim Hong-do (1745–c. 1806), a court painter and one of Korea's most prolific artists (Plate 27 and enlargement in Plate 17). This very long screen painting (*hwagwŏn*) dates from the end of the 1700s or early 1800s and depicts an inaugural celebration to welcome the new governor of P'yŏngyang. Four dances are represented in the central performing area, one of which is Ch'ŏyongmu.[19] The question that immediately arises is whether these dances were actually all performed simultaneously —as in a kind of "four-ring circus"—or whether the artist simply chose to show all of the dances in what is essentially a composite picture. Such dances are never performed simultaneously today.

There is another intriguing feature in this painting. In all of the previously shown pictorial images the dancers wear baggy pants or pantaloons underneath the long tunic—attire suggesting male dancers. In this painting the tunic is shortened and the under-garment is a skirt—suggesting female dancers. It is also interesting to note that in this painting all of the other dancers appear to be female and, except for the musicians at the bottom of the painting, the individuals flanking the performing space are all women. In the previous paintings, any additional dancers and individuals lining the performing space were all men.

Ch'ŏyongmu authority Kim Ch'ŏn-hŭng identified a reference to a female Ch'ŏyongmu dancer in the mid-twentieth century. If this painting accurately documents reality, then women danced Ch'ŏyongmu by the early nineteenth century. However, at least by the time of the 1923 reconstruction, it was believed the dance's movements were more suited to men than to women, and it was men who were enlisted to perform the dance. From that time until the mid-1990s, the dance has almost always been performed by men. On the few occasions when it is performed by women, they wear pantaloons. Again, an historical pictorial image and contemporary performance are not in agreement.

Before looking at another illustration, note that here, as in all of the other examples thus far, there are only five Ch'ŏyong dancers, and all wear masks.

An important source of documentation for court banquets of the late Chosŏn dynasty are the *ŭigwe*, records of the superintendency for royal ceremonies. Most *ŭigwe* are text manuscripts, but some are paintings or woodblock prints. These documents are often identified on the basis of the size of the banquet they describe: those that describe large royal banquets (*chinch'an ŭigwe*), those that describe medium-sized royal banquets (*chinyŏn ŭigwe*), and those that describe small royal banquets (*chinjak ŭigwe*).[20] Numerous court records of each of these types exist from banquets held at different times. Two of these *ŭigwe* contain particularly interesting illustrations of Ch'ŏyongmu. A line drawing of Ch'ŏyongmu in an 1828 record of a small court banquet (*Sunjo muja chinjak ŭigwe*), shows nine dancers (Figure 9); five are attired in masks and pantaloon-clad Ch'ŏyong costumes similar to those seen today, and are positioned so that four dancers form a circle surrounding the fifth dancer—a formation commonly shown in other documents and one seen in contemporary performances. But there are four male dancers in typical court dance attire placed between each of the dancers wearing Ch'ŏyong costumes and masks in the circle.

In an 1829 large banquet record (*Sunjo kich'uk chinch'an ŭigwe*) (Figure 18) we see the same configuration, but this time the four dancers in between the regular Ch'ŏyong dancers are women. In a painting from the late 1700s or early 1800s (attributed to Kim Hong-do) we see a similar configuration, but this time all five regular pantaloon-clad Ch'ŏyong dancers are in the circle and seven female dancers are interspersed among them (Plate 28). In addition, the five Ch'ŏyong dancers appear in the diamond formation at the top of the painting. As pointed out previously, the diamond formation is present in today's performances. Likewise, a circular formation is seen today. But the intermixing of female and male dancers is not seen when Ch'ŏyongmu is performed today, nor does a group of five dancers in a diamond formation perform simultaneously with a group of dancers in a circular formation.

Most contemporary performers and dance scholars do not recall seeing performances or other illustrations in which either male or female performers intermingle with the regular Ch'ŏyongmu dancers. The only explanation offered for these groupings is that court dances sometimes employ not only the major dancers, but also attendants who carry ceremonial implements and sing. While it is possible the male and female dancers in ceremonial attire in these three illustrations are attendants who would normally appear at the sides of the performing area, the use of such attendants would have been unusual. *Chukkanja*, as the attendants and the implements they carry are known, are used in dances of Chinese origin, and, as pointed out earlier, Ch'ŏyongmu is considered to be of Korean origin.

The placement of the diamond and circle formations in the same image bears an interesting resemblance to the careful arrangement of Chinese characters shown in these same two formations in the *Akhak kwebŏm*

Figure 18. Ch'ŏyongmu illustration from *Sunjo kich'uk chinch'an ŭigwe* (1829). Courtesy of Kyujanggak, Seoul National University.

illustration presented earlier (Figure 6). Although one explanation for the placement of words meaning "before" and "after" in conjunction with the *Ahkak kwebŏm* processional suggests a sequence of events, the 1829 large banquet painting contains no explanatory text. Thus, it is not clear whether the two configurations were performed simultaneously or were juxtaposed by the painter. We might also question whether the male and female dancers in the 1829 drawing actually performed together or if their juxtaposition, too, was a matter of artistic license. Art historian Park Jeong-hye (1997:140) says painters could not easily represent all the details of the banquet on a two-dimensional picture plane; sometimes a painter's discretion or ability yielded changes in the paintings.[21] Hence, the juxtaposition may have been done at the artist's discretion.

It is interesting to note that while Chinese characters in the *Akhak kwebŏm* illustration identified the dancers in the diamond formation as one of the five colors or five directions, in the painting attributed to Kim Hong-do Korean writing identifies each of the dancers in the diamond formation specifically as one of the *spirits* of each of the five directions. Because of the presence at the bottom of the illustration of the platform and two lotus flowers that were part of the suite of three dances done for entertainment, as well as the identification of the dancers at the top of the illustration as spirits of the directions, it is easy to speculate that this represents *both* versions of Ch'ŏyongmu—the ritualistic New Year version to expel evil spirits as well as the version performed for entertainment. But the question still remains regarding the simultaneity of their performance.

The final illustration, from a document recording an 1848 large banquet (*Hŏnjong mushin chinch'an ŭigwe*) (Figure 8), shows only the five pantaloon-clad and masked Ch'ŏyong dancers in quite static positions in the diamond formation. This static quality is unusual in today's performance of the dance.

Although the examples here were presented in approximate chronological order, they do not constitute a full catalogue of representations of Ch'ŏyongmu. Nor has all the potential information that might be gleaned from each image and related text been pointed out. I will now, however, identify several historical events and propose a potential relationship between artists and choreographers based on this sampling.

A Ch'ŏyong dance is first described and illustrated in a late thirteenth-century document, and subsequently in numerous documents up through the twentieth century. Despite this documentation of a lengthy history, there have been at least two breaks in the tradition of performing a Ch'ŏyong dance. Political battles at various times in Korea's history created several forced "pauses." Each time, however, the dance was reconstructed, either from the memories of living dancers or on the basis of extant documents, such as those described here.

The dance performed most often today is said to replicate the version reconstructed in 1923. Following a hiatus in court performances during the early days of the Japanese occupation, Ch'ŏyongmu was reconstructed by young boy musicians. At that time, it was only the Ch'ŏyong dance that was restaged, not the set of three dances constituting the suite described earlier. Thus, claims of "authenticity" regarding the dance performed today are based on the belief that it is essentially a continuation of the dance reconstructed in 1923, which, in turn, is considered "authentic" and "accurate" because it was based on information contained in historical documents. In subsequent years, other extant documents were consulted to refine performance details as well as to reconstruct the other two dances of the suite, but, with only one exception (the 1983 performance), no effort was made to perform the dances as a suite.

A significant departure from the independent performance of a Ch'ŏyong dance with five masked dancers was staged in 1983. Based, in part, on some of the same pictorial representations described here, National Living Treasure Kim Ch'ŏn-hŭng staged the full suite of dances that included the Intangible Cultural Asset version of Ch'ŏyongmu. The most significant feature of the performance, however, was its conclusion. Following each of the three dances in the suite, all performers joined together in a kind of grand finale. During this culminating section, female dancers joined the male Ch'ŏyongmu dancers to dance, at one point, in between each of the masked Ch'ŏyong figures and, at another point, in another circle surrounding the masked Ch'ŏyong figures (Plate 29). In mixing the masked male and unmasked female dancers, Kim replicated the illustration in the 1829 pictorial court record and the mid-eighteenth/early-nineteenth century genre painting. In other words, we know that interspersing unmasked female dancers with the five masked Ch'ŏyong dancers in this 1983 performance was consciously based, at least in part, on pictorial representations in historical documents.

In addition, Kim, says that at the time of the 1923 reconstruction, no masks from former times could be located. Therefore, new masks were made—specifically based on the illustration contained in the *Akhak kwebŏm* (personal communication 21 Oct. 1990), which continues to serve as the model for today's masks. Again, we know, with certainty, that something contained in the reconstruction and continued today was consciously based on pictorial representations in historical documents.

Where does this lead with regard to the relationship between pictorial documentation, contemporary performance, and choreographers? Although the examples presented suggest both similarities and differences between former performances and those at the end of the twentieth century, and while they suggest possible information in relation to costume details, gender of dancers, additional dancers beyond the five wearing Ch'ŏyong masks, group formations, and some movement elements, they also pose many questions, questions regarding the juxtaposition of formations in a single representation, the gender of the dancers, and the inclusion of more than five dancers—whether wearing masks or not. Since we know that there have been several breaks in the continuity of Ch'ŏyongmu performances and that the dance has been reconstructed several times specifically based on various historical documents, I propose one further question—Who choreographed today's Ch'ŏyongmu?—and a possible answer to it.

When dances are selected for Intangible Cultural Asset status there is a great deal of concern with authenticity, and researchers strive to identify "the original" version of each dance. (See discussion of authenticity in Chapter 3.) But what constitutes authenticity and an original version? We know that Ch'ŏyongmu was reconstructed at least twice. And we know that textual and pictorial documents served as the basis for two of these reconstructions. Although many of these documents purportedly record actual events, we also know that movement is extremely difficult to represent accurately in a two-dimensional medium (either textual or pictorial). It is very possible that while documenters, particularly those creating pictorial documents, attempted to record the actuality of individual events, they also took artistic license. Although based on reality, they in fact may have created a kind of mythical performance. When people later tried to reconstruct Ch'ŏyongmu after periods of inactivity and turned to pictorial documentation for inspiration, they created a performance based on artistic license taken by the documents' creators—ultimately creating a new reality based on a mythical reality. In other words, artists may have, unwittingly, become contributors to the choreography, and identity, of today's Ch'ŏyongmu.

5
Chinju Kŏmmu

Prologue

Eight female dancers walk casually into the performing space. They wear long light-blue skirts and long-sleeved blouses. Atop this traditional clothing of Korean women, they wear long dark-blue jackets styled after those of male military officials of former times. Each dancer's hair is pulled back tightly at the nape of the neck into a chignon, through which is thrust a long hairpin—both typical of older Korean women in the past. On top of their heads they sport round, flat, black hats, each with a peacock feather and red tassel dropping lazily over the side and a chain of large red and yellow beads draped loosely beneath the chin—again reminiscent of former male military attire. The dancers' long, multicolored sleeves that are separate from those of their blouses and that are fastened at the wrist with drawstrings—typical of female court dancers of an earlier era—hang almost to the ground, and from within each sleeve the hand grasps a sword not much longer than a dagger. Small metal ornaments dangle loosely from the metal blade and a red tassel suspended from the handle spins through the air as the sword is manipulated.

The dancers position themselves in two lines facing each other, both lines perpendicular to the audience. They slowly lower themselves to a kneel, quietly place their swords on the ground beside them, and rise to begin the dance.

They continually bend and extend their knees as they walk slowly through a series of formations in which the lines merge, open into two lines parallel to the audience, change to a square, and merge and open several more times.

When they are again in their two lines perpendicular to the audience they begin a walking sequence with a strong backward tilt of the torso and an opening of the arms sideward at shoulder height, palms facing upward. The next sequence is a series of slow walks in which the dancers change their physical relationship to the partner they have been facing. As the movement pattern concludes the dancers remove the long sleeves fastened at their wrists and drop them to the floor at the sides of the performing area.

The dancers continue with a series of formation changes and an arm pattern in which they quickly open their cupped hands and simultaneously turn their arms to display their palms. At the conclusion of this sequence they add the backward torso tilt to the hand-opening movement.

Again the dancers change their group formation, this time moving their hands and wrists as if holding and manipulating the swords.

Upon returning to their two lines perpendicular to the audience they sit, grasp the long "tails" of their jackets, and move them to reveal the red inner lining. The dancers then tie the ends of their jacket tails behind their backs and while still seated move their hands and wrists again as if holding and manipulating the swords.

They pick up one sword and then the other, and flick their wrists while bending and extending their elbows and turning their forearms. The metal ornaments on the swords clang gently and the tassels spin as the sword blades trace arcs in space—movements that are ornamental rather than realistic representations of combat motions.

The dancers stand and change formations again, continuing to manipulate the swords as they advance and retreat, and then form a circle.

By this time the tempo has increased and the dancers do a series of individual turns as they progress around the circle, all the while continuing the complex arm movement and wrist flicking. The turns are reminiscent of movements most often seen in dances performed by men and the concurrent sword manipulation ornaments the movement rather than displaying fighting actions.

The tempo slows, the dancers walk around the circle—still manipulating their swords—form a single straight line parallel to the audience, bow, and quietly exit by backing away from the performing area.

No story has been told. Although a suggestion of military action has been offered, the strongest impression is that of a kaleidoscopic ensemble that groups and regroups amidst a flurry and swish of sword blades—all with the calm dignity of a regal group of dancers.

The Dance Name

Kŏmmu is most frequently glossed in English as "Knife Dance," and occasionally as "Sword Dance." "*Kŏm*" is the Sino-Korean word for "sword," and "*mu*" is from the Sino-Korean "*muyong*," meaning "dance." Illustrations in mid-nineteenth century court documents show dancers using a

A
CLOSER
LOOK

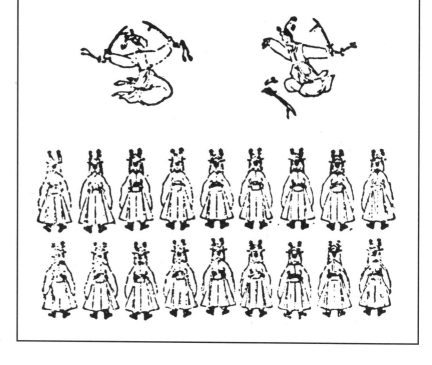

fairly long implement that we would probably identify today as a sword
(Figure 19); most of today's implements are relatively short (approxi-
mately fourteen inches), and would more likely be considered knives.
The dance is occasionally referred to as "K'al ch'um," "*k'al*," the pure-
Korean word for "knife," "sword," or "dagger," and "*ch'um*," the pure-
Korean word for "dance." "Kŏmmu" is used more frequently than "K'al
ch'um," and the terms "knife" and "sword" are used interchangeably
here, as they are by Koreans when identifying such dances in English.

Many different dances are performed today with knives. Historical
documents indicate some kind of knife or sword dance was formerly performed in the court, and one version performed today is classified as a
court dance. Most of today's knife dances, however, are identified as folk
dance or new dance (see Chapter 2), are recently choreographed by different dancers or teachers, and are performed in a formal theater setting.
There is a great deal of emphasis in these dances on virtuosic manipulation of the knife.

There is one knife dance that stands apart from many of these spectacle-
oriented versions. The full name of the dance is Chinju P'al Kŏmmu. A
small but bustling city approximately two hundred sixty miles south of
the capital of Seoul, and surrounding both sides of the Nam River, Chinju
played a key role in several of Korea's battles against the Japanese. Despite attempts to maintain its stand, Chinju succumbed, a number of times,
to the powerful blows of its island neighbor. But there is a strong tie between one battle and Chinju P'al Kŏmmu (discussed shortly), and today

the city is the home of the dance. "*P'al*" is the Korean word for the number eight, and it is the version of this dance performed by eight women that was designated an Intangible Cultural Asset by the Korean government in 1967. Hence, the title of the dance indicates the city with which it is associated, the number of dancers, and the implement used in the dance. The title of the dance is generally shortened to "Chinju Kŏmmu."

The blade and handle of the knife used in Chinju Kŏmmu are firmly rather than loosely connected (Plate 30) and many of the dance movements are different from those of other knife dances. Chinju Kŏmmu displays features common to court dances performed today: a large number of female performers, movements that are slow and stately and that emphasize changing group formations, and a quality of contained composure reflecting Chosŏn dynasty Confucian ideals of femininity (discussed shortly). In contrast, it has a vigorous concluding section of rapid turns that is typically found, in a more elaborate variation, in masculine folk dances, and several sections in which the front surface of the torso and the palms of the hands are given prominence—movements that, despite their decorous performance, stand out blatantly as the antithesis of female Korean deportment. Although the dancers begin their performance wearing multicolored sleeves similar to those in court dances, they soon remove them in order to manipulate the knives. The knives used are different from those in other knife dances today, and the movements emphasizing the palms and torso are not found in any other dances still performed.

Thus, Chinju Kŏmmu shows clear links to both court and folk forms. How did such a blending of movement characteristics come to be? Although legendary and historical accounts do not always concur, frequently intertwine fact and fiction, and leave many unanswered questions, they do shed light on a number of things that contributed to these seemingly contradictory features—the unusual blending of masculine and feminine movements, and court and folk characteristics.

Legendary Origin

Two stories are referred to when tracing the origins of knife dances in Korea, one about an individual known as Kwanch'ang, and the other about an individual known as Hwang Ch'ang-nang. Together they actually contain references to three knife dances. The stories are found in the thirteenth-century *Samguk yusa* and the seventeenth-century *Tonggyŏng chapki*.

THE STORY OF KWANCH'ANG

During the Shilla dynasty (57 B.C.–A.D. 935) an institution known as *hwarang* was established. The *hwarang* were young boys trained in Korea's cultural and military arts. Commonly referred to as "flower boys" (because of large flowers on the hats they wore), the boys were highly educated loyal patriots, and are frequently compared to the knights of medieval Europe.[1] The oldest reference to a sword dance relates to a *hwarang*, and is found in the *Samguk yusa* (Memorabilia of the Three Kingdoms), a work completed some time in the late thirteenth century by the Buddhist monk, Iryŏn (1206–1289). The story takes place at a time when the kingdoms of Shilla and Paekche were at war with each other, and tells of Kwanch'ang (645–660), a sixteen-year-old *hwarang*.[2] The son of a soldier named P'umil, Kwanch'ang was an expert horseman and archer. In the year 660 his father sent him to the enemy camp of Paekche to help on the battlefield. There, Kwanch'ang was captured, but the enemy general, Kyebaek, refused to kill Kwanch'ang because of his youth, and sent Kwanch'ang back to the Shilla camp.

Kwanch'ang's father was greatly distressed because military conventions of the Shilla period required that a soldier either die in battle or return only after killing his enemy. So P'umil sent his son, once again, to the enemy camp of Paekche to try to achieve a victory. This time Kwanch'ang was captured and beheaded by Kyebaek.

> When his horse returned to the Shilla lines with the boy's head tied to the saddle, P'umil grasped his son's head and wiped off the blood with his sleeve. "My son's face is as when he was alive," he said. "He was able to die in the service of the king. There is nothing to regret." (Henthorn 1971:45)

In sorrow, Kwanch'ang's father made a mask of the boy's face and during funeral rituals the soldiers performed a sword dance[3] (Sŏng Kye-ok, personal communication 19 July 1983).

Although a mask is referred to in this story, it is not clear whether the dancers wore masks or if a mask was used simply as a reminder of the young soldier. Because soldiers performed the dance, the dancers were undoubtedly male.

THE STORY OF HWANG CH'ANG-NANG

Although the *Samguk yusa* story is the oldest reference to a sword dance it is not the one most frequently referred to as documenting the origin of today's knife dances. The more commonly related story comes from the folklore chapter of the *Tonggyŏng chapki* (Capital Miscellany), a text compiled in the late 1600s that also describes events in Korea during the Three Kingdoms period (57 B.C.–A.D. 935), but primarily in the area of Kyŏngju, the capital of Shilla. The story tells of a seven-year-old *hwarang* identified as Hwang Ch'ang-nang. Like Kwanch'ang, Hwang Ch'ang-nang is said to have lived during the Shilla dynasty (57 B.C.–A.D. 935) at a time when the kingdoms of Shilla and Paekche were at war with each other. People from the Shilla kingdom contrived a plot, and sent seven-year-old Hwang to Paekche to dance in the streets. The king of Paekche

heard of the beauty of the young boy's dancing and invited him to perform in the court. While performing a sword dance before the king the
young boy seized the opportunity to help his homeland by killing the
enemy king with his dance weapons. Hwang was then captured and executed. According to the *Tonggyŏng chapki* the people in Hwang's homeland of Shilla created a mask with Hwang's features and performed a
sword dance to commemorate the courageous act of their young dancer-
hero, Hwang Ch'ang-nang.

The story of Hwang Ch'ang-nang actually contains two sword dances:
the solo of the young warrior originally performed in the streets and subsequently performed, at least in part, before the king, and that of an unknown number of dancers performed to honor the young warrior after
his death. Although there is reference to a mask in connection with the
dance to honor Hwang, it is unclear if the dancers wore masks during
the dance or simply constructed them prior to performing; there is no
reference, however, to the young boy wearing a mask while he danced.
Hwang's dance was clearly a male solo dance, but we do not know the
number of dancers who commemorated his courageous act, or whether
they were male or female. And there are no indications regarding resem-
blances between Hwang Ch'ang-nang's dance movements and those of
the people who celebrated his courageous act. Thus, the major common-
ality between the two dances referred to in this story is the use of swords.

COMPARISON OF THE STORIES

There are a number of similarities in the legendary stories of Kwanch'ang
and Hwang Ch'ang-nang. Both are based on incidents occurring during
the war between the kingdoms of Shilla and Paekche and both involve
valorous deeds of young *hwarang*. However, the ages of the boys are different; Kwanch'ang was sixteen years old and Hwang Ch'ang-nang only
seven years old. Although Hwang Ch'ang-nang danced, Kwanch'ang
never did—it was only soldiers who danced to honor him. Both stories
mention the use of swords in a commemorative group dance. Although it
is unclear if the dancers wore masks, both stories indicate some kind of
mask used in association with the dance. And the names of seven-year-old
Hwang Ch'ang-nang and sixteen-year-old Kwanch'ang are very similar,
particularly if one takes into account that "*rang*" (from "*hwarang*," which
is pronounced "*nang*" in certain contexts) may have been a suffix added
to the names of individuals who were *hwarang* (Rutt 1961:7).

Except possibly for the group dance in the second story, the dance in
both legendary versions was performed by men; contemporary performers are women. Whether today's dance has roots in the solo dance of the
young boy dancer who killed an enemy king or in the group dances performed by others to commemorate the heroic deeds of one of the two
young boys is not clear. According to a writer in the 1950s, one story is
simply an adaptation of the other: The story of Kwanch'ang, the sixteen-

year-old warrior, is the original story, and the story of Hwang Ch'ang-nang, the seven-year-old dancer, is a later adaptation (Zong 1956:36–37). This is plausible since many historical documents simply replicate information in previously written material. Additionally, the stories merge in a later portion of the *Tonggyŏng chapki* (in *Chinjushisa* 1979:1176). In a section dealing with Kwanch'ang (the name of the boy in the earlier *Samguk yusa* story), documents of Yi Ch'ŏm (1345–1405), a notable person of the late Koryŏ/early Chosŏn dynasties, are cited. The reference indicates that in 1385, during the eleventh year of the reign of King U (r. 1374–1388), Yi Ch'ŏm was in Kyŏngju. An officer sponsored a feast at which a young boy performed a masked dance in a courtyard. Yi Ch'ŏm inquired about the dance and was told it had been performed during the Shilla dynasty by Hwang Ch'ang-nang (the name of the boy in the *Tonggyŏng chapki* story). In the story contained in the documents of Yi Ch'ŏm the dance was clearly a solo performed by a young boy wearing a mask. Although we are told the dance originated in a sword dance, it is not clear if the performer at the officer's feast actually used a sword in his dance.

The fact that the story referring to a dance by Hwang Ch'ang-nang was contained in a document relating to Kwanch'ang suggests that one of the stories was, indeed, an adaptation of the other. If this is the case, the names of the young boys described in the stories may have either been confused or used interchangeably. It is interesting to note that in the story of the dance performed at the officer's feast, although the dance was performed for an important dignitary, it was not performed in the royal court.

The earliest reference to a sword dance (in the *Samguk yusa*) indicates it was performed for entertainment, both in the city streets and in the royal court. One of the later references (the second reference in the *Tonggyŏng chapki*) suggests this same function was served in an open courtyard at the house of an important person. And both references indicate it was done as a commemorative act, in one case (that of the *Samguk yusa*) specifically during a funeral ritual. A twentieth-century writer (Zong 1956:37) states that a mask was used by the people of Shilla in a sword dance to soothe the spirits of the dead. If all of these accounts are accurate, early sword dances were performed for several different reasons and in several different contexts.

Nineteenth- and Twentieth-Century Documentation

SWORD DANCES IN GENERAL

Beyond legendary origins, today's Chinju Kŏmmu is sometimes attributed to performances in the court and sometimes to village performances. If sword dances were part of the early court dance repertoire it would be logical to find mention of them in the 1493 *Akhak kwebŏm*, one of the

Figure 20. Kŏmmu
(Sword Dance) illustra-
tion from *Sunjo kich'uk
chinch'an ŭigwe* (1829).
Courtesy of Kyujanggak,
Seoul National University.

oldest records of court dance and music. This text mentions a number of dances, but not a sword dance. If such a dance was performed prior to the fifteenth century, therefore, it is likely it belonged to repertoire outside the court.

Significant references to knife dances do not appear until the late eighteenth and early nineteenth centuries. Knife dances performed in the court are documented in pictorial form (*ŭigwe*, records of court banquets, see Chapter 4) in records from the nineteenth century (Figures 19, 20, 21, and 22). What is interesting to note in these illustrations is that in the first, the performers are two men, and in others, the performers are four women.

There are several records of knife dance performances outside the court. A late eighteenth- or early nineteenth-century painting by Kim Hong-do records the inauguration celebration of the governor of P'yŏngyang; it

Figure 21. Kŏmmu
(Sword Dance) illustra-
tion from *Hŏnjong
mushin chinch'an ŭigwe*
(1848). Courtesy of Kyu-
janggak, Seoul National
University.

Figure 22. Kŏmmu (Sword Dance) illustration from *Kyobang kayo* (1872). Courtesy National Library of Korea.

includes two women brandishing swords who dance before a dignitary and guests (Plate 17). In the *Kyobang kayo* (Text Collection of Court Entertainers' Training Institute), published in 1872, Chŏng Hyŏn-suk describes activities of female entertainers from the provinces, particularly the city of Chinju. The text mentions ten court dances, one of which is a sword dance, performed at a particular festival in Chinju (see Non'gae Pyŏlche discussion later). Some rather vague general descriptions of sword dance movements are given, and an illustration shows four female performers and the accompanying musicians (Figure 22). Text accompanying this illustration indicates that two of the performers are young female entertainers (*kisaeng*), and two are child female entertainers. Thus, by the nineteenth century sources reflect a sword dance performed outside the court as well as for court functions, and indicate both male and female performers. And at least by 1872, a sword dance was performed in Chinju.

Although the text in some of these early documents suggests some movements, the earliest vivid description comes from a westerner living in Korea. In an 1896 English-language text a foreigner gives a lively description of a dance performed by female entertainers he saw at the royal court in Seoul.

The dancers are as usual clothed in voluminous garments of striking colors. Long and brilliantly colored sleeves reach down to and beyond the hand. False hair is added to make an elaborate headdress in which many gay ornaments are fastened. The dance is done in stockinged feet, and as the sword dance is the most lively of all, robes are caught up and the sleeves turned back out of the way. The girls pirouette between swords laid on the floor and as the music becomes more lively they bend to one side and the other near the swords until at last they have them in their hands, then the music quickens and the swords flash this way and that as the dancer wheels and glides about in graceful motion. A good dancer will work so fast and twirl her swords so dexterously as to give one the impression that the blade must have passed through her neck. This dance is also done in men's clothes at times, but the cut of the garments of the sexes is so much alike as to present little external difference except that the colors of the men's are either white or of one shade, and the mass of hair worn by the dancer ordinarily is replaced by a simple hat. (Allen 1896:384)

While the description indicates that men's clothing was sometimes worn, it implies the dance was always performed by women. Note that none of the pictorial sources shows the dancers wearing masks, nor does the English-language description. This leads to the conclusion that, while a sword dance may originally have been performed by men in various contexts for the general population, during the latter part of the Chosŏn dynasty (1392–1910) it became part of the repertoire of dances performed at court banquets by both men and women, and if a mask was previously worn by the dancers, it was abandoned.

DEVELOPMENT IN CHINJU

It is not until the mid-twentieth century that texts specifically mention a "Chinju" sword dance. In order to convince the government that what is now known as Chinju Kŏmmu should be designated an Important Intangible Cultural Asset, Kim Ch'ŏn-hŭng (see Chapter 7 for biographical information), Pak Hŏn-bong (a wealthy Chinju arts supporter), and Yi Ki-yŏng conducted research and jointly authored a report in 1966. This report justifies the proposed designation by stating that although many sword dances existed at the time, it was the version of the dance performed in Chinju that had the longest history and demonstrated the "highest artistic quality and great value" (1966:3). The dance's longevity is justified on the basis of the memories of several important dancers living at the time (see discussion below). The report also describes the dance's costume and some of its movement patterns (in a general way), and identifies individuals believed to be the perpetuators of the old version.

Historical details about Chinju Kŏmmu (only a few of which are part of the 1966 report) are elaborated on in a volume published thirteen years later. The 1979 *Chinjushisa* (History of the City of Chinju) is the major historical document of the city of Chinju. The text links Chinju and the royal court via *kisaeng*. This institution of female entertainers, established during the Koryŏ period (918–1392) and believed by many to be patterned after a similar one in T'ang China, involved a hierarchy of women who served in unofficial and official capacities with the local and/or central government. Various titles indicated the status of these women, based on their abilities and government affiliation, with "*kisaeng*" being the general term for "female entertainer." *Kisaeng* received education in the arts that was usually reserved for the upper-class literati. They were particularly adept in dance and music, and some were skillful at composing songs. Although the services provided by *kisaeng* brought them recognition and often admiration, their official social status was quite low.[4]

During the Chosŏn dynasty there were twelve government *kisaeng* unions established in major provincial government areas to train young women entertainers for government officials in the area as well as for large, important banquets of the central government. Chinju was the location of one such union. A 1906 claim by a foreigner visiting the city that "there were more *kisaeng* in Chinju than flies" (*Chinjushisa* 1979:1174) is indicative of the quantity of *kisaeng* for which this area was known. The Chinju *kisaeng* are attributed with perpetuating a distinctive type of sword dance. The precise origin of this sword dance, however, particularly in relation to the court, is difficult to ascertain. Some information suggests it originated in Chinju, and some suggests it came to Chinju from the royal court.

According to the *Chinjushisa*, Ch'oe Wan-ja (the professional name of Ch'oe Sun-i, 1883–1967) was a famous *kisaeng* employed by the Chinju government. At that time it was common practice for officials of the central court in Seoul to augment the number of court *kisaeng* for special occasions by summoning outstanding women from among the entertainers in outlying areas. The report prepared for Chinju Kŏmmu's designation as an Intangible Cultural Asset states that Ch'oe went to Seoul when she was fourteen years old (1896, according to the Korean method of determining age) (Kim Ch'ŏn-hŭng et al. 1966:11–12), but the *Chinjushisa* states that, in 1900, at the age of eighteen (according to Korean age reckoning), Ch'oe was selected as a *changagwŏn'gi* (also known as *sŏnsanggi*, "selected, chosen entertainer"), the highest ranking of female entertainers (1979:1174). Thus, some time between 1896 and 1900 Ch'oe undoubtedly began to serve as a court entertainer, and danced at royal banquets.

Sometime during the Japanese occupation of Korea (1910–1945) Ch'oe returned to Chinju. Precisely when is not known, but based on the dates when elderly dancers alive in 1983 say they studied with her, it was prior to 1920. According to the *Chinjushisa* (1979:1174), Ch'oe was responsible for introducing a sword dance to the people of Chinju. This is contradicted, however, in the 1872 *Kyobang kayo*, which states that a sword dance was performed outside of the court, and specifically in Chinju, at least by the late 1800s. The claim that Ch'oe introduced a sword dance to Chinju is further contradicted by two older Chinju Kŏmmu dancers: One states that Ch'oe Wan-ja told her she went to Seoul to perform Chinju Kŏmmu at the court when she was a young girl (Ch'oe Ye-bun, personal communication 12 July 1983), and another says that a sword dance was part of the basic training course for Chinju *kisaeng*, and Ch'oe Wan-ja knew a sword dance before going to Seoul (Sŏng Kye-ok, personal communication 19 July 1983). These senior dancers, then, suggest that some kind of sword dance existed in Chinju, and was known by Ch'oe, prior to her dancing in the royal court. The 1966 report says that Ch'oe specifically learned Chinju Kŏmmu, the special version of the dance that was from Chinju, when she was nine years old, during her training in Chinju (p. 11). The 1828, 1829, and 1948 records of court events at which a sword dance was performed, on the one hand, and the 1896 reference by a foreigner to a sword dance performed in the court, reinforce the notion that a sword dance was part of the court dance repertoire prior to Ch'oe Wan-ja's arrival in Seoul.

It is probable that sword dances developed concurrently in various contexts. If Ch'oe had, indeed, learned such a dance as part of her training in the Chinju entertainers' institute, it is likely it would have continued to be taught and performed in her absence, and it is possible she taught the Chinju version to *kisaeng* in the court. If a sword dance was also performed in the court prior to Ch'oe's arrival, it is possible there was a sharing of the two versions among the *kisaeng*, that Ch'oe brought the court version back to Chinju, or that there was a mixing of the various versions —either by Ch'oe, herself, or by Ch'oe and other *kisaeng* in the court. Obviously it is not clear what the origin of the version of the sword dance now known as Chinju Kŏmmu is. Based on the fact that movements in today's version share some features with court dance and some with folk dance, as well as having several quite distinctive movements, it is most likely that, regardless of where the dance originated, at some time there was a merging of several versions.

EARLY CHINJU PERFORMERS

Originally the training of *kisaeng* took place in the royal court and in official regional institutes, but this function was taken over by private schools in the early 1900s. It is said that these schools each taught their own specialties, such as literature, music, or dance (Lee Byong-won 1979:80), and regardless of whether the dance known as Chinju Kŏmmu originated in the court or in Chinju, it eventually became the specialty of the Chinju *kisaeng*.

The *Chinjushisa* quotes Ch'oe Wan-ja as stating that the Chinju Female Entertainers' Union (Chinju Kisaeng Chohap) held a kind of workshop (*sasŭp*) for seven days every March at which a sword dance was taught (1979:1179). This is corroborated by a former *kisaeng* (Yi Yul-lye, personal communication 15 June 1983). It is possible this practice stopped in the 1920s, but resumed again.[5] One senior dancer (Yi Yul-lye, personal communication 15 June 1983) recalls that young women were recruited in the mid-1930s by the entertainers' union specifically to learn a sword dance. Although thirty to forty women applied and began the seven-day session, many dropped out after several days because of the difficulty of portions of the dance (in particular, a section known as *yŏnp'ungdae*, described later). At the conclusion of the seven-day training period, four of the remaining women were chosen to perform the dance.[6]

FROM PAST TO PRESENT

Three major changes have occurred in the Chinju sword dance since at least the late 1950s: The dance came to be performed in a formal theater for entertainment purposes only, instead of in the court and in other locations for various celebratory events; it was performed by eight people instead of the possible one, two, or four reflected in early documents; and the dance was considerably shortened.

While performed in the court for entertainment purposes, the physical environment in which a sword dance was done would have been quite different from the western-style proscenium-arch theaters of today. Thus, it is possible the changed physical environment contributed to changes in the nature of dance movements and overall choreography.

Changes in the number of dancers and the length of the dance are attributed to Pak Hŏn-bong (1907–1977, also known as Kisan), a strong supporter of the performing arts.[7] In the late 1950s, following a break in the performance tradition during the latter part of the Japanese occupation (sometime after the 1930s workshop), Pak requested that eight women reconstruct the Chinju sword dance. (There is no record of why he specifically wanted eight dancers.) According to one of the dancers involved in the reconstruction, it was not difficult to bring the dance to life again; in spite of the fact that it had not been performed for a while, it was still very much alive in their memories because they had performed it so many times (Yi Yul-lye, personal communication 15 June 1983). Pak was then instrumental in having Chinju P'al Kŏmmu, the full name of the dance as it is usually performed today, designated Intangible Cultural Asset number twelve on January 16, 1967.

In preparation for bestowing the governmental honor, and because of the advancing age of the earlier Chinju Kŏmmu performers (particularly Ch'oe Wan-ja, who was then in her eighties), in 1966 a cultural institute in Chinju recruited women to learn and carry on the tradition of Chinju Kŏmmu. A recruiting scheme similar to that of the earlier *kisaeng* union was established, but this time drawing on women who were not *kisaeng*. Middle-aged housewives were recruited rather than younger women because of the fear that younger women would leave Chinju to marry or attend college, and hence would not contribute to the preservation of the dance.

Training sessions financed by the city and offered free to participants were organized. Fifty women began the session taught by Yi Yul-lye (a student in the earlier *kisaeng* workshop), but only five completed the training. Explanations given for the high attrition include the difficulty of the dance (the same reason given for the dropping out of dancers when Ch'oe Wan-ja originally taught a sword dance to members of the *kisaeng* union in the 1930s) and the time it took to learn the dance, which was considered an inappropriate amount of time for a woman to spend away from home. Because the version of the dance to be designated an Intangible Cultural Asset required eight dancers, and only five had completed the training, three additional sessions were conducted until two groups of eight dancers could be selected (one to be designated *poyuja* and the other *isuja*—see Chapter 3). Unfortunately Ch'oe Wan-ja, the woman probably most responsible for many of the movements performed in today's dance, died shortly before Chinju P'al Kŏmmu was honored. The four dancers originally selected from the entertainers' union to perform in the mid-1930s, and four "second generation" dancers selected from the 1966 workshop, were designated National Living Treasures.[8]

At the time the dance was declared an Intangible Cultural Asset the government issued a commemorative postage stamp (Plate 31). Although the dance was identified on the stamp only as Kŏmmu, it is specifically Chinju Kŏmmu that received recognition and that was pictured, and Ch'oe Wan-ja is consistently given credit for either creating, developing in a form close to the present-day version, or introducing to Chinju after having learned elsewhere (probably in the court), the dance.

Today the dance is largely passed on at the Chinju Muhyŏng Munhwajae Chŏnsu Hoegwan, a facility much like a performing arts academy at which individuals who have been designated as *poyuja* or *isuja* practice and teach their various art forms.[9] The dance is also taught at Chinju Teachers College (where its instructors are the *poyuja* who teach at Chŏnsu Hoegwan), and at several private dance studios in Chinju. In the late 1980s, performers of the National Center for Korean Traditional Performing Arts in Seoul began to include Chinju Kŏmmu in their repertoire. A number of dancers from the Center went to Chinju to learn it, and they now perform it as part of regular programs of traditional dance and music in Seoul.

NON'GAE PYŎLCHE

Apart from government-sponsored performances of Intangible Cultural Assets, the major occasion on which Chinju Kŏmmu is performed today is an annual ritual to commemorate a young Korean woman, Non'gae (Plate 32). Non'gae became a heroine in Chinju in the late sixteenth century. The city played a pivotal role in Korean battles with the Japanese, but was often unsuccessful. Because of her reputation as an entertainer, in October of 1592 Non'gae's presence was requested at a Japanese victory celebration held inside the Chinju castle. She graciously met her obligation to fill the leisure time of the Japanese officials, but maintained her loyalty to Korea and privately lamented the death of her Korean sponsor. Overcome with grief in anticipation of the fate awaiting her countrymen, she lured Japanese General Rokusuke Ketanimura to the precipice of a cliff overlooking the Nam River. To show support of her homeland, while embracing him in an assumed air of affection she pulled him over the brink to their mutual deaths in the water below.

In 1905 a visitor to Korea added details to the story when he related a version told to him.

> An interesting story is told of a dancing girl of this town. When the Japanese took possession of the place she was appropriated by one of the Japanese generals. One day while they were feasting in a summer-house on the wall overlooking the river, she began to weep. He asked her the reason and she replied, "You have come here and driven away our people and our king. I do not know whether my sovereign is living, and yet I sit here and feast. I can hardly claim to be better than the beasts, to sit here and make merry. I must put an end to my life." Thereupon she threw her arms about her paramour and flung herself and him over the edge, thus ending her weary life and helping to avenge her native land at the same time. For this reason she was canonized at a later date and her spirit was worshipped at this place each year by royal edict. (in Hulbert 1962 Volume II:15)

To honor Non'gae a shrine was built alongside the river where she jumped to her death (Plates 33 and 34). The rock from which she jumped was given the name Ŭiam, "righteous rock," to commemorate her heroic deed, and an annual celebration, known as the Non'gae Pyŏlche, was established. (The festival is sometimes referred to as the Ŭiam Pyŏlche; "*pyŏlche*" meaning "special festival.") The event occurs in early August, according to the solar calendar. Chinju Kŏmmu is performed at this time in Ch'oksŏngnu, a large pavilion adjacent to the Non'gae shrine on the grounds of the old Chinju Fortress (Plate 35).

The August 7, 1983, Non'gae Pyŏlche was described as the three hundred eighty-ninth ceremony, indicating that the celebration was begun in 1594, a little more than a year after Non'gae's death. Precisely when Chinju Kŏmmu became a part of celebratory activities is not known, but the use of the dance to mark the anniversary of Non'gae's death returns it to a commemorative function, like that described in its legendary origins relating to Kwanch'ang and Hwang Ch'ang-nang.

Today, performances of Chinju Kŏmmu may be seen in Chinju as part of the annual Non'gae Pyŏlche activities, at the annual Kaech'ŏn Art Festival held in the fall, and at occasional performances in Chinju sponsored by the Chŏnsu Hoegwan; at periodic performances by dancers of the National Center for Korean Traditional Performing Arts in Seoul; and at events outside of Chinju at which the Chinju dancers are invited to perform, including the annual performance of Intangible Cultural Assets held in Seoul.

COSTUME

The most distinctive features of the Chinju Kŏmmu costume are color—particularly red and a dark, vibrant blue—and the hat, outer jacket, and sleeves (the latter worn at the beginning of the dance but subsequently removed) (Plate 36). The foundation of the costume is the *ch'ima* and *chŏgori*—the traditional-style floor-length skirt and blouse worn by Korean women. The skirt is dark blue; the blouse is a very light blue with narrow borders at the neck and edge of the sleeve of the same dark blue as the skirt. A red inset under the arm runs from the shoulder area to approximately halfway between the elbow and the wrist. The tie that fastens the blouse is the same dark blue as the skirt. Wrapped around the skirt to keep its bulk from getting in the way is a narrow tasseled cord, which is tied in a bow at the front of the waist.

A *chŏnbok*, or military-style jacket, is worn over the *chŏgori* and *ch'ima*. It is based on the *ku kunbok*, the uniform worn by high-ranking officers of the Chosŏn dynasty. The outer portion of the *chŏnbok* is the same blue as the skirt, and the inner lining, which is important when the jacket is manipulated during the dance (Plate 37), is the same red as the sleeve insets. The *chŏnbok* is comprised of four panels, two in front and two in back. The back panels are stitched together from the neck about halfway to the waist. Each front panel is fastened to a corresponding back panel by means of a narrow band under the arm. The two front panels are tied together with a narrow band of blue material fastened to each.

On top of the *chŏnbok* is a wide red sash known as a *hongtti*, or *hongsaek chŏndae*. This is placed across the chest and under the arms, and is tied in a large bow at the back, just below the shoulder blades, the ends of the bow trailing almost to the floor.

On the dancer's head is a military-style hat known as a *chŏllip*. The hat is black, has a narrow brim, and is adorned with a dark feather and red yarn tassle. The feather was originally a peacock feather, but today is that of a chicken dyed to approximate the colors of a peacock feather. The hat is tied onto the dancer's head under the chin with a black ribbon, and has a loose loop of large yellow and red beads fastened at each side and that hangs below the chin. Generally made of plastic today, these beads replace semiprecious stones (e.g., coral, amber, and quartz) used previously by military officers. The hat is made more secure on the dancer's head by tying a narrow black ribbon across the forehead, looping it through the ties on the hat, and tying it tightly in a bow at the back of the dancer's head.

The hairstyle is based on one worn by women of the royal court. The hair is parted in the center and pulled back tightly. It is gathered into a chignon at the nape of the neck, wrapped with hair that has been braided, and a red ribbon is fastened across the chignon. A long hairpin runs horizontally through the bundled hair.

Instead of the thick boots that were a part of former military attire, the dancers wear the traditional Korean *pŏsŏn*. These are tight-fitting, moderately padded white socks with a slightly up-turned toe.

In addition to the sleeves that are part of the blouse, the dancers also wear an extra pair of multicolored sleeves, known as *hansam* or *saektong*, at the beginning of the dance. These sleeves are fastened at the wrist by a drawstring or piece of elastic and are tubular in shape. They are twenty-seven inches long (extending about halfway to the floor when the arms are down at the sides of the body), twenty-six inches in circumference, and have multicolored stripes that are one inch wide following the circumference of the sleeve. Starting at the edge of the sleeve farthest from the wrist the stripes are dark blue, yellow, magenta, light blue, red, and white, with this color sequence repeating the length of the sleeve. Although similar to the sleeves worn in court dances, the Chinju Kŏmmu sleeves are shorter and the bands of color are narrower and more in number.

KNIVES

One of the most important items for the dance is the knives manipulated by the performers (Plate 30). Until his death, these were specially made for the Chinju dancers by Kim Tŏg-yong, a National Living Treasure for metal work (the type found on hinges and locks on Korean chests). Kim had a workshop in Chungmu, a port city approximately fifty-three miles south of Chinju.

The knives are constructed theatrical properties: The blades are not sharp, and both blade and handle are ornamented. The blade is nine inches long and almost 1 inch wide, and is a mixture of nickle and white brass known as *paekt'ong*. Its most significant features are its moveable parts, which are made of tin. One-and-one-half inches from the tip of the blade a small metal loop fastens a one-inch-long hollow, cone-shaped piece of tin with a saw-toothed edge at its broad end to the blade by means of a small hole in the blade. This allows the cone-shaped piece to swing freely as the knife is manipulated, and because of the way in which it is fastened, it easily strikes the blade to create a jingling sound. A short red tassel dangles from inside the cone (this is not shown in the illustration here).

Unlike the implements used in most other knife dances, in which the blade and handle are connected via metal loops that allow the blade to swing freely, the Chinju Kŏmmu blade and handle are firmly fastened to each other. The blade and handle are connected via a narrow metal T-shaped rod. The horizontal portion of the rod is affixed to the base of the blade and the vertical portion inserts into the handle. One-quarter inch of the vertical part of the rod is left exposed between the blade and the handle. Surrounding this exposed portion are three flat thin disks made of tin. They are primarily oval in shape, with scalloped edges, and are in graduated sizes. The largest, which is two-and-three-quarter inches across its widest part, is situated closest to the handle. Because of the distance between the blade and the handle, these disks bounce back and forth as the knife is manipulated and make a delicate clanging sound.

The handle, which is made of wood, is four inches long and one inch in diameter. It is covered with red cloth affixed with glue. Thin gold-colored metal caps—each one inch wide—cover each end, and a red tassel is fastened to the extremity of the handle by means of a thin red cord looped through a small hole drilled near the base end of the handle. The tassel is red silk, with gold thread binding it near the top, the overall length being approximately eight inches, of which one inch is the binding.

MUSIC

The earliest musical accompaniment for Chinju Kŏmmu is not known. Dancers today say the music was originally played by an ensemble comprising *kayagŭm*, *yanggŭm*, *kŏmun'go*, *changgo*, *puk*, *p'iri*, and *taegŭm*. The 1872 *Kyobang kayo* illustration (Figure 22) shows only six musicians. Because of the simplicity of the line drawing and the fact that one musician is shown from the back, it is impossible to know for certain which instruments are depicted. The clearest representations appear to be *changgo*, *p'iri*, *haegŭm*, and either *puk* or *ching*.

According to Ch'oe Wan-ja, Pon Yŏngsan Hoesang (also known as Sang Yŏngsan Hoesang or Kin Yongsan Hoesang), the first section from the court music piece Yŏngsan Hoesang, had been used to accompany the dance until 1921, but then gradually stopped being used because "it took too much time," and the original musicians were too old or died, and younger musicians could not play the music[10] (in *Chinjushisa* 1979: 1180). According to Kim Ch'ŏn-hŭng, who was involved in writing the report to have Chinju Kŏmmu designated an Intangible Cultural Asset, in 1951 musicians from Yiwangjik Aakpu (the forerunner of today's National Center for Korean Traditional Performing Arts) were asked to go to Chinju to help with the music (personal communication 11 Dec. 1990). At that time the Chinju dancers and musicians said that the earlier music had been too difficult, and they requested assistance in developing a simpler form that could be played by younger musicians.

At some time an *ajaeng* was added to the ensemble, but at no time was there any singing. Today, few Chinju people can play the court-style music and it is very costly to hire a full ensemble or to bring to Chinju musicians who can play this type of music. Frequently, therefore, only the percussion accompaniment of the *puk* and *changgo* are used. While this would appear to provide a thin accompaniment, because of the nature of the movement, the effect of performing the dance to a small ensemble of only percussion instruments is hypnotic.

As with much Korean music there are many changes in rhythm as the dance progresses. It begins with a pattern of six beats per measure and then progresses through five variations of patterns of four beats per measure.[11] At the beginning of the dance the tempo is extremely slow (typically twenty to twenty-five pulses per minute). The tempo increases with each metric change, shifting early in the dance (to approximately fifty pulses per minute), and concluding with a rapid tempo (approximately 110 pulses per minute). Just prior to the final increase in tempo, there is a short section in which the tempo is slower.

As in Ch'ŏyongmu, the dancers' movements directly relate to the structure of the accompanying music; as the tempo increases, so does the speed of the dance movements. The movements also adhere closely to the underlying metrical pulse, with movements coinciding to the basic pulse rather than creating their own rhythmic structure.

MOVEMENT CHARACTERISTICS

Older dancers in the 1980s say the version of the dance they originally performed lasted one hour, and Ch'oe Wan-ja indicated that the dance "took too much time" (*Chinjushisa* 1979:1180). The dance taught in the 1960s was forty-five minutes long. (See Appendix 3 for a narrative description of this version of the dance.) The complete dance performed today by eight dancers is generally approximately twenty minutes long. One explanation for shortening the dance is that it was too hot in the summer at the time of the Non'gae Pyŏlche to perform the number of repetitions that occurred in the longer version of the dance (Yi Ŭm-jŏn, personal communication 16 June 1983). In the shorter version of the dance the series of square formations at the beginning, which are repeated and are done to a very slow tempo, are eliminated.

Movements in the dance are an interesting blend of those usually considered typical of court dance, those usually considered typical of folk dance, and several not found in any other Korean dances still performed. In addition, a portion of the dance involves the manipulation of knives, which has given the dance its name.

As with Ch'ŏyongmu, the movements in Chinju Kŏmmu do not portray a narrative representation of any of the possible legendary origins of the dance. Some of the movements are, however, explained as being pantomimic (these are discussed below), and the overall nature of the dance (as suggested in the concluding section of this chapter) does reflect the dance's possible militaristic origin.

Appendix 3 contains a detailed verbal description of how the dance progresses. As with Ch'ŏyongmu, here I describe predominant movement characteristics and analyze the use of space to suggest a major contributor to the dynamics of the dance. I then explore issues relating to gender in the dance. As also with the discussion of Ch'ŏyongmu, Labanotation examples are provided for readers familiar with this system, but reading these examples is not necessary to understand the verbal comments that follow.

Number of Performers. If the story of Kwanch'ang is factual, a knife dance was originally performed by a group of men (soldiers during a funeral ritual). If the later story of the nobleman's feast is factual, there is evidence of a solo dance performed by a male dancer. And if the story of Hwang Ch'ang-nang is factual, it was a solo dance performed by a male dancer or a group dance to honor Hwang.

At some time there was a change to both male and female performers. Court records of the Chosŏn dynasty contain illustrations with either two male dancers or two or four female dancers. When Chinju Kŏmmu was performed at the Non'gae Pyŏlche in the 1930s, it was performed by four female dancers, and when it was reconstructed in 1966, it was performed by eight female dancers. When it was designated an Intangible Cultural Asset it was the version performed by eight female dancers that was recognized.[12] Fixing the number of performers at eight may have had symbolic significance. In earlier times when dances were done before the king of a tributary nation, there were only four performers; when done before the emperor of China, there were eight performers. Hence, using eight dancers for the newly revived Chinju sword dance may have served as a symbol of the stature accorded it.

Chinju Kŏmmu is sometimes performed today by only four female dancers. This is done when eight dancers are not available, or when the performing space is small and cannot accomodate eight. When performed by four dancers the opening formation changes are eliminated, since they can only be done by eight performers. No changes are made, however, in the other movement sequences.

Knife Manipulation. When the knife is held the fingers and thumb surround the handle—the fingers wrapping around the handle in one direction and the thumb in the opposite direction, much like the position established when making a fist. Although strength is used to punctuate some movements, throughout the manipulation of the knife the handle is grasped loosely. Support is provided primarily by the thumb and first finger. The grasp of the remaining fingers loosens and tightens to allow the knife blade to swing or to stop its momentum.

There are two primary movements performed with the knives. In one the blade swings back and forth in an arc and in the other it traces a full outward circle. To produce the arc the dancer simply alternately folds her wrist over its front and back surfaces. This movement is supported by a small amount of twisting in the lower arm and by bending and extending the elbow; the elbow extends to propel the blade outward (away from the dancer's body) to the peak of the arc and bends as the blade swings inward (toward the dancer's body).

To produce the full outward circle the dancer combines an inward and outward twisting of the lower arm with a bending and extending of the arm and a slight folding and unfolding of the wrist. This movement begins with the arm bent, the knife blade pointing backward and resting on the outside surface of the upper arm, about halfway between the elbow and the shoulder. The arm extends as the twisting, unfolding, and folding propel the blade forward and away from the body and bends as the blade circles outward to be stopped abruptly as it strikes the upper arm in the position from which it began.

Although "sword" or "knife" is the identifying feature of the dance, the use of these implements during the twenty-minute dance is minimal: movements in the first fifteen minutes of the dance have no relationship at all to the knives, the next two minutes include movements without the knives but as if manipulating them, and it is only during the last three minutes of the dance that manipulation of the knives becomes important.

Despite the reference to the dance's military origin in the costume and the use of knives, construction of the knives and the ways in which they are manipulated have taken on a purely aesthetic function—for both eyes and ears. Some movements forecast the use of the knives, using the wrist and turning the lower arm as if holding the knife when, in fact, it is still lying on the ground. Others simply enhance the knife movements; although the knives are brandished to trace arcs or circles in space during the latter portion of the dance, the looseness of the grasp, the flexible wrists, and the nature of the movements is such that the knife manipulation is purely ornamental. Except for one possible instance, these movements bear no relationship to any kind of stabbing, slicing, or piercing that might be done in combat with a real weapon. And because the moveable portions of the knife jingle and clang as the knife is manipulated, they contribute to the sound of the accompanying music. Hence, ornamentation is provided to both the eyes and ears.

Use of Sleeves. An unusual feature of the dance is the inclusion of the extra sleeves that are removed a little more than ten minutes into the dance. As mentioned earlier, slightly different sleeves are found in other court dances, where they are gently flicked during the course of dancing, but are *never* removed. Although a few of the arm movements in the early part of Chinju Kŏmmu specifically manipulate the sleeves, such action is minimal compared to that typically found in court dances.

Palm-Display Movement. In court dances the palms are concealed inside long sleeves.[13] In folk dances performed by women the palms may be turned upward but this usually happens only briefly, and the movement does not conclude until the arm is turned inward and the wrist relaxes so that the hand points slightly downward, resulting in concealing the palm. Hence, if the palms are shown, it is only in passing. In Chinju Kŏmmu, arm movements often conclude in the same palm-concealing gesture, but in one section of the dance this is preceded by a blatant display of the palm.

The palm-display movement begins with one arm extended forward at shoulder height and the other overhead, both turned so the palms face upward (Figure 23). The fingers are laterally closed and rounded so the palm surfaces of the fingers lightly touch the palm surface of the thumb. The fingers then open and straighten quickly, exposing the palms, before the

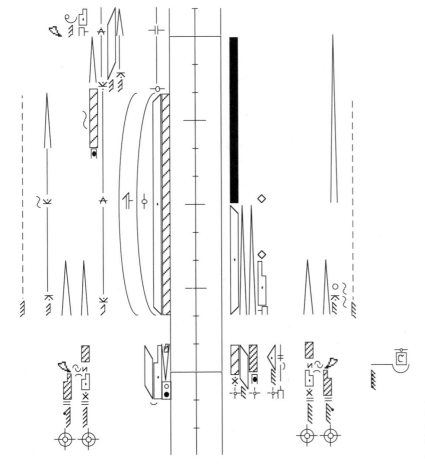

Figure 23. Labanotation score of palm-display movement from Chinju Kŏmmu. Notation by Judy Van Zile.

arms begin excursions through the horizontal and vertical planes: As the forward arm opens sideward at shoulder height, the high arm lowers down to the side of the body.

That this movement appears in no other Korean dance performed to-day and is so unlike any movement found in other dances makes one wonder about its origin. Unfortunately the name by which the movement is identified, *ipch'um*, does not provide a clue. "*Ch'um*" is simply the pure-Korean word for "dance." Dictionary translations and those provided by Chinju Kŏmmu dancers indicate "*ip*" means "mouth," "tongue," "speech," "words," "a beak," and "one's taste." While it is possible to imagine the opening of the curled fingers symbolizing speech, the opening of one's mouth, or the opening of a beak, this does not bear any rela-tionship to the nature of the dance or its origin. Although not attempting to translate the word "*ipch'um*," one senior dancer says the movement resembles the opening of the petals of a flower (Ch'oe Ye-bun, personal communication 18 March 1991). Some senior dancers say the movement symbolizes the shooting of a bow and arrow. This is plausible in rela-tion to the military nature of the supposed origin of the dance, but is not logical when considering that the early stories all specifically describe a *sword* dance.

Torso-Display Movement. Although the arms are often extended sideward at shoulder height in Korean dances performed by women, there is a tendency to move them forward a bit so they point slightly to the diagonal rather than sideward, and to round the shoulders a little to make the front surface of the chest slightly concave. (This is less common in court dances.) This de-emphasizes the female anatomy. The leaning back of the torso with arms spread wide found in Chinju Kŏmmu (Plate 38 and Figure 26) is the direct antithesis of this type of movement. Following a rather sedate walking pattern, the dancers place one foot slightly forward of the other, tilt their torsos backward at almost a forty-five degree angle from the vertical, and open their arms sideward at shoulder height with their palms facing upward. This torso-display movement both exposes the palms and opens out the chest area in a manner highly unusual in Korean dance as well as in Korean society.[14]

USE OF SPACE

The reader is referred back to the several paragraphs at the beginning of this chapter for a broad description of how the dance progresses, and to Appendix 3 for a more detailed description of the entire dance. The use of space in the dance reflects the dualities described earlier: female and male costume components, movements reminiscent of both folk dance and court dance, young and old performers, and the early honoring of a young boy as opposed to the contemporary honoring of a young woman. Again, Labanotation examples are provided to illustrate the following discussion, but are not necessary to comprehend it.

Use of Territory and Relationships Between Dancers. Initially appearing to be singularly focused, and potentially obscured by the slow tempo at which movements are performed, opening sequences create floor patterns easily interpreted as representing military practice or actual battle formations. The dancers pair off in two lines facing each other throughout much of the dance. As shown in the floor plans (Figure 24, Example 1A — note that floor patterns here are given from the dancers' perspective), this is introduced at the beginning after the dancers place their swords on the ground and align themselves in two rows perpendicular to the audience — a formation clearly establishing two opposing groups. A confrontational attitude is reinforced as the lines advance and penetrate each other to form a single line perpendicular to the audience and then retrace their steps, directly facing an opponent the entire time (Figure 24, Examples 1B through 1D).

A lengthy pattern follows (Figure 24, Examples 2 and 3) in which the formation dissolves into a square that stretches to a rectangle, reorients to form the two opposing lines and then the single line — but this time par-

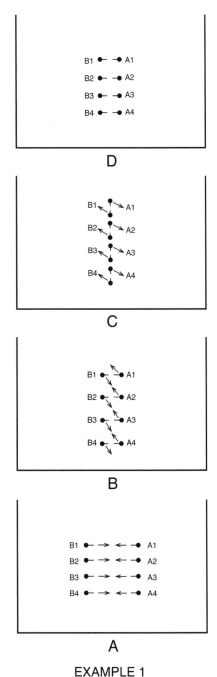

D

C

B

A

EXAMPLE 1

Figure 24. Floor plans of dancers' spatial pathways for Chinju Kŏmmu, from the perspective of the performer.

allel to the audience—and then repeats the square, rectangle, and line shapes, finally returning to the opening configuration. Throughout all of these groupings and regroupings, however, the dancers consistently maintain a face-to-face relationship with a partner.

The focus then shifts to *en masse* advancing and retreating rather than changing geometric formations. The dancers maintain their facing toward each other as they collectively advance and retreat (Figure 24, Example 4). They then advance while facing each other, the two lines pass through each other, and the dancers retreat, but while retreating they face away from each other (Figure 24, Example 5).

Another kind of confrontational advancing and retreating occurs when the two lines of dancers face each other and one line advances while the other retreats (Figure 24, Example 6).

Up to this point the emphasis is on two opposing sets of "troops" that advance and retreat, interspersing these actions with moments of more direct, one-on-one "combat" before returning to the "larger battlefield." The one-on-one moments created by relationships among dancers (as shown in Figure 24, Examples 1C and 2D) are reinforced through individual movement sequences such as that shown in Figure 26. In this sequence the sets of partners almost embrace each other as each places one hand on a partner's shoulder and the other on the partner's hip.

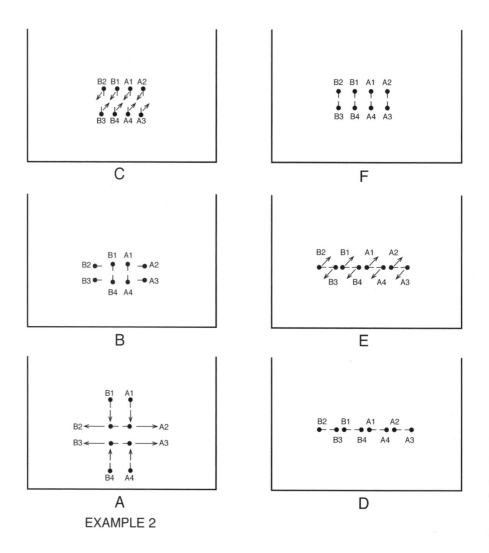

Figure 24 (cont.)

EXAMPLE 2

The use of group or partner formations to simulate military drill or battle changes somewhat abruptly near the end of the dance (Figure 24, Example 7) when the two opposing lines dissolve into a single circle in which the dancers perform movements emphasizing a virtuosic display rather than any sort of relationship to each other. The circle returns to two opposing lines and this circle/line alternation repeats two more times.

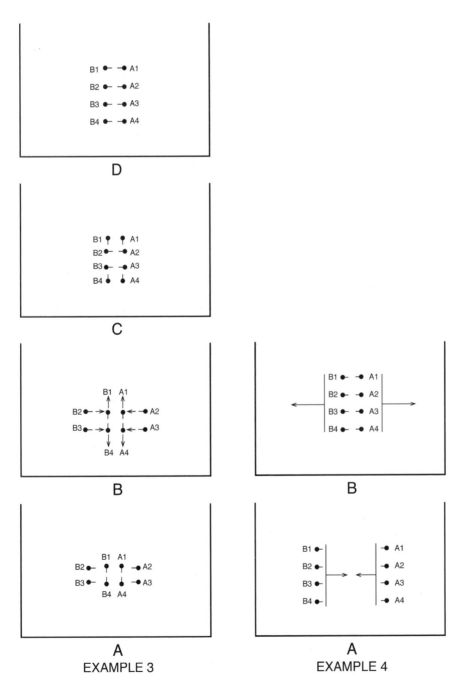

Figure 24 (cont.)

The dance concludes with a single line of performers parallel to and facing the audience, and the dancers bow before leaving the performing space.

Throughout the dance the overriding use of territory suggests a mock battle or a field for military drill with an emphasis that shifts between group maneuvers and a sense of paired combat, but that resolves into an explicit acknowledgment of a theatrical presentation. A duality is established between the group as a whole and individually paired relationships, as well as between military suggestion and theatrical presentation.

The strongest singular focus throughout the dance is on unison and symmetrical movement. The only exceptions are in very slight modifications, as when some dancers step forward while others step backward in order to shift between the square and rectangle formation (e.g., Figure 24, Example 2A and B), and when the two lines face each other and one moves forward (or advances) while the other moves backward (or retreats—Figure 24, Example 6). And despite the implication of military drill, ex-

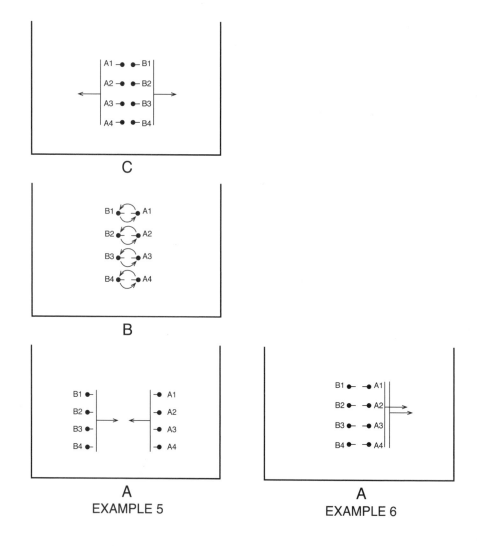

Figure 24 (cont.)

C

B

A
EXAMPLE 5

A
EXAMPLE 6

cept for a very subtle suggestion in formation (Figure 24, Example 6), movements never involve action and reaction—there is never, for instance, a thrusting action by an individual or group followed by a response to the thrust from another individual or group. In this aspect, also, there is a clearly singular focus.

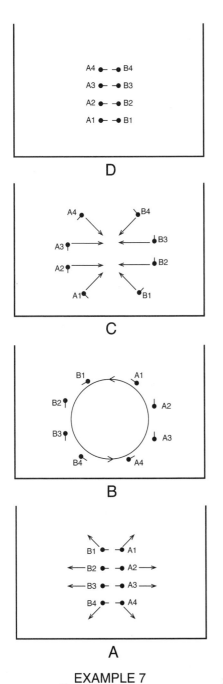

D

C

B

A

EXAMPLE 7

Figure 24 (cont.)

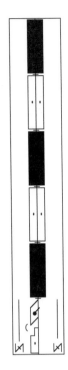

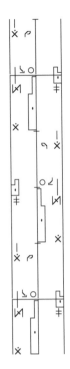

Figure 25. Labanotation scores of walking patterns from Chinju Kŏmmu. Notation by Judy Van Zile.

EXAMPLE 1   EXAMPLE 2   EXAMPLE 3

Use of Personal Space. Throughout most of the dance the basic body attitude of the performers involves a comfortably held, upright torso that emphasizes verticality. The verticality is reinforced in the constant rising and sinking movements of the dancers (Figure 25). This begins simply (Figure 25, Example 1) when each dancer steps forward with a comfortably straight knee, brings her feet together, and then bends and extends her knees several times before stepping out again. This action is enlarged when the knee of the gesturing leg lifts and there is a small, brief bending of the supporting leg in anticipation of the succeeding forward step (Figure 25, Example 2), and is enlarged even further when the dancer rises onto the ball of her supporting foot while lifting the knee of her gesturing leg and then lowers the heel of her supporting foot and bends her supporting leg before stepping forward (Figure 25, Example 3).

The incessant rising and sinking establishes the vertical as a constant in the body that is counterposed against the horizontality of the floor patterns traced by the group. Variations in individual movement sequences are also counterposed against the vertical emphasis, creating a dual tension *within* the body.

This dual bodily tension is established from the very beginning. While the dancers emphasize horizontality as they move smoothly through intricate floor patterns, they perform the basic walking pattern that emphasizes verticality within their bodies. But to this is added a horizontal countertension in the arms, created by the extension of one arm or both arms sideward at shoulder level most of the time. Thus, the pulls within the body create another level of duality as they occur concurrently with the horizontal spatial pull of the floor patterns and the opposing group relationships. And the rising and sinking together with advancing and retreating results in movement that cycles through the sagittal plane.

Elaborate involvement with territory and group relationships gives way in the middle part of the dance to elaborate involvement with personal space and the kinesphere. From the moment the dancers sit on the floor until they rise with their weapons in hand, the emphasis is on personal, rather than group, preparation for combat. At an increased tempo, the dancers tie the tails of their jackets behind their backs to eliminate the encumberance of clothing. They prepare for the use of weaponry with the forearm and wrist movements described previously. Their preparation intensifies as they manipulate one and then both of the swords that lay on the ground up until this point. Despite the fact that they are facing each other in opposing lines, however, the movements are not directed at an opponent. Instead, the dancers appear to prepare their own bodies for battle rather than engage in direct combat or group activity. Hence, a duality is created in transitioning from other-focused (regardless of whether the "other" is an individual or group) to self-focused movement.

A movement that could be perceived as both self- and other-focused, but that resolves into an other-focused movement, is the torso-display. Following the sedate walking pattern described earlier, the dancers abruptly assume a fourth position (one foot forward of the other; Figure 26, at the beginning of the second measure) in which they tilt their torsos backward with their arms opened sideward at shoulder height, the palms facing upward. The movement can be perceived as self-directed in that it quite

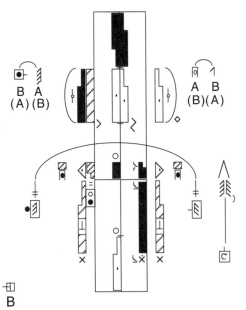

Figure 26. Labanotation scores of torso-display movement from Chinju Kŏmmu. Notation by Judy Van Zile.

overtly exposes the self, but other-directed in that it displays the self to an other. It quickly dissolves, however, into an other-directed movement when the dancers return to an upright position and almost embrace each other.

An intricate, multilayered spatial emphasis is created in the distinctive palm-display (Figure 23). The initial position of this movement (one arm forward at shoulder height, the other overhead, fingers closed) establishes a dual linear pull in both the sagittal and vertical dimensions. As the fingers open and straighten quickly, exposing the palms, the arms begin excursions through the horizontal and vertical planes: As the forward arm opens sideward at shoulder height, the high arm lowers down to the side of the body. This creates a shift to a dual planar pull. At the same time the arms open, however, the forward arm lifts and lowers slightly two times (through the folding and unfolding of the elbow and then the slight lifting and lowering of the whole arm) before it comes to rest in its sideward destination with the palm facing downward. This up-down "floating" softens what would otherwise be a harsh "slicing" through the two planes. The combination of linear, planar, and floating emphases is augmented further when this sequence is done concurrently with the basic walking pattern that emphasizes verticality. This results in a highly complex orchestration of body parts, each of which has its own spatial focus.

Another intricate, multilayered spatial emphasis is created in a sequence using a movement referred to as "flying." Known as *yŏnp'ungdae*, this is the movement described by early dancers as being difficult and the reason many dropped out of training sessions (Plate 39). The movement is a barrel turn that is softened so it does not include elevation and extreme forward and backward arching of the torso.[15] The sequence is done three times, and it involves the dancers forming a circle and moving halfway around it in a counterclockwise direction while performing a series of the modified barrel turns in which they revolve counterclockwise around their own axes. The first time they do this, they simply hold their arms in a position extended to the open, low-level diagonals (in relation to their own bodies). Their hands grasp their swords and the blades point backward, resting on their upper arms. The second time, however, both arms are extended forward and upward, flicking the swords from side to side —all simultaneous with the progression around the group circle and turning around one's own axis. The entire pattern is repeated a third time, but one arm traces a sweeping arc through a tipped horizontal plane while the wrist unfolds so that the sword enhances this arc, and then both arms repeat the side-to-side flicking of the swords. And as this entire sequence is performed, the knees continue to bend and extend while carrying the body through space—again, a complex orchestration of body parts in which each has its own spatial focus. This section occurs near the end of the dance, and drives the performance to a conclusion that is climactic in terms of tempo, movement intricacy, and spatial complexity.

While Chinju Kŏmmu begins slowly and with quite simple use of space, it becomes both quicker and increasingly complex spatially as it progresses. This development contributes not only to an interesting theatrical performance, but to a metaphoric ritual of battle—a presentation that harmonizes the decorum of female performers with the dance's legendary origin of male battle.

RELATIONSHIP TO CONTEMPORARY COURT AND
FOLK VERSIONS OF THE KNIFE DANCE

Differing views regarding the classification of Chinju Kŏmmu as a court dance or as a folk dance are understandable when looking at the movements in relation to those most typically found in each of these categories. The slow, measured walks with which the dance begins are identical to patterns seen in court dances performed today. Changing geometric formations are also typical of court dances, although the specific formations used in Chinju Kŏmmu are unique. While the sleeves are manipulated in several instances, this type of movement is extremely sparse in Chinju Kŏmmu, and does not play the integral role it does in court dances. Although the 1896 description of a court knife dance cited earlier indicates that the performers wore multicolored sleeves, in the court version of *kŏmmu* performed today long sleeves are not worn during any part of the dance. And in court dances performed today in which sleeves are worn, they are never removed during the performance, as they are in Chinju Kŏmmu.

Changes in rhythmic accompaniment are typical in court dances, but with the exception of Ch'ŏyongmu, which probably originated outside the court, the lively tempos and accompanying lively movements of Chinju Kŏmmu are not present in court dances. The livelier rhythms and movements of Chinju Kŏmmu are more similar to those of folk dances. The barrel turns, although found in one other court dance, Musanhyang—where they are performed by a solo dancer, are more typical of the folk tradition of farmers' band dance and music. In the farmers' tradition this pattern becomes so lively as to carry the dancers into leaps in which their bodies are almost parallel to the ground while turning. In Chinju Kŏmmu there is a lifting of the center of weight during the turns while the torso tilts forward and then backward, but the feet always maintain contact with the floor. In the court knife dance the bending and extending of the knees while turning is exaggerated, but there is no tilting of the torso. These turns are considered the most difficult part of the dance, and it is because of their difficulty that many former would-be dancers terminated their training.

Knives are manipulated not only in Chinju Kŏmmu but also in the court *kŏmmu* performed today and in the more modern folk dance versions. In the latter two types of knife dance the implements used are loosely joined at the juncture of the knife blade and the handle in such a way that when manipulated the blade swings freely. Dancers capitalize on this movement potential (particularly in the folk versions), and the dance frequently employs lengthy sections of dazzling knife twirling. Because the knives used in Chinju Kŏmmu are rigid, their potential for contributing to movement is more limited. Hence, simpler movements of the wrist and lower arm are employed than in other knife dances. In addition, a large portion of Chinju Kŏmmu is performed without the knives.

When the use of a knife with a loosely connected handle and blade began is not known. Some say this is the type of knife used very early; following Hwang Ch'ang-nang's slaying of the king of Paekche the knife structure was changed to prevent future court knife dancers from doing any harm with their dance implements. Illustrations in documents of late-nineteenth-century court banquets, however, show rigid knives (for example, Figures 19–22), and Korean musicologist Chang Sa-hun believes the "broken hilt" knives of other dances came into use with the establishment of female entertainers' unions between 1905 and 1910 (personal communication 22 July 1983). If this is, indeed, the case, it would be an additional argument for the age of the Chinju version of the dance.

Some dancers today believe the movements of Chinju Kŏmmu are more "courtly" than those in today's court knife dance. They feel the slow, dignified movements of Chinju Kŏmmu reflect the restraint of the Confucian Chosŏn dynasty. An element contributing to this is the lack of emphasis on shoulder movement. One of the most pervasive features of traditional dances as they are performed today is the raising and lowering of the shoulders in what appears to be a response to the breathing process. This movement, referred to as ŏkkae ch'um, or "shoulder dance," is subtle in court dances and exaggerated in folk dances. Chinju Kŏmmu dancers today emphasize the simplicity of their dance, and although the torso is held in a relatively relaxed manner, the shoulders are not allowed to respond to movement in the rest of the body as they are in other dances.

The most directly military, or combative, movements are those in which the two lines of dancers advance toward each other, and then one line advances while the other retreats. This is the only movement to which several dancers ascribe a military origin. One senior dancer (Yi Ŭm-jŏn, personal communication 16 July 1983) remembers asking her teacher, Ch'oe Wan-ja, the meanings of some movements. Ch'oe told her the version of the barrel turns done with movements for one knife were symbolic of beheading someone.

In traditional female attire the skirt is fastened tightly across the breasts. Placing the arms on a slight forward diagonal in a horizontal plane, with the arms inwardly turned and the shoulders pulled forward a little, creates a concave chest area. This position, together with the clothing worn by women, minimizes the visual presence of the female anatomy. Hence, a movement in which the arms are spread wide to openly project the front surface of the body, as in the torso-display, is unusual (see Note 14).

Additionally, women, particularly in the court, were taught to conceal the palms of their hands. Again, the open display of the palms in Chinju

Kŏmmu goes directly counter to accepted codes of movement and use of the body.

It might be that within the context of a military-based dance the torso- and palm-display movements are ways of showing a willingness to be vulnerable and that no weapon is concealed in the hands. It is also possible such movements would have been acceptable for men to do, and that when the transition from male to female performers occurred this movement was never changed. And the implement may have played a more important role in the dance when it was longer than it is today. The incompleteness of the limited historical records, however, makes these notions strictly conjectural.

What is not conjectural, however, is that what probably began as a military dance or as a symbolic dance to commemorate heroic military deeds has become a purely aesthetic enterprise. And although knives are integral to the dance and prominent because they figure in the most lively portion (at its conclusion), they are not the most unique feature of Chinju Kŏmmu.

For Men or Women?

I now re-examine Chinju Kŏmmu's historical development from the perspective of the gender of its performers and the functions it has served, as well as gender implications of movements in the dance. I propose that although the dance, as performed today, retains clear suggestions of *both* male-female and masculine-feminine characteristics, and while features of these dichotomous categories contributed to the development of the dance and, indeed, to its very survival, ultimately gender is *not* what the dance is about.[16]

The original dance in the first legendary story described previously was performed by a young boy; it is not clear in that story, however, whether the people who danced to commemorate the death of the young boy dancer were male or female. The fellow soldiers who danced in the second legendary story were undoubtedly men. In the nineteenth- and twentieth-century paintings and line drawings, some dancers are men and some are women. Despite the probability that men or boys were the earliest performers of sword dances, and that nineteenth- and twentieth-century documents provide illustrations of both men and women performing sword dances (although not concurrently), we do know that a sword dance became the purview of female entertainers (*kisaeng*). We also know that when Chinju Kŏmmu was reconstructed in the 1960s in preparation for its designation as an Intangible Cultural Asset, female housewives were invited to learn the dance—specifically because it was felt they would be more likely to remain in the city and could, therefore, contribute to perpetuating the dance. And today the primary performers and teachers of Chinju Kŏmmu are women in the city of Chinju who have been designated by the government to perpetuate the dance.

Thus, although we cannot always trace the reasons, there have clearly been changes in the gender of the performers of knife dances. And whether Chinju Kŏmmu has always been performed by women or experienced a similar change remains unknown.

The costume worn by sword dancers as the dance developed into the version known today as Chinju Kŏmmu has also undoubtedly changed. It is, of course, logical that if the early dancers were men, and if the dance was done in relation to military activities, the attire worn would be masculine and have military attributes. Indeed, illustrations in the court documents described earlier show differences in the clothing worn by male and female dancers (compare, for example, Figures 19 and 20). These differences are also described in the 1896 publication by a foreigner, quoted previously, who saw a sword dance performed at the royal court in Seoul. After describing the elaborate female hairstyle of the performers, their "voluminous garments" that are "caught up" and sleeves that are "turned back" to accommodate the vigorous movements of the dance, the author refers to male *or* female attire worn by female dancers (Allen 1896:384). As described earlier, today's costume brings together an unusual combination of items based on clothing traditionally worn by Korean women, by military men, and by women court dancers.

Although perhaps originally performed for ritual or celebratory purposes, Chinju Kŏmmu became a well-known dance performed by women for the entertainment pleasure of men. It is performed today for entertainment or to display cultural manifestations of Korea's past, and in Chinju at an annual festival to honor the woman known as Non'gae. What is particularly intriguing in relation to gender is that at this festival to honor a woman, eight women clad in costumes based on both male military attire and traditional female attire perform a dance with roots that apparently lie in a dance of men, with movement qualities that, although suggestive, have been transformed to a quality more appropriate to women.

The quality of the movements used in today's Chinju Kŏmmu is predominantly soft and gentle, characteristics epitomizing femininity in the Confucian-dominated Chosŏn courts.[17] This quality is sometimes layered on top of less feminine movements, such as exposing the palms and the torso, which are the direct antithesis of the traditional humble and gentle female deportment.

No one knows the reason for these movements, unusual for Korean women as well as for Korean dance in general, nor any meaning that may have been derived from them. Nor does anyone know when such movements became part of Chinju Kŏmmu. While there are several possible explanations, all of them are speculative. One native Korean dance researcher believes that the palm displaying movement was present in dances performed in the court during the Chosŏn dynasty, and that this movement has been preserved *only* in Chinju Kŏmmu (from Han Ok-hŭi via Gary Rector, personal communication 11 June 1983). In former times court dances were sometimes performed by men, and, as previously mentioned, several illustrations substantiate this. Therefore, it is possible this type of movement was originally appropriately performed by male court dancers, and was not transformed when women began to perform the dance. Thus, Chinju Kŏmmu, as performed today, may retain movements originally performed in the court by male dancers, and the dance may originally have been a court dance.

A second possibility, expressed by a Chinju dance teacher, relates to the story of the origin of the dance. She feels the displaying of the palms and torso area are strong, courageous movements and are an attempt to incorporate into the dance a sense of the strength and courage of the young boy dancer who killed the enemy king (Kim Chŏng-ae, personal communication 21 July 1983). If this is accurate, the origin and meaning of the dance provided acceptable reasons for women to perform movements that otherwise would have been unacceptable.

A third possibility lies in the Chinju environment in which the dance is said to have evolved or to have been preserved. Because the dance was originally perpetuated in this region by *kisaeng*, the dancers, either because of their artistic or their social functions, may have been allowed to take liberties with movement and the display of their bodies inappropriate for other women. This explanation is tenuous, however, in light of the notion that the use of long sleeves by court dancers who were *kisaeng* may have originated in the inappropriateness of women showing their hands before the king. Would not a *kisaeng* show similar respect to patrons outside the court?

A fourth possibility is that standards of female propriety inhibiting the display of the palms and torso area were imposed during the Chosŏn dynasty, with its strong Confucian ideals. If this is the case, movements displaying these body parts may be indicative of a considerably older dance style, a style preserved today only in Chinju Kŏmmu.

The notion of Chinju Kŏmmu predating the Chosŏn period is supported in the government report submitted in 1966 in preparation for Intangible Cultural Asset designation. This document justifies the government's recognition by asserting that although there were many versions of sword dances performed at the time the report was written, and although the Chinju version had changed the overall movements from harsh to soft and graceful (Kim Ch'ŏn-hŭng et al. 1966:27), the Chinju version was the most "authentic"[18] (ibid.:10). The report goes on to state that during the Chosŏn period two versions of a sword dance were performed in the royal court: one by male dancers for a male audience; the other by female dancers for a female audience[19] (ibid.:21). Furthermore, the report, together with subsequent documentation and the memories of older dancers alive in the 1980s, establishes women as the performers, since the early 1900s, of what is now known as Chinju Kŏmmu. The earliest of these female performers were *kisaeng*.

When dancers were recruited for the workshop in preparation for Chinju Kŏmmu's designation as an Intangible Cultural Asset, it was specifically women who were recruited. A subsequent generation of dancers was selected from individuals who responded to a recruiting scheme that focused on middle-aged housewives. But many people had dropped out of these workshop sessions, giving as one reason the inappropriateness for women to spend as much time away from home as was necessary to learn the dance. Confucian notions of the place of women and the low stature of *kisaeng* had left indelible marks.[20]

A second reason women gave for dropping out of the workshop was the difficulty of the "flying" movement (*yŏnp'ungdae*, the barrel turn—see Note 15). This movement, done in a vigorous manner that propels the dancer off the floor, is performed by men dancers in, for example, farmers' band dance and music (*nongak*). But in Chinju Kŏmmu the movement is modified so the dancers do not leave the ground. This modification better suits models of stereotypic Confucian feminine decorum, but retains the essence of the more vigorous movement most usually associated with men dancers, from which it derives.[21]

The focus on middle-aged housewives points to a significant difference between early generations of female dancers and those of later generations: The first generation were all young professional entertainers who had learned a number of arts skills; from the time of the dance's designation as an Intangible Cultural Asset, the primary dancers were housewives who were not professionals and whose arts skills focused specifically on Chinju Kŏmmu. This generation maintained their positions as housewives while simultaneously assuming their roles as perpetuators of Chinju Kŏmmu. Hence, at the same time they continued the stereotypic role of the woman belonging to the house, they were entrusted with the continuation of one of Korea's officially designated cultural artifacts, and were in positions of significant recognition.

The primary administrative force behind the perpetuation of Chinju Kŏmmu at the end of the twentieth century was Sŏng Kye-ok. Her involvement with the dance reflects a number of things relating to gender and societal attitudes. Because of a strict Confucian upbringing, Sŏng spent her early days studying Chinese literature (Sŏng Kye-ok, personal communication 25 June 1983). Her parents maintained the commonly held belief that dance was performed by female entertainers, whose status was low despite their importance in government functions. Although she had a keen interest in dance, it was not until her husband died that Sŏng began to study it. She was then torn between her freedom to learn dance and her family obligation to support her five children. The latter necessity led to developing a strong business sense, and it was not until the mid-1970s that she became actively involved with the Chinju Kŏmmu dancers. Because of her sophisticated educational background and her business acumen, she has served as coordinator for the activities of the Chinju Kŏmmu dancers since the 1980s.

What can we make of this complex and not-always-known historical background in relation to gender issues and the way Chinju Kŏmmu is performed today? Chinju Kŏmmu's development has led to a dance that includes many movements stereotypically characteristic of other older Korean dances, some of which are performed primarily by women and some primarily by men. Additionally, some of the costume components are, or were, typically worn by women and some by men. All of these features are distinctively present rather than being combined in an androgynous manner. The intent of the dance is not primarily to represent literally its likely military origins nor to represent women or men. The 1967 designation of Chinju Kŏmmu as an Intangible Cultural Asset was, like many other such designations, recognition of something that displayed a distinctively Korean identity, and at least in this case, without regard for gender representation. It was an acknowledgment of something considered important from Korea's past selected to create a Korean identity in the present, regardless of gender issues.

It is intriguing that a dance attributed to male military roots is now performed to celebrate the heroic deed of a woman (Non'gae) important in the history of the city of Chinju. It is also intriguing that a dance with such roots became the purview first of young female entertainers and eventually of middle-aged housewives; housewives continued a role usually assumed in the past by *kisaeng*—entertaining and perpetuating the arts. Equally fascinating from a movement perspective is why a movement associated with stronger dances most usually performed by men (the "flying" movement), and several movements that directly contradict notions of femininity prevalent in Korea at least at one time in history (the palm-display and torso-display), have been retained together with movements that are more stereotypically feminine. It is tempting to connect these less feminine (in a Confucian framework) dance movements to forces of the 1920s that sought liberation for women from some of the strictures of Confucianism (see, for example, Kim Yung-hee 1994). But there is insufficient evidence to establish a cause-effect relationship: Available information does not allow us to assign meaning to these features nor to ascertain a clear rationale for their existence.[22]

Chinju Kŏmmu may be on the brink of another gender-related change, however. In 1990, young professional women dancers of the National Center for Korean Traditional Performing Arts, a government-sponsored institute in Seoul, began to perform Chinju Kŏmmu. They modified the full, loose-fitting costume by wrapping the skirt tightly in a style that is traditional when women are working and want to keep their full skirt out of the way, and that reveals the contours of the female body. While for working women such a display was undoubtedly inadvertent, for the viewer of Chinju Kŏmmu it specifically calls attention to the fact that the performers are women. And the dance these women perform has a very light, uplifting, and almost joyous quality. All of these features constitute a sharp contrast to the full-figured image of Chinju's housewife-dancers and their weighty performance quality. It is easy to envision this as the beginning of another significant change in one of Korea's officially designated dance treasures, and in this case one that could alter the previous lack of emphasis on gender and the identity of the dance.

6

Movement in Shamanic Contexts

An Inquiry

Shamanism has been practiced in Korea for centuries. Although attitudes toward shamanism changed as other belief systems were introduced or advocated, shamanism is practiced today, even in highly westernized big cities.[1] Movement is an important ingredient in shaman rituals, known as *kut*. In addition, there is a potentially intimate relationship between shamanism and the contemporary concert dance form known as salp'uri (see Chapter 1 and discussion below), and concert dances are created today that are inspired by shaman practices and that are intended to suggest shamanism.

In this chapter I examine movement in three shaman-related presentations given in formal theater settings. One was staged in Hawai'i by Yi Chi-san, a visiting shaman from Kyŏnggi Province near Seoul, and the late Halla Pai Huhm, a dancer and teacher from Korea and later resident of Hawai'i (see Chapter 9 for further discussion of Halla Pai Huhm, and note 2 of Chapter 9); one was staged in Korea by Chŏng Chae-man, a professional dancer and teacher; one was staged in Korea by shamans from Chindo island. Movement features of these presentations are then briefly related to movements of shamans when executing *kut*.

The three presentations that are my focus did not occur in "first existence" contexts, that is, they are not *kut*.[2] All three took place in formal theater settings before paying audiences. Some performers were shamans and some were not. My intention is not to provide a full analysis of shamanic movement, its meaning, and the role it plays in ritual. Rather, I use materials involving presentations *by* shamans and representations *of* shamans as the basis for raising questions; questions relating to the nature of structured movements Koreans use as emblems of shamanism, and questions ultimately relating to the nature of structured movements used by shamans in *kut*.

The basis for the analysis of the movement is videotaped documentation of three distinct events.[3] A number of recurring elements emerge when looking at movements used in these nonritual contexts by both shamans and nonshaman dancers, which suggest movements that broadly represent shaman activities.

Issues of aesthetics and ritual efficacy emerge as important themes in the contexts of the performances examined here. The complex interconnections between the structural accuracy of a performance and the intent of an event are particularly relevant. These issues do not create a dichotomy, but reflect interrelated forces impinging on a single event. Performers may be concerned with presentational accuracy as an end in itself, which is usually the case in western theater contexts, or may be concerned with an end beyond presentation, which is usually the case in ritual contexts. But ritual can also be a form of theater, and presentational accuracy may be a necessary component to ritual efficacy. Focus may be not just on how an event is done or why, but on doing it in a particular way in order to achieve a goal beyond the event itself.[4]

All of these issues are brought to the fore in the context of the Hawaʻi performance. This two-pronged event, which included participation by a shaman as well as by a dance teacher and her students, demonstrates issues of both ritual efficacy and theatrical aesthetics. When the shaman performs, the intent appears to be to approximate—or even to create—portions of a *kut* on stage, complete with dancers who assume the role of clients. The shaman is concerned with accuracy of movements necessary to satisfy the requirements of a ritual, rather than with the details of performance execution needed to create movement that is aesthetically pleasing to watch; his ultimate intent is communicating with spirits rather than creating a visual display for the audience. The dancer and her students, on the other hand, demonstrate a concern with performance accuracy that creates theatrically pleasing dances rather than ritual efficacy—shaman movements from creativity inspired by a *kut*. Some of these dances are connected to form a kind of suite, much like the *kŏri* (sections) of a *kut*, while others are simply independent units.

In the second context examined, there is also a concern with visual aesthetics. In this case, however, there is an attempt to interconnect a series of dances so that together they suggest an entire shaman ritual. No attempt is made to replicate a *kut*, only to suggest one through movement that creates its own danced drama that is an end in itself.

In the third context there is, as in the first, an attempt to replicate portions of a *kut*. But here the performance is done as if showing spectators what they might see at a ritual without a clear concern for either theatrical aesthetics or ritual efficacy; with the exception of one segment, the intent appears to be merely to display a number of activities that form parts of a *kut*. There is a concern with doing things correctly, but there is no visible presence of any client (either real or representative). And, while the theatrical setting is acknowledged, there is not the concern for an overriding theatrical aesthetic that was present in the Korean performance staged by a dancer. In addition, however, a relatively structured dance —specifically performed for spectators—has become part of the depiction by shamans of shaman ritual.

For the performers, in some of these contexts it appears that the correct feeling leads to the correct movement, while in others, correct movement appears to lead to a correct feeling. And in several, there is a merging of conventionally recognized Korean "dance" movements with structured shaman movements.[5]

The state of mind of the performer, whether shaman or dancer, is another issue relevant here. Theoreticians of acting in western drama debate the necessary state of mind for the performing artist to function effectively. One side believes that a good performer must be simultaneously "in" a different state of mind and "not" in it: The performer must be sufficiently immersed in the character being portrayed to lure the audience into the cultural fiction that is theater, and at the same time must be outside of the character so as to be in control of the theatrical situation. The analysis here suggests the movement used in shaman rituals is not entirely spontaneous or improvised, and it is performed for both the spirits and human clients. As such, in the context of a *kut*, the shaman treads a thin line between these two states of mind, using structured movement as a kind of balancing pole to enter into a particular state of being as well as to reflect that a particular state of being has been achieved.

Although I do not focus on structured movements in actual *kut*, features of the movements I examine raise important questions for studies of Korean shaman ritual. Foremost among these are: What kinds of movements recur in shaman-related events? Are these movements rooted in *kut* and have they, therefore, come to represent shamanic activities? How structured, or choreographed (and therefore taught) are the movements used in *kut*? Is the nature and role of structured movement in shaman rituals changing?

The Hawaʻi Performance

In 1976 Halla Pai Huhm, a native of Korea who studied various Korean dance forms and lived and taught dance in Hawaʻi from the mid-1900s until her death in 1994, invited Yi Chi-san, a male shaman from Kyŏnggi Province, to participate with her and her students in a two-evening theater performance. Huhm had studied shamanism and shaman ritual with Yi in Korea and published a book recording his practice (see Huhm 1980). My analysis is based on viewing the 1976 performance as well as videotapes of it, examining the printed program, and interviewing Halla Huhm and several other performance participants.[6]

The students who participated included individuals of Korean and non-

Korean ancestry, and ranged in age from young children to adults. They
had studied Korean dance as an avocation for varying lengths of time.
The performance took place in a conventional western proscenium-arch
theatre, with two tables placed upstage, parallel to the audience. The
tables were elaborately laden with fruit and other paraphernalia, and
were framed by pictures, banners, and streamers—all of the sort typically
found at *kut*. A flat cut-out of a tree was set at one side of the stage, and
musicians were seated at the other side.[7]

The September 3 and 4 programs were in ten clear sections, six performed on the first evening and four on the second.[8] (See Appendixes 4
and 5 for outlines of each program.) The approximately two-hour programs were different (two subsections of two sections were performed in
slightly modified variations on each night), except for one section, which
was performed both evenings. Of the ten sections, seven were identified in
the printed program distributed to the audience as *kŏri*, each with a specific and conventional *kŏri* name. The section performed identically on
both evenings was not identified as a *kŏri*, but as "Byoltang assi [Pyŏltang
asshi]" (Woman of the Separate Cottage) and was a series of pantomime
sequences, performed mainly by children, of various village scenes, some
related to shaman activities. The other section not identified as a *kŏri* was
titled "Mudang kibon dongjak [tongjak] chom [ch'um]" (Basic Shaman
Movements) and was a demonstration by Huhm of what was described in
the printed program as "various fundamental movements basic to all
shaman dances."

Each *kŏri* section was a kind of suite that included a solo by Yi, which
was something he might perform in the context of a *kut* (e.g., Plate 40),
and one or more dances choreographed by Huhm and performed by her
and her students. It is interesting to note that no distinction was made in
the program between the "authentic" shaman material performed by Yi
and the theatrically choreographed dance, nor was there identification,
by name, of Huhm's choreographed dances. Furthermore, in performance
there was no break between individual components of the *kŏri*, although
the audience applauded at the end of some sections within a *kŏri*. In an
interview (8 Nov. 1992) Huhm described the combination of authentic
and choreographed material as all belonging to a single unit, and considered the traditional identification of *kŏri* appropriate to the newly structured unit. She stated she did not think the audience needed more detailed
information and the dances included in each segment were sufficiently related (in either theme or movement) to Yi's ritual components for the *kŏri*
label to be all that was needed.

Appendixes 4 and 5 outline the content of each evening's presentation.
Sections are labeled as identified in the printed program. Based on my
knowledge of Korean dance and of Huhm's repertoire, as well as consultation with Huhm, I have provided subsection labels for each of the units.
(Some of these units were given Korean names by Huhm, some only English names, and some no names.) The subsections performed as solos by

Yi are referred to with the label "ritual" to suggest their apparent intent to replicate portions of a *kut.*

Each part of the programs performed by Yi had its own distinctive quality. Several features stand out because of the frequency with which they occurred. Predominant body configurations and movement sequences were:

1. An overall orientation that shifts between the onstage musicians, the onstage altars, onstage dancers acting as clients, and occasionally the audience;
2. A zigzag floor pattern traced with simple walking steps;
3. Large steps and a basic stance in which the feet are spread broadly apart;
4. Outwardly turned legs;
5. Counterclockwise turns and circular paths, generally performed with arms stretched sideward at shoulder height; and
6. Jumping.

Although there are times when movements are executed with a sense of wild, and what appears to be almost uncontrolled, abandon, the overall quality of Yi's movement conveys a sense of nonchalance, jaunty casualness, and lightness. This quality is the result of several elements. First, despite the strong underlying pulse of the musical accompaniment, Yi only occasionally steps or bounces to this pulse; more frequently he executes patterns that simply coexist with the music rather than conform to any particular rhythmic pattern established by it. At times, his movements appear to be metrically random—there is no underlying pulse to which they relate; at other times, they appear to have their own rhythm or pulse. Second, although an overall orientation to the audience, musicians, altar tables, or onstage clients is maintained, many movements do not have a clear spatial focus; they are simply done, rather than being directed toward a particular object, person, or direction. Third, Yi often performs a bounce in which, in addition to bending and extending his knees slightly, he shifts his weight from one foot to the other, creating a side-to-side rocking movement. This contributes to the indirect spatial focus, and in turn to the nonchalant quality. And fourth, he is very light on his feet. Despite jumps, a sometimes flatfooted walk, and large and sometimes cumbersome costumes, he tends to carry his weight on the balls of his feet and maintain an upward focus rather than landing heavily or driving downward into the ground.

The zigzag floor patterns Yi traces also have a casual, nonchalant quality (see Figure 27). He performs them with very simple walking steps that often have no direct relationship to the underlying musical pulse. The basic pattern involves a frontal orientation toward the audience or toward the altar. If toward the audience, Yi turns toward one downstage corner, takes two steps forward, turns approximately one-quarter of the way toward the other downstage corner, and then takes two steps backward. Despite the basic orientation, however, Yi's pattern and directions are not

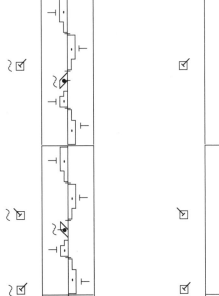

**Yi Chi-san Basic Version
(NOTE: timing is only
approximate)**　　　　**Halla Huhm Basic Version**

Figure 27. Labanotation scores of zigzag floor patterns from Hawai'i shaman-related performance. Notation by Judy Van Zile.

rigid: He occasionally takes an extra step, and diagonal facings are sometimes interrupted with backward steps moving directly upstage or downstage rather than relating to the corners of the performing space. Yi's predominant widespread stance also deflects each of the steps into slightly sideward or diagonal directions rather than pure forward-backward (sagittal) directions. In short, the overall zigzag shape of the floor pattern is important, but not the details of how it is created.

A sense of nonchalance is also found in Yi's jumps. Although by definition such movements involve a time when the weight is suspended and both feet are off the ground, there is seldom a sense of up-and-down-ness to Yi's performance of them. They give the impression of extending the light quality and of carrying the weight on the balls of the feet, with frequent side-to-side shifts that prevent any clear sense of a single dimension. All of these features that convey nonchalance and lightness contribute to a self-absorbed presence; an individual intent on doing particular activities, but with an ultimate goal that lies beyond the activities themselves.

In an interview (8 Sept. 1992), Huhm said Yi's movements had served as inspiration for the dances she choreographed for the program. There are traces of many of Yi's movements in Huhm's choreography, but two movements predominate: the zigzag spatial pathway and jumping. Huhm considered these movements the most important (personal communication 8 Nov. 1992). Although it is clear her versions of these movements derive from those of Yi, the manner and quality in which she and her students perform them are quite distinct. She gives the zigzag pathway a sense of directionality (Figure 27). She and her students precisely face the corners of the performing space and "slice" directly forward or backward in their stepping. They perform the stepping in a specific rhythmic pattern that both relates directly to the music and involves an elaboration of the simple sequence of two steps forward and two steps backward performed by Yi. The result of these variations is that the pathways performed by Huhm and her students are angular—both literally and qualitatively—while those performed by Yi are ambling and almost rounded. The same kinds of differences are seen in the jumping. Huhm and her students perform the jumps in direct relationship to the accompanying music and emphasize "going up and down" rather than simply "leaving the ground." Again, there is a clear spatial orientation in the movements of Huhm and her students.

The overall impression of the two performances is of an alternation between an individual performing sequences of loosely structured movement and an individual or group of individuals performing tightly choreographed dances comprised of movements that are variations or elaborations of selected portions of the former. Additionally, Yi sometimes integrates his movements with the performance of tasks in which he manipulates objects—brandishing knives or balancing on top of knife blades, holding flags or musical instruments, balancing a pot on his head, bowing toward the altar or different directions, and so on. Even the movements that do not manipulate objects take on the appearance of tasks performed to accomplish an end beyond themselves. There seems to be a larger, overriding purpose, in this case a fictitious intent to summon spirits (but for "pretend" purposes) for visible but nonetheless "pretend" clients. In order to accomplish this larger goal, certain movements must be done, but their precise execution is not important; movement functions as a means to an end beyond the performance for an audience.

The movements Huhm choreographed, on the other hand, had a clear sense of being portions of dance pieces and hence of being both the means and the end. Even though many movement sequences were based on those used in shaman rituals, they were selected and/or altered for their aesthetic value. When Huhm's dancers pulled one flag from a bundle of five, they were doing a task done by Yi (and other shamans) as part of certain rituals, but the flourish with which they did it contributed significantly to the visual design of the stage picture.[9] Although much of what Yi performed was visually and aesthetically interesting, that was not why he was doing it; the movement was only a means to another end.

In addition, Yi's orientation shifted between altar, musicians, "clients," and audience, but was either inwardly or "other worldly" focused; Huhm and her dancers maintained an orientation toward the audience—they were presenting a performance for conscious viewing by an audience rather than for accidental or coincidental observation by spectators.

Some of Huhm's choreographic decisions came from a desire to have a group of dancers perform in unison and from a sense of theatrical aesthetics. She said that when learning movements from Yi, he did not always perform them the same way (personal communication 8 Nov. 1992). The zigzag floor pattern, in particular, was problematic. She described this sequence as a kind of meandering that the shaman does until the desired spirit possesses him. Hence, precision in performance is not important; the shaman simply "roams," becoming more or less agitated, and repeats the pattern as necessary while awaiting the arrival of the spirit. This explains the reason for a clearly recognizable zigzag pattern in Yi's performance and the quality of his movement, as well as the transformation of that quality and the precision of movement detail in Huhm's choreographed version. Some of Huhm's choreographic choices were made because of the diverse abilities of her students, all of whom were considerably less adept than Yi in shamanic movement.

In sum, Yi seemed intent on creating excerpts of a *kut* on stage. Movements he performed and the manner in which he performed them were only important for their contribution to ritual accuracy and hence ritual efficacy, not as an aesthetic end in themselves. For Huhm and her students, on the other hand, movements were performed to suggest their shaman source, but, more importantly, to present an aesthetically pleasing dance performance.

Chŏng Chae-man's Salp'uri Kut

The analysis of Chŏng's performance is based on a videotape.[10] The twenty-nine-minute dance is structured in four sections, several of which have subsections, and all but one of which revolve around Chŏng (Plate 41). It includes members of his professional dance company and is performed on a conventional western proscenium-arch stage. The stage is bare, but special effects are created by dramatic lighting changes.

The dance begins with a seven-minute solo by Chŏng. The lights come up dimly to reveal him seated onstage alone, facing upstage. He bows several times, then slowly rises and manipulates paper streamers he is holding, turning both clockwise and counterclockwise as he does so, all of which takes approximately three minutes.[11] He throws the paper streamers offstage and begins a sequence resembling many of those common to the staged dance salp'uri, but with a quality alternating between the introverted quietness typical of salp'uri and an extremely extroverted, strong, melodramatic quality. (See Chapter 1 for a general description of salp'uri, and further comments in the discussion section below.) He also performs small jumps, often seen in *kut* but not usual in salp'uri, and travels a great deal through the performing space.

The second section, of approximately five minutes, is an intensification of the first, with some additional movement material. It begins with Chŏng leading a group of women in a large counterclockwise circular procession culminating with their prostrating themselves on the stage in a circle around him. This is reminiscent of a moment in salp'uri when a solo dancer sits and bends forward at the waist to an almost prone position, but in salp'uri the movement is done to facilitate picking up a scarf that has been dropped to the floor rather than in association with another performer. Chŏng continues with movements similar to those in the second part of the first section, but with more abrupt and stronger accents and interludes of skips, jumps, leaps, and hops. The intensity builds as Chŏng appears to be alternately angry and frenzied, the women eventually rise, and a group of men enter to carry Chŏng, in a prone position, offstage.

In the third section a group of women manipulate long scarves in a manner similar to salp'uri. Despite the continuing increase in the intensity of the music, the dancers' movements are relatively calm, displaying the quiet suspensions and releases found in many Korean dances. This section lasts for only about two minutes.

Although there is a brief subdued solo by a woman in the final section, the conclusion focuses on developing a feeling of group frenzy. Clusters of men and women run back and forth across the stage, manipulate poles with streamers affixed to them, and intersperse their locomotion with brief moments of jumping and more stylized, dancelike movements reprised from earlier sections. The climax is reached when Chŏng re-enters: he splits a long, dark-colored piece of cloth by running through it;[12] he jumps frantically and falls to the stage floor trembling; he is "revived" by female "clients" who stand over him, each rubbing her hands together in circles in a movement executed by clients in rituals; and the entire group of performers strikes a tableau.

The overriding impressions created by Salp'uri Kut are those of a powerful and very commanding male soloist, masses of people in almost continual motion traveling through the performing space to arrive in a final group pose, and an extremely dramatic build in intensity—all performed by highly trained dancers executing tightly choreographed patterns. The focus is entirely audience-oriented. In contrast to shaman rituals and attempts to replicate them on a stage, an altar table of any sort, singing, and much of the paraphernalia manipulated by shamans are conspicuously absent. The primary intent seems to be to draw inspiration from shaman rituals in order to create a dance that is an abstraction of shamanism, rather than to depict an actual ritual. A fictitious event is created depicting a *kut* without in any way replicating it. Selected movements from both *kut* and salp'uri are incorporated, but they merge and are elaborated to create their own aesthetically appealing danced drama *about* a *kut*. This contrasts with the performance of the shaman, Yi Chi-san, in the Hawa'i program, in which an attempt was made to create a real event, but with a fictitious purpose that required ritual efficacy. It also contrasts

with the performance of Huhm and her students in the Hawaʻi performance, in which an attempt was made to *represent* shamanic activities
without replicating them.

Chindo Sshikkim Kut

My analysis of this event is based on a videotape of a November 1985
performance at the Munye Theater in Seoul,[13] part of a series of presentations of performance forms that have been designated Intangible Cultural
Assets (see Chapter 3). The performance took place on a proscenium-arch
stage, with a small altar table stage right containing several kinds of food
and backed by a folding screen with calligraphy, placed at a slight angle
facing the audience. The remainder of the stage was empty, except for five
musicians seated stage left.[14] The featured performers were three females.

The program, lasting eighty minutes, contained eight sections (out-
lined in Appendix 6), each corresponding to a *kŏri*, and each marked by a
change in the performing personnel. The sections ranged in length from
six to thirteen minutes, and six were performed by only a single individual. Based on the differing nature of the activities within them, several
sections appeared to have subsections.[15]

Sections one, two, three, five, and seven were almost entirely singing: A
soloist sang primarily from center stage, focusing mostly on the audience
but occasionally on the musicians or the altar. Only in section seven did
the performer place herself at the altar in a seated position and remain
there throughout. Movement involved a little simple walking and occasionally walking in which the performer carefully stepped on her heel and
then rolled through to the rest of her foot, all within the center stage area;
extending the right arm to the side or forward-right-diagonal at shoulder
level; and a chest/shoulder impulse—all movements typically found in
many Korean dance forms. In section five the performer occasionally
executed symmetrical arm gestures, unlike the asymmetrical ones most
frequently seen in Korean dance. In the first section the performer manipulated paper streamers; in the second she held a small tree branch and
played a *changgo* while standing; in the fifth she held a small bowl with a
candle in it; and in the seventh she played a gong. When the paper streamers were used they were sometimes simply held in the outstretched hand,
were sometimes flipped backward and draped over a shoulder, and sometimes traced S-shaped curves in front of the body as the arms alternately
moved up and down in small arcs.[16] (See Plate 42.)

All sections included accompanying instrumental music. Sections four,
six, and eight were substantially different from the others: Section four
involved only movement; section six involved manipulation of many objects; and section eight involved singing, movement, and manipulation of
objects. In section four a performer covered the white attire she had worn
in all previous sections with a white cloak and a red banner draped across

one shoulder, and performed a dance that was clearly presented to the audience. This had the same features and overall choreographic structure as many versions of salp'uri dances, but also several distinctive features. First, in most salp'uri the dancer carries and manipulates a silk scarf; in this section of Chindo Sshikkim Kut the performer held and manipulated paper streamers. Second, in most salp'uri, arm gestures are largely asymmetrical: They are performed by only one arm at a time or, when performed with both arms simultaneously, each arm does a different movement. While the performer of Sshikkim Kut used many asymmetrical arm gestures in this section, she also did some that were symmetrical, particularly when dividing the paper streamers into two bundles and manipulating them. Third, she sat in front of the musicians and talked and laughed with them—something not seen in salp'uri performances.

Section six has three subsections that involve singing and movement centering around objects. In the first subsection, two performers hold between them a long cloth with loosely tied knots in it. They sing and, with several abrupt arm movements, thrust the cloth into arcs that eventually untie the knots. In the second subsection, a straw mat tightly rolled around clothes and tied shut is held vertically (stood on end) on the stage floor by one of the performers. Another performer then sings as a bowl of rice and a pot lid are placed on top of the mat; the whole configuration is brushed with water from the bowls and disassembled, with the mat unrolled in front of the altar to reveal the clothes; and more clothes are placed on top of the mat. One performer seats herself at the edge of the mat. In the third subsection one performer stands near the altar and sings while placing a small bundle of paper streamers on the head of the seated performer. In addition to the movements needed to manipulate the various objects, there is some manipulation of the paper streamers in S-shaped curves as in previous sections, but the focus of movement in this section remains on manipulating various objects.

The eighth and concluding section involves singing, manipulation of objects, and other movements seen in previous sections. All three performers assist in stretching a long piece of cloth across the width of the stage, which is then held by people standing offstage so that it is suspended above the stage floor. One performer holds the clothes that were wrapped in the straw mat, one holds paper streamers, and one holds a decorated object. The object is unidentifiable in the videotape, but may be a paper boat, a hat worn in one of the previous sections, or a small spirit shrine. All three begin at the stage-right end of the cloth and sing as they slowly move toward stage left, retreat a little, advance, retreat, and advance again. As they traverse the length of cloth they place the objects they are holding over it and move them along its length. They periodically lift the objects from the cloth, trace arcs with them, and perform movements seen previously. They then bundle the cloth, which is held by one of them, perform movements they have each done before, bow to the audience, and leave the stage.

The overall impression of the performance of Chindo Sshikkim Kut, with the exception of section four, is that singing serves as the primary focal point, manipulating objects occasionally takes over, and structured movement serves to punctuate the singing and task-oriented movements. Movements, particularly in section four, are the same as those that predominate in many Korean dance forms, especially in contemporary theatrical versions of salp'uri. These include initiation of movement in the chest area, lifting and lowering the shoulders, walking that emphasizes stepping first on the heel of the foot and then carefully rolling the rest of the foot down, inwardly rotated arms extended to the open diagonals at shoulder height, relaxed wrists that allow the hand to point downward when the arm is extended, and the tracing of S-shaped curves (usually done with only one arm and while holding a scarf rather than the paper streamers of Sshikkim Kut).

The sections appear to be disconnected, and the performers bow at the end of each in a public acknowledgment that they have "performed for an audience." Particular activities are done in a manner suggesting that they are simply to be done. There is an aura of "this is what we would do at a *kut*" rather than "we are trying to communicate with spirits." The performers are not intensely involved in what they are doing, and hence the performance recreates the *form* of a *kut* but not the *intent*. In the salp'uri-like section (section four), the impression is that one is watching a well-trained mover performing a highly structured dance interlude among the other activities.

Relationship Between Shamanism and Salp'uri

Connections are often made between contemporary theatrical versions of salp'uri and shamanism. Dancers and dance teachers consistently point out that salp'uri has its roots in shamanism. The basis of the concert form of this dance seen today is generally attributed to Han Sŏng-jun, who is said to have choreographed it in Seoul in the mid-1930s, and to have named it after a rhythm and dance used in shaman rituals in South Chŏlla Province (Loken-Kim and Crump 1993:14; Ku Hee-seo 1997:156; and Kim Kyoung-ae 1997:178). Howard (1989:174 and 248) points to changes that occurred in Chindo Sshikkim Kut to prepare it for designation as an Intangible Cultural Asset, as well as changes that have taken place since its designation, indicating the effect of recent theatrical dance forms on it, particularly as performed by what he refers to as the "Asset Team," the individuals designated by the government to perpetuate this ritual. Huhm, who studied salp'uri with Han Sŏng-jun in the 1930s, believed that despite contemporary dancers' attributions of the concert dance to Han, today's version is quite different from that taught by him (personal communication 8 Nov. 1992). According to her, in Han's version the dancer was frequently stationary or almost stationary and sang a great deal; today's dancers are in almost constant motion and do not sing. (Her description of Han's version of the dance is, interestingly, similar to some of the sections of Chindo Sshikkim Kut analyzed here, in which singing predominates.) Although the dance may originally have had strong ties to shamanism, Huhm believed its present theatrical manifestation is related to shamanism in name only, and that it is a direct descendant of a dance developed by female court entertainers (*kisaeng*) during the twentieth century.

Korean scholar Chŏng Pyŏng-ho concurs with Huhm:

> Originally called *Sugŏnch'um* because it is performed with a long handkerchief (*sugŏn*), [it] was renamed under Japanese colonial rule [1910–1945] by . . . Han Sŏng-jun. Though the term *salp'uri* refers to the expulsion of evil spirits and bad luck, the dance does not contain any direct reference to shamanic exorcism. It is merely a beautiful dance performed to the accompaniment of shamanic music from the southern region. (Chung Byung-ho 1997b:146).

Chŏng also states that Han was an instructor at a *kyobang*, a place where female entertainers were taught the performing arts (ibid.). Loken-Kim, citing Kim On-gyŏng, indicates that the female entertainers' version of salp'uri was based specifically on one part of what she calls Honam Sshikkim Kut, that is, Sshikkim Kut from the southwestern provinces (1989:129–130). Ku Hee-seo (1997:164) states that To Salp'uri, a particular version of salp'uri performed by Kim Suk-cha, a dancer and member of a family of hereditary shamans, derived from the Todang Kut of Kyŏnggi Province. If all these comments are accurate, it is possible some versions of salp'uri are directly tied to shaman dance and some are not.

Kendall suggests numerous connections between "dancing girls" and shamans (1991–1992:54–56), and posits that shamans and female entertainers "may have borrowed elements of each others' performance" (ibid.:60). Howard points to links based on performance and class (1992). Shaman Pak In-o (in Guillemoz 1998:75) states that in the past shamans "were often recruited from among the ranks of dancers." Unfortunately, the current state of Korean dance history does not allow us to know just how much, if any, of Han's choreography was based on ritual dance, how much of what is seen in contemporary salp'uri has affected the movements performed today by Chindo shamans, and whether specific movements originated among shamans, female entertainers, or other dancers. But, as noted above, relationships between today's concert dance and Chindo Sshikkim Kut are extremely strong.

Howard (personal communication, undated) notes that shamans have been joined by nonshamans in the Chindo Asset Team. He confirms that two of the three performers in the Munye Theater performance are shamans, only one of whom is designated a perpetuator of the tradition, and that the performer in section four, the section similar to today's concert versions of salp'uri, was more extensively trained as a dancer than a shaman.

The Three Events: Similarities and Differences

The events described can be compared in terms of identity of the performers, relationship of the events to actual shaman rituals, and predominant movements. The Hawaʻi performance included both a shaman and nonshaman dancers, each in separate but alternating sections of the program; the Chŏng Chae-man performance was done entirely by dancers, but with Chŏng assuming the role of a shaman in the last portion; the Chindo performance was done by both shamans and a nonshaman. However, all three events were consciously staged; none was an actual *kut*. In Hawaʻi, the portions done by Huhm's students were performances for a theater audience. Yi Chi-san's segments, on the other hand, had a sense of genuine ritual, of "I am a shaman doing a *kut* here on stage." His orientation toward objects and altars and his naturalistic manner gave his performance a quality of concern with accomplishing something beyond the literal tasks being executed, rather than with performing precise movements presented for observation. His inconsistent performance of the zigzag floor pattern and Huhm's explanation of the purpose of this movement reinforce this notion. When Huhm performed, she was *enacting* the role of a shaman; although her movements were precise and generally tightly choreographed, she presented herself to the audience "as if" she were a shaman. When Yi Chi-san performed, there was a sense of *being present* at an actual *kut*; when Huhm performed, there was a sense of a *kut* being *suggested*; when Huhm's students performed there was an awareness of *dances*.

The Chŏng performance made no attempt to be an actual *kut*. No typical *kut* paraphernalia were present on the stage, only a limited number of handheld objects used in *kut* were employed, there was no singing, and there was no purpose beyond the stage presentation itself. Although Chŏng included several typical shaman activities (such as splitting the cloth), there was no sense of experiencing all or a portion of a *kut*. The only "*kut* experience" for the viewer was at a qualitative level: a sense of intensity, at times of frenzy, that was being experienced by someone *else* for the audience to *observe*, rather than directly *participate in*. This performance was an abstraction based on elements of shamanism; it presented a dance to elicit a "*kut*-like experience" at a superficial level rather than to depict the reality of a *kut* and provide for communication with the spirit world.

The Chindo performance also was presentational in nature. Although the performers did many of the same things they would do in a *kut*, the primary orientation was toward the audience. There was, as in Chŏng's performance, no sense of being present at a *kut*, since there was no sense of communication with the spirit world. But in addition, the performers displayed an awareness of how things were being done.

The movements used by Yi Chi-san and the Chindo performers were quite different. The zigzag floor patterns and jumping of Yi are not present in Sshikkim Kut. Likewise, the single-arm extension, careful use of the foot, suspended movements, shoulder movements, and chest initiation of the Chindo performers are not seen in the movements of Yi. Interestingly, Chŏng's movements combine elements of both the Chindo and Yi performances.

It is logical that the movements of Halla Huhm and her students and Chŏng and his performers—all of whom are dancers—would be carefully selected, arranged, and "dancelike." But it is noteworthy that the movements of the Chindo performers had a polish that might be expected of trained dancers. Howard (personal communication, undated) reports that not only is one Chindo performer a trained dancer, but dance has become part of the routine training of the Chindo "Asset Team."

Relationships to Other Shaman Events

In addition to the three performances described, I examined several videotapes of portions of shaman rituals performed by Kim Kŭm-hwa, a shaman originally from Hwanghae Province and now living in Seoul[17] (JVC 1990 and Asia Society 1978). Although it is not always clear precisely how much of the material in these tapes comes from actual *kut* as opposed to staged *kut*, a number of movement features recur:

1. Counterclockwise turning (either slowly or quickly), often with arms stretched sideward at shoulder height;
2. Jumps that are both light and have a strong sense of verticality;
3. Movements of the arms in front of the body that trace S-shaped curves in space (generally while holding knives) as well as pure up-and-down movements of the arms; and
4. An occasional overall jaunty quality.

The counterclockwise turning, jumps, and jaunty quality are reminiscent of movements of Yi Chi-san; the S-shaped curves are reminiscent of movements of the Chindo performers.

In one Kim Kŭm-hwa excerpt (Asia Society 1978) clients participate at the end of the ritual by moving. Although their movements are not polished like those of individuals with dance training, they appear to copy the jumping with vertical emphasis and up-and-down arm movements used by Kim. Do they execute these kinds of movements because they have been told to perform them, because they have seen them performed by shamans, because they think or know that they are the right movements to do at a *kut*, or because they are similar to Korean dance movements they have seen in other contexts? Kendall (1991–1992:57) suggests

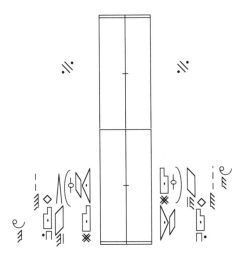

Figure 28. Labanotation score of
arm movements demonstrated by
shaman initiate in Kendall and Lee
1991 videotape. Notation by Judy
Van Zile.

that women who dance in the portion of the *kut* known as *mugam* imitate
movements done by the shaman when possessed.

In another videotape, made in Korea by Laurel Kendall and Diana Lee
(1991) of an initiation *kut*, the initiate performs some of the same movements as Yi Chi-san and Kim Kŭm-hwa—counterclockwise turning,
jumping that emphasizes verticality, and movement of the arms up and
down in front of the body. The senior shaman coaxes the initiate to jump
and demonstrates an arm movement she wants her to do that is similar to
one found in many Korean dance forms (Figure 28). Although the context
here is a *kut*, we are told the young initiate is having difficulty allowing
the spirits to descend, and the senior shaman seems to attempt to use
accuracy of movement as a device to instill the appropriate feelings in the
initiate so the ritual can proceed as it should. In other words, correct
movement serves as a vehicle for achieving a state of inspiration.

Conclusions

My analysis is phenomenological in approach: The primary emphasis is
on describing and making interconnections between what is seen and the
impressions of the spectator, rather than in seeking symbolic meanings of
movement or the intent of the performer—particularly in their original
kut context. While I have provided detailed descriptions for three shaman-
related presentations given in formal theater settings, the movements
have been briefly juxtaposed against movements observed in actual *kut*.
Together, these descriptions embrace shamanic movement performed in
three contexts: by shamans in theatrical presentations, by nonshamans in
theatrical presentations, and by shamans in rituals. Since it was not possible to examine the same performers in more than one context, it is not
possible to draw definitive conclusions regarding potential differences
due to settings. The analysis, however, allows for some generalizations to

be made, and supports the notion of the tenacity of movement: In all of the contexts examined there are recurring movement themes. The fact that these themes occur in both *kut* and non-*kut* contexts and are performed by shamans and nonshamans suggests that they are taught or learned and that they are signifiers of things shamanic in a variety of contexts.[18]

One telling example relating to movement instruction and shamanic representation through movement is Yi Chi-san's zigzag floor pattern. His performance demonstrates the importance of this overall shape, but not of the precise manner of stepping that creates it. And herein lies a seeming contradiction. Halla Huhm's book on shamanism (1980), which is based on her studies with Yi, includes extensive diagrams detailing the precise order, placement, and rhythm of stepping to create the zigzag pattern. Are these her "dancerly" interpretations of Yi's teachings? Similar diagrams are included in a recently published manual for shamans.[19] Huhm's book and the manual, together with the performances I have observed, corroborate an interrelationship between aesthetics and ritual efficacy mentioned at the beginning of this chapter. It appears that a basic structure is sufficiently important to the fulfillment of a ritual intent to be taught, but the state of mind of the performer—which can lead to performance variations—supersedes precise replication of a taught movement pattern. Laurel Kendall and Diana Lee's videotape further suggests the relationship between taught movement and a state of mind. In this case not only is the neophyte shaman taught a movement pattern, but the emphasis is on achieving a particular state of mind by correctly executing it. Both of these instances suggest that correctly performed movement is used to achieve a desired state of mind, but once that state has been achieved, the movement execution can dissolve to individual performance style. And since the movement has been learned, its essence is retained while undergoing an overlay of improvised and/or personal style.[20]

Of shamans examined here performing in theatrical contexts, Yi Chi-san gives the appearance of simply replicating, on stage, excerpts of what he might normally do in a *kut*. Although he surely made choices of what to do, he duplicated what he would do in a ritual, giving primary attention to successfully completing portions of a *kut* on stage rather than to pleasing the aesthetic theatrical sensibilities of spectators. The Chindo performers, likewise, made choices in what to present on stage, but they more clearly had an audience in mind. It is not possible to determine what movements, if any, were modified for theatrical presentation without observing shamans in rituals. It is noteworthy, however, that none of the shamans appeared to enter an altered state of consciousness or performed movements indicative of a particularly frenzied state. It was only the dancer, Chŏng, who acted "as if" transported mentally.

Of the nonshaman performers, the structure of the movements used by Halla Huhm shows a clear intent to replicate or draw inspiration from shaman rituals: While she chose to modify or not duplicate some of the performance *quality* present in the source of her inspiration (Yi Chi-san), she retained the essence of the *movement structure*. The performance staged by Chŏng, on the other hand, relies most heavily on the physical trappings of shamans, particularly costumes and handheld implements, and the qualitative nature of an ecstatic state. But he has translated these elements into his own notions of "aesthetically pleasing" and "theatrical," overlaying them heavily with typical Korean dance movements in an effort to provide a highly theatrical symbolic, or abstracted, *kut*.

Many people believe the movement in shaman ritual is purely spontaneous—when the spirits descend and/or the shaman is possessed by spirits, he or she is "moved"—both spiritually and literally. The resulting physical movement is considered improvised or controlled by the spirits. Guillemoz indicates that some shamans say they are taught by the spirits (1998:82). Kendall states that for clients who participate in the *mugam* portion of a *kut* "the successful dancer's actions are considered involuntary, willed by the presence of a personal spirit" (1977:38). But the recurring motifs in the examples analyzed here and the existence of at least two teaching manuals suggest otherwise.[21] Kendall indicates that clients may actually be taught correct movements during a *kut*: "If the woman remains bashful, one of the *mansin* [*manshin*—shamans] or a friend will clasp the woman's arms and move them *in the correct manner* or dance in front of her to coach her" (1977:40—emphasis added). The fact that movement is taught, however, does not preclude the possibility of a performer being in some otherworldly frame of mind, since movement patterns may be sufficiently ingrained that they are repeated regardless of the performer's state of mind, or learned sequences may be so inextricably connected to the context in which they were learned that they are "automatically" done when an altered state of mind is reached.

This analysis has identified a number of recurring movement themes, but further study is needed to ascertain if differences observed may be attributed to different shamans, different genders, different types of shamans (i.e., hereditary or god-descended), different contexts, geographic origin of the shamans and the *kut* they perform, or other causes. The recurrence of movement themes suggests that movement has become an emblem that can be used, at will, to represent things shamanic, and that in some cases it is taught—either formally or informally. Further research might determine precisely what the boundaries of structured movement are in relation to ritual efficacy: what must be performed and how much improvisation—or individual style—is allowable. My analysis supports ideas relating to interconnections between shamans and dancers, some of which may have occurred in former times, and some of which have probably been motivated by the current government preservation system. Precisely which movement components have been influenced by dance, and which movements in theatrical dance are the result of shaman influences, must be left to further research.

Ultimately, my analysis points to the importance of giving serious and detailed consideration to movement in and related to shamanism. This could shed new light on the nature and ingredients of *kut*, the meanings of its various components, and interconnections between structured movement in shamanic activities and dance—what movement activities contribute to the identity of shamans and shaman ritual.

7

Kim Ch'ŏn-hŭng

*Portrait of a Performing Artist
and Teacher*

Kim Ch'ŏn-hŭng is one of Korea's foremost senior court dance and music performers and teachers. He began his training as a musician, but moved on to learn dance as well. During his more than ninety years he lived through extraordinary times. In 1910, a little more than a year after his birth, Korea became a colony of Japan. Although Japan sought cultural assimilation of the Korean people as part of colonization, during its thirty-five years of overlordship, Japanese policies changed many times. In general, the 1910s were a period of extreme repression marked by governmental restructuring as the Japanese took control and set up educational systems. Following a major independence demonstration in 1919, the Japanese loosened control a bit, allowing for the publication of Korean-language newspapers and magazines as well as the establishment of organizations dedicated to the study of Korean culture. In 1931 Japan's invasion of Manchuria contributed to intensification of control in Korea, negating many of the leniencies of the 1920s and adding censorship to priorities. In 1937 Japan's invasion of China began the Sino-Japanese war, again contributing to increased pressures in Korea. This time policies mandated that Koreans worship at Shinto shrines honoring the Japanese rulers. In 1941 the war expanded into the Pacific, and Koreans were forced to take on Japanese names.

The end of World War II in 1945 eventually led, in 1948, to the division of Korea into the Republic of Korea in the south (South Korea) and the Democratic People's Republic of Korea in the north (North Korea). Family members were geographically separated, many never to reunite. And 1950 to 1953 saw the Korean War, pitting Koreans in the divided peninsula against each other.

As South Korea sought to rebuild itself and re-establish a distinct national identity, in 1962 the government implemented a law to help perpetuate Korea's traditional intangible cultural heritage (see Chapter 3). This had a major impact on advocacy for the performing arts, including dance and music. The phenomenal economic growth of the 1970s and 1980s contributed to an extraordinary dance boom, while the downturn of the 1990s brought restraint and funding cutbacks. Throughout all of these events Kim Ch'ŏn-hŭng endured and flourished, sustaining his involvement in the performing arts.

This chapter is based on my interviews with Kim, his family members, and his colleagues, and on his memoirs published in the February to December 1990 issues of *Ch'um*, an important dance magazine in Korea. (These memoirs were collected and expanded on in Kim Ch'ŏn-hŭng 1995.) Unlike other chapters that are intended to both provide information and analyze events and issues, the purpose of this chapter is to tell a personal story. My intent is to convey a portrait of the life of a performer and teacher that captures his personality, describe facets of dance and music training and performance, and present a picture of life during the times in which an important dance figure lived. I have tried, therefore to retain the style of comments in Kim's memoirs and conversations, and have omitted conventional scholarly citations and notes. Visual images of Kim may be found in Plates 3 and 43, and Figures 29–32.

*   *   *

The tiny, almost fragile-looking figure quickly ascending the stairs to his second-floor office at the National Center for Korean Traditional Performing Arts brings to mind a young tree, firmly rooted in the soil, but gently giving way to the wind. The smile on his face is pervasive, and as it spreads his eyes become thin slits and almost disappear. This wisp of a man, who stands only five feet, four inches tall and who could so easily become lost in a crowd, is strong and of considerable stature in Korean culture. Although born during the turbulent year of Korea's transition from a Japanese protectorate to a Japanese colony, and living half his life in a country that was seeking independence, he attributes his longevity to his childhood involvement with sports and athletic games. His contributions to Korean culture, which include dancing before Korea's last king in Ch'angdŏk Palace and playing music for an elaborate ceremony to relocate the tomb of Korea's last queen, were formally recognized twice by the Korean government when he was designated a Human Cultural Asset for his expertise in important performing art forms of Korea.

Kim Ch'ŏn-hŭng was born on February 9, 1909, according to the lunar calendar (March 30 in the solar calendar), in Imukkol, a village near the southern part of Seoul. He was the third of five sons of a carpenter. The smile he bears today belies the hardships he has endured. His two younger brothers died in infancy, and he has vivid memories of the loud wailing of relatives at the funeral of his grandmother and of glimpsing her lifeless body through a window. In 1924 his father came home from work ill. Kim was only fifteen at the time. While their mother was away at

Plate 1. Kain Chŏnmoktan (Beautiful Women Picking Peonies), a court dance, performed by members of the National Center for Korean Traditional Performing Arts. Courtesy of Kungnip Kugagwŏn.

Plate 2. A musician from the National Center for Korean Traditional Performing Arts plays the *pak.*
Photo by Park Seung-u. Courtesy of Art Space Korea.

Plate 3. Kim Ch'ŏn-hŭng performs Ch'unaengjŏn (Nightingale in Springtime), a court dance, in Hawai'i (1995). Photo by Judy Van Zile.

Plate 4. Hangmu (Crane Dance), a court dance. Photo by Chung Su-mi.

Plate 5. Ch'ŏyongmu (Dance of Ch'ŏyong), a court dance, performed by members of the National Center for Korean Traditional Performing Arts. Courtesy of Kungnip Kugagwŏn.

Plate 6. Ilmu, Confucian shrine dance. Photo by Park Seung-u. Courtesy of Art Space Korea.

Plate 7. Kosŏng Ogwangdae, masked dance-drama from Kosŏng. Photo by Park Seung-u. Courtesy of Art Space Korea.

Plate 8. Yangju P'yŏlsandae Nori, masked dance-drama from Yangju. Photo by Park Seung-u. Courtesy of Art Space Korea.

Plate 9. Nongak, farmers' band dance and music. Photo by Judy Van Zile.

Plate 10. Nongak, farmers' band dance and music. Photo by Judy Van Zile.

Plate 11. Chindo shaman Kim Tae-rye ("holder" of Intangible Cultural Asset number seventy-two) performs a major memorial service (February 1983). Musicians, led by Pak Pyŭn-ch'ŭn, are members of the "asset team." Photo by Keith Howard. Courtesy of Keith Howard.

Plate 12. Monks of the Pongwŏn Temple perform Parach'um (Buddhist Cymbal Dance) at the Yŏngsanjae celebration. Photo by Park Seung-u. Courtesy of Art Space Korea.

Plate 13. Kim Suk-cha performs Salp'uri. Photo by Park Seung-u. Courtesy of Art Space Korea.

Plate 14. Yi Mae-bang performs Sŭngmu, a theatrical version of the Buddhist Monk's Dance. Photo by Park Seung-u. Courtesy of Art Space Korea.

Plate 15. Puch'aech'um (Fan Dance), performed by members of Korea's National Dance Company (1978).
Photo by Charles Kennard.

Plate 16. Puch'aech'um (Fan Dance), performed by members of Korea's National Dance Company (1978).
Photo by Charles Kennard.

Plate 17. Detail of hand scroll, Inaugural Celebrations Welcoming the New Governor of P'yŏngyang, attributed to Kim Hong-do (late eighteenth/early nineteenth century). Courtesy of National Museum of Korea.

Plate 18. Painting of Ch'ŏyongmu (1724). From Lee Duhyon (Yi Tu-hyŏn), *Han'guk kamyŏnguk* (Korean Mask Dance Drama). Korea: Research Institute of Korean Mask Dance Drama. Courtesy of Yi Tu-hyŏn.

Plate 19. Mask for Ch'ŏyongmu. Photo by Judy Van Zile.

Plate 20. Ch'ŏyongmu dancer. Photo by Judy Van Zile.

Plate 21. Dancers of the National Center for Korean Traditional Performing Arts dance Ch'ŏyongmu. Courtesy of Kungnip Kugagwŏn.

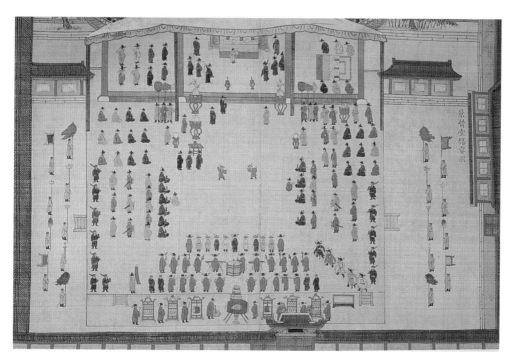

Plate 22. Detail of King Sukjong's Banquet for the Society of Elders, from *Kisa kyechŏp* (Album of Gathering for Officials Over the Age of Seventy) (1719–1720). Color on silk, original 44.0 ˇ 67.7 cm. Photo by Kim Chin-yo, et al., Ho-Am Art Museum.

Plate 23. Detail of King Sukjong's Banquet for the Society of Elders, from *Kisa kyechŏp* (Album of Gathering for Officials Over the Age of Seventy) (1719–1720). Color on silk, original 44.0 ˇ 67.7 cm. Photo by Kim Chin-yo, et al., Ho-Am Art Museum.

Plate 24. Detail of Elder Ministers Returning from Banquet Sponsored by King Sukjong, from *Kisa kyechŏp* (Album of Gathering for Officials Over the Age of Seventy) (1719–1720). Color on silk, original 44.0 ˇ 67.7 cm. Photo by Kim Chin-yo, et al., Ho-Am Art Museum.

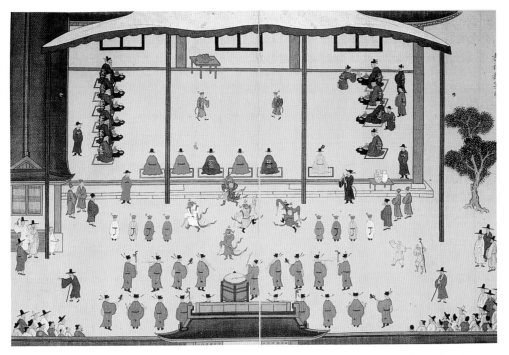

Plate 25. Detail of King Sukjong's Private Party for Elder Ministers, from *Kisa kyechŏp* (Album of Gathering for Officials Over the Age of Seventy) (1719–1720). Color on silk, original 44.0 ˇ 67.7 cm. Photo by Kim Chin-yo, et al., Ho-Am Art Museum.

Plate 26. Detail of King Sukjong's Private Party for Elder Ministers, from *Kisa kyechŏp* (Album of Gathering for Officials Over the Age of Seventy) (1719–1720). Color on silk, original 44.0 ˇ 67.7 cm. Photo by Kim Chin-yo, et al., Ho-Am Art Museum.

Plate 27. Hand scroll, Inaugural Celebrations Welcoming New Governor of P'yŏngyang, attributed to Kim Hong-do (late eighteenth/early nineteenth century). Courtesy of National Museum of Korea.

Plate 28. Painting of Ch'ŏyongmu attributed to Kim Hong-do (mid-eighteenth/early nineteenth century). Courtesy Kim Hak-su.

Plate 29. Kim Ch'ŏn-hŭng's reconstruction of Hak Yŏnhwadae Ch'ŏyongmu Hapsŏl (1983). Courtesy of Kungnip Kugagwŏn.

Plate 30. Knives used in Chinju Kŏmmu. Photo by Judy Van Zile.

Plate 31. Postage stamp issued upon designation of Chinju Kŏmmu as an Intangible Cultural Asset.

Plate 32. Picture of Non'gae in the Chinju Shrine dedicated to her. Photo by Judy Van Zile.

Plate 33. The shrine dedicated to Non'gae and the Chinju pavilion (Ch'oksŏngnu) in which Chinju Kŏmmu is performed today. Photo by Judy Van Zile.

Plate 34. Entrance to the Chinju shrine to Non'gae. Photo by Judy Van Zile.

Plate 35. Ch'oksŏngnu, the Chinju pavilion in which Chinju Kŏmmu is performed today. Photo by Judy Van Zile.

Plate 36. Dancers of the National Center for Korean Traditional Performing Arts perform Chinju Kŏmmu. Courtesy of Kungnip Kugagwŏn.

Plate 37. Yi Suk-yŏng, a student of the Halla Huhm Dance Studio, performs the movement from Chinju Kŏmmu in which the red lining of the jacket is displayed. Photo by Judy Van Zile.

Plate 38. The torso-display movement of Chinju Kŏmmu, in a performance by dancers from the National Center for Korean Traditional Performing Arts. Courtesy of Kungnip Kugagwŏn.

Plate 39. Yŏnp'ungdae, the "flying" movement from Chinju Kŏmmu, in a performance by dancers from the National Center for Korean Traditional Performing Arts. Courtesy of Art Space Korea.

Plate 40. Yi Chi-san, a shaman from Seoul, performs in a theatrical concert of shaman dance in Hawai'i (1976). Photo by William Feltz. Courtesy of William Feltz.

Plate 41. Chŏng Chae-man's dance company performs Salp'uri Kut. Courtesy of Chŏng Chae-man.

Plate 42. The Chindo shaman Yi Wan-sun performs a family ritual in Imhoe district (January 1990). Waving the paper streamers in S-shaped patterns, she encourages the spirits to dance. Photo by Keith Howard. Courtesy of Keith Howard.

Plate 43. Kim Ch'ŏn-hŭng makes a point while lecturing (1982). Photo by Judy Van Zile.

Figure 29. Kim Ch'ŏn-hŭng plays the *changgo*. Courtesy of Chung-won Meyer.

work, he and his brothers took turns looking after their father, never thinking to consult a doctor. When their father's health did not improve and they finally took him to a physician, it was too late; he died on August 19. Despite Kim's young age at the time, he remembers his father's strong nationalistic spirit and the countless hardships he underwent to keep the family together.

The following year the central beam in the family house broke during one of Korea's worst floods. The damage was severe, but the family was unable to purchase a new home of their own. Instead, they had to rent a house, and this was the beginning of more than thirty household moves.

Figure 30. Kim Ch'ŏn-hŭng teaches at the Halla Huhm Dance Studio in Hawai'i (1963). Courtesy of Halla Huhm Dance Collection.

Kim recalls hearing older people say that you only move to a new house when you die. In his typically sprightly manner he says that must mean that he overcame death more than thirty times. In fact, Kim narrowly escaped death: During the Korean War, a bomb struck his house just as he left it after locking things up in an effort to protect the family. Not long afterward, many of Kim's family members were separated; he still does not know if some of them are alive.

But the difficult times have been interspersed with special moments, and more than ninety years have brought many happy memories. Early childhood days were spent playing soccer, baseball, and tennis. When baseball was first introduced, purchasing equipment was beyond the means of the common people. So they made balls from old socks and the yarn of worn-out sweaters. But after fainting when a ball hit him in the eye, his baseball days were replaced by soccer. Trying to play soccer on the ice in winter while wearing only the simple straw shoes of the less wealthy people was a particular challenge.

Despite the political upheaval and tight controls of the early days of the Japanese occupation, "instant street theaters" were popular. At the young age of only five or six, Kim imitated the groups he saw in the streets: He sometimes used a white cloth to delineate an impromptu stage, donned his mother's clothes for costumes, and put on his own performances.

Hard work was a part of family life from the days when Kim was a young boy. His father's carpentry skills were constantly put to use. Each time the family moved they searched for an inexpensive house that was in need of repair. The whole family would pitch in to assist with renovating and fixing things so that when the house was eventually sold they could reap a profit.

While he was still very young, Kim's mother opened a shop in the family's house. She refurbished the matted stuffing in mattresses, and Kim would help by running small errands. Later, his mother helped augment the family's income by working part-time at Namdaemun Market (one of Seoul's major markets) drying persimmons and shelling nuts to make biscuits and candies. Kim fondly recalls the treat of sampling these sugary-sweet delicacies, and the gentle warmth of his mother.

Days at Kyungmyŏng School were particularly memorable. Sitting on a traditional-style small wooden platform (*pyŏngsang*), with a fire to keep away insects, the students recited Chinese poems, a traditional part of Confucian-based education. And Christmas always meant a visit to the

Figure 31. Kim Ch'ŏn-hŭng performs Salp'uri, 1985. Courtesy of Halla Huhm Dance Collection.

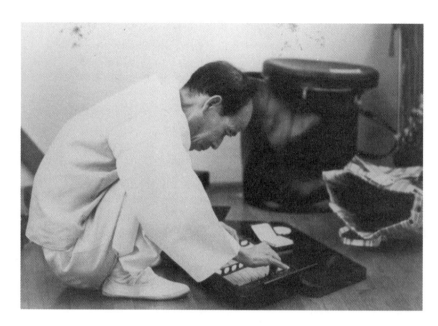

Figure 32. Kim Ch'ŏn-hŭng prepares the *yanggŭm* for a Hawai'i performance (1974). Photo by Mary Jo Freshley. Courtesy of Halla Huhm Dance Collection.

church next door to the school to receive a gift—even if the children were not practicing Christians, and even if this was the only time they visited the church. This early confluence of traditional practices (in the case of Confucianism, imported centuries earlier from China) and those imported from the west (in this instance, Christianity, imported in the eighteenth century but not widely accepted until the nineteenth century), would resurface many times during his life.

In July of 1922, shortly before Kyungmyŏng School was closed by the Japanese, at the age of thirteen Kim began to study at Yiwangjik Aakpu. This school was originally established in 1392 as an official government organization under the jurisdiction of the royal court. Its purpose was to train several hundred musicians and dancers to perform in official ceremonies and at royal banquets. After the beginning of the Japanese occupation in 1910, and with the elimination of vestiges of the former court, the school became a private association. With Japanese restrictions somewhat lessened in the 1920s, Aakpu began taking on new students. Kim was one of nine young boys selected to become the second group of students to enter the school. He knew very little about the kind of music taught there, but was lured by the opportunity to continue to study other subjects as well. The recommendation of a friend of his father, who was the father of a student in the school's first class, led to his acceptance, which included a modest monetary stipend and all of his school supplies. Since Kim came from a poor family, it was this financial assistance that enabled him to continue his education, and that provided the beginning of his lifelong involvement with the performing arts.

This was a major turning point for Kim. He began to learn to play the musical instruments of the royal court—not just one instrument, but many of them. Instruction began with the percussion instruments and then proceeded to the string and wind instruments. Melodies and rhythm patterns were first learned by singing them. Then students learned the techniques of playing the various instruments.

Melody patterns of the *p'yŏnjong*—a set of large metal bells suspended from a standing wooden frame—were particularly difficult to remember. Kim's creativity led to the development of his own study method. He drew pictures of the bells, in their proper arrangement, on the wall of his house and practiced striking the imaginary instruments with a stick. At that time walls were made of a mixture of soil, straw, sand, and cow dung that was packed together and then covered with paper. Kim's repeated banging on the imaginary instruments he had drawn on the wall eventually put holes in the paper, and the wall's inner content spewed into the room, littering the floor with dust and dirt. Fortunately, his family was understanding. And when examination time came and he drew the slip of paper indicating which of the more than a dozen pieces he had learned he would have to play, his creative practicing method yielded good results—he performed well.

Days at Aakpu were not just study days. One of the teachers encouraged the students to play tennis, and in 1927 set up a tennis court in the front yard of the school. Between his continuing involvement with soccer and his new interest in tennis, as Kim could afford to buy them he eventually wore out many pairs of sneakers over the years. And when table tennis was introduced to Korea in the 1930s, Aakpu's recreational activities expanded as students and teachers played together at night.

And there was mountain climbing, creating memories of beautiful trees and the dew on flower petals reflecting the rising sun; rowing rented boats along the river to get back to the city; and satisfying an outdoor hunger with wine, spicy pickled vegetables, bean curd casserole, and dried fish while standing amid the noisy crowds at the food carts in the streets.

A surprise came shortly after starting classes at Aakpu. Kim was one of eleven students selected from the school's all-male population to study dance. Prior to the Japanese occupation, dance had been done primarily by female entertainers (*kisaeng*). When the Japanese assumed rule, they disbanded the official institution of female court entertainers. The boys' previous education had focused solely on music, but in anticipation of a special event, the school staff sought handsome young boys they thought could learn to dance relatively quickly. The boys knew little about the dances and did not know why they had been selected to learn them, but they dutifully stood behind their teachers and imitated the movements they had never seen before—movements they found quite unusual. As they caught glimpses of each other, they couldn't help but giggle at the sight of their young male classmates' attempts at being graceful.

Studies intensified as a very special day approached. Despite the fact that Korea was now officially a colony of Japan, there was to be a celebration to honor the fiftieth birthday of Sunjong, Korea's last king. Sunjong's reign began in 1907, but ended with his deposition when Japan imposed colonial status in 1910. Although Sungjong had been exiled to Japan, he was allowed to return to Korea periodically, and the Japanese allowed celebratory events to take place during his return.

A little more than two months after beginning their dance studies the young boys found themselves unpacking their bags at Ch'angdŏk Palace to participate in the event, and to encounter still more new experiences. Although they had rehearsed their dancing many times, they had never performed before. Since this was a real performance for a former king and special dignitaries, they had to put makeup on their faces. As he mixed the hard dried powder square with water to create a substance he could apply to his face, Kim discovered himself in front of something else he had never seen before—a white porcelain sink. The houses he had known did not have their own water facilities—water had to be carried to the house from a shared well. As these new experiences unfolded there were constant exchanges of delight, and outbursts of laughter at the sight of the transformation of fellow classmates into dancers fit for a royal audience.

When the time for the performance came the young dancers nervously entered the palace room, hands together and eyes downcast, as they had rehearsed so many times. Upon reaching their assigned places they lifted their gaze. Kim vividly recalls seeing the king in his royal seat with elaborate tables of food and flickering candles on either side. Behind the king were guests from Japan and other people of high rank, including Yi Hang-gu, whose father, Yi Wan-yong, was considered by many to be the traitor who sold Korea to the Japanese.

A wooden clapper, known as a *pak*, sounded the introduction to the grandiose music of the court. Nervousness overtook Kim, together with a feeling of difficulty in moving his hands and feet. A brief spell of dizziness eventually gave way to relaxation. With his mind finally at ease, Kim was able to dance as he had practiced, and the performance ended without any major mistakes. While the young dancers and musicians rested afterward in their dressing room, a table was ceremoniously brought in covered with some of the most remarkable foods the young students had ever seen. Their teacher explained that these were special foods served at court banquets, foods identified in the Korean language as those "sent down by a royal person" (*sach'an*). March 25, 1923, was a truly memorable day for a young boy about to turn fourteen. In fact, it was a memorable day for all of Korea: It was the first major court-style event since the beginning of the Japanese occupation in 1910, and the last such event ever. Kim believes that because of that event much of the court music and dance repertoire was revived and would later be remembered, following liberation in 1945, when it could again be performed and passed on to future generations.

During the year following the palace performance, in 1924, a short vacation trip with his brother contributed to both good and bad memories for Kim. His eldest brother worked in the freight department of the train station in Seoul. Since his brother and their family received twelve free train tickets each year, in December Kim and his brother embarked on an adventure to Manchuria. But Kim's excitement over his first long train trip was tempered by the tedium of Japanese police continually boarding the train and checking passengers and luggage. Despite leniency in some areas, Japanese authorities still maintained strict controls at border areas and unreasoned harassment of Koreans was common.

After more than twelve hours the train crossed a steel bridge over the Amnok River and entered Manchuria. Large buildings in a traditional style of Chinese architecture, rickshaws, and rickshaw men with their hair in long braids caught Kim's attention. He and his brother strolled through the streets, taking in all the new sights. Then they shopped for gifts to take home—sugar, wine, and especially Chinese cigarettes, which were valued as a special treat since their cost in Korea made them accessible only to the wealthy. As they purchased their treasures they were particularly mindful of what they understood to be the quotas they could bring back to Korea, especially the restriction of ten packs of cigarettes.

With sightseeing and shopping done they decided to return across the border for dinner before heading back to Seoul. Again the Japanese inspected passengers and luggage, but this time more thoroughly than before. As Kim and his brother approached the exit gate on the Korean side of the border they were stopped. A policeman searched their luggage and without any explanation said they must go to the police station. They had no choice but to accompany the officers. Once at the station they were questioned and accused of smuggling; they had ten packs of cigarettes and only two were allowed. Kim and his brother felt certain this was just harassment, and that they had known the proper restrictions, but they had no recourse. They gave up their purchases, paid a fine, were forced to ask for forgiveness, and were ordered to leave immediately.

The street outside was dark and cold. As they walked, Kim watched his brother looking straight ahead, but focusing on nothing. The sadness they felt from their treatment by the police was augmented by their increasing hunger, but the bitterness faded as they entered a restaurant with a straw mat on the floor and large steamy pots of boiling noodles. Memories of winter surfaced, with icicles on the roof reflecting the sunlight, skating on the frozen Han River, ice sellers doing rituals in hopes that the weather would stay cold so they could easily obtain their goods, and *naengmyŏn*— cold noodles that somehow tasted best in the winter.

Following his trip to Manchuria, Kim's musical studies intensified. During his first two years at Aakpu students learned the music played at Confucian rituals. In the third year of their studies each student began to specialize in a particular musical instrument. The instrument was not of their own choosing, however; teachers assigned the instruments based on each student's physique and a related assumption of physical abilities. Because of Kim's small stature and health problems (suffered from his early teenage years and forcing constant decisions between tolerating pain and yielding to potentially addictive medication) his teachers thought he did not have the stamina or strength necessary to play wind and percussion instruments. So he began to specialize in the *haegŭm*, a two-stringed fiddle used since the Koryŏ period (918–1392). The *haegŭm* continued to be the primary focus of Kim's musical studies for many years. In 1967, he was designated a Human Cultural Asset for his expertise on this instrument as played for special ceremonies at Chongmyo, a Confucian shrine dedicated to royal ancestors.

In March of 1926, at the age of seventeen, Kim graduated from Aakpu. As was typical at the time, he and his fourteen classmates became teachers at the school, and continued their studies in an advanced curriculum as well as their performing for special events.

The month following graduation brought both an important performance and considerable turmoil in Seoul. On April 26, Sunjong, Korea's last king, died. Just three years earlier Kim and his classmates had danced at Sunjong's fiftieth birthday celebration. Now they would perform on a sadder occasion. Protocol mandated a forty-day mourning period before the king was buried. In addition, it was necessary to move the tomb of the last queen, Queen Min, who had been assassinated in 1895, so that the final resting places of these important people would be together. Both events would bring with them elaborate ceremonies, and both would lure hundreds of thousands of grief-filled Koreans to the streets of Seoul.

Prior to these events, political activities among Koreans had escalated and there was keen interest in pushing, once again, toward independence. Seven years earlier, at the time of the former King Kojong's 1919 funeral, political activists took advantage of the gathering of throngs of people in the city of Seoul. The execution of funeral rites became a time for a massive demonstration. But hopes for a peaceful showing of concerns for independence failed, and there was a great deal of brutality. Because of the date on which the demonstration occurred, it became known as the March First Movement. Now, in 1926, the Koreans had lived through seven more years of Japanese occupation and sought a successful reprisal. But the Japanese remembered the March First Movement that had taken place under similar circumstances. Wary of possible uprisings, the militia was on guard against the anticipated high level of emotion.

On June 9, 1926, there was a ceremony, similar to a funeral, to move Queen Min's body. Kim and members of the Aakpu staff provided music as part of the festivities, with Kim playing his primary instrument, the *haegŭm*. The next day there were ceremonial activities for the burial of the king, and the political upheaval of what became known as the June 10th Independence Movement. Young people distributed fliers as they shouted, "Long live Korean independence." As had happened during the March First Movement, tensions rose. There was much shouting, and people were arrested and tortured.

By the young age of seventeen, Kim had experienced what many people only read about in history books and fairy tales—the repercussions of an occupied country, political movements seeking independence, and performances at a royal birthday and funeral rites.

But the practicalities of life moved on, and Kim and his former classmates continued their teaching, performing, and studying. Ha Kyu-il, a vocalist who was well-known among the common people, was invited to teach. Because there had previously been no written documentation for this music, Ha worked to devise a detailed notation system as he was teaching. This contributed to the eventual publication of notated scores of numerous songs that are still sung today, scores to which Kim contributed, and eventually to Kim's own authorship, in 1971, of the *Chŏngak yanggŭmbo*, a book of scores for the *yanggŭm*.

Kim stayed at Aakpu for many years, expanding his performing abilities, gaining experience in teaching a number of musical instruments, contributing to the documentation of instrumental music traditions, and performing in a variety of contexts. Together with Aakpu colleagues, from 1927 to 1931 he performed in outdoor music concerts at Ch'anggyŏngwŏn (the name used for Ch'anggyŏnggung, a palace used as a public park at that time) at cherry blossom time in the spring. He also performed in live broadcasts of traditional music at Korea's first radio station, and in the late 1930s he participated in recording music for the performance tours of Ch'oe Sŭng-hŭi, one of the earliest of Korea's dancers to experiment with creating new dance forms (see Chapter 8).

Despite his commitment to Aakpu and the strong relationships he developed there, the school was not to be Kim's permanent place of employment. Although dance and music performers had been important contributors to events of the royal court prior to the Japanese occupation, as individuals they were not looked on favorably, even in the days of the court. Their inferior status continued, and even increased, at various times during the occupation. Sometimes family relationships were severed for those indulging in the performing arts. Kim's family looked favorably on his teaching and performing, but his income was never high. As Japanese control began to tighten once again it affected the administration of Aakpu. Problems emerged regarding equitable treatment and advancement among the staff, all of which impacted salaries. In June of 1940, after eighteen years as a student and then staff member at an institution where he thought he would stay forever, Kim decided it was time to move on. Fortunately for traditional Korean dance and music, this move was only temporary, and Kim continued his involvement with the performing arts in other contexts.

Supporting a wife and four children on his meager salary while various groups strove for political superiority made life very difficult. Although jostled in his career pursuits, Kim managed to maintain contact with dance and music. Through colleagues, when he left Aakpu he obtained a position at a *kwŏnbŏn* (the Chosŏn Kwŏnbŏn Kisaeng Yŏnsŭpso). When the Japanese took over and the court was abolished, the *kwŏnbŏn*, or public entertainers' school, became the primary training institution for female dancers. Kim's work at the *kwŏnbŏn* was administrative, involving supervision to insure that the young women were properly trained and scheduling the women to go to restaurants, bars, and private houses to perform. His new job provided him the opportunity to renew his previous brief encounter with dance; he was continually drawn to watching the women's dance classes. Within only a year, however, he lost his job. To curtail expenses so that more funds would be available for escalating war activities, the Japanese placed restrictions on entertainment, and several *kwŏnbŏn* were combined. Many staff members were laid off, and since Kim did not have seniority, he was not asked to continue. He moved on to a restaurant and bar to assist with the female entertainers there.

In 1942, in an effort to maintain morale among Japanese soldiers and Koreans sent to work in military-related activities, the Japanese government formed three performing groups to travel around the countryside and entertain the workers. Kim responded to a newspaper announcement, sang the mandatory "audition song," and became a musician with Chosŏn Aktae, the group established to perform folk music and dance. During his travels Kim performed for workers at carbide and cement factories and coal mines. He liked to travel and was always excited to see new places. He collected small rocks as mementos of the many mines where he performed, but his precious keepsakes were all lost later during the Korean War.

When winter set in, and travel became difficult, the groups returned to Seoul and were disbanded. Kim then discovered that for people not supported by the Japanese government, as he had been while performing with Chosŏn Aktae, life was extremely harsh. Food rationing was severe, and even for those who could scrape together money, meat and staples were in short supply. Colleagues suggested that Kim find employment as a musician accompanying shaman rituals. For many this reflected still further degradation for a performing artist. Although dance was an important part of royal activities during the Chosŏn dynasty, dancers themselves were not highly regarded. This stigma increased with the termination of the court and the establishment of female entertainers' unions and schools. As Kim moved from the formal school that succeeded the institution that had trained court dancers and musicians to his association with the entertainers' schools, he broadened his relationships with people generally considered lower class. Participating in shaman rituals meant being involved with individuals who were regarded even lower still. Initially uncomfortable at the prospect of working in such an environment, Kim feared the approaching winter. Ultimately, the well-being of his wife and four children took precedence.

Since dance was part of many shaman rituals, this was a chance for Kim to reconnect, once again, with this aspect of his earlier training and to broaden his familiarity with different kinds of dance. Despite the inferior status many ascribed to dancers, Kim was growing to love this art form. Following his dance debut at the king's birthday party in 1923 and his graduation from Aakpu in 1926, he continued, at various times, to learn more about dance. Because the Japanese prohibited the performance of court dance from 1910 to 1922, the dances Kim learned at Aakpu were reconstructions of those that had been performed in the days of Korea's last royal court. During his brief involvement with female entertainers, he was exposed to some new choreographies and folk dances. While accompanying shaman rituals in the early 1940s, he was able to expand the scope of his dance knowledge even further and became increasingly committed to both dance and music.

In the mid-1950s, following the end of the Korean War, South Korea experienced a nationalistic surge and efforts were made in many areas to re-establish a solid Korean identity. In this environment, Kim opened his own dance studio in Seoul. In 1956 his students gave their first recital. During this time he also rejoined the staff of Aakpu, which became known as Kungnip Kugagwŏn, the National Classical Music Institute (and in the late 1990s, as the National Center for Korean Traditional Performing Arts). He began to create dances of his own, choreographing more than five dance-dramas based on traditional Korean stories. Concurrent with his efforts at innovative ways to present Korean dance, he always maintained strong movement ties to older, more traditional forms.

In 1960 Kim received the Seoul City Cultural Award (Seoul-shi Munhwasang) for his experimental presentations of traditional dance; he choreographed Ch'ŏyongnang, a dance-drama based on the traditional story of Ch'ŏyong (see Chapter 4). This was the first time the award was presented to a dancer. He subsequently received ten prizes from the Korean National Academy of Arts for his contributions in the areas of dance and music. In 1968 the government designated him a National Living Treasure for Royal Ancestor Shrine music and dance. In 1971 he was again designated a National Living Treasure, this time for Ch'ŏyongmu, an important court dance he had learned from his teachers at Aakpu, who had reconstructed the dance from historical documents (see Chapter 4). Many times he returned to such documents himself to try to reconstruct dances on his own, and in 1983 he staged a reconstruction of Hak Yŏnhwadae Ch'ŏyongmu Hapsŏl, a suite of three court dances (see Chapter 4). Each of the three dances had been reconstructed previously, but this was the first time an attempt was made to find a way to combine them as a suite, as described in court documents. In 1997 he was presented an award by the *Chosŏn Ilbo* (a major Korean newspaper) for his contributions to the perpetuation of traditional Korean dance through research, writing, teaching, and performing.

Kim's exposure to dances of other countries increased over the years. During the colonial period he saw dances performed by Japanese *geisha* (female entertainers comparable to Korean *kisaeng*). In 1945, after liberation, he saw a Chinese ribbon dance, which, he believes, influenced some of the ways Korean dancers manipulate their sleeves. In 1964, while on a performing tour in the United States, he was particularly struck by the quality and creativity he saw in a performance of the famous American modern dance company of José Limón.

Kim saw many kinds of dance, but was never tempted to try to learn anything other than Korean dance, nor to incorporate dance styles from other countries into his own choreography. He believes, however, that the kinds of experimentation occurring in dance in Korea today are important. He tells his students they are more fortunate than he: Having studied only Korean dance, he stands on only one leg; with their opportunities to study both Korean dance and foreign dance, they stand on two legs. But he is quick to add that any dance style is difficult to master fully, and therefore it is important to have a solid foundation and pursue a single focus. He also believes there is so much variety in Korean dance that it is not necessary to borrow from foreign dance; it is possible to be creative from a purely Korean dance base.

Although primarily involved with dance and music as a teacher and performer, Kim's early music studies were not limited to learning how to play different instruments; they included learning how to make instruments as well. He was taught how to construct a *p'iri*, a double reed instrument, and had to go to a funeral home to obtain the correct wood, which was the same as that used to make coffins. He used a knife, a drill, and wire to adjust the thickness of the wood, the size of the finger holes, and the distance between the holes in order to make an instrument that would produce the best tones. In 1932 the Japanese government instructed the Aakpu staff to make a set of *p'yŏnjong* (the large metal bells) and *p'yŏn'gyŏng* (a set of large jade chimes) to send to Manchuria for the coronation of Pu Yi, the last emperor of China. Kim observed the process of smelting metal for the bells and obtaining and cutting the jade. When the jade chimes were near to completion, one of Kim's teachers gave him a pitch pipe and asked him to help tune the instrument. All of these experiences helped him, in later years, to maintain his own musical instruments.

Following his days as a student and then staff member of the former court music school, his involvement with the female entertainers' union, and performances as a roving musician and shaman ritual accompanist, Kim was invited to teach music at Ewha Woman's University and Seoul National University. Since that time he has continued to teach at universities in Korea as well as abroad, and has taught both music and dance.

Kim's active life of study, performing, and teaching did not prevent him from having a rich family life. In 1931 he married Pak Chun-ju, the sister of a fellow Aakpu student. Over the years they had eight children—five girls and three boys. Poverty and difficult times during war years led to the early deaths of two of the girls, and the 1990 death of a son left only five children, all but one of whom live in the United States. In 1994 his wife passed away.

There was always much love in Kim's family. His children say that he was an even-tempered person, and seldom got angry. He was always quiet, and his wife told stories of how he seldom spoke when they first got married. His children who resided there often encouraged him to move to the United States, but he felt that doing so would create a burden for them. He would have to learn to drive and do things he wasn't used to in order to maintain the kind of independence he had when he was in his more familiar surroundings in Korea. And as long as he was in Korea, he could continue active involvement in teaching and performing at many different places.

When Kim's children were young, they were never really aware of what their father did. Kim Chŏng-wŏn, his second oldest daughter, recalls being surprised at seeing her father's students perform in a dance program in the 1950s; she had no idea he was so involved with dance and that he was so good at training dancers. When she expressed an interest in learning to perform, her father tried to discourage her. He was all too familiar with the negative attitudes toward dancers. When she persisted he finally said it would be all right, but that she would have to learn from someone else. She did so, but eventually her father agreed to teach her, and when he opened his own studio she became his assistant.

Through performances and teaching Kim Ch'ŏn-hŭng has contributed to spreading Korean dance worldwide, but perhaps his greatest influence outside Korea has been felt in Hawai'i. In the 1960s Korean dancer Halla Huhm, who had moved to Hawai'i in the mid-1900s and set up a dance studio there (see Chapter 9), returned to Korea to study with him. She subsequently invited Kim to visit and teach at her studio. She also sponsored Kim's second oldest daughter, who emigrated to the United States and assisted at the dance studio. Huhm and Kim's daughter, as well as Kim himself, taught classes at the University of Hawai'i.

Throughout all of his experiences Kim maintained a sense of humor. He took childlike delight in small pranks and in turning dark things into lighthearted jokes. This attitude permeates his relationships with people, his teaching, and his studying. The *yanggŭm*, Kim's secondary instrument, is difficult to play. A dulcimer with fourteen sets of wire strings stretched over and through round holes bored in two metal bridges, the strings are struck with a small, light, padded bamboo beater held in the right hand. Since all the strings are close together, a tremendous amount of spatial sensitivity is needed to strike the correct string. When he was young, Kim and other students would hold contests to see who could play *yanggŭm* best at night—in total darkness.

While he was overseeing activities at the *kwŏnbŏn*, Kim realized that the young women were particularly averse to practicing a difficult movement pattern in the summer heat. Whenever it came time to rehearse *yŏnp'ungdae*, a movement involving many rapid turns, the women decided not to exert themselves. To motivate them he promised a reward: If they would work hard, he would treat them all to Popsicles. Practice sessions perked up, and he provided treats for everyone.

Once when he was preparing his students at Ewha University for a Christmas performance, Kim realized that the student who played the *tanso*, a small flute, was not particularly strong musically. He felt it would enhance the performance to have another student, who was more skillful, play from backstage at the same time. Following the performance a colleague told him that he had heard the *tanso* played incorrectly at one point, but that at the same time he also heard the correct melody coming from somewhere else. Kim revealed his camouflage, and he and his colleague had many a good laugh each time they thought about the incident.

On another occasion, when some young female entertainers came to perform at the radio station with Kim and his male colleagues in the 1930s, the gentlemen told the women that if they wanted to play well they first had to bow to the microphone. The men all smiled with glee as the young women got up *en masse* and dutifully paid their respects to the equipment of modern technology.

Professor Yi Hye-gu, a prominent Korean ethnomusicologist, provides an analogy for Korean culture that can readily be used to describe the life of Kim Ch'ŏn-hŭng. Yi describes Korean culture as being like a sand castle built by a child at the edge of the water: The child builds the castle, waves come in and tear it down, and eventually the child rebuilds the castle. In a similar fashion, Korean culture was built up, then torn down by foreign invasions, either through war or simply through contact and exposure, and then the Koreans built it up again.

Kim Ch'ŏn-hŭng could easily be compared to the child, continually involved with the castle of traditional Korean dance and music. He has endured many hardships and, indeed, turned them to his advantage; he has taken bleak moments and made light of them so they could be tolerated; he has experienced tremendous modernization over his long years; and he has always remained faithful to Korea's traditional performing arts. He believes he was chosen to do court dance and music, this was his destiny. He always accepted what life placed before him and made the best of it, and he always worked to maintain the identity of traditional Korean culture.

Part III

BEYOND KOREA'S SHORES

8

Ch'oe Sŭng-hŭi

A Korean Dancer in the United States

On December 19, 1937, the elegantly appointed Chichibu Maru set sail from Tokyo for San Francisco. Among the 138 passengers on board was a young woman who had appeared in a film and become known as "the dancing princess of the peninsula."[1] Lines of people had circled the Seoul and Tokyo theaters in hopes of obtaining tickets for her farewell performances. The parents of this twenty-six-year-old woman, whose beauty captivated people everywhere she went, had once been aristocrats of Seoul. Although born Ch'oe Sŭng-hŭi, she had become known as Sai Shoki, the Japanese pronunciation of her name. When she returned to Tokyo three years later she would bring with her newspaper clippings, photographs, and other memorabilia documenting her performances in the Americas. She would go on to perform for military troops in China and Manchuria, set up a major dance institution in North Korea, be elected a representative of the People's Congress, and receive a medal from the North Korean government. By the late 1960s her husband was purged and downgraded to a low-class subway laborer, her daughter publicly criticized her, and she was stripped of her congressional position and forced to work at tasks having nothing to do with the arts (Takashima Yusaburo and Chŏng Pyŏng-ho 1994).

What did U.S. audiences think of the dancing of this young woman? How did her travels affect her development as an artist? How did she fare in the West as Japanese impact spread throughout the world and the United States was on the brink of entering World War II? In this chapter I examine the North American tour of Ch'oe Sŭng-hŭi: how she was presented to the public, the nature of her performances, and how, according to the press, she was received.

Biographical Sketch

There is no definitive literature available on details of Ch'oe's life. Much that exists is more effusively laudatory than analytical, and, because of her involvement with Japan and both North and South Korea during politically volatile times, there are significant gaps in information. Comments are often more concerned with political issues (such as reclaiming Ch'oe and her importance to Korean dance or justifying her Japanese support) than with efforts to substantiate facts. Biographical information presented here, therefore, is neither extensive nor definitive; it gives a sketch of Ch'oe's life and selected events that provide a backdrop against which to better understand her American tour.[2]

Ch'oe Sŭng-hŭi was born into an upper-class (*yangban*) family on November 24, 1911, a little more than one year after Korea officially became a colony of Japan. Unlike Korean dancers of previous generations whose education was limited almost entirely to dance and other art forms, Ch'oe received a public school education.[3] She skipped several grades in elementary school and graduated from Sukmyŏng Women's High School in 1922, where she excelled in most subjects and was particularly noted for her singing ability. Ch'oe wanted to study at a music school in Tokyo, but was too young to apply. By this time she became familiar with the financial trials that would mark much of her early artistic life; her father's alcoholism, as well as land policies implemented by Japan, deprived the family of its former wealth.[4] She remained in Korea until 1926.

In the spring of that year, at the urging of her brother she attended a performance by visiting Japanese modern dancer Ishii Baku. Mesmerized by what she saw, she became interested in studying dance; but she was also concerned with prevailing attitudes toward dancers. In an autobiography written when she was only twenty-five years old she said:

> I thought dance was something low and crude. But with the influence of my brother's words, as I watched the stage my whole being was quickly attracted . . . by some kind of powerful inspiration. . . . Ishii's famous works . . . have a powerful underlying feeling that evoked the spirit hiding at the bottom of my heart . . . (in Hirabayashi Hisae 1977:188)

Encouraged by her brother, Ch'oe met with Ishii to inquire about studying with him and, much to the chagrin of her family, particularly her mother, she followed Ishii back to Japan. She studied with him for about eight years, with several periods during which they severed their student-teacher relationship and then resumed it. Throughout those years she performed both in Seoul and Tokyo, at some times with Ishii's company and at others independently. She opened a dance studio in Seoul, but because of financial difficulties it was short-lived.

While continuing her dance studies and establishing a performing career, in 1931 Ch'oe married An Mak, a political activist who played a major role in her life. Over the years they had a daughter, who became a dancer, and a son, and An completed a university degree in Russian literature. In 1935 Ch'oe signed a contract to star in a movie based, at least in part, on her life. The title of the film, *Hanto no Maihimei*, The Dancing Princess of the Peninsula, was the way in which Ch'oe was often referred to in later years. Ch'oe's career began to escalate, and in addition to success as a dancer she became a popular female icon, appearing in newspaper advertisements for stationery, makeup, and snacks.

In 1936 plans began to evolve for an international performing tour. In a letter dated February 23, 1937, addressed to the American Secretary of State in Washington, O. Gaylord Marsh, then American Consul General in Seoul, indicated his presence at the farewell performance of "Miss Sai Shoki" and stated she was "said to have obtained, as a result of a performance at the American Embassy in Tokyo, a contract for six months in the United States."[5] Japanese occupation policies sought to eliminate the Korean language and Ch'oe Sŭng-hŭi had become known as Sai Shoki, the Japanese pronunciation of her name. Accompanying Gaylord's letter was a copy of an article attributed to *The Seoul Press* (Anonymous 1937a), in which Marsh is quoted as saying that Sai was "remarkable," and predicted "an outstanding future for her." Following the performance Marsh attended, Ch'oe returned to Tokyo for a series of farewell performances before departing in December for a tour to North and South America and Europe. It is generally believed Ch'oe was the first Korean dancer to perform in the United States.

Upon completing her two-year performing tour, Ch'oe returned to Japan at the end of 1940, just before the United States entered World War II. Prior to her tour Japan had become Ch'oe's primary home, but when she returned, she began to move back and forth between Japan, Korea, and China, at some times to perform and at other times to flee the rapidly changing political pressures. In July of 1945, she and her family went to what became North Korea when the peninsula was officially divided.

Ch'oe performed in North Korea, set up a school, and eventually became a government officer. Her school gained national support and she received a medal for her contributions to the arts. Her husband became increasingly involved in political activities, but, because of his views, lost favor with the North Korean government. A 1986 Japanese publication said Ch'oe, her daughter, and her husband had been arrested and executed, but gave no dates (in Takashima Yusaburo and Chŏng Pyŏng-ho 1994:214). The same year a Korean dancer resident in Japan reported that name lists published annually in North Korea had included Ch'oe until 1964, but not after that time (ibid.).[6]

Ch'oe is widely known in both Korea and Japan—among dancers as well as nondancers, and is considered, by many, to be the founder of the type of dance now known as *shinmuyong*, or new dance. (See Chapters 1 and 2.)

Dance Training and Experiences
Prior to International Tour

Ch'oe describes her introduction to dance as coming from her father:

> When my father was in a good mood he stayed at home relaxing
> and when he drank too much he got carried away and showed me a
> dance called Kutkŏri ch'um. . . . In Korea this dance was presented
> at parties when people started getting drunk. While I watched him
> dance Kutkori ch'um I was memorizing it without even knowing it.
> (in Hirabayashi Hisae 1977:187)

Ch'oe's formal training, however, did not begin until 1926, the year she
followed Ishii Baku, the Japanese modern dancer she saw perform in
Seoul, to Tokyo. The training she received there was based largely on the
modern dance schooling of her teacher.

Ishii's dance training and influences were diverse. In Japan he studied
Japanese dance, ballet (Cecchetti style, from an Italian resident in Japan),
and some modern dance (with a man who had been influenced by early
U.S. modern dancer Isadora Duncan and the eurhythmics of the Swiss
Emile Jacques-Dalcroze). He toured Europe and was greatly impressed
by new developments in modern dance there, particularly the German
expressionist works of Mary Wigman, and was later influenced by the
works of U.S. modern dancers Ruth St. Denis and Ted Shawn (whose
Denishawn company performed in Japan in 1925 and 1926).[7] Despite his
initial training in ballet, Ishii questioned its validity and favored modern
dance, but believed directly importing western dance was boring and that
there was a limit to simply imitating its form. He wanted to create a new
kind of Japanese dance that was not just an imitation of other forms, and
was concerned with issues of humanity and modern society. His works
were noted for being harsh, often dealing with issues of social injustice
and poverty in a realistic manner. Ishii believed dance should not be technique first and then thoughts and emotions layered on top; thoughts and
emotions must germinate first, and then technique and form will follow.

As Ishii's work developed he made a conscious effort to reject traditional Japanese dance, which he felt was trapped in the past. But he eventually came to believe that his roots had subconsciously imbued his dance
with both a Japanese feeling and originality, and that one must "reconstruct one's own ethnic spirit using an international or universal technique"
(Hirabayashi Hisae 1977:193). Ishii's dance is characterized by a Japanese dancer and writer as being "his own style, neither German nor American. He created Japanese narrative dance, using Western music and an
interesting combination of dance elements, including mime" (Wakamatsu
Miki 1995:210).

Ishii was initially reluctant to take Ch'oe on as a student because of
her lack of training in, and even exposure to, dance. He did decide to

accept her, though, and because of the poverty into which her family had slipped by this time, he and his wife helped to support her during her studies in Japan.

Ishii was a strict taskmaster. As he began to see Ch'oe develop as a dancer in a style originating in the West, and acknowledged the impact of his Japanese roots on the essence of his own dancing, he became concerned with Ch'oe's rejection of her Korean heritage. Since traditional Korean dance was then in a period of decline (due to Japanese policies and concerns with modernization), he told Ch'oe that if she did not do Korean dance he wondered who would. At that time Han Sŏng-jun, a famous Korean dancer who was developing a new dance style strongly rooted in traditional Korean forms, was in Japan. Ch'oe studied with him, but only briefly. This planted seeds for her interest in the dance of her own people, leading to some explorations of traditional Korean dance when she returned to Korea.

As Ch'oe matured both personally and in dance, she began to develop ideas about how to integrate her western training and the dance heritage of her birthplace. She became dissatisfied with performing only the works of Ishii and wanted to follow her own artistic vision. Since Ishii insisted on loyalty, this, together with personality differences, created tension between them, and she returned to Seoul to work independently. Ultimately the two reconciled their differences, and Ch'oe studied again, for a short time, with Ishii, and then embarked on her own career.

Ch'oe's initial performances in Korea were not well received, and she eventually shifted away from the style advocated by Ishii. She became intent on developing a new style of Korean dance, one that was "Korean in essence but that was capable of responding to and expressing modern concerns" (in Choe Sang-cheul 1996:211–212). She subsequently became extremely popular in both Korea and Japan. Her physical beauty was a constant source of comment and people flocked to her performances. Despite Korea's colonized status and the foreign influences on her dance, she was identified as being Korean and "was worshipped as an authentic symbol of ethnicity. When she performed in a public government building in Seoul people formed a line almost one kilometer long to buy tickets" (Chŏng Pyŏng-ho in Takashima Yusaburo and Chŏng Pyŏng-ho 1994:37).

A Japanese writer describes Ch'oe's dance by saying she "is not just dancing Korean dance as it is. She makes the old into the new and the weak into the strong and revitalizes what had died" (Kawabata Yasunari in Takashima Yusaburo and Chŏng Pyŏng-ho 1994:148). Some members of her audience considered this inappropriate and criticized her for doing traditional dance in nontraditional ways (Nishikawa Tadahiro in Takashima Yusaburo and Chŏng Pyŏng-ho 1994:148). Conflicting views from audiences and critics prevailed—in Korea, Japan, and subsequently in the United States. An interesting view of the nature of what she did is provided in comments prior to her departure for the United States by her own teacher, Ishii Baku, who said her Korean dances are just entertainment for the audience. Such a thing as reviving Korean dance should be done on the side. . . . Bringing joy to people and moving people are two different things in meaning. Her Korean dance was effective in simply bringing people joy. However, her mission in artistic dance does not end there.[8] (in Takashima Yusaburo and Chŏng Pyŏng-ho 1994:166)

Had Ch'oe known about and understood these words of her teacher, she may have been better prepared for the early reviews she received in the United States.

Outline of the U.S. Tour and Repertoire

Ch'oe began her U.S. tour on the heels of the Depression, at a time when many young American dancers were struggling to establish modern dance. Audiences in New York, Los Angeles, and San Francisco, in particular, were being exposed to choreographic experimentation. In addition, several Asian performers, most notably Indian dancer Uday Shankar, were touring and awakening audiences to vastly different styles of dance than they had previously seen. Newspapers carried advertisements as well as advance stories on upcoming dance events, and reviews of performances, often authored by music specialists or any journalist who happened to be available on a particular performance date, were frequent.

Before detailing the way in which Ch'oe was presented and received in the United States, I will briefly outline her performances and provide a few summary comments on some of the dances she performed. This will contextualize the performances and show some of the relationships between her repertoire and Korean dance in general, facilitating a deeper understanding of the discussion to follow. Because Ch'oe became known professionally in Japan and Korea by the Japanese pronunciation of her name, and because it was the Japanese version that appeared in all American publications and documents, I use the name Sai Shoki from this point on. This is in no way intended to take sides in debates relating to Ch'oe's political allegiances nor to the name by which she *should* be known. It is, rather, to accurately reflect how she was known in the United States, and to avoid confusion when referring here to direct quotes from American sources in which she is identified as Sai Shoki.[9]

According to the letter of Consul General O. Gaylord Marsh, Sai had an initial contract for $150,000 to perform for six months in the United States (Marsh 1937). But sponsorship of her performances changed, and Sai extended her tour to include South America and Europe as well as the United States. When she first set out, she was accompanied by "Japanese pianist Koshun Lee," who played for her early performances, and also by her husband, who served as both percussionist for performances and personal manager.

I have confirmed ten performances Sai gave in the United States.[10] Appendix 7 provides dates, times, theaters, and, where known, local sponsors and managing companies for these performances. Following her San Francisco arrival on January 11, 1938, Sai's U.S. debut occurred eleven days later on January 22. She then left for Los Angeles, where she performed once in February, and moved on to New York City for two performances in February and March. There was then a hiatus of eight months in Sai's performing activities, most likely because of political events and management problems (discussed below). Her financial situation apparently became difficult, and she began to model for a painter in New York (Takashima Yusaburo and Chŏng Pyŏng-ho 1994:219). Her next documented U.S. performance did not occur until November, again in New York City, after which she left for Europe, where she performed extensively in numerous countries.

As the war intensified in Europe, Sai returned to the United States and performed five more times. Essentially retracing her first U.S. circuit, she performed twice in New York, in December of 1939 and February of 1940, and added a February performance in Chicago before returning to the west coast for performances in Los Angeles in March and San Francisco in April. Her travels then took her to Central and South America for performances. As war tensions increased and the United States was poised to enter the struggles, Sai returned to San Francisco and departed, on November 24, 1940, for Tokyo.

Confirming the repertoire Sai performed in the United States is problematic. Because performance repertoire often changes from the time an announcement and printed program are produced, the surest indication of a particular dance actually having been performed is its acknowledgment in a postperformance review. But not all dances performed are commented on in reviews. Complicating efforts to identify the repertoire, and potential links to dances she performed prior to her U.S. tour, is that the titles of Sai's dances were translated into English from either Korean or Japanese, and translations were inconsistent. It is also possible that, even though dance titles remained constant, Sai modified choreography of individual dances and may, herself, have changed some titles.

Based on notes in printed programs, newspaper coverage, and photographs, Appendix 8 identifies individual dances Sai likely performed in the United States and gives a brief description of each. During the course of her U.S. appearances Sai probably performed some two dozen different dances, with each program including between twelve and fifteen items. In three of the dances, Dream of Youth, Greatest General Under the Sun, and Korean Vagabond, Sai wore masks. The mask in Korean Vagabond is similar to those used today in the traditional masked-dance drama of Pongsan, and this dance of Sai's appears to have been based on the traditional form. How closely Korean Vagabond resembled traditional dance movements, however, is not known (Figure 33). The hat that is part of the mask of Greatest General Under the Sun is in the style of that worn for-

Figure 33. Ch'oe Sŭng-hŭi performs Korean Vagabond (Dance Collection, New York Public Library).

merly by court officials, but the mask is unlike any worn in traditional dance forms (Figure 34). The story that, according to printed programs and brochures, served as the basis for this dance (see Appendix 8), is rooted in Korean customs. Dream of Youth also appears to be based on traditional practices, but the absence of photographs prevents making clear links to older dances.

Bodhisattva is a particularly intriguing dance for two reasons. First, it would be quite unusual for a Korean woman to publicly expose her body (or even suggest its exposure, if the basis of the costume was a kind of body stocking) in the manner in which it is revealed in the costume of this dance (Figure 35). Second, the similarity between the primary photograph of this dance and photographs of American dancer Ruth St. Denis is quite extraordinary (Figure 36 and 37). (This is discussed later in this chapter.)

The dance identified variously as Scarf Dance, Geisha Dance (*geisha* being the Japanese term for a dance entertainer), and Kisaeng Dance[11] appears to be some version of what is identified today as salp'uri, a dance variously attributed to traditional shaman dances and the choreography of Han Sŏng-jun, the Korean with whom Sai studied very briefly. (See Chapters 1 and 6 for further comments on salp'uri.) The Drum Dance (Figure 38), which in her fourth U.S. performance Sai began to include, together with the Scarf Dance, as a suite known as Kisaeng Dances, is photographically similar to dances performed today titled Changgoch'um, a dance in which an hourglass-shaped drum is fastened to the dancer's

Figure 34. Ch'oe Sŭng-hŭi performs Greatest General Under the Sun (Dance Collection, New York Public Library).

Figure 35. Ch'oe Sŭng-hŭi performs Bodhisattva. Photo courtesy of Soichi Sunami (Dance Collection, New York Public Library). Courtesy of the Sunami family.

waist, and that has roots in traditional farmers' dance and music (see Chapter 1).

Buddhist Temptress resembles dances now known as sŭngmu, or monk's dance (Figure 39). Today the original version of this dance is also generally attributed to Han Sŏng-jun, but a title, in English or Korean, never includes the word "temptress." One story of the dance's origin, which tells of a young woman who sought to tempt a Buddhist monk, is described in some of Sai's programs. But her coquettish interpretation,

Figure 36. Ruth St. Denis performs Kuan Yin. Courtesy of the Jane Sherman Collection.

Figure 37. Ruth St. Denis performs Kwannon. Photo by Soichi Sunami (Jane Sherman Collection). Courtesy of the Sunami family.

reflected in photographs and newspaper comments, is never a part of today's version of the dance.

There is little documentation describing Two Court Dances and the Sleeve Dance (Figure 40), but it is likely these bore some similarity, in costume if nothing else, to dances previously done for entertainment in the royal courts. Several uncaptioned photographs show Sai in a costume resembling those seen in court documents and used in court dances performed today, but she sports a rather broad smile that would have been unlikely in the days of the Confucian court[12] (Figure 41).

Dances such as Young Korean Bridegroom (Figure 42), Whalyang, Two Folk Dances, and Three Traditional Rhythms appear to have some grounding in traditional Korean customs. It is impossible to determine for certain if Young Korean Bridegroom is an English title for Ehea Noara,

Figure 38. Ch'oe Sŭng-hŭi in a studio portrait with the drum she used in Drum Dance. Photo by Soichi Sunami (Dance Collection, New York Public Library). Courtesy of the Sunami family.

Figure 39. Ch'oe Sŭng-hŭi performs Buddhist Temptress. Photo by Chester Kohn (Dance Collection, New York Public Library). Courtesy of Dance Magazine.

Figure 40. Ch'oe Sŭng-hŭi performs Sleeve Dance. Photo by Soichi Sunami (Dance Collection, New York Public Library). Courtesy of the Sunami family.

Figure 41. Ch'oe Sŭng-hŭi performs Ancient Spring (Dance Collection, New York Public Library).

a dance that seems to have been her signature piece in Japan and Korea. The popularity in Japan, Korea, and the United States of dances with these two titles, captioned photographs of Ehea Noara from Japan and Korea and Young Korean Bridegroom in the United States, several advance announcements including the title Ehea Noara, and the fact that the words "*ehea*" and "*noara*" have no meaning in Korean and therefore could not be translated, all suggest these dances might be one and the same.

Although program notes describe Sword Dance as Sai's attempt to reconstruct a dance of the past, and there is, indeed, such a dance performed today (see Chapter 5), the costume for this dance bears no relationship whatever to the costume used now nor to any pictorial representations of the dance from the Chosŏn dynasty.

It is most likely the majority of the dances Sai performed in the United States were choreographed and performed prior to her arrival on American shores, and that she rechoreographed some of them while abroad. Despite changes that occurred in her program from her first U.S. performance to her last, these changes were largely the result of substituting dances from an already-choreographed repertoire and reordering the program.

Advance Announcements and Newspaper Reviews

Sai's American debut was preceded by considerable press coverage. In February of 1937 she gave a farewell performance in Seoul to sold-out

Figure 42. Ch'oe Sŭng-hŭi performs Young Korean Bridegroom (Dance Collection, New York Public Library).

houses. In addition to quoting then–American Consul General Marsh as describing Sai as "remarkable," the author of a *Seoul Press* article continued by stating his belief that during her U.S. tour Sai would "win the hearts of [the] American audience" (Anonymous 1937a). In December of 1937, a month before Sai arrived in the United States, the *Chicago Tribune* included Sai in a photo essay titled "They All Dance" (Anonymous 1937b). At the top of a page containing photographs of Lithuanian, Viennese, Scottish, and Native-American dancers, Sai was shown in a decidedly un-Korean costume and pose with a caption stating, "Rhythm is a universal thing and dancing an international, although varied[,] expression of it. Sai Shoki, Corean [*sic*] dancer, adds a touch of swing to the famed cherry blossom number she will do on her world tour." There are several noteworthy aspects of this photo and its caption: Sai is identified as Korean and not Japanese, despite Korea's colonial status at the time; cherry blossom dances are most often associated with Japan and not Korea;[13] and the costume and dance pose are much more akin to a style of modern dance found in Europe and the United States at the time and beginning to be practiced in Japan than to anything traditionally either Japanese or Korean. Although a similar photograph is included at the end of an elaborate publicity brochure (Figure 43) produced by Hurok Attractions (probably after Sai's west-coast and first New York performances and prior to her November 1938 New York performance, the latter her first managed by Hurok), such photographs were not used in other U.S. newspapers, and during her U.S. tour Sai never performed a dance such as that suggested in the photograph. (Although Sai's early studies and choreographies were akin to western modern dance of the time, beginning in the 1930s she turned to Korean sources as the basis for her creativity (Choe Sang-cheul, personal communication 15 June 1998).)

Almost three dozen articles and advertisements then appeared prior to Sai's San Francisco and Los Angeles performances. These were indicative of the large number of advance stories and photographs publicizing her subsequent performances, and they ranged from small display ads to captioned photographs and stories listing the dances she would perform. (Source citations are not provided here for quoted or paraphrased material appearing in multiple newspapers. Once an article has been cited, it is subsequently referenced in abbreviated format, using only the author's name or the name of the newspaper.)

SAN FRANCISCO DEBUT

Advance information dealing with her first performance in San Francisco commented on Sai's reputation, highlighting her as the "ace box office attraction" and "unspoiled darling" of Japan, Korea, Manchuria, and North China. English-language papers noted her "novel program" that included "religious and ceremonial dances of her country, comic and character sketches, and ancient dances of war." They described her pro-

Figure 43. Ch'oe Sŭng-hŭi in a western-style modern dance portrait (Dance Collection, New York Public Library).

gram as comprising "native Korean dances which are purported to be both exotic and beautiful," and promising "rare glimpses of the traditional dances and music of her native land." Also noted were "elaborate" and "vivid Eastern costumes," designed by "noted Korean artist Chung Wan Kim" (Kim Chŏng-wŏn) and "native musicians" providing "exotic accompaniment." Several papers simply listed anticipated repertoire items to be performed.

None of the English-language newspapers gave coverage to Sai's own comments, in contrast to the Japanese-language *Shinsokai Asahi*. Information contained in some of the latter might have had a significant impact on the way Sai's non-Japanese-speaking audience responded to what they saw. In a January 13 article she is quoted as saying some traditional dances are "too long to perform on stage or too short and simple to perform on stage. So I wanted to create something original and new which fits this contemporary era." The writer goes on to say Sai "has re-interpreted

Korean indigenous dance and re-created pieces" (Anonymous 1938d).
These statements would have contributed to significantly different expectations than English-language sources touting "native Korean dances."

Although four reviewers of Sai's U.S. debut performance in San Francisco found positive things to comment on, all were less than enthusiastic:
"[A]nyone who expected deep revelations of the mystic East . . . was dis-
appointed" (Fried 1938); the "program remained on an even keel of
mildly pleasant, unexciting entertainment" (Frankenstein 1938); "slightly
dull, slightly boring, slightly entertaining"[14] (Fisher 1938). One of the
major criticisms of the reviewers was that the program "lacked bold variety of pace, idea and movement" (Fried), and the "dances were too much
alike" (Fisher). One reviewer offers stronger comments, saying Sai's "solemn portrayal of old Korean scenes, the execution of which involved
more parading around the stage than actual dancing, was a slow motion
feat in itself, while the cloying winsomeness of her comic sketches was
quite in a class by itself" (Costello 1938). That Sai's dances had subtle
variety or minimal dynamics in relation to what San Francisco audiences
might have been used to or expected is hinted at in this statement as well
as in that of another writer who commented on the "very slight physical
exertion required" (Fisher). Sai's subtlety was a negative attribute for her
reviewers, another of whom stated her "vocabulary of gesture and movement is limited" (Frankenstein). One reviewer felt the second half of the
program "devoted to ancient court dances, had far more interest, intrinsically and artistically, than [the] opening folk dances, which had covered a
wide variety of subjects . . . with too little variation in tempo" (Fisher).

Minimal insights into specific dances are provided with indications that
Sai was "always cute, usually pretty (especially as the Flower Girl)," that
Arirang was "somber in mood" and "particularly impressive because of
its more thoughtful aspects," and that Sai was "flirtatious" as a "geisha
girl" (note the use of the Japanese term for a female entertainer rather
than the Korean *kisaeng*) and "coy" as a "Buddhist priestess" (Fisher).

Most writers commented on Sai's physical beauty, albeit in orientalist
terms popular at the time and expressions considered demeaningly gen-
dered by the end of the twentieth century. They described her as "excep-
tionally comely" (Fried), "a very pretty girl" (Frankenstein), and a
"charming little lady" (Fisher) with a "confident, delicately flirtatious
smile" (Fried). One writer spoke of her "softly feminine Eastern poise and
elasticity" (Fried). Reviewers also noted her "wardrobe of beautiful costumes" (Fisher), but one writer commented on them being "silken modern fancies derived from Oriental traditions, . . . sometimes . . . charming[,] . . . often . . . entirely too chic" (Fried).

All four writers were singularly unimpressed with Sai's musical accompaniment, which program notes and reviews indicate was provided primarily by piano and occasionally by Korean percussion instruments.
One writer observed that the "Western harmonizations of Korean motifs
sounded all wrong for a trans-Pacific dance evening" (Fried) and another

questioned "the wisdom and authenticity of piano accompaniments [*sic*]" (Fisher). The latter writer apparently followed up on this troublesome feature and reported she learned "it was only the bad advice given the dancer by friends in the Orient that made her use the piano instead of her Korean orchestra."

Although suggesting a strong orientalist bent, the most concise summary of reviewers' responses is the *San Francisco Chronicle* writer's remark that the performance "seemed more like the sort of thing a somewhat conventional and old-fashioned Occidental artist might bring back from the orient rather than the kind of thing one expected from an artist reared and trained in the traditions of the Far East" (Frankenstein). This clearly reinforces the possibility responses might have been different had reviewers been privy to Sai's own remarks regarding her choreographic intent, as well as details regarding her dance training.

Only two of the four reviews, both of which were unfavorable, were published prior to Sai's January 24 departure from San Francisco. Nevertheless, the Japanese-language *Shinsokai Asahi* reported Sai's "wonderful success" (Anonymous 1938d). Were different yardsticks used to measure success? Was the Japanese press, for political reasons, inclined to support Sai regardless of the views of others? In a *New World-Sun Daily* article published prior to her San Francisco debut Sai is quoted as saying, "If I am a success here I am sure that I shall be successful on my present trip around the world" (in Anonymous 1938f); an almost identical quote is given in a January 12, 1938, *San Francisco Chronicle* article (Anonymous 1938c). Based on subsequent reviews and changes in her program, Sai apparently heeded the comments of her English-language reviewers in an effort to please them and hence be successful. Surely she needed strong conviction and confidence as she proceeded to Los Angeles and New York.

LOS ANGELES DEBUT

Advance publicity for Sai's Los Angeles performance was as extensive as that in San Francisco. Recurring patterns in content and phrasing suggest much specific information was likely provided in advance materials prepared by Sai's managing company (and/or her husband). Frequent statements occur regarding her box office attraction in eastern countries and equal popularity among Chinese and Japanese people, ranking her with Mei Lan-fang and describing her as the Korean Pavlova,[15] and calling attention to her native musicians playing exotic music (despite San Francisco reviewers' negative comments about her nonnative music). Previous descriptions of her elaborate costumes were augmented in the caption of one photograph informing readers that Korean artist-designer "Kim Chung Wan [Kim Chŏng-wŏn] had . . . won first prize in the Oriental exhibit at the Paris Exposition last year" for his paintings (Anonymous 1938a). One article, headlined "A Korean artist designs costumes for a dancer," stated that Kim "attracted widespread attention last Autumn by doing portraits of Stalin, Hitler and the duke of Windsor" (Anonymous 1938b).

Sai's two Los Angeles reviews are more favorable than those from San Francisco. Headlines read "Dance Star Lauded" (Swisher 1938) and "Sai Shoki, Exotic Korean Dancer, Thrills" (Anonymous 1938e). Supporting comments indicated she "won instantaneous favor" (Swisher) and "unanimous approval" (Anonymous) and presented a "fascinating dance recital" that "enthralled her patrons" (Anonymous). General comments about Sai's attractiveness, such as "slim, bright eyed and lovely to look upon" (Swisher) and her coquettish artistry (Anonymous), were much simpler and a bit less demeaning than those in San Francisco papers. Again, note was made of "eye-filling costumes" (Anonymous) that were "exquisite in color and design" (Swisher), but music was evaluated more positively than in San Francisco: "[S]imple native court and folk music . . . [on piano] gave the dancer musical support along with excellent percussion accompaniments [sic]" (Swisher). Both reviewers noted a large audience, and both commented on the fact that spectators were "Oriental and Occidental" (Swisher), although one couched this statement more diplomatically by saying that among the audience "were many countrymen and not a few noted dance and screen stars" (Anonymous).

Considerably more space than in the San Francisco reviews was given in each Los Angeles review to suggesting details of the dances performed. One described Sai generally as a "mime and comedian of persuasive ability," indicating the "later portions of the program were invested with much good humor, both delicately piquant and of the earth," and "it was especially in the circumscribed choreographic patterns and stage designs of the tradition-inspired court dances that Sai Shoki proved indisputable and perfectly poised mistress of the art of projecting herself and her intent across the footlights" (Swisher). The same writer commented more fully on individual dances by saying:

> [D]elineations of such formal dance modes as "Court Lady of Shiragi" [Figure 44] and "Fresco of Rakuro" were contrasted effectively with the universally human poignancy of her "Buddhist Temptress" and "Korean Sweetheart's Farewell." The closing "Young Korean Bridegroom," the gaily colorful "Seoul Fortune Teller," the enchanting blandishments of the "Korean Dancing Girl," the "Festival Dance" and "Peasant Girl" were charming entertainment as well as graceful art. . . . A mask of forbidding ferocity in the satiric "Korean General" and one of great grotesquerie in the "Korean Vagabond" made these dances memorable. In them, too, the artist's hands—at other times flower-like in their exquisite delicacy—became amazingly strong and masculine in appearance.

The other reviewer indicated Sai's "Buddhist temptress and dagger dances were acclaimed the evening's favorites" (Anonymous).

Figure 44. Ch'oe Sŭng-hŭi performs Court Lady of Shiragi. Photo by Soichi Sunami (Dance Collection, New York Public Library). Courtesy of the Sunami family.

Why was Sai reviewed so differently in Los Angeles? No program is available from her San Francisco performance. However, specific mention in reviews from that city of six dances that were also performed in Los Angeles, and mention of the same six dances in the printed program and reviews of her first New York performance after she left Los Angeles, make it likely the entire program in all three cities was identical. A change in reception, therefore, is probably not linked to a change in Sai's repertoire, but possibly to modifications to individual dances. One noticeable difference is that at least three of the four San Francisco reviews were written by music critics (credentials of the fourth reviewer are not known); it is no wonder they focused harshly on music, and likely they were less attuned to dance than one of the Los Angeles writers and many later New York writers, who were dance critics.[16]

FIRST NEW YORK PERFORMANCES

Advance announcements in New York newspapers tended to be briefer than those in San Francisco and Los Angeles, and most often focused on listing titles of dances to be performed. The occasional photographs accompanying performance announcements featured Sai in full costume and dance poses, unlike many of those in California that were simply portraits of the sort one would find on a society page—e.g., Sai attired in a western-style woman's suit and hat with veil.

Reviewers of Sai's February 20, 1938, New York debut performance at the Guild Theatre generally reflected less of an orientalist tendency than those of her previous performances. Although many of the comments were substantively similar to those of west-coast writers, they tended to be less harshly stated than the San Francisco reviews and three were somewhat positive. All commented on Sai's physical beauty and charm, most on her elaborate costumes, and most on what they considered the inappropriateness of piano accompaniment arranged in a western style. One writer noted a "predominantly Japanese" audience that was "most responsive to Miss Shoki's native evocations"[17] (Sanborn 1938). It is unclear if the writer was suggesting ethnic-Japanese or national-Japanese, given the inability of many Americans to distinguish between Japanese and Korean people ethnically, and the fact that Korea was then occupied by Japan, which meant Sai was traveling on a Japanese passport. Sai was, however, always billed as Korean.

New York writers tended to group the dances, but not always in the same way. One delineated lyrical and character dances (Martin 1938a), one sorted dances on the basis of whether Sai performed as a male or female character (JDB 1938), and one singled out "folk dances" (Gilfond 1938). Korean Vagabond was identified by one writer as "the program's high mark" (Martin), and another described it as disclosing "a light humorous touch which won . . . insistent applause . . . and brought about a repetition of the dance" (JDB). A third writer disagreed by indicating Young Korean Bridegroom "brought the most applause," and suggests a rationale for audience favorites in saying that the character dances (which included Korean Vagabond and Young Korean Bridegroom) "were more picturesque and active, and therefore more appreciated" (Kaye 1938). This rationale is corroborated by a comment from another writer that dances demonstrating "vivacity and color," which according to descriptions again included Korean Vagabond and Young Korean Bridegroom, "were welcomed" (Martin). Interestingly, none of the reviewers reiterated the "peasant, court and war dance" categorization in some advance announcements, and the "exotic" descriptor used in display ads for the performance appeared only once, in a headline (JDB).

While one writer enjoyed much of the program's simplicity, stating Sai's "art in her opening contribution was often subtly appealing because of its fragile delicacy of approach and the exquisitely lovely costumes" (JDB), other reviewers reiterated comments of their west-coast counterparts with such remarks as "at present her art seems a bit too mild for these rough-and-tumble precincts" (Martin), "after a while the dancing struck one uninitiated in Korean lore as repetitious and colorless" (Sanborn), "for a New York audience, somewhat sparse, but agreeable enough if taken for what they were: illustrations of folk movement" (Kaye), and the major "interest for an audience in her work lies not in her form but in what the dancer brings by way of native and national materials from Japanese Korea" (Gilfond). The latter comment is particularly interesting in its recognition of Sai as representing the colonized Korea, as well as in the assumption that her dances represented what was "native and national." If Sai was, indeed, the first Korean to perform in the United States, one can only wonder how the writer knew what was "native and national." One writer proposed Sai's dance "would be more effective in joint recital with a contrasting artist," suggesting the New York audience might find her dances of greater interest in smaller doses (Kaye). Sai did, however, generate some kind of charisma, since a return engagement at the Guild Theatre nine months later attracted a large audience, and a reviewer of that event reflected back in time and described this first performance as a "sound if unsensational success" (Kolodin 1938).

Sai's next New York performance was at the 92nd Street Y (Young Men's Hebrew Association) on March 5, 1938, an event that attracted little attention in the press, and apparently no reviews.[18]

Sai performed a second time at New York's Guild Theatre on November 6 of the same year. Three of the reviewers who had written about her first Guild Theatre program were joined by an additional three in commenting on this performance, which included most of the better-received dances from the earlier program as well as several dances new to American audiences. Although negative views of some of the same features of her earlier Guild Theatre performance continued, there were more favorable comments this time. Two reviewers specifically noted changes since her first performance: "[I]n the intervening months she has acquired considerable knowledge in the matter of arranging a program for American audiences, and in general has found more of the tempo of the local recital world" (Martin 1938b); and "there is much to indicate that she has progressed, at least for American audiences" (KT 1938). Both of these comments are noteworthy because they suggest Sai modified her program to cater to her specific audience.

Sai's physical beauty continued to receive comment, as did her costumes. But there was a significant change in comments on music. Sai apparently heeded the cries of her earlier reviewers and this time used music described in advance material and in the printed program as "authentic native accompaniments [*sic*] in recorded form." Reviewers indicated there was also an off-stage percussionist. These changes elicited statements of "immeasurable improvement" (Martin), "added greatly to the spirit" (KT), and "strange sounds that do not seem too strange to Occidental ears" (Anonymous 1939). One can only wonder, however, if these comments were inspired, at least in part, by Sai's dispensing with piano accompaniment (no pianist is credited in the program, as for previous performances), and the statement in the program that "the records of old

Korean music used in this program were specially recorded for Sai Shoki's dances." (As noted in Chapter 7, Kim Ch'ŏn-hŭng participated in sessions to record music for Sai's tour.)

The audience for this performance is described as quite large, and one reviewer noted it included "not only . . . compatriots but . . . a liberal number of other dance lovers" (Kolodin 1938), suggesting that her first audience was largely either Japanese, Korean, or both.

Korean Vagabond and other masked dances continued to receive strong, positive comments, but several of her new dances were singled out for recognition. Chief among these was Bodhisattva, a dance she had performed in Japan but one she had not previously danced in the United States. One reviewer and photographs provide a glimpse of this dance (Figure 35): "Attired in a glittering crown and strings of sparkling brilliants that set off her lovely figure to shrewd advantage [described as "generously revealing" by a later writer (Kaye 1939)], Sai Shoki mimed the static ideal of [the Buddhist] faith with simple eloquent movements of her hands and arms, without altering her one constant posture" (Kolodin). Bodhisattva was so popular that, spurred on by audience response, Sai repeated it as an encore.

Sai's mimetic ability was also noted by several reviewers who singled out dances capitalizing on this talent, including Seoul Fortune Teller; Whalyang, "a gay lampoon of a Korean youth" (Kolodin); Dream of Youth, "a tart commentary on aging muscles" (RCB 1938); Buddhist Temptress, which demonstrated "her suppleness and grace" (RCB); and Greatest General Under the Sun, a masked dance in which she portrayed a "strutting Korean general" (Kaye).

Despite these positive comments, reviewers remained unimpressed with the overall nature of Sai's repertoire. One writer stated that although "the dancer's concern for line and detail, her sense of effective climax, were the stuff of genuine artistry," the program "suffered from a plenitude of brief numbers whose slight substance would have profited by more expansion and comment" (Kolodin). This comment is interesting in light of Sai's own statement referred to earlier that some traditional Korean dances were too long to perform on stage. Other writers said "her work depends for its effectiveness rather on its pictorial suggestiveness than on technical brilliance or depth of content" (JDB), and "many of the impressions are charming, though it must be admitted that as a whole they are extremely fragile and do not spread too well over an entire program" (Martin). Despite these concerns, there was clearly an attraction about Sai, reflected in such statements as: "[W]ithin the framework that she established for herself, Sai Shoki achieved some rare and charming effects" (Kolodin); "her dances are devoted rather to the creation of decorative Korean impressions than to the reproduction of authentic traditional material, and in this purpose they succeed well within their limitations" (Martin); and "it is a charming and exotic performance that this Korean dancer puts on. But when one says that, there is not much left to add" (Kaye).

Following Sai's second Guild Theatre appearance she departed to spend almost a year in Europe, where she performed many more times than during her year in the United States, participated in dance events such as competitions, at which she served as judge, that exposed her to a broad variety of kinds of dance, and undoubtedly saw a vast array of performances.[19] Whether because of these new experiences, attempts to counter criticisms in her American reviews by revising individual dances in her repertoire or substituting alternate dances, new information contained in advance publicity, knowledge and familiarity on the part of the audience that comes with repeated performances, or other reasons, Sai's return performance in New York was significantly more favorably received than her earlier performances there. While some reviewers continued to note a similarity between many dances in her repertoire and an evenness to the entire performance that was tedious for an American audience, the reviews stand in marked contrast to those of her first U.S. performances.

A statement in the printed program for her December 28, 1939, performance was referred to frequently in reviews: "Korean dance is almost a lost art. The program has been created by Sai Shoki on original sources." The impact of this on reviewers is suggested in the explicit comment of one that since Sai did not claim authenticity, "the critic is free to enjoy her work for what it is, a delightful creation by a dancer with a delicate and fascinating talent" (GNB 1940). This is reiterated in another review in which the author said: "I am by no means an authority on the Corean [*sic*] dance, so I can't say whether or not Sai Shoki succeeded in representing honestly the characteristics of her race. I do know that she has a well disciplined body, potentially wide movement range and that she offers a pleasurable experience in the theater" (Terry 1939). Still another writer states: "[S]he admits that the Korean dance is 'almost a lost art,' and her work therefore consists of recreations, built on research. But it is authentic in spirit, and certainly beautiful to watch" (Kaye 1940). Sai's public acknowledgment that she was not trying to accurately reproduce traditional dances (more accessible than when cited in the English-language Japanese newspaper in San Francisco) gave at least some critics freedom to relax and simply accept what they saw.

Although few of the new dances Sai introduced in this program were singled out for recognition, for several reviewers they contributed to varying the program more than previous dances. Reviewers noted that her repertoire achieved "a rather remarkable variety" despite "the slenderness of its material," which "succeeded in making a most engaging evening" (Martin 1939); "her program in its entirety [is] a distinct pleasure to watch, not only for its novelty but for the perfection of its presentation" (GNB); and "she succeeded in keeping her audience interested and enthusiastic throughout the evening" (Sabin 1940).

Reviewers continued to comment on Sai's physical beauty and grace, the appeal of her costumes, and what they considered the greater appropriateness of her recorded musical accompaniment than the piano renditions in her first U.S. performances. Korean Vagabond, Dream of Youth, Bodhisattva, and Whalyang, noted positively in reviews of previous performances, continued as audience favorites. Only three new dances were sometimes singled out, with Three Traditional Rhythms described as "charming" (Martin) and "very well done" (Kaye); Melody of the Jade Flute as having "an exquisite grace" (Sabin); and Sleeve Dance as being "excellent" (Sabin).

More generalized comments suggest reviewers were beginning to look seriously at the dancing itself, and not trying to read "cultural messages" into it. One writer comments on "the care with which her dances have been composed and her very real qualities as a theatrical personality" (Kolodin 1939); another says that "as the program progressed, one gradually warmed to the gentle child-like dances, to the shy humor and to the personal beauty of Sai Shoki herself" (Terry); a third states "her movement is strong and certain beneath the lightness of its application and her program in its entirety a distinct pleasure to watch, not only for its novelty but for the perfection of its presentation," and whether "formal and precise, . . . representing a merry wanderer, . . . or . . . arresting and sculptural, . . . her work has a personal quality which one can only call charming" (GNB); and a fourth writes that "her quiet command of an audience is as fascinating to watch as is her controlled dancing" (Vitak 1940a).

CHICAGO PERFORMANCE

Sai gave one performance in Chicago before returning to the west coast. Three advance announcements were more varied than those of her previous performances in other locations. One included a photograph of her Seoul Fortune Teller dance with a caption indicating she was bringing "the dances of Asia" to Chicago (Anonymous 1940c), another offered a brief biographical sketch (Anonymous 1940a) (based on information contained in the elaborate brochure produced by Hurok Attractions, her managing company at the time), and the third included a head-shot of Sai sporting a western-style hat and the more Los Angeles–style information indicating the train on which she arrived from New York and that she was "en route to Hollywood, where she is to appear in a moving picture"[20] (Anonymous 1940b).

There is only one known review of Sai's Chicago performance, and it resembles those of her final New York performance, summarizing the earlier reviews rather succinctly but extending more lavish praise. The writer tells us Sai "won the approval of her audience thru the diversified interest of her repertoire, the polished excellence of her technique, and the graciousness of her appealing personality" (Cecil Smith 1940). The writer also provides insights into the U.S. dance context in which Sai was performing, and thereby suggests the yardstick against which she was measured:

Any followers of the dance who expected to encounter dancing of the meticulously stylized, subtly symbolic variety of Uday Shan-Kar [*sic*] found a surprise in store. Sai Shoki is by no means a religious or ritualistic dancer, and her one picturesque representation of Buddha bore more kinship to Angna Enters' purely pictorial madonna than to Shan-Kar's [*sic*] traditional Siva dances.[21]

One earlier reviewer had juxtaposed Sai's Bodhisattva against the East-Indian dance of Shankar by saying, "In a sense this was reminiscent of Shan-Kar's [*sic*] superb 'Indra,' though Sai Shoki's delicate accomplishment was hardly of this rarefied altitude"[22] (Kolodin 1938). The Chicago reviewer also reiterated Sai's distinctive abilities in mime and character studies, and stated that "when she turned away from theatrical divertissements to actual Korean dance forms, she lost none of her warm humanness and none of her skilled showmanship" (Cecil Smith). Unlike other writers, he confessed his lack of knowledge about Korean dance in stating: "[I]f we may judge from Sai Shoki's compositions, the Korean dance does not try to turn its movements into abstractions, or to require specialized concentration from the audience." Although he had not seen previous performances by Sai, unless he had been alerted through advance announcements, he was able to set aside concerns with authenticity and focus on what he saw, an attitude that only came over time for New York reviewers.

RETURN TO LOS ANGELES

Advance announcements for Sai's return performance in Los Angeles used information, and in some cases precise verbiage, contained in the Hurok brochure. For example, the *Hollywood Citizen News* claimed Sai's dances "reveal the soul of the Orient" (Anonymous 1940d), a statement made by New York's Dalton Schools President Helen Parkhurst in her comments in the brochure. Text also sometimes paraphrased reviews from other places cited in the brochure.

Sai's March 30, 1940, Los Angeles performance was even more well-received than her first in that city. One writer stated "an exotic spell of the east was cast over dance fans," describing the program as "a charming highlight in the dance season" and Sai as "one of the most accomplished dancers to come out of the east since Shan-kar [*sic*] and Mei Lan Fang [*sic*]" (Rialtan 1940). Three specifically commented on her varied program (Rialtan, Swisher 1940, and Vitak 1940b), and one elaborated on this variety by indicating "the repertory ranges through drum dances, scarf dances, sword dances, comedy numbers and the serious [Bodhisattva] offering" (Rialtan). The same writer who provided views on almost all of the items in Sai's first Los Angeles program commented briefly, but glowingly, on all but one of the dances in this second program (Swisher), and another singled out the masked dances and Sword Dance, indicating the latter was "one of her best numbers" (Vitak). Comments regarding Sai's physical beauty and charm, elaborate costumes, and music followed the pattern established in other reviews after her return from Europe.

In addition to the types of comments by then routinely included in her U.S. advance notices, those for Sai's San Francisco performance on April 7, 1940, almost consistently commented on her success in the United States and Europe and said this would be her last U.S. performance before she left for South America. The Japanese-language *Shinsokai Asahi* restated views expressed in some of her last New York performances, indicating "she has changed her program and improved her technique compared to that of two years ago" (Anonymous 1940e).

Despite all the local acknowledgment of success elsewhere since her first San Francisco performance, Sai's second appearance there received mixed reviews. One writer reiterated sentiment expressed by reviewers in other cities by stating "her work would seem to have gained a little in fluency, but her virtues remain more personal than artistic," and describing Sai as a "capable entertainer, but as an artist of the dance she has a vast amount to learn" (Frankenstein 1940). Another writer sweepingly praised the performance, saying it was "as interesting a presentation of Oriental dance as has ever been revealed to local audiences" and describing Sai as "an exquisite exponent of an exquisite art" who "more than proved her right to be regarded as a distinguished artist" (Fisher 1940). An English-language, Japanese-published newspaper touted "San Francisco Lauded Miss Shoki's Appearance" and reported that she returned "to score another triumph" (Anonymous 1940h). A Japanese-language newspaper took a more reportorial stance by stating that her "satisfying program receive[d] a storm of applause" and was "received with support and warm love" (Anonymous 1940i). Bodhisattva was singled out for excellence in two of the reviews (Anonymous 1940h and Fisher), and one singled out additional dances that were audience favorites in many geographic locales: the masked dances, Melody of the Jade Flute, and Three Traditional Rhythms (Fisher).

Analysis

While there were strong similarities in the repertoire performed by Sai at various U.S. venues prior to her European tour, there were some differences. More significant differences occurred when she returned from Europe. While her first three presentations, which occurred within one month, were undoubtedly identical, she introduced Bodhisattva and Drum Dance in her fourth performance. By her fifth program (the third in New York), she introduced Ancient Prisoner, Dream of Youth, Invocation to Buddha, and Whalyang. Ancient Prisoner went unnoticed in reviews and was not performed again. Invocation to Buddha received minimal, but negative, comment, and was also not performed again. All of the other new additions, however, received favorable reviews, and were consistently performed in subsequent programs. With the exception of Drum Dance, about which there is little comment in reviews, all of these additions relied heavily on story content conveyed through mime. It is likely these dances were added by Sai in the belief that her audience would respond more favorably to them than to more abstract dances for which they were substituted.

Although it received favorable mention on several occasions, Young Korean Bridegroom was dropped from programs following Sai's return from Europe.

When Sai returned from her year in Europe, she introduced (in her December 28, 1939, New York performance) five dances new to American audiences: Melody of the Jade Flute, Sleeve Dance, Three Traditional Rhythms, and Two Court Dances. Descriptions in printed programs and the titles of these dances suggest a stereotypic image of "the Orient." Except for Two Court Dances, Sai continued to perform these dances in her remaining U.S. performances.

By making these changes to her programs I believe Sai was seeking ways to satisfy her audiences' (as represented by her reviewers') aesthetic preferences and imagined visions of what constituted either Korean or "oriental" dance. She herself expressed a desire to achieve "international attention" (in Choe Sang-cheul 1996:6) and success. In the United States this translated into making her dances more palatable to an Occidental audience that originally saw a sameness in what she did. This is reflected, for example, in one reviewer's comment from her last major New York performance that Sai "has not made the mistake of bringing Korean dances to us out of the whole cloth. Rather she has heightened them dramatically for Occidental eyes" (Anonymous 1939). Another reviewer of the same performance indicated that since her last performance "she has acquired considerable knowledge in the matter of arranging a program [sequencing the dances of a single performance] for American audiences" (Martin 1938b). Adapting to her American audience was also noted following her return performances in Los Angeles (Rialtan 1940) and San Francisco (Fisher 1940). It is difficult to know, however, whether the latter were independent observations of reviewers or if, once commented on by New York writers, this perspective was incorporated into advance materials for her second west-coast performances. Sai, herself, reiterated this perspective, but clearly stated a concern with creating an image of the East when she said, just prior to her final San Francisco performance, "My program . . . will be entirely Korean. . . . I have gained much experience since my appearance here two years ago and have modified my program to give an exclusively oriental tone" (in Anonymous 1940g).

While some of Sai's dances remained on her programs throughout her two performance seasons, most notably Greatest General Under the Sun, Korean Vagabond, Scarf Dance, Seoul Fortune Teller, and Sword Dance, which were performed in almost all programs, Sai states that she choreographed twenty new works while on tour (Ch'oe Sŭng-hŭi 1990:549). Titles of dances she performed in the United States, however, are the same or similar to titles of dances she performed in Korea and Japan prior to her tour abroad.[23] Since Sai is said to have often modified both her choreography and the costumes she used for individual dances (Choe Sangcheul, personal communication 15 June 1998), it is possible she simply rechoreographed dances she had done previously, based on what she thought American audiences would like.

What is particularly interesting about three of her most frequently performed dances in the United States, Scarf Dance, Seoul Fortune Teller, and Sword Dance, as well as the Drum Dance Sai added in her fourth performance, is that various versions of these dances are still performed in Korea today. They serve as icons of Korean dance in performances for visitors to Korea, as part of programs performed outside of Korea, and in popular-oriented performances. They are part of the style of dance identified as *shinmuyong*, or "new dance," for which Sai is often described as a major innovator (see Chapters 1 and 2). Although originally choreographed and performed in Korea and Japan, the popularity of these dances in the United States may have contributed to their ongoing popularity in Korea. A potentially intriguing possibility: The constructed view of Korean dance that evolved during Sai's 1938–1940 U.S. performances, which was the result of Sai's own training, her views about modernizing dance while rooting it in past tradition (a common view about culture in general in Korea at the time), and her choices based on U.S. responses, may have contributed to a lasting set of Korean dance icons.

Constructed images of "the orient" were common in the 1930s and 1940s. People fantasized about the "exotic other" when they had little, if any, direct knowledge about countries that were far away and often unknown. Such images are reflected in the advance press coverage of Sai as well as in reviews. Her frequent billing as an "exotic dancer," stereotyping broad expanses of the Asian world by describing her "dances of the Orient," and criticizing her for "characterizing" Korean dance rather than actually doing Korean dance all reflect an assumed concept of the "other." At the same time, however, there was acknowledgment that Sai should, and indeed did, modify her presentations for her U.S. audiences. Since Sai was purported to be the first Korean dancer to perform in the United States, the basis for what constituted Korean dance in the eyes of American writers and audience members could only have been in the imaginations of those watching and writing.

One dance that stands out in relation to imagined notions of Korea is Bodhisattva. This was a particularly popular dance, and response often contributed to its repetition in a single performance. Reviewers noted its association with Buddhism (albeit sometimes in terms that simply reiterated advance information or notes in the printed program) and described its sculptural representation of spirituality. Based on photographs of the dance, however, the major similarity to Korean Buddhist images lies in Sai's use of hand gestures; a costume as revealing as that worn by Sai is not depicted in Buddhist images in Korea. In contrast, the similarity between photographs of Sai in this dance and two photographs of early American modern dancer Ruth St. Denis is quite extraordinary. St. Denis and the Denishawn company performed in Asia from 1925 to 1926, and according to information for their September–October 1925 performance in Japan, "substitute and new dances" included Kuan Yin, St. Denis's "Bodhisatva style [*sic*]" piece[24] (Schlundt 1962:58) (Figure 36). Although these particular performances were prior to Sai's arrival in Japan, the Denishawn performances had a strong impact on Japan's dancers, and the Denishawn company performed there again in 1926; Sai went to Japan in the spring of that year, and the Denishawn Company performed there in October and November. One company member tells of the snapping camera shutters during the first performances and later consequences:

> We soon found the results of all this photography on postcards that were sold in the lobby of the theatre and in other places around the city. . . . [W]hen we returned to play Japan again more than a year later, we found they had served another purpose: in many of the popular modern theatres we saw Japanese dancing girls performing our numbers with almost the exact steps. And they were wearing duplicates of our costumes. (Sherman 1976:43).

Ted Shawn, St. Denis's partner, said of their return to Japan after performances in other Asian countries: "Not the least of our irritations was the sight of local companies trying to copy Denishawn. . . . The Japanese stage was 'lousy with Denishawn imitations: music, movements, costumes'" (Shawn 1960:202). It is possible Sai saw St. Denis perform Kuan Yin or other Asian-inspired dances during the company's return engagement,[25] that she was aware of these dances through the "copied" performances of other Japanese dancers, or that she heard about them.

A short film excerpt of Bodhisattva[26] shows Sai standing in an upright position (as in Figure 35) and executing only small, slow movements of her hands and arms, as described by one American reviewer. She performs a small, slow torso twist to the left and then the right one time, but otherwise remains fixed in one spot. Denishawn dancer Jane Sherman describes St. Denis's Kuan Yin as follows:

> With the opening four slow, soft, mysterious bars of music, a dim blue light comes up to reveal the figure of Kuan Yin standing at center stage in absolute stillness. Her hands are lightly crossed before her chest, her head is tilted with eyes down, her left hip thrusts slightly out to the side. When the brooding Satie melody begins, she moves one hand with stately grace, then the other. As the light brightens, the expression on her face—with its sober mouth, its

eyes downcast—is seen to be one of utmost tenderness. She steps forward, bare feet hidden by the long skirt, heavy gold scarf trailing. She stops. With hands seemingly attached at the wrists, she gradually unfolds her long fingers up with the right, down with the left. She reverses this fragile gesture when the music repeats the phrase.

With each deliberate step, her body, her robe, her scarf fall into such perfect place that at any pause RSD [Ruth St. Denis] becomes a significant statue of the goddess. At the final *pianissimo* chords, the brief solo ends stage center in the same pose with which it had begun. (Sherman 1979:41)

American critics' comments on Bodhisattva, together with the extant film excerpt and photographs, indicate Sai's dance was remarkably similar to that of St. Denis. It is quite intriguing, however, that no American critics commented on this similarity. (Kuan Yin had premiered in December, 1919. Kwannon, which may have simply been a revision of Kuan Yin, premiered in April, 1929.) Whether her dance was an imitation of St. Denis's or not, it is most probable Sai, like others, was strongly influenced by the Denishawn performances. If this was the case, it was not only the Occident that was into orientalizing; one part of the orient was orientalizing another, through an image based on an Occidental filter.

Politics came into play in some of Sai's U.S. experiences. Although traveling with a Japanese passport and using the Japanese pronunciation of her name, with only one exception, a headline in the April 3, 1940, *San Francisco News* reading "Japanese Dancer at Curran [Theater] Sunday" (Anonymous 1940f), Sai was always presented as a Korean dancer.[27] One writer alluded to Korea's then-colonial status by describing Sai as "a Korean by birth" (Fisher 1940). Occasional newspaper comments about the audience identified some of its members variously as "fellow compatriots," Japanese, Koreans, or, in one instance, "members of the local Japanese colony" (Anonymous 1940f). An advance article in the *Hollywood Citizen News* announced that the Japanese consul would be present at Sai's second Los Angeles performance (Anonymous 1940d).

Stronger political issues are reflected in items prior, but related, to Sai's U.S. debut. When then–Consul General Marsh sent his February 23, 1937, letter from Seoul to the American Secretary of State, he indicated he was calling attention to his attendance at Sai's performance "only in connection with the prestige of the American Consulate General, the particular circumstances of the performance, and the numerous courtesies shown me since my arrival." He then pointed out that despite the turning away of many people who held either complimentary or purchased tickets, seats were vacated near the Governor General's box for him and his companions, all by way of showing, symbolically, the good relations between Japan and the United States. This rapport was explicitly stated by the author of the *Seoul Press* newspaper article Marsh included with his letter when he said Sai's forthcoming U.S. tour "would by her presence there help promote the long-standing friendly relations between America and Japan" (Anonymous 1937a). Little did anyone know how much this relationship would change by the end of her tour.

Promoting relations between Korea and Japan during the intense colonial period may have been on the mind of Japanese dancer Ishii Baku when he debated whether or not to take Sai on as a student. He is quoted as saying, "I began to think that it might be important to have an excellent dancer come from Korea to soften the relationship between two ethnic people, and also for the Korean people to be known in the world" (in Hirabayashi Hisae 1977:189).

Among somewhat garbled comments about Sai being of "Chinese origin," one San Francisco writer stated she was from "an area of China that has been under Japanese influence long enough to be Japanese in culture and education" (Anonymous 1938c). While it is accurate Sai received a Japanese education (a Japanese school system had been instituted in Korea shortly after the 1910 colonial period began), she was developing as a dancer at a time when a sense of Korean identity was very much in the minds of Koreans.

Whether because of a specific incident in Los Angeles or the larger political arena, the caption to a January 25, 1938, photograph of Sai in the *Los Angeles Evening News* indicated she "ignored completely the obvious friction between her countrymen and the Japanese members of the welcoming committee" (Anonymous 1938a). Such friction occurring directly in connection with Sai's performances is never mentioned in any American newspapers. It is, however, discussed by Korean writer Chŏng Pyŏng-ho (1995: 144–149 and Chŏng Byŏng-ho 1997:98) and in comments by Sai herself. Chŏng says during Sai's first appearances in San Francisco and Los Angeles people thought she had come to advertise Japanese culture and that Korean immigrants and Jews demonstrated outside the theaters where she performed (1995:144–149). (If demonstrations did, indeed, happen, protests may have been related to Japan's alliance with Germany and perceptions that Sai was representing the Japanese.) He believes limited attendance at her early New York performances, which is not substantiated by comments in reviews, is attributable to similar demonstrations, and to the fact that because Sai used the Japanese pronunciation of her name, many Koreans believed she had betrayed her country. Meanwhile, a Japanese newspaper in Japan claimed she was doing anti-Japanese activities (in Chŏng Pyŏng-ho 1995), and Chŏng further states that she was "forced to make an anti-Japanese speech by Korean residents in the U.S.A." (1997:98). Since Sai was traveling on a Japanese passport, however, she had to maintain allegiance to Japan and had to continue to use the name Sai Shoki instead of Ch'oe Sŭng-hŭi if she wanted to continue her performing tour. And any involvement of Jews in protesting against Sai did not prevent the New York Young Men's Hebrew Association (the 92nd Street Y) from sponsoring her performance on March 5, 1938.

Sai describes her insecurity and fear resulting from anti-Japanese sentiment, and says that she was threatened and told to speak out in radio broadcasts and sell anti-Japanese buttons at her performances. She attributes a weak New York performance to the fact that the Japanese consulate had requested police protection for her backstage (1940, in Ch'oe Sŭng-hŭi 1999:94), surely a distraction for her performance focus.

According to Chŏng it was because of this tumultuous period in her U.S. tour that Sai tried to assert her Korean identity by hiring a Korean musician to replace the Japanese pianist who had accompanied her first performances. It was also at this time that Metropolitan Music Company, sponsor of her early New York performances, wanted to cancel her contract (according to Chŏng because they were a Jewish company and wanted to avoid becoming involved in political issues), and that Sai decided she wanted to go to Europe (Chŏng Pyŏng-ho 1995:141, 150).

An American military intelligence report prepared May 25, 1942, regarding "Japanese activities in Columbia [sic—South America]," states:

Sai Shoki. A Korean danseuse, who came to Bogota in October, 1940. She is reported to be an international spy, and when she was here, there were many secret conferences in restaurants and private residences with suspicious people. (Military Attaché Report)

Views are divided on the political beliefs and allegiances of the dancer born Ch'oe Sŭng-hŭi. Based on her activities following her return to Japan, her own views undoubtedly changed at various times, and many believe she was significantly influenced by the political beliefs of her husband. But the politics most significantly affecting her U.S. performances were aesthetic politics. Although press coverage sometimes touted authenticity, Ch'oe herself claimed only that she was doing *Korean* dance, not purely *traditional* Korean dance. In fact, some early writers in Japan and Korea praised her for creating new versions of traditional dances (see, e.g., Kim Ch'ŏng-uk 1999:78–81). Ch'oe had little training in "traditions of the Far East," as one American writer assumed (Fried 1938). In many ways her dancing reflected transitions occurring in the dance world in Korea at the time (see Chapters 1 and 2), transitions undoubtedly unknown to her U.S. audience and critics.

Ch'oe succeeded in modifying the content of her U.S. programs to suit what she thought would satisfy the American view of what constituted Korean dance, perhaps completely independent of what her own aesthetic preferences might have been. There is no question that she had a strong, positive impact on audiences, particularly during her later performances. But reviewers' favorable comments were often qualified. Ch'oe was less successful, however, in establishing herself as a serious artist in the eyes of most American reviewers, many of whom echoed her own teacher's comment regarding entertainment and artistry, summarized in one review of her final U.S. performance in San Francisco: She is a "capable entertainer, but as an artist of the dance she has a vast amount to learn" (Frankenstein 1940).

Ch'oe Sŭng-hŭi returned to perform in east Asian and east European countries for at least fifteen years, and had a profound impact on dance developments in Korea. Her dances may not have had the depth U.S. audiences and her own Japanese teacher considered necessary for true artistic works. But she exposed U.S. audiences to her vision of Korean dance and they, in turn, had an impact on that vision. An impact that is still seen in what identifies Korean dance today.

9
Korean Dance in Hawai'i
Immigrant Issues and
Cultural Ownership

In 1991 Connie Chang, a young Korean-American woman from Hawai'i, described the importance of her experiences with Korean dance:

> Looking back at my eight years with the [Korean dance] studio, I cannot express to you the significance it has had on my life as a second generation Korean-American. . . .
>
> . . . What I have experienced about the Korean culture through art could not have come so richly through any other method.
>
> . . . I learned about Korean history. Korean traditions and Korean values. These were values and traditions my parents were raised with, but ones I could not understan[d] or appreciate until discovering the history behind them because they were so different from my own. (p. 16)

These sentiments underline issues raised at a 1996 conference on Koreans abroad. In his report on that event, Kim Moon-hwan states one issue clarified at the conference was that "national identity must be realized within the context of the new world environment" (1996:81). Historian Kang Man-gil "warned that the preservation of traditional Korean culture in the context of [an] emigrant society should be pursued in a harmonious, positive manner which contributes to the development of the host society as well as humanity in general" (in Kim Moon-hwan 1996:81). In a statement applicable to dance as well as music, musician Hwang Pyŏng-gi "emphasized the importance of understanding a culture's musical attributes and techniques to understanding the culture itself." He commented on efforts in Korea to rediscover the values of traditional culture as a way to overcome an emptiness and sense of loss that accompanied a declining national identity experienced by Koreans during the rapid modernization and industrialization of their country (ibid.), an emptiness and loss I believe is experienced similarly among all immigrant groups.

The nature of Korean dance activities in Hawai'i, and their significance to those directly involved in them as well as to the broader Hawai'i community, exemplify the points made at the 1996 conference. In this chapter I describe some of these Hawai'i activities, the roles they have played in the lives of individuals and the community at large, and several issues raised by the continuation of Korean dance in one North American community.

The first Korean dance activities in Hawai'i may have occurred as early as 1922.[1] Local immigrants with some dance experience in their original homeland participated in the early performances, and guest performers and teachers have come to the islands from time to time. Until her death in 1994, however, no one contributed so significantly nor for such an extended period of time to Korean culture in the islands, through dance, as Halla Pai Huhm, a woman whose name has become synonymous with Korean dance in this island state.[2] When recognizing her in 1979 as the first Outstanding Korean in Hawai'i, a spokesman of the Korean Community Council described her as working "quietly but arduously in promoting and exposing Korean culture." The council also acknowledged "her extraordinary generosity and personal dignity while perpetuating the image of the Korean community in the larger Honolulu Community" (Anonymous 1979b).

Halla Pai Huhm

Halla Pai Huhm was born in Pusan in 1922.[3] At the age of five she and four siblings went to Japan, where she was raised by Pae Ku-ja. It is generally believed that Pae Ku-ja was Huhm's cousin (the daughter of her father's sister), but Huhm often referred to her as her sister. Pae, a performer who, in addition to Korean dance, had studied ballet and modern dance in Europe, began to pass on her knowledge and skill to her young relative. Huhm learned dance at the same time she worked toward earning a Bachelor of Science degree in Home Economics at Jitsen Women's University in Tokyo. With the start of World War II she returned to Korea, where she met John Huhm, a Hawai'i-born Korean-American serving in the U.S. military. She married Huhm, and immigrated to Hawai'i with him in 1949 or 1950.[4]

In her new home Huhm began to pursue the artistic talents she developed in Korea and Japan. These were first displayed in flower arranging (Figure 45), but she soon began teaching dance informally to students in her home. Her abilities in both dance and acting became increasingly apparent to the people of Hawai'i through performing activities. In 1954 she played the role of Lotus Blossom, a *geisha*, in the Honolulu Commu-

Figure 45. Halla Huhm (center) teaches a flower-arranging class at a Japanese school in Hawai'i (c. 1949). Courtesy of Halla Huhm Dance Collection.

nity Theatre's production of *Teahouse of the August Moon*. Newspaper articles about the highly successful production touted both her acting and dancing ability. Interestingly, the dancing was Okinawan. This was not unusual, however; Huhm had studied several dance forms before coming to Hawai'i, and was actively involved with Japanese, Chinese, Okinawan, and Filipino dance groups. After establishing her own studio in the early 1950s, she included some of these diverse dance forms in recitals.[5] In 1959, she began teaching Korean dance at the University of Hawai'i's Mānoa campus.

Huhm kept scrapbooks of photographs, letters, and newspaper clippings that document her activities in Hawai'i. Besides reflecting the nature and quantity of her involvements, many of these items attest to her artistic talent. They continually describe her ability as a performer and choreographer: "a mime and dancer of extraordinary talent," "a number of [her] creations rise to the level of great art," "an artist of the first rank." The clippings and letters also speak of her generosity. Over the years she gave of herself and of her students through performances and activities for countless functions sponsored by a vast array of community organizations: Hawai'i state fairs, the Honolulu Academy of Arts (Figure 46), the

Women's Society of the Korean Christian Church, the Honolulu Symphony, a convention of the Hawai'i Dance Masters of America, and benefits for the Cancer Society and the Korean Wounded Veterans' Association.

Among accolades she received are recognition by the government of the Republic of Korea (including citations from the Ministry of Education, the Ministry of Public Information, and the Consulate General of the Republic of Korea), the legislature of the State of Hawai'i (both the Senate and House of Representatives), and the American Smithsonian Institution. Her 1980 cultural medal from the Korean government (Pogwan Munhwa Hunjang) is particularly noteworthy, since she was the first overseas individual awarded this recognition. She received letters of appreciation from such organizations as the Soroptomists and the Jaycees and such individuals as U.S. Senator Daniel Inouye, who spoke of her willingness to spread Korean culture and serve the community.

Many of Huhm's Hawai'i activities continued despite limited financial resources. Shortly after her arrival in the islands she worked in a variety of jobs in order to take care of her most basic needs. Later, after opening

Figure 46. Halla Huhm poses for students at the Honolulu Academy of Arts, Hawai'i (1958). Photo by Raymond Sato (Honolulu Academy of Arts).

her studio, she worked for a travel agency, taking tour groups to Japan and Korea, in order to pay rent for studio space and allow many young students to forego tuition payments. Few people in the community realized the expense involved in performing—the cost of fabrics to make costumes and then maintain them, travel to sustain ties with the dance community in Korea and continue her own studies, and obtaining tapes of music to accompany her dances, since there were no Korean musicians in Hawai'i.[6] But she never asked for performing fees; if an event would contribute to knowledge about Korean culture and further worthwhile causes, those were sufficient reasons to perform.

Although the foundation of her dance training came from Pae Ku-ja, Huhm never stopped studying. She invited guests to teach at her studio (Figure 30) and her Hawai'i-Japan-Korea travel circle frequently included stopovers to continue dance studies. Her teachers were some of Korea's most well-known dance masters; she always sought out specialists from whom she could learn particular types of dance. She studied traditional dance with Han Sŏng-jun, a man acknowledged throughout Korea for both his retention of traditional movement characteristics and innovative choreography; Buddhist ritual music and dance from Pak Song-am, a priest formally recognized by the Korean government for expertise in this area; shaman rituals and dance from Yi Chi-san, a shaman from the Seoul area; salp'uri, a solo dance form considered by many to be the epitome of Korean dance (see Chapters 1 and 6), from Kim Mok-hwa; and court dance from Kim Ch'ŏn-hŭng, a dancer recognized by the Korean government for his traditional dance knowledge and ability. (See Chapter 7 for a biography of Kim Ch'ŏn-hŭng.)

In 1983 Huhm was invited to return to Korea as an Assistant Professor in the Dance Department of Ch'ŏngju University of Education. For five years she taught traditional dance to future teachers in her homeland—a significant comment on the validity of her Korean dance knowledge, despite her long residence abroad. (While she was away, her Hawai'i studio was maintained by Mary Jo Freshley—see below.)

To recognize the abilities of her students and try to instill in them the importance of their contributing to the perpetuation of Korean culture, in 1963 Huhm began a system of awarding certificates of achievement to students that is based on a system she learned in Japan.[7] The highest certificate awards students the name of Pai, and designates them as instructors in the Pai tradition Huhm continued from Pae Ku-ja.

Huhm's persistence in keeping Korean dance alive in Hawai'i never ceased. Over the years she extended her performances to include presentations on many of Hawai'i's islands. Although enrollments in her studio classes fluctuated, the Halla Pai Huhm Korean Dance Studio has been the only continuous source of Korean dance and music in the state. In 1989 Halla Huhm and her studio were honored with an invitation to be part of the performing arts delegation when Hawai'i was the featured state at the Smithsonian Institution's Festival of American Folklife in Washington, D.C.

In 1993 Hawai'i celebrated the ninetieth anniversary of Korean immigration to the state. On January 13, 1903, the first boatload of Koreans had arrived at Hawai'i's shores from the port city of Inch'ŏn. This marked the beginning of Korean immigration to Hawai'i, and subsequently to the mainland United States. The 1993 festivities highlighted the impact of Koreans on the Hawai'i community. To celebrate the contributions of Halla Huhm to Hawai'i's understanding of Korean culture, tribute performances were held in January in Honolulu and Hilo.[8] The program featured thirty-seven dancers ranging in age from six to fifty-eight years old. Although most of the performers were of Korean ancestry, two were of European ancestry and one was Hawaiian-Portuguese, only a suggestion of the varied ethnicities of students at Halla Huhm's studio over the years. Performers also reflected the diverse nonstudio lives of those who studied with Huhm: a European-American elementary school physical education teacher who studied with Huhm for more than thirty years and earned the Pai name and teaching certificate; a recent visitor from Korea who studied in Seoul with well-known dancer Yi Mae-bang; two homemakers who were born in Korea and recently immigrated to Hawai'i; and the youngest performer, a second-generation Korean who only began her studies of Korean dance several months earlier.

The January performance was a retrospective of some of the many works choreographed by Huhm. It demonstrated her interest in both traditional Korean dance and creativity, as well as her concern with showcasing the varying abilities of her students. Huhm herself performed Noin Ch'um, The Old Man's Dance (Figures 47 and 48). Inspired by a mask made in Japan, she choreographed and first presented this dance in the 1950s.[9] Noin Ch'um came to be a favorite of Hawai'i audiences because of the poignancy and believability of the character portrayed. Huhm also performed the role of the teacher in Yedo, The Way of Art, originally choreographed in 1990. In a manner representative of the way she taught at her studio, the dance depicted the almost ritualistic passing on of dance traditions from teacher to student.

The evening concluded with a colorful pastiche of drum dances. As the entire cast of dancers circled the stage weaving long, colorful streamers in maypole fashion, the Honolulu audience rose to offer a standing ovation to the woman described earlier in the evening by Donald Kim, chairman of the sponsoring committee, as a "pillar of Korean culture in Hawai'i."

One year later, on January 29, 1994, Halla Pai Huhm died.

*Benefits of Participating in Activities
of the Halla Huhm Dance Studio*

Two of Huhm's primary interests were contributing to knowledge about Korean culture and furthering worthwhile causes. Toward those ends, studio performances were a part of both Korean celebrations and multi-

Figure 47. Halla Huhm performs Noin Ch'um (Old Man's Dance) (1993). Photo by Cory Lum. Courtesy Halla Huhm Dance Collection.

cultural programs in the community, as well as events to support humanitarian causes. In the 1950s, students performed at fundraisers for support groups during the Korean War. Over the years they performed at Korean weddings and birthday celebrations;[10] for local festivals showcasing the many ethnic groups represented in Hawai'i's population; in public school programs; for events sponsored by the Korean Consulate; and in studio recitals.

Huhm's commitment to Korean culture and her strong sense of discipline were qualities she expected in her students. Besides teaching a repertoire of dances representative of the traditional culture of the ethnic heritage of many students, she was concerned with the personal development of those who studied with her. Stern scoldings sometimes led to tears, but invariably to an understanding of Korean culture and appropriate behavior. Ultimately these lessons were directed at teaching the cultural values of her homeland and helping each student become the kind of dignified person she herself was often described as being.

While the experiences and feelings of the people who studied at her studio prior to Huhm's death are highly individual, the role played for many individuals by Korean dance, the studio, and Huhm can be summarized in further comments from the letter written by Connie Chang, the Korean-American quoted earlier, who was one of Huhm's students. Chang states:

> Saturday afternoons at Mrs. Huhm's studio were the only window through which I could view and actively participate in the traditions of my ancestors.
>
> As a child, I was embarrassed to have my American friends know that I did Korean folk dancing. I chose to enjoy it privately and keep the world of Mrs. Huhm's studio and its close-knit community of dancers distinct from my life as a regular kid growing up in America. . . .
>
> I had been afraid that I would be teased if anyone found out I didn't do the "normal" kind of dancing. But to my surprise and delight, I awed my high school classmates and teachers with a Korean Drum Dance [during my senior year in high school]. Contrary to the sneers I expected, other students complimented me and asked, when did I start, how did I get so good and where could they learn Korean folk dancing. In addition to my personal satisfaction, I felt I was doing right in sharing my culture.
>
> . . . I sometimes wonder if [I would have come] to terms with my

Figure 48. Halla Huhm performs Noin Ch'um (Old Man's Dance) (1993). Photo by Cory Lum. Courtesy Halla Huhm Dance Collection.

heritage . . . if I did not have the opportunity to experience and share part of it with other people. . . .

Aside from bringing entertainment and culture to generations of Hawai'i and U.S. residents, unknowingly Mrs. Huhm has helped me conquer my childhood feelings of inferiority as a[n] Asian-American because she was so full of pride for her culture and so generous in bringing it to others. (1991:16)

These comments reinforce conclusions drawn by Nishiguchi in her 1982 study of the studio. It is clear that dance provided for Chang, and continues to provide for others, a strong visual symbol for Koreans within Hawai'i's multicultural community. It reinforces a sense of Korean identity among those of Korean heritage, introduces the non-Korean community to the culture of origin of some of its members, and contributes to preserving selected facets of Korean tradition. And since dance is used by many ethnic groups in Hawai'i as a symbol of identity, Korean dance functions in a manner appropriate to the larger community.

Because most individuals who participate in studio activities are at least part Korean, it would be easy to consider the studio an "ethnocentric organization," and to then conclude, as proposed by Yu Eui-young, that although it helps to preserve Korean culture, it also "enforce[s] cultural and social isolation" (1981:22). Since participating in dances of a particular cultural heritage is one way to show that you are clearly a part of the Hawai'i community, however, participating in studio activities facilitates *integrating* with the larger environment at the same time it affords opportunities for subgroup identification.[11]

The Halla Huhm Studio is still active.[12] My own spring 1997 interviews with studio participants indicate that Nishiguchi's 1982 conclusions and the views stated by Chang in 1991 parallel the functions the studio continues to serve. For many younger second- and third-generation Korean-Americans, their primary knowledge of Korea comes from what they learn at the studio. In addition to information gleaned from verbal explanations, they experience facets of Korean culture by kinesthetically embodying them.

Like Chang, some students prefer to keep their Korean identity to themselves and initially use the studio as a way to connect privately with that part of their heritage.[13] But privacy cannot be maintained for long: Those at the studio are often called upon to participate in public programs, including a generally annual public recital.

For some students, performing is an important reason for taking lessons. They like the opportunity to wear the elegant traditional garments and like to have people see them doing something Korean. This also appears to be important for some parents of the younger students. Parents reconnect vicariously with their homeland through the Korean dance performances of their children, and these performances provide a way in which the parents can publicly reassert their own Korean identity through their offspring.

Participating in studio performances means extra rehearsals, back-stage preparations, and the energy and tension of performing before an audience. This fosters a microcommunity among the participants, a community based on shared participation in something easily identifiable as Korean (costumes, movement, music), and one that contributes to friendships, a benefit expressed by many students. Because this shared experience is often publicly performed, it also makes a statement to the individual and others about things Korean, and contributes to a time when individuals can feel special, thus supporting the development of a positive self-image.

Besides youngsters, at the start of the twenty-first century the studio also has a number of older students. Several recent female immigrants in their fifties go to the studio to participate in an activity they were never able to be a part of in their homeland, and a small group of older Korean men find classes in masked-dance a time to bond and the basis for performance opportunities that allow them to showcase their physical abilities. Many also use their studio time as a way to connect with individuals who speak Korean; depending primarily on where they were born, some students speak almost entirely Korean to each other at the studio.[14]

Cultural Confrontation

Despite the benefits of ethnic identity, development of positive self-image, and friendship, benefits that much literature on Korean-Americans describes as coming from involvement with Korean-language schools, Korean churches, and other culturally based activities,[15] the studio is not always fully supported by individuals of Korean heritage. Often, support is little more than lip service. In some instances, involvement with Korean dance leads to difficult choices that reflect issues arising when two cultures confront each other in the lives of immigrants. A fifty-two-year-old third-generation Korean-American believes that Halla Huhm was often used by the Korean community. At the same time her contributions were acknowledged, she was not given the financial or moral support that would have made sustaining the studio easier. One student in the early 1980s indicated "the Korean community is usually only supportive of the studio when they want a favor—a free program or for us to bail them out when another group has failed to come through" (in Nishiguchi 1982:42). There has generally been at least a small group, however, that is very supportive of studio activities.[16] Although never formalized, from time to time efforts were made to establish an official parents' support group.

At the same time parents choose to send their young children to the studio and older students choose to attend classes, many do not make a commitment beyond minimal involvement. For example, by sending their children to the studio some parents relinquish responsibility for educating their own children about their mother culture. Some parents are preoccupied with financial subsistence or their own activities and do not wish to make time to pass on their heritage to their children.[17] Others are sufficiently removed from Korean culture themselves that they are unable to instill a knowledge of Korea in their own children. Rather than attempting to learn themselves, or to find ways to support studio activities beyond the payment of modest tuition fees, they simply deposit their children at the studio for an hour every Saturday and have someone else do the job for them.[18] A middle-aged, upper-class Korean believes some consider the studio little more than a baby-sitting service with a dose of culture attached to it. Thus, at the same time the studio attracts participation at one level, many do not willingly participate at other levels.[19]

To many older Korean-Americans dance still carries with it the stigma of the *kisaeng* established during the war years—the notion of a woman of loose morals whose dancing was only part of an evening's entertainment. Posted on a bulletin board at the studio in the late 1990s was a copy of a letter to students and parents asking them not to use the name of the studio or its dances without consulting with Mary Jo Freshley, the woman currently in charge of the studio. The letter also states that "Mrs. Huhm worked very hard to present Korean dance as an *art* form and the image which we project whenever and wherever we dance should reflect that philosophy" (emphasis in original). Whatever connotations have been associated with Korean dance in other places and at other times, and regardless of what goes on at Korean bars in the community, the studio has always been concerned with the respectful use of Korean dance as an art form. Choy and Sutton (1991) state that for women of the Hyung Jay (Hyŏngje) Club of Hawai'i who danced in the 1920s and 1930s, Korean dance and music

> became primarily a symbol of Koreanness, no longer representing the royal courts, Confucianism, Buddhism or shamanism from which these arts had sprung. Neither did they represent anything other than Koreanness to the Hawaiian community at large.
>
> Though professional musicians and dancers ranked very low on the social ladder in the Korea that . . . first-generation immigrants had left just after the turn of the century, performances by upwardly mobile young people, particularly for upper class audiences at the Honolulu Academy of Arts, was a different matter. There was no risk of social stigma.

This attitude did not always prevail, however. Despite the fact that dance can be an enjoyable way to connect with Korean culture, it is difficult to forget associations of the past and reconcile them with current beliefs. The dilemma, according to a third-generation Korean-American businessman, is whether to participate in an activity that easily instills a sense of ethnic or national identity, but that at the same time carries negative connotations for some people.[20] This issue surfaces in relation to the repertoire that is taught and performed at the studio. Halla Huhm was interested in researching and teaching to her students many of the different kinds of dances done in Korea. In addition to the elegant dances performed in Korea's former courts, she learned dances performed as part of Buddhist and shaman rituals. Like her counterparts in Korea, she adapted these materials into a theatrical framework, in her case to demonstrate to Hawai'i audiences the diverse kinds of dance that are part of Korea's culture. In 1976 she invited Yi Chi-san, an important shaman from Seoul, to teach dance movements that are part of shaman rituals to her students and to perform in a recital with them (see Chapter 6). The program also included several dances based on movements used by shamans. A number of parents refused to allow their children to participate in this event. On another occasion she taught students a dance that originated in Buddhist ritual, and again some parents would not allow their children to participate. Despite the fact that Huhm did not attempt to re-create shaman or Buddhist rituals, but rather tried to show, in a highly theatrical way, a facet of Korean culture (as is common in performances in Korea today— see, for example, Chapter 6), parents were unable to reconcile their western Christian beliefs (many Hawai'i-Koreans are Christian) with a theatrical presentation that was about their mother culture.

Cultural Ownership

Yet another issue of cultural confrontation surfaced with the demise of Halla Huhm, an issue relating to how the studio is being continued and to cultural ownership. Over the years a number of individuals served as assistants to Halla Huhm, individuals of diverse ethnic and national heritages. These included people she helped come to Hawai'i from Korea, several young women who had studied in university dance programs in Korea, and local residents of Okinawan and Japanese ancestry. Most maintained their studio affiliation for several years and then moved on to other things. Since 1994, the gray-haired woman telling students to relax their arms, bend their knees more, and listen to the music as she counts in Korean has been Mary Jo Freshley. When I was speaking with a young student about her experiences at the studio, the student asked, "You mean Ms. Freshley isn't Korean?" Many young Korean-Americans who began their dance studies after Halla Huhm died are unaware that their teacher today is not Korean. Although she is not sufficiently fluent to speak Korean all the time, Freshley's instructions to the students are liberally sprinkled with Korean phrases.[21] When she helps them dress for a performance she identifies each of the costume components with their Korean names.[22] She tells the young Korean-Americans things about Korea and Korean dance that, in some cases, even their parents, who were born in Korea, do not know. In fact, the born-in-Korea parents of one of these young students asked if Freshley could talk to her child's grade-school class about Korea.

Mary Jo Freshley, who now runs the Halla Huhm Dance Studio, was born of European ancestry in Ohio in 1934. Although she studied many kinds of dance in college, her interest in Korean dance did not begin until after she moved to Hawai'i in 1961 to teach physical education to elementary-level students. Piqued by her exposure to Korean dance in a University of Hawai'i class taught by Halla Huhm, she continued her studies at the Halla Huhm Dance Studio. In the early days, her classes were mostly private lessons, since she was older than most of the other students. Interestingly, at that time a number of students were of Japanese ancestry.[23]

Over time, Freshley's studies became more intense, and in the 1970s she began to assist at the studio. In 1974, when a Korean assistant left, Freshley and a local resident of Japanese ancestry began to teach entire classes at the studio rather than just assisting Huhm.

Freshley's knowledge of Korean dance and culture did not come solely from her work at the studio, however. In 1972 she spent three-and-a-half weeks in Korea with other students on a study tour arranged by Halla Huhm. Since then she has returned to Korea more than six times for periods ranging from several weeks to three months, during which she, like Huhm, studied with some of Korea's finest dance masters. Her teachers were some of the same as those who had instructed Huhm (particularly Kim Ch'ŏn-hŭng), as well others, most notably Kim Pyŏng-sŏp, a recognized performer and teacher of Korean farmers' band dance and music (*nongak*), and members of the well-known contemporary SamulNori group.

Freshley's dance knowledge and abilities were formally acknowledged by Halla Huhm. In 1975 she was given the designation of instructor, together with the name Pai Myung-sa. She is one of only about a dozen individuals who earned this certificate, and is the only one still actively engaged in studying and teaching Korean dance.

Since Huhm's death, Freshley has been the primary teacher at the Halla Huhm Studio. In addition to handling business matters, which include responding to countless requests to do performances for Korean and non-Korean functions, raising funds for the studio, and obtaining costumes, music, and dance and music equipment from Korea, she teaches Korean dance to individuals who are, for the most part, of Korean ancestry, while she, herself, is entirely of European ancestry. In 1991 a young Korean woman, Kim Chi-a, who had studied dance at Seoul Institute of the Arts, came to Hawai'i to attend college. In 1992 she began to attend classes at the Halla Huhm Studio, and today she serves as Freshley's assistant.

This raises the issue of cultural ownership. Is it "correct" or "appropriate" for a member of one culture, or ethnicity, to teach the dances of another culture, or ethnicity? While some Koreans and some non-Koreans in the Hawai'i community have asked this question, it has not even occurred to others. Freshley's knowledge and dedication are recognized today by virtually everyone affiliated with the studio, as well as by those who observe studio activities from the outside. Koreans as well as non-Koreans stand in awe of her knowledge of Korean dance. They admire her efforts to learn the Korean language and her ongoing study trips to Korea. They sometimes wonder what drives her to so aggressively engage in the practice and support of another culture. (One young student wonders if she had a Korean boyfriend at some time.)

To those who ask if Freshley's teaching of Korean dance is appropriate, "Why not?" is the answer from many students and parents: They believe she knows more than anyone else in Hawai'i of Korean ancestry, that she is totally committed, and that there is no Korean in Hawai'i who can do what she does. One student says that some older Koreans feel ashamed that Freshley knows so much more about Korea than they do.

Freshley believes Huhm was always looking for a student of Korean ancestry who could one day take over the studio. But the studio has never been able to pay a full-time salary to any teacher. Halla Huhm, herself, could not sustain a livelihood solely through teaching Korean dance. The financial situation, a personal declining interest in dance, and various other personal circumstances prevented the few Koreans who did assist at the studio from developing a strong commitment, a commitment Freshley sustained and was able to pursue because she had a full-time teaching position elsewhere.[24]

Coinciding with the death of Halla Huhm was Freshley's retirement from her grade-school teaching position. Since 1994 she has devoted herself full-time to the studio. She draws no salary from studio income, however. Funds are used to pay studio rent, purchase costumes and musical instruments, and, on the rare occasion there is a surplus, to help subsidize dance study trips to Korea for students or the visit of a guest instructor. She continues the same goals and practices established by Halla Huhm, despite the fact that she is not Korean. She describes her goals as helping people gain a sense of what Korean culture is like through dance and music; perpetuating the repertoire of Halla Huhm, showing the diversity of Korean culture through the diversity of Korea's dances, and educating both children and their parents (personal communication 17 Feb. 1997).

Freshley, like Halla Huhm in the past, is concerned about the future of the studio. And, like Huhm, she is anxious to find someone of Korean ancestry to continue what Huhm began. Some members of the Korean-American community would have preferred to see someone of Korean ancestry take over leadership of the studio when Huhm died. A very small number of people say that while Freshley knows the repertoire and understands a tremendous amount about Korean culture and the dances, there is a quality to her movement that will always be missing because she is not Korean. This is countered by those who say she may not have an ounce of

Korean heritage, but she has far more understanding of things Korean than many Korean-Americans. No one with the knowledge and commitment of Freshley has yet come forward with an interest in working with, or taking over, the studio. Indeed, if it were not for Freshley, the studio would not exist.

For now, the studio continues in much the same way it always has. It represents Korean culture in a manner appropriate to the Hawai'i community, contributes to knowledge about Korean culture among those of both Korean and non-Korean ancestry, and serves as a gathering place for individuals of Korean heritage—for some, simply a place to acquire deep friendships; for others, a place to come to understand part of their ethnic roots and come to grips with their bicultural identity. A middle-aged, third-generation Korean-American businessman believes many Korean-Americans in Hawai'i consider studying dance at the studio to be part of their education as young Koreans: Just as many Americans ask, "Weren't you a girl scout?", Koreans in Hawai'i, he says, ask, "Didn't you go to the Halla Huhm Studio?" At least for the present, the responsibility for the studio rests in the hands of a European-American—an ironic reminder of the conflicting issues confronting various generations of immigrant groups, and issues relating to the ownership of artistic forms evolving from specific cultural sources.

Afterword

In reflecting on the diverse chapters here I was reminded of American poet John Godfrey Saxe's rendition of an Asian story:

> It was six men of Indostan
> To learning much inclined,
> Who went to see the Elephant
> (Though all of them were blind),
> That each by observation
> Might satisfy his mind.
>
> The First approached the Elephant,
> And happening to fall
> Against his broad and sturdy side,
> At once began to bawl:
> "God bless me! but the Elephant
> Is very like a wall!"
>
> The Second, feeling of the tusk,
> Cried, "Ho! what have we here
> So very round and smooth and sharp?
> To me 'tis mighty clear
> This wonder of an Elephant
> Is very like a spear!"
>
> The Third approached the animal,
> And happening to take
> The squirming trunk within his hands,
> Thus boldly up and spake:

"I see," quoth he, "the Elephant
Is very like a snake!"

. . .

And so these men of Indostan
Disputed loud and long,
Each in his own opinion
Exceeding stiff and strong,
Though each was partly in the right,
And all were in the wrong!

As I thought about the various perspectives presented here I questioned their interrelatedness. The moral to Saxe's poem began to haunt me.

So oft in theologic wars,
The disputants, I ween,
Rail on in utter ignorance
Of what each other mean,
And prate about an Elephant
Not one of them has seen!

Had I really done justice to Korean dance? Would readers leave this volume with disconnected bits and pieces of information about dance in Korea?

In the Introduction I stated my intention to present a series of perspectives rather than a definitive study. I believe these diverse perspectives shed light on a whole, both the "whole" of Korean dance and how dance fits into the "whole" of Korean society—in the past as well as today. The thread that runs through the perspectives and that binds them together is identity, which is at the core of much that we do and many of the choices we make. And, like Korean dance, we each have many identities, all of which constantly change.

When Koreans had a royal court, dance reflected the hierarchical structure that existed and included both court and village forms. As they modernized they created a new kind of dance and chose to label it in a way that reflected their concern with keeping up with countries they considered more advanced. When Ch'oe Sŭng-hŭi sought to establish a positive reputation in the United States, she modified her performances to reflect an identity she thought was *expected* of her and her dances. When individuals of Korean ancestry in another country wanted to publicly present their heritage, they chose dance as one vehicle for doing so. And Korean immigrants, as well as people like Kim Ch'ŏn-hŭng, chose images of the past to construct their identities in the present. What constitutes Korean dance has now spread beyond Korea's shores.

The terminology used to identify dance in general and various kinds of dance in particular has evolved with changing ideas of what is important and how to best identify dance and dances. It has also responded to changing political circumstances that contribute to how people must, or choose to, identify themselves.

The histories of Ch'ŏyongmu and Chinju Kŏmmu reflect changing identities of individual dances, yet each retains an essence that allows it to continue to be identified as essentially the same dance. Today performances of both serve as a way to mark an identity of the past that is integral to an identity of the present.

As movements used in shaman rituals became the source for out-of-context, or new-context, presentations, people delineated distinctly identifiable shamanic movement features, some of which are shared with other kinds of Korean dance and some of which are unique.

There are those who lament changes that have occurred in Korea's dances from the past, and those who fault the government's National Treasure System for freezing them in a way that changes their original meanings. In reality, however, traditions of the past were never static. They, too, were constantly evolving. Today, symbols of the past are created by selecting isolated moments from former times, perhaps "authentic," perhaps constructed. But as time moves on, just as the original dances changed, so too do the meanings of the newly created symbols. As time moves on, meanings of dances or of symbols they have become can never be the same. Near the end of the twentieth century Korean students described their use of masked dance-drama as a way to reconnect with the past, to breathe "together with the ancestors" and reclaim themselves "by becoming one with the spirit" of them (in Choi Chungmoo 1995:111). The past has become the basis for constructing a modern identity. And although in some cases frozen in form, the dances of the past are, indeed, part of a living tradition, but one that has a new meaning and that lives in a different way than in the past.

As cultures become increasingly homogeneous, they concurrently seek ways to reflect their uniqueness. And the body, through dance, is an ideally suited "vehicle" or "container" for establishing and presenting identity (see Jonathan Friedman in Ness 1997:97). By retaining, even in modified form, traditions of the past, dancers can "quote and cite their antecedents, . . . partake of or modify or rebel against known traditions, . . . [and] innovate consciously in a genre or create a new tradition *knowing* their works are a departure" (Erdman 1996:292, emphasis in original). Korea specialist Clark Sorensen (1995) provides an intriguing discussion of contemporary uses of shaman and older folk practices by students, stating that they

> encode highly specific and widely understood politico-cultural messages that powerfully express opposition to the class structure of present-day industrial Korea, to government-business relations, to the secular rationalism of certain types of government-patronized

modernization theory, to Korea's place in the world economy, and to the cosmopolitan orientation of the establishment. (p. 328)

Such transformed uses of older practices highlight the tension between modernization and tradition and emphasize the importance of the past to the present and the future.

As Korea began sending dancers abroad older dance forms

> were thought to represent indigenous Korean culture best, and these projected an identity that satisfied the Western expectation of the Far East as different from the West. . . . the emphasis on traditional arts also created an image of Korea as a country with a long history but without much interesting contemporary culture. (Kim Youngna 2000:119–120)

Today modern dancers and dance companies as well as groups performing court dance and older village dance forms are presented abroad. Today there is a concern with showing Korea's past as well as its present.

In the end it is not a question of tradition *versus* modernity, but tradition *plus* modernity. In an increasingly homogenized world, symbols of uniqueness are particularly important. In Korea dance serves as a visual symbol of both uniqueness *and* modernity, and a powerful way to communicate messages of many kinds to oneself as well as to others. The institutions and mechanisms created to support dance reflect this dual pull.

Dance is an important area of study in its own right, but it cannot be dislodged from the culture of which it is a part. In fact, it is an intriguing entry point to many facets of that culture. Much English-language literature on Korea deals with such things as politics and economy, but ignores dance. Dance often serves as a cultural ambassador and is exported or displayed to represent Korea, but it is important to go beyond its colorful entertainment value to come to important deeper understandings.

Each chapter of this text could easily expand to an entire volume, and none would fully represent either Korean dance or Korean culture. What I observed that forms the basis of the material presented here existed at a particular time, and at that time only. I do not pretend to be an unbiased presentor of aspects of Korean dance. As I studied the dance in various ways I became emotionally attached to it. As I became acquainted with dancers, teachers, and researchers I established professional and social relationships. Despite efforts to do so, I could not be objective in what I saw or analyzed nor in how I reported my understandings. The way I examined and understood what I saw existed at a particular moment and in a particular context. By the time you read this, I will have seen more, and will surely see things differently.

I believe Saxe was correct in pointing out that no single perspective yields the entire picture, but I believe he was incorrect in his conclusion. With due respect to Mr. Saxe, I propose a different moral to his poem:

To think about the things we see
We cast a long and serious glance.
From here, from there, from everywhere,
We seek the perfect stance
To join the views as best we can
So we may know the ultimate dance.

Afterword

Detailed Description of Ch'ŏyongmu

Section I (entrance—10 measures)

The dancers begin offstage left (to the right, from the audience perspective), with their arms akimbo, long sleeves hanging down toward the floor, and hands—from inside their sleeves—grasping their waists. They stand in a line, one behind the other, with Blue at the head of the line followed, in order, by Red, Yellow, Black, and White. (Traditionally the dancers are identified by the predominant color of their costumes.)

The musical excerpt from Sujech'ŏn, to a rhythm of 10 beats per measure, begins. The dancers remain in their places for 9 beats, then rise onto the balls of their feet as if taking a deep breath before beginning. They execute a slow, almost laborious walking pattern that carries them onstage in a single file. The pattern is repeated until all the dancers are properly aligned across the stage, at which time the player of the *pak* provides a signal that calls for one more measure of the pattern to be performed before moving on to the next section. During this last repetition the dancers turn, during one of the steps in the pattern, in order to end facing the audience.

During the second execution of the 10-beat movement pattern the dancers thrust their right arms upward and then return their hands to their waists in such a fashion that their sleeves come to rest draped over their right shoulders. This is repeated with the left arm during the third execution of the 10-beat walking phrase.

The total number of times the walking pattern is done depends on the size of the stage, usually averaging 7 to 9 times in all. What is important is that the dancers have sufficient time to allow them to perform the walking pattern to the slow, dignified tempo, and arrive evenly spaced across the back of the stage facing the audience—five elegant beings with large, slightly mysterious masks, hands resting on their waists and white sleeves resting on their shoulders.

Section II (song)

The dancers stand in their places and bob their heads slightly as they, or offstage musicians, sing Ŏllak, the first song.

Section III (bows—5 measures)

The music now changes to Hyangdan Kyoju, but remains in a 10-beat rhythmic pattern, and the dancers execute a series of bows to the audience and each other. They begin by tilting their torsos forward to bow toward the audience. As they bow and then return to an upright position they lower their arms, lift them, and return their hands to their waists. This time their sleeves simply drop toward the floor.

With their hands on their waists they perform a portion of the walking pattern of Section I during which they turn so that the two outer dancers on either side face each other, and then bow to each other. Yellow—the center dancer—turns to face stage left and bows to an imaginary person.

The dancers turn to face the opposite sides of the stage, bow again, and then all turn to face the audience.

Section IV (walking forward—2 measures)

This short section comprises a walking pattern that is almost identical to that used in the dancers' entrance, but that progresses directly toward the audience. At the beginning of the sequence the dancers thrust their arms upward, propelling their long sleeves upward toward the forward diagonals, and then return their hands once again to their waists as their sleeves drop again toward the floor. The variation of the initial walking pattern and sleeve thrusting are then repeated.

Section V (square formation—3 measures)

With their hands on their waists the dancers perform the same basic pattern used in their entrance walk, but this time each makes minor adjustments so that after performing the sequence three times they end in a square formation with Blue stage right near the audience, Red stage right at the back of the stage, White stage left near the audience, Black stage left at the back of the stage, and Yellow in the center. Blue and White face each other from opposite sides of the stage, as do Red and Black, while Yellow faces the audience. (All except Yellow face inward toward the center line of the stage.)

Section VI (rocking with sleeve thrusts—9 measures)

The music changes to the Sang Yŏngsan Hoesang section of Yŏngsan Hoesang, still in a 10-beat per measure phrase.

The dancers now begin a pattern involving an alternation of bending and extending the knees combined with a tilting and returning to upright of the torso, interspersed with changing the supporting stance from a position in which the feet are spread so that one is diagonally forward of the other to one in which they are side by side. The first time the sequence is done the right arm thrusts upward, propelling the sleeve to the forward diagonal and the arm then lowers as the hand is placed on the waist. The second time the left arm thrusts upward and the hand is placed on the waist, and the third time both arms project upward and the hands return to the waist.

The legs then bend and extend as the arms lower and lift to circle inward, and then lift and circle slightly outward before returning the hands to the waist.

The legs then bend and extend again, accompanied by a turn so that all dancers except Yellow face the opposite directions (away from the center line of the stage). Yellow does not turn, and remains facing the audience. Except for the concluding measure to adjust facings, the entire sequence is then repeated.

Section VII (counterclockwise circle—12 measures)

The dancers all perform a variation of the entrance walk, Yellow making a small counterclockwise circle in the center of the stage and the other dancers, one behind the other, making a large counterclockwise circle around Yellow. By now the tempo has increased, and although the music is still in a 10-beat rhythmic pattern, the dance phrase is 15 beats long. (This is the portion described in the section on music in the text in which movement and music adhere to a common underlying pulse, but because of differing phrase lengths they change their relationship to each other—shifting from being out of synchrony to being aligned.)

The pattern comprises 5 steps forward and 1 backward, interspersed with a bending of both knees and then extending one while the other lifts. As this is done both arms thrust upward to the forward diagonals, propelling the sleeves outward, lower in a circular fashion to a position behind the back, and then lift so one hand is near the side of the head and the other is pulled in close to the body at chest height. This sequence of arm movements is done during the first 2 steps, and then repeats on the other side during the second 2 steps.

During the fifth step the arms thrust upward and lower to behind the back again, and on the final step backward both arms simply lift to the side and then bend so each hand is near one side of the head—a kind of preparation to begin the 15-count phrase again.

The pattern is done a total of 6 times in the circular configuration. It is then done 2 more times while the dancers adjust their step directions and facings so that they move into a single line across the stage as at the beginning of the dance, and then open out into a diamond formation with Black center stage nearest the audience, Red center stage farthest from the audience, Blue stage right, White stage left, and Yellow again in the center. Yellow faces the audience and all other dancers face Yellow.

The overall effect of this sequence is of a kaleidoscopic turning, closing, and then opening. As the rising-walking-sinking pattern is done the dancers repeatedly thrust their arms open and then almost wrap them around their bodies; after the open circular formation the dancers close into a straight line only to open out again into the diamond formation.

Section VIII (duets—17 measures)

The music changes to a 6-beat rhythmic pattern, and the dancers perform 2 stepping sequences in place that are identical to the previous stepping pattern but that are performed to the different rhythm.

A 24-count pattern now begins in which Yellow dances, in turn, with each of the other dancers. He progresses in a clockwise direction, beginning with Black, then Blue, then Red, and finally White. The stepping pattern is basically the same as those done previously—step, close, bend, and lift—with a total of 8 steps, but this time there is a clear relationship between the 2 performing dancers. On the first 2 steps they advance toward each other. On the next 2 they separate slightly to the right and then return so they are directly in front of each other. They then turn so their backs are toward each other, each moves forward so they separate a bit from each other, they turn once again to face each other, and then separate slightly to the left. The torso tilts and turns during each stepping sequence, making a swinging arc from one side to the other.

The arms begin low in front of the body, right arm crossed slightly in front of the left. The right arm thrusts upward to the open forward diagonal and then returns to low and in front of the body, and then the left arm thrusts upward. This time, however, the sleeves are not thrust outward, but remain hanging down toward the ground; in lieu of propelling the sleeves, this time the arms appear to punch upward. This arm movement is done 3 times during the first 3 steps. On the fourth step both arms thrust forward and upward and the sleeves are propelled in the same direction. Both arms then lower to the sides at shoulder height. The right hand is quickly drawn in near to the head so that it can be thrust upward and to the side, propelling the sleeve into the same direction, and then lowers to behind the back. Both arms remain still on the next step, and then the left arm draws in quickly so that the hand is near the side of the head in order that it can repeat the sideward thrusting, and lower to behind the back. The arms remain still on the last step, and then lower quickly to the crossed position in front of the body to prepare for the next repetition of the pattern. The dancers who remain still, awaiting their turn to dance with Yellow, simply rest their hands on their waists.

The 24-count pattern repeats as Yellow dances, in turn, with each of the remaining dancers.

Section IX (canon—16 measures)

A similar 24-count pattern is now done in canon form—a form in which a pattern originally done by one or more performers repeats, each time with an increasing number of performers. Yellow faces Black and both dancers perform the pattern, Yellow turns to face Blue and all three dancers perform the pattern, Yellow turns to face Red and all four dancers perform the pattern, and finally Yellow faces White and all five dancers perform together.

The pattern performed comprises the step-close-sink-lift footwork done repeatedly, progressing forward, backward, sideward, and returning to the starting place. The arms repeatedly thrust forward and upward to propel the sleeves in the same direction; first both arms together, then each arm separately, then both together three times. The dancers conclude the pattern by lowering their arms, circling them upward and inward, and then lowering them again to prepare to repeat the complete sequence.

The overall effect of this section is of increasing intensity. The thrusting of the sleeves is much more frequent than in previous sections and is done more times with both arms simultaneously than separately, the tempo has increased, and the canon form that gradually adds more dancers to the number performing at one time leads to a stage alive with rising-sinking, torso-swinging, sleeve-thrusting beings.

Section X (clockwise circle—24 measures)

Yellow now moves to a position behind White, and the group of five dancers progresses in a large clockwise circle around the stage. They execute the same basic pattern as in the preceding section, but this time the first 2 steps carry them forward around the circle, the next moves them slightly toward the center of the circle, the next slightly away from the center, the next 3 carry them forward around the circle, and the final step carries them back before they repeat the complete pattern. The 24-count pattern is performed a total of 4 times in the circle formation. It is then repeated again with slight modifications to the step directions so the dancers can regroup themselves into a straight line as at the beginning of the dance, and it is performed a final time with the step directions adjusted so the line of dancers retreats toward the back of the stage.

Section XI (song)

After the lengthy flurry of swishing sleeves and changing group formations, the dancers quietly place their hands on their hips and stand in their places and bob their heads slightly as they, or offstage musicians, sing Up'yŏn, the second unaccompanied song.

Section XII (advancing and retreating with sleeve thrusting—4 measures)

The music resumes a 6-beat rhythmic pattern, but the dancers pause for 6 beats before starting to dance again. Except for the direction of the steps, the footwork of the next pattern is the same as previously—a 24-count sequence comprising a step, close, sink, and lift—but the sleeve-thrusting pattern is different. This time the first 4 steps advance forward and the last 4 retreat. Starting with both arms bent so the hands are near the right shoulder, they thrust forward and upward to propel the sleeves in the same direction. They then lower and lift to the starting position, but this time both hands are near the left shoulder. The thrusting, lowering, and repositioning to the opposite shoulder continues. The arms thrust forward on the first step, and then rest near the shoulder on the second step; they then continue to alternate between thrusting and resting. The overall effect of this section is increasing intensity as the dancers seem to thrust a great burden from one shoulder and then the other.

Section XIII (advancing and retreating with sleeve thrusting followed by exit)

The step-close-sink-lift footwork pattern continues, and the thrust-lower-lift to the shoulder arm pattern continues, but this time the arms thrust on each step. The dancers advance with 4 steps, retreat with 4 steps, and then all turn to face stage right as Blue leads the dancers in a counter-clockwise arc before leading them all to exit upstage left.

In this final section the arms attract the greatest attention. But the increased tempo, greater quantity of movement activity, continual rising and sinking, changing of direction of progression, and frequently recurring thrusting of the sleeves all lead to a dynamic exit of the five dancers.

Description of an Abridged Version
of Ch'ŏyongmu

An example of an abridged version of the dance—demonstrating elimination of some repetition and of several entire sections—was performed by members of the National Center for Korean Traditional Performing Arts in November of 1990. The nature of modifications is summarized below.

Sections I and II (entrance and first song)—Not performed; dancers simply begin in a line onstage.

Section III (bows)—Dancers bow only once—to the audience; they do not bow to each other.

Section IV (walking forward)—Performed as in long version.

Section V (square formation)—Performed as in long version.

Section VI (rocking with sleeve thrusts)—The basic pattern is performed only once—with the dancers facing each other; there is no repetition with the dancers facing away from each other.

Section VII (counterclockwise circle)—Not performed.

Section VIII (duets)—Only half of this section is performed: Yellow dances, in turn, with Black and Blue.

Section IX (canon)—Only half of this section is performed: Yellow dances with Black, Blue, and Red, and then all dance together.

Section X (clockwise circle)—Performed as in long version.

Section XI (song)—Performed as in long version.

Section XII (advancing and retreating with sleeve thrusting)—Performed as in long version, but with fewer repetitions.

Section XIII (advancing and retreating with sleeve thrusting followed by exit)—Performed as in long version but with fewer repetitions of advancing and retreating.

Detailed Description of Chinju Kŏmmu

Section I (entrance)

The dancers enter the performing space wearing the long multicolored sleeves that are attached at their wrists. From within the sleeve each hand grasps the handle of a knife. The performers simply walk to their starting positions in two lines, four in each line. Both lines are perpendicular to the audience, with the dancers in one line facing those across from them in the other line.

Section II (square formations)

The accompanying music begins with a slow 6-beat-per-measure rhythmic pattern, to which the dancers bend their knees and place their knives on the ground, where they remain until needed. They then walk slowly, alternately bending and extending their knees several times after each step. This locomotor pattern is used while they move through a series of formations in which the lines merge and separate in a kaleidoscopic opening and closing fashion. At one point after the lines merge the dancers open out into a square formation, then two parallel lines (parallel to the audience), merge into a single line, open again into a square, and then re-form two lines perpendicular to the audience.

Section III (partner-relationships)

The accompaniment changes to a 4-beat-per-measure rhythm in which the underlying pulse is slightly quicker, and the dancers continue the walking pattern in several different relationships with the partner they have been facing, beginning with a strong tilt of the torso backward in which the arms open sideward at shoulder height with the palms facing upward. The sequence concludes with a walking pattern that takes each line of four dancers to opposite sides of the performing area, where they remove their sleeves and drop them to the floor.

Section IV (palm-display)

The dancers then continue with a series of formation changes during which they continually repeat an arm pattern involving the abrupt opening of their cupped hands with arms turned to display their palms. At the conclusion of this sequence the dancers add the backward torso tilt to the hand-opening movement.

Section V (advancing and retreating)

The accompaniment changes to a faster 4-beat-per-measure pattern to which the dancers perform a livelier walking sequence in which the emphasis is on a lifting of the center of weight. This time the locomotor pattern is done while tracing a series of advancing and retreating floor patterns, and is accompanied by moving the arms and wrists as if holding and manipulating the knives.

Section VI (seated preparation)

The dancers then sit in two lines facing each other, the lines perpendicular to the audience as at the start of the dance. They carefully grasp the ends of the front panels of their jackets and twist their lower arms to alternately reveal the red inner lining and the blue outer surface. Then they tie the ends of their jackets behind their backs and repeat some of the arm movements they did previously as if manipulating the knives. They pick up one knife and dance with it, and then the other.

Section VII (standing knife dance)

When the rhythm changes to a slow 4-beat-per-measure pattern, the dancers stand and then briefly change formation.

The rhythm then changes back to a fast 4-beat-per-measure pattern as the dancers perform a series of advancing and retreating movements while doing the same arm movements they did previously, but now with knives in hand.

They then form a circle and move halfway around it in a counterclockwise direction executing a series of simplified barrel turns (also in a counterclockwise direction) without arm movement. They re-form their two lines, repeat the advancing and retreating patterns, re-form the circle, and move halfway around the circle again while doing barrel turns. This time, however, they add arm and knife movements during the turns. The entire pattern is repeated a third time with a different arm movement to manipulate the knives during the barrel turns.

Section VIII (concluding)

The rhythm changes to a slow 4-beat-per-measure pattern as the dancers walk in a circle while manipulating the knives and conclude in a single line parallel to, and facing, the audience. To a faster 4-beat-per-measure rhythmic pattern the dancers briefly manipulate their knives, bow, and exit by backing away from the performing area.

Outline of September 3 Program of the Hawai'i Shaman-related Performance

SECTION	SUBSECTION	PERFORMER(S)	GENERAL DESCRIPTION	PREDOMINANT MOVEMENT FEATURES
I. Pulsa kŏri	A. Sŭngmu (5 minutes)	11 students	abbreviated version of Buddhist Monk's Dance (adapted for theatrical presentation)	elaborated drum-playing movements
	B. Ritual (12 minutes)	Yi Chi-san	singing while holding a fan and bell tree, standing on a large clay pot, talking with dancers enacting the role of clients at a *kut*, and dancing with a large pair of cymbals	· zigzag pathways through space · alternate facing to four directions · turning counterclockwise · gentle bouncing · jumps with feet astride · manipulation of costume sleeves and cymbals to enhance overall visual design
	C. Parach'um (3 minutes)	10 students	abbreviated, choreographed-for-the-theater version of the Buddhist Cymbal Dance	· some zigzag pathways through space · gentle jumping · turning both clockwise and counterclockwise
II. Taegam kŏri	A. Transition (2 minutes)	3 students	dancers wearing military vests and hats trace floor patterns while each holds a wood/cardboard trident and knife	movements unrelated to those of any other sections

SECTION	SUBSECTION	PERFORMER(S)	GENERAL DESCRIPTION	PREDOMINANT MOVEMENT FEATURES
	B. Ritual (12 minutes)	Yi Chi-san	wearing military-style clothing, walks through the audience to get to the stage; manipulates knife, fan, costume, and pig's feet from the altar table; balances large pot on his head; dances while manipulating his costume; interacts with "clients"	· zigzag pathways through space · turning counterclockwise · "wild" jumping · side-to-side swagger with jumps (including shifting of hips from side to side) · small leg lifts
	C. Small Changgo (7 minutes)	8 students	dancers manipulate and play a very small drum while dancing	
III. Hoku kŏri [Hogu kŏri]	A. Goddess Hogu (5 minutes)	4 students and Halla Pai Huhm	representation of the goddess Hogu, with Huhm interacting with "clients"	· zigzag pathways through space in a syncopated rhythm · turns counterclockwise · bouncing
	B. Sŏnyurak (7 minutes)	20 students	Huhm's version of the Boat Dance, a traditional court dance	
IV. Byoltang assi [Pyŏltang asshi]	(14 minutes)	students	primarily mime sequences performed largely by children, depicting various scenes in a village	(not analyzed here)
V. Mudang kibon dongjak chom [Mudang kibon tongjak ch'um]	(5 minutes)	Halla Pai Huhm	demonstration of movements described in the printed program as "basic to all shaman dances"	· zigzag pathway through space · jumps emphasizing verticality · hopping on one leg

SECTION	SUBSECTION	PERFORMER(S)	GENERAL DESCRIPTION	PREDOMINANT MOVEMENT FEATURES
VI. Chaktu kŏri	A. Mudang Ch'um (4 minutes)	14 students	dancers manipulate a long scarf, bell tree, and a large fan; 2 dancers mime a shaman and client	· zigzag pathways through space · vertical jumping · hops on one leg
	B. (2 minutes)	8 students	dancers each hold a wood/cardboard knife and a trident	· movements unrelated to those of any other section except IIA
	C. Ritual (23 minutes)	Yi Chi-san	brandishing of knives, standing barefooted on up-turned knife blades, manipulation of knives	· bows to four directions · jumps · zigzag pathways through space · circling the knives in a clockwise direction · turning counterclockwise · shoulder "shudders"
	D. Flag Dance (5 minutes)	10 students	dancers each manip-ulate five flags of different colors	· zigzag pathways through space · vertical jumping

Note: Order is as in the printed program. In performance, sections IV and V were reversed.

APPENDIX 5

Outline of September 4 Program of the Hawai'i Shaman-related Performance

SECTION	SUBSECTION	PERFORMER(S)	GENERAL DESCRIPTION	PREDOMINANT MOVEMENT FEATURES
I. Chon'an kŏri	A. Fairy Dance (8 minutes)	20 students	dancers attired in semi-court style	· simple walking · geometric group formations · manipulation of a nonfolding fan and very long scarf
	B. Ritual (11 minutes)	Yi Chi-san	wears costume of a king; manipulates long sleeves, knives, and five flags of different colors; some singing	· simple, slow walking · zigzag pathways through space · gentle rising and sinking on steps · gentle jumps in wide stride
II. Byoltang assi [Pyŏltang asshi]	(14 minutes)	students	repeat of section from first evening	(not analyzed here)
III. Sinchang kŏri [Shinchang kŏri]	A. Mudang Ch'um (6 minutes)	14 students	slightly longer version of VI A performed on first night	
	B. Flag Dance (15 minutes)	Halla Pai Huhm and 10 students	section VI D of previous night's program, preceded by 10-minute solo by Halla Huhm; dancers manipulate five flags of different colors	· "wild" jumping · zigzag pathways through space · some light jumping and some wild jumping

SECTION	SUBSECTION	PERFORMER(S)	GENERAL DESCRIPTION	PREDOMINANT MOVEMENT FEATURES
IV. Chin no ki kut [Chinogwi kut]	A. (9 minutes)	Halla Pai Huhm	dances with a dead codfish tied to her back and then with a long scarf; talking and singing; manipulation of long scarf	· vertical jumping · turns counter-clockwise
	B. Ritual (18 minutes)	Yi Chi-san; 8 students performing as villagers	alternately holds and manipulates a fan, bell tree, and paper money	· walking in counter-clockwise circle · gentle bouncing with step-touch walking pattern · zigzag pathways through space
	C. (5 minutes)	Halla Pai Huhm	sings and then dances	similar to many salp'uri movements (suspensions, asymmetry, chest initiations)
	D. Ritual (16 minutes)	Yi Chi-San	interaction with "clients"; sings and dances with paper money and clothing; plays cymbals and manipulates paper money while dancing and then splits two long white cloths by walking through their lengths	walking with bounce
	E. Buk Ch'um [Pukch'um] (5 minutes)	8 students (all other dancers join for a final bow)	4 dancers carry a drum, which the other 4 dancers play on	movements not related to those of previous sections

Outline of Chindo Sshikkim Kut Performance

SECTION	SUBSECTION	PERFORMER(S)	GENERAL DESCRIPTION	PREDOMINANT MOVEMENT FEATURES
I.		soloist	primarily singing	· minimal movement; primarily standing center-stage with right arm extended to forward-right-diagonal at shoulder height · simple walking in center-stage area · some manipulation of paper streamers in S-shaped curves · small clockwise and counterclockwise arced pathways through space
II.	A. holding small tree branch and changgo	soloist	primarily singing	simple striking of one head of the changgo while holding it in an upright position
	B. holding small tree branch and paper streamers	same soloist as section A	primarily singing	· minimal movement; primarily standing center-stage with right arm extended to forward-right-diagonal at shoulder height · simple walking in center-stage area · some manipulation of paper streamers in S-shaped curves · small complete clockwise and counterclockwise circular pathways through space

SECTION	SUBSECTION	PERFORMER(S)	GENERAL DESCRIPTION	PREDOMINANT MOVEMENT FEATURES
III.		soloist	primarily singing	· minimal movement; primarily standing center-stage with right arm extended to forward-right-diagonal at shoulder height · simple walking in center-stage area · no use of handheld properties except at the end (grasping paper streamers and waving them briefly over the altar table)
IV.		soloist	· salp'uri-style dance · sits in front of musicians and talks and laughs with them	· manipulates paper streamers · both asymmetrical and symmetrical arm gestures · careful rolling through the foot as it takes weight · suspended movements · impulses in chest and shoulder area
V.		soloist	primarily singing	· minimal movement; primarily standing centerstage · occasionally right arm extended to forward-right-diagonal at shoulder height in isolation; occasionally both arms extended—right to forward-right-diagonal and left to forward-left-diagonal, at shoulder height · simple walking in center-stage area · no use of handheld properties except at the end—a small bowl with a lit candle in it that was taken from the altar table

SECTION	SUBSECTION	PERFORMER(S)	GENERAL DESCRIPTION	PREDOMINANT MOVEMENT FEATURES
VI.	A. Knotted cloth	2 performers	primarily singing	abrupt arm movements to thrust, in order to untie the knots it contains, a long cloth held between them
	B. Rolled mat	2 performers (one appearing to function as a client)	primarily singing and manipulation of objects	only those movements needed to manipulate the objects
	C. At the altar	2 performers (one appearing to function as a client)	entirely singing	
VII.		1 performer	entirely singing and playing of a gong	
VIII.		3 performers	primarily singing and manipulation of objects	each performer does some movements to manipulate an object being held (clothes, paper streamers, and an unidentified object)

Documented U.S. Performances
of Ch'oe Sŭng-hŭi

DATE	CITY	THEATER	LOCAL SPONSOR	MANAGING COMPANY
1/22/38	San Francisco	Community Theatre		Fritz Horwitz
2/2/38 Wednesday 8:30 P.M.	Los Angeles	Wilshire Ebell Theatre	Western Dance Guild	Fritz Horwitz
2/20/38 Sunday 3:00 P.M.	New York	Guild Theatre		Metropolitan Music Bureau
3/5/38 Saturday 9:00 P.M.	New York	Theresa L. Kaufmann Auditorium	Dance Theatre of the Y.M.H.A. (92nd Street Y)	Metropolitan Music Bureau
11/6/38 Sunday 8:30 P.M.	New York	Guild Theatre		Hurok Attractions
12/28/39 Thursday evening	New York	St. James Theatre	Frances Hawkins, in association with Jean Rosenthal	
2/17/40	New York	McMillin Theatre	Institute of Arts and Sciences, Columbia University	
2/22/40	Chicago	Civic Theater		
3/30/40 Saturday evening	Los Angeles	Hollywood Women's Club Concert Hall		
4/7/40	San Francisco	Curran Theatre	Tom C. Girton	

American Repertoire of
Ch'oe Sŭng-hŭi

Descriptions are based on publicity brochures, printed programs, and reviewers' comments.

Where dances assumed to be the same were presented with different titles, the most frequently used title appears first. Titles in parentheses indicate possible Korean titles of dances, based on titles and descriptions of dances in Korean-language sources.

Ancient Honeymoon Dance (Shinhon Yŏhaeng)

(no description available)

Ancient Prisoner, Choonhyang in Prison
(Kamoge Kach'in Ch'unhyang)

The dance of anguish of the heroine of a traditional story (*Ch'unyang*) who is imprisoned for refusing to entertain an official because she had a lower-class lover.

Bodhisattva
(Kwanŭm Posal, Posalmu, Pohyŏn Posal, Kamu Posal)

A figure representing a Buddhist "saint" stands on a lotus-flower pedestal, moving only her arms and hands in movements symbolizing the attainment of enlightenment.

Buddhist Temptress (Pulgyoŭi Yobu, Sŭngmu, Tosŭngŭi Yuhok)

A representation of Whang Chin-i, a Korean woman who is said to have seduced a monk with her dancing more than 600 years ago. Whang disguised herself as a monk and beat on drums while she danced. During the piece Ch'oe played a drum suspended in a standing frame.

Court Lady of Shiragi (Shilla Kungnyŏŭi Ch'um)

A dance displaying the beauty of a court woman from the period known in Korean as the Shilla dynasty. The dancer manipulates two feathered fans.

Dream of Youth, Old Pipe Smoker
(Shinno Shimbullo, Ch'ŏngch'un, Changch'un Pullojigok)

A masked dance in which an old man reminisces about his youth while smoking his pipe and drinking. He attempts to dance as he did in former times, but his aging muscles won't allow him to.

Festival Dance, Korean Festival, Harvest Dance
(Kaŭlgŏji Ch'um, Maŭrŭi P'ungjak)

Rejoicing to celebrate a harvest.

Flower Girl, Peasant Girl
(Nonggaŭi Ch'ŏnyŏ, Nongch'on Sonyŏŭi Ch'um)

A young girl from the countryside joyfully picks flowers during the spring.

Fresco of Rakuro
(Nangnangŭi Pyŏkhwa'esŏ, Shillaŭi Pyŏkhwa'esŏ)

A male figure from a painting said to be 2,000 years old.

Greatest General Under the Sun, Korean General,
Tenka Daishogun (Ch'ŏnha Taejanggun)

A masked dance portraying a man who thinks himself the wisest and greatest general on earth.

Invocation to Buddha
(Sŏgwangsaŭi Ach'im, Puch'ŏe Taehan Kido)

A monk gives himself up to prayer by counting his rosary and sounding his bells.

Kisaeng Dances (Kisaengch'um)

Dances done by performers to entertain upper class men.
  Drum Dance (Changgoch'um)
    Rooted in traditional farmers' dance and music, the dancer plays the changgo, an hour-glass shaped drum, that is tied to her body with sashes over her shoulder and around her waist.
  Scarf Dance, Geisha Dance, Korean Dancing Girl (Sugŏnch'um)
    Possibly rooted in shaman dance, the dancer manipulates a long scarf while performing.

Korean Vagabond, Masked Dance
(Pongsan T'alch'um)

Based on an excerpt from the Pongsan masked dance-drama.

Melody of the Jade Flute
(Okchŏgŭi Kok, Pich'wi P'iriŭi Mellodi)

Shows the fantasy of the playing of a jade flute by young angels, which precedes a great event on earth.

Seoul Fortune Teller (Sŏurŭi Chŏmjaengi, Munyŏŭi Ch'um)

A deceitful fortune teller tries to persuade people to give her money or rice.

Sleeve Dance
(Paekche Kungnyŏŭi Ch'um, Shilla Kungnyŏŭi Ch'um)

A dance said to have originally been popular among waiting women in the court.

Sword Dance, Dagger Dance (Kŏmmu)

Originally created to portray the manly appearance and heroic spirit of ancient warriors, the dance became more delicate when performed by female entertainers. Ch'oe attempted to restore the dance to its original feeling.

Three Traditional Rhythms (Segajiŭi Korian Mellodi)

Although described as a dance "based on the three fundamental movements of Korean dance," the title is undoubtedly based on the dance's accompaniment by three traditional rhythms, one fast, one slow, and one medium in tempo. (There are no movements described today as the "three basic movements.")

Two Court Dances

Two dances said to have originally been performed at royal ceremonies.

Two Folk Tunes

    Arirang (Korean Sweetheart's Farewell)
       A dance accompanied by a folk song telling of the sorrow of parting
       and memories of happy times with a lover.
    Shinkosan Tariang
       A twentieth-century folk song.

War Dance of Kokurai
(Koguryŏŭi Chŏnmu, Koguryŏŭi Suin)

Based on an ancient painting, a warrior demonstrates various phases of battle, during which he brandishes a sword and then a bow and arrow.

Whalyang (Hallyang, Hwarangŭi Ch'um)

A handsome young man dances to entertain young women.

Young Korean Bridegroom, Child Bridegroom
(Ch'oriptong, Sae Shillang, Kkoma Shillang)

Traditionally, Korean boys of fourteen or fifteen years would be ceremonially married. Wearing the traditional hat of men (*kat*) and traditional garments, a young boy shows his happiness.

CHRONOLOGY

1919	Death of King Kojong; March First Independence Movement
1922	Kim Ch'ŏn-hŭng begins studying at Yiwangjik Aakpu; Ch'oe Sŭng-hŭi graduates from high school; possible first Korean dance activities in Hawai'i; Halla Pai Huhm is born in Pusan
1923	First major court-style event with music and dance since beginning of Japanese occupation, and last such event ever; Ch'ŏyongmu is reconstructed
1924	Father of Kim Ch'ŏn-hŭng dies
1925–1926	American modern dance company of Ruth St. Denis and Ted Shawn, Denishawn Dance Company, performs in Asia, including Japan
1926	Performance in Seoul of modern dance by Japanese dancer Ishii Baku; Kim Ch'ŏn-hŭng graduates from Yiwangjik Aakpu; Sunjong, Korea's last king, dies; June 10th Independence Movement
1931	Japan invades Manchuria; Kim Ch'ŏn-hŭng marries Pak Chun-ju; Ch'oe Sŭng-hŭi marries An Mak
1932	Yiwangjik Aakpu staff makes a set of metal bells and jade chimes to send to Manchuria for coronation of Pu Yi, last emperor of China
1934	Establishment of American Dance Festival in the United States; Mary Jo Freshley is born in Ohio
1935	Ch'oe Sŭng-hŭi signs a contract to star in a movie based, in part, on her life
1937	Japan's invasion of China begins the Sino-Japanese War; Ch'oe Sŭng-hŭi sets sail from Tokyo for performances in the United States
1938–1940	Ch'oe Sŭng-hŭi performs in the United States, Europe, and South and Central America
1940	Kim Ch'ŏn-hŭng leaves Yiwangjik Aakpu; Ch'oe Sŭng-hŭi returns to Japan
1941	United States enters World War II
1942	Japanese government forms performing groups, including Chosŏn Aktae, to perform for Japanese and Korean soldiers
1945	Ch'oe Sŭng-hŭi and her family go to what will become North Korea
1948	Division of Korea into the Republic of Korea in the south and the Democratic People's Republic of Korea in the north
1949?–1950?	Halla Huhm immigrates to Hawai'i
1950	Japan establishes a Cultural Properties Protection Law (Bunkazai Hogohō), to preserve both tangible and intangible objects; Halla Huhm opens her dance studio in Hawai'i
1950–1953	Korean War
1951	Musicians from Aakpu go to Chinju to assist in re-establishing music to accompany Chinju Kŏmmu
1953	Pak Oe-sŏn goes to Japan to study ballet and modern dance
1954	Im Sŏng-nam returns from studying ballet in Japan and begins to train many Korean ballet performers; Halla Huhm performs a geisha dancer in Honolulu Community Theatre production of *Teahouse of the August Moon*

1955	Former court music institute is established in Seoul as the National Classical Music Institute (now the National Center for Korean Traditional Performing Arts)
1959	Premiere of Ch'ŏyongnang, a dance-drama based on the Ch'ŏyong legend, choreographed by Kim Ch'ŏn-hŭng
1960	Kim Ch'ŏn-hŭng receives the Seoul City Cultural Award for his choreography of Chŏyongnang
1961	Mary Jo Freshley moves to Hawai'i and begins to study Korean dance
1962	Government of South Korea passes the Law on the Protection of Cultural Properties (Munhwajae Pohopŏp)
1963	Ewha Woman's University establishes the first dance department in a four-year university; Yuk Wan-sun returns to Korea from the United States and establishes the Graham technique of modern dance at Ewha
1966	Completion of report leading to designation of Chinju Kŏmmu as an Intangible Cultural Asset
1967	Kim Ch'ŏn-hŭng is designated a Human Cultural Asset for expertise on the *haegŭm* as played in Chongmyo cheryeak; Chinju Kŏmmu designated an Intangible Cultural Asset; Ch'oe Wan-ja dies
1969	Korea's Cultural Property Preservation Bureau begins to sponsor annual performances of Intangible Cultural Assets
1971	Ch'ŏyongmu is recognized as Intangible Cultural Asset number thirty-nine; Kim Ch'ŏn-hŭng authors *Chŏngak yanggŭmbo*, a book of musical scores for the *yanggŭm*
1974	Mary Jo Freshley begins to assist in teaching classes at the Halla Huhm Dance Studio
1974	Mary Jo Freshley is given the designation of "instructor" by Halla Huhm
1976	Publication of first issue of *Ch'um* (Dance) magazine; Kim Mae-ja establishes Ch'angmuhoe (Creative Dance Company); Halla Huhm stages a performance with shaman Yi Chi-san
1977	Premiere of Kim Mae-ja's The Silk Road (Pidan Kil)
1979	Halla Huhm is recognized as the first Outstanding Korean in Hawai'i by the Korean Community Council in Hawai'i
1980	Yuk Wan-sun brings forty Korean students to the American Dance Festival in the United States; Halla Huhm receives a cultural medal from the government of South Korea
1983	Kim Ch'ŏn-hŭng restages the Hak Yonhwadae Ch'ŏyongmu Hapsŏl court dance suite; Halla Huhm returns to Korea as Assistant Professor of Dance at Chongju University of Education
1986	Universal Ballet Company premieres Shim Ch'ŏng
1988	Seoul hosts the Olympic games and includes dance and music in many official ceremonies; Halla Huhm returns to Hawai'i
1989	Halla Huhm and her studio are honored with an invitation to participate with the Hawai'i delegation at the Smithsonian Institution's Festival of American Folklife in Washington, D.C.

1990   Premiere of Mun Il-chi's Rice Plant (Pyŏ), Nam Chŏng-ho's Hey, Children, What's Beyond the Mountain (Aiya, Chŏ San Nŏmŏe Muŏshi?), and Kuk Su-ho's Myth of Mount Paektu (Paektusan Shin'gok); An Ae-sun's Meeting (Mannam) wins the Grand Prize at the Seoul Dance Festival; the first American Dance Festival in Seoul is established

1992   Establishment, by Ministry of Culture and Sports, of Korean National University of Arts (Han'guk Yesul Chonghap Hakkyo); designation, by Korean Government, as the Year of Dance; Cultural Property Preservation Bureau implements a code of conduct for National Living Treasures

1994   Halla Huhm dies; Mary Jo Freshley assumes full responsibility for operating the Halla Huhm Dance Studio; Pak Chun-ju, wife of Kim Ch'ŏn-hŭng, dies

1996   Korean National University of Arts establishes School of Dance

1997   Serious downturn in Korea's economy; Kim Ch'ŏn-hŭng receives award from *Chosŏn Ilbo* for contributions to perpetuating traditional Korean dance

Notes

1. The Many Faces of Korean Dance (pp. 3–29)

1. The concepts of "tradition" and "traditional" are complex, and the terms are not universally defined. For a summary of some meanings associated with them see Killick 1998:11–23. I use "traditional" here because it is the most common gloss of the term used by Koreans for a particular kind of dance. For further discussion of issues relating to this categorization see Chapter 2. In many traditional performing art forms in Korea what are commonly compartmentalized in the West into such things as music, dance, drama, and acrobatics are conceived of as a single entity. This is particularly apparent in, for example, the many "drum dances." Additionally, the playing of many musicial instruments incorporates highly choreographed, or structured, movement sequences. Since the focus here is on dance, music is only briefly touched on.

2. The men were known as *mudong*, the women as *kisaeng*. Although a law was passed in 1477 to replace female dancers with young boys, it was unsuccessful (Heyman 1964:11). During the mid- and late-Chosŏn dynasty (1392–1910) boys are said to have performed for kings, princes, and guests, and women for queens, princesses, and occasionally male members of the royal household (ibid.: 14). For an overview of the *kisaeng* tradition see Loken-Kim 1989:36–51, 65–69 and Lee Byong-won 1979.

3. For historical background on individual court dances and descriptions of other dances see, for example, Heyman 1964.

4. These dances were originally performed by men. According to Loken-Kim, women began to perform them in the 1980s (1989:89). This undoubtedly occurred when the high school students began to perform them.

5. For discussions of political uses of masked dance-drama and other traditional dance forms see Choi Chungmoo 1995 and Yang Jong-sung 1988 and 1994.

6. *Nongak* literally means "farmers' music." Koreans often refer to this genre in English as "farmers' music" or "farmers' dance." Ethnomusicologist Keith Howard (see, e.g., his 1990 publication, especially Chapter 2) glosses the term "farmers' band music" or "percussion band music." Because the genre to which I refer throughout this volume is comprised of choreographed, or structured, movement as well as percussion music, I have chosen to gloss the term in a way that reflects both of these important ingredients—hence, "farmers' band dance and music." For a discussion of the assumed inclusion of dance in some Korean terms literally referring only to music, see Chapter 2.

7. Defining "dance," as opposed to movement systems that are structured but not considered dance, is a task that goes beyond this volume. For discussions of the topic see, for example, Hanna 1979, Kaeppler 1989, and Kealiinohomoku 1983.

8. For discussions of *mŏt* in relation to many aspects of Korean culture, see the Autumn 1998 issue of *Koreana*.

9. In a January 1998 lecture in Hawai'i, Korean musician Yi Chi-yŏng described the importance of the curved line in traditional Korean music when discussing the way pitch changes are made. She also commented that one way to show the beauty of this line was by a momentary stopping, or suspension, of the tone, or by showing "empty space." This suggests that a suspension, or pause (the "motion in stillness" in dance), is a shared feature of dance and music.

10. Except for limited interactions with China and Japan, its closest neighbors, for many years the Korean government sustained a strong isolationist policy, contributing to much of the western world's identification of the country as the Hermit Kingdom. An 1876 treaty of amity with Japan was followed shortly by commerce and navigation treaties with the United States, Great Britain, Germany, Russia, and France, hence opening Korea to the rest of the world and making the appellation of the Hermit Kingdom no longer relevant.

11. Loken-Kim (1989:81) presents a somewhat similar classification scheme to that presented here in which she identifies three categories: traditional, transitional, and modern. Her system, however, was delineated to describe the way in which dancers were trained, rather than the dances themselves; it only relates to the dances by implication. She labels

> those dancers "traditional," who received their training in *kwŏnbŏn* [schools for female entertainers], *chaeinchong* [*chaeinch'ŏng*—schools for traditional artists], or privately from family members or pre-theatrical troupes. "Transitional" dancers are those who have received their training in private studios, often from traditional dancers, but have adapted the dances for the stage. "Modern" dancers are those who have attended high school or colleges where they were exposed to non-Korean forms of dance such as ballet and modern. (Ibid.)

Fouser (1994) uses the term "Koreanesque" to identify a category that exemplifies some of the characteristics in what I describe here as "derived," and Killick (1998) introduces the term "traditionesque." It is also possible to identify this "derived" category as "modern dance," since in many cases its intent was to modernize the traditional. This supports American dance critic and historian George Jackson's belief that modern dance was not just a phenomenon of the western world, but that "at the last turn of the century just about every country with professional performers saw some modernization of the art of dance—be it the formal aspects, the movement technique, or the dramatic and emotional contents of the choreography" (1999). See also Anderson 1997:272–290.

12. The first such theater is generally identified as Hyŏmnyulsa, built in 1902 and later renamed Wŏn'gaksa. Killick, however, states that this theater was originally known as Hŭidae, and that there may have been other indoor theaters prior to 1902. See Killick 1998:54–58.

13. Yang Jong-sung describes the use of sŭngmu in such a television commercial (1994:136).

14. Because there are many different dances identified as salp'uri, I use this term with a lower-case "s" to refer to them generically. This format is also followed for sŭngmu and changgoch'um, discussed later in this chapter.

15. Han Sŏng-jun began his performing studies under his grandfather, learning tightrope walking, drumming, and some southern styles of village dances, including shaman dances. While he was teaching female entertainers (*kisaeng*), he recreated and arranged many village folk dances for theatrical performance (Choi Haeree 1995:173).

16. *Han* is a particularly important emotion in Korean culture, often said to be the result of the country's continual involvement in war. Hyun Young Hak (*sic*), a Korean theologian, describes it as

> a sense of unresolved resentment against injustice suffered, a sense of helplessness because of the overwhelming odds against, a feeling of total abandonment . . . , a feeling of acute pain and sorrow in one's guts and bowels making the whole body writhe and wriggle, and an obstinate urge to take "revenge" and to right the wrong all these constitute. (in Chung Hyunkyung 1990:42)

Korean writer Elaine H. Kim states it is "the anguished feeling of being far from what you wanted, a longing that never went away, but ate and slept with you every day of your life . . . by no means a hopeless feeling, however" (1989:82–83).

17. German expressionist modern dance, known as both *ausdruckstanz* ("ex-

pressionist dance") and *neue tanz* ("new dance"), is generally believed to have begun at the end of World War I, in approximately 1918. Mary Wigman, considered by many to be one of the style's leading figures, greatly influenced a number of Japanese dancers. The style advocated the expression of personal emotion through movement; movement was initiated by the dancer's emotion. Although some practitioners advocated group performance (such as Rudolf Von Laban, with his movement choirs), the style was dominated by solo performances. Although continuing on into the mid-1900s, the style is most often associated with the 1920s. For discussions of this style see, for example, Manning 1993 and Partsch-Bergsohn 1994.

18. During her first and subsequent visits to the United States, Yuk was exposed to the technique of many American modern dancers, including Merce Cunningham and Donald McKayle. She believes that writers and critics place too much emphasis on the impact of the Graham style on her work (personal communication 26 March 1999). But an examination of her choreography, even works created near the end of the twentieth century, reveals a strong Graham imprint.

19. The choreographers were Han Sang-gun, Chu Ong-nyŏ, and Hong Kyŏng-hŭi.

20. For an interesting description and analysis of this event see Sorensen 1995.

21. Loken-Kim identifies the spontaneous dances done at drinking parties, by nonshaman participants and shamans at shaman rituals or at parties associated with shaman rituals, and in nightclubs and discotheques as *hŏt'ŭnch'um* (1989:138–142).

22. The festival originally took place in Bennington, Vermont. It relocated in 1948 to the campus of Connecticut College in New London, and in 1978 to its present home at Duke University in Durham, North Carolina.

2. *Korean Dance Terminology (pp. 30–50)*

1. This chapter was inspired by discussions with Choi Haeree while she was working on her M.A. thesis at the University of Hawai'i. While some of the ideas grew out of material in her thesis (particularly her Chapter 2), I have considerably expanded on these and deepened the theoretical analysis. Portions of this chapter are based on Van Zile (1993) and several chapters of Choi's 1995 thesis. For ease of reading, we agreed that except where citing material originally drawn from other sources, crediting her contribution to the ideas presented here in this note was more desirable than including in-text citations for information taken from her thesis or my own 1993 publication. I claim sole responsibility, however, for the analysis and theoretical discussion.

2. Sohn Ho-min states:

> The vocabulary is composed of native words (41%), Chinese character (or Sino-Korean) words (54%), and loan-words (5%). Native words denote daily necessities of food, clothing and shelter, basic actions, activities and states, lower-level numerals, body parts, natural objects, etc. The native stock includes thousands of onomatopoeic and mimetic words as well as thousands of idioms and proverbs that reflect traditional culture and society. Due to their ideographic and monosyllabic nature, Chinese characters are easily combined and recombined to coin new terms as new cultural objects and subtle concepts are created. Even the title of the country (*Han'guk* "Korea") is a Sino-Korean word. So are most institutional terms, traditional cultural terms, personal names, and place names (one exception is *Seoul*, which is a native word). Sino-Korean words are pronounced not like contemporary Chinese but more like Classical Chinese, but without tones. . . . There are about 14,000 loan-words in Korean, of which almost 90% are from English. (1993:11)

Martina Deuchler (personal communication 18 Nov. 1997) states that when *han'gŭl* was initially introduced people used entirely *han'gŭl* or entirely classical Chinese. It was only gradually that a mixture began to occur.

3. Robert Provine (personal communication 3 Jan. 1998) indicates that in a listing of "qualifying examinations in various subjects" in the *Kyŏngguk taejŏn* (Confucian Dynasty Code of Law, compiled between 1460 and 1484), "exams for the *aksaeng* ("musicians") include both *aak* [a kind of music] and the two dances (*mumu* and *munmu*); exams for the *akkong* (also 'musicians') include *tangak*, *hyangak* [both assumed to be types of music] and various dances." In his 1984 *Han'guk muyong kaeron* [Introduction to Korean Dance] (p. 24), Korean musicologist Chang Sa-hun states that you can have music without dance, but there can be no dance without music.

4. According to Sohn Ho-min (undated 1998 personal communication) the more standard romanization is *taensŭ*, although the word is still pronounced by many as represented in the spelling *ttaensŭ*.

5. Ohtani Kimiko (1991:25) states that the term originated in 1904, when Tsubouchi used it in the table of contents of a book that was announced but never published. Ito Sachiyo (1979:268) attributes the origin of the word to 1905.

6. According to Shuhei Kikkawa (in Ohtani 1991:25), Tsubouchi later stated that "for scientific research a comprehensive word which could be applied to all kinds of dance was required." For other discussions of Japanese dance terminology see Kozo 1983 and Pronko 1985.

7. Although *wu* and *yong* exist independently in Chinese, they are not used together (Daniel Cole, personal communication 22 Oct. 1997).

8. Loken-Kim says the concept of *Han'guk muyong* came into being in 1947 (1989:80). Prior to that time the country was referred to as Chosŏn. Thus, since the country was not known as Han'guk previously, there would have been no concept of *Han'guk muyong*. In addition, as dance became a subject taught at universities and ballet and modern dance were taught as well as older Korean forms, "*Han'guk muyong*" was a way to differentiate "our" dances from "foreign" dances (Christine Loken-Kim, personal communication 26 Jan. 1998).

9. Some Korean dance scholars have their own groupings within the *Han'guk muyong*, or Korean dance, category, groupings that are not always clearly defined and that do not always agree with each other. For example, in 1997 Chŏng Pyŏng-ho divided *chŏnt'ong muyong* into four groups based on function—folk dance (which includes farmers' band dance and music, masked dance-dramas, and other village dances), ritual dance (which includes shaman dance, Buddhist dance, Confucian dance, and several funerary dances), *kyobang* dance (which includes dances described in this volume as theatrical folk dance, *kyobang* referring to the place where professional female entertainers were trained), and court dance (Chung Byung-ho 1997b). In an earlier publication (Chŏng Pyŏng-ho 1992:31), Chŏng identified the categories as classical dance (*kojŏnmu* or *yenŭng muyong*), folk dance (*minsok muyong*), ritual dance (*ŭishik muyong*), and court dance (*kungjung muyong* or *chŏngjae*).

10. Killick indicates that *chŏnt'ong* was a "loan-word" from Japanese (a Chinese-derived term employed first in Japan and exported from there to Korea), and that prior to its use Koreans identified "traditional" things as *koyu*, referring to "inherent" and "inherited" (1998:47). He further states that the concept of "traditional music," as differentiated from that of western origin, did not become prominent until the 1920s, and that it ultimately related to concerns with national identity (ibid.:88–89).

11. Kim Ch'ŏn-hŭng, the senior court dance master at the beginning of the twenty-first century, occasionally uses the term *pŏmmu* for this category (personal communication 1995). *Pŏmmu* combines the Chinese characters meaning "method," "way," or "law," and "dance," producing "conservative dance" or "orthodox dance," which describes the nature of the movements used in dances in this category. Some (e.g., Chŏng Pyŏng-ho, personal communication 13 June 1998) consider this term relevant only for Buddhist dance, since *pŏp*, the first Chinese character in the term, generally relates to Buddhism and Buddhist practices.

12. I use the mid-fifteenth century date because it was apparently in the 1493 *Akhak kwebŏm* that *tangak* and *hyangak* were officially established as two "opposing" categories. The terms were used earlier, including in the *Koryŏsa akchi*

(completed in 1451 and published in 1454), on which much of the *Akhak kwebŏm* is based, in varied contexts. For example, Pratt states:

> In the early Tang (618–907) the Chinese had described music in terms of "elegant music" (*ya-yueh* [Korean: *aak*]), which included ritual and ceremonial court music, "popular music" (*suyu*) and "foreign music" (*huyue*). By this time the Koreans were well accustomed to Chinese music and gave it the title *tangak* ("music of Tang"), in contrast to their own music and that of other countries which eventually came to be known as *hyangak* ("native music"). In 1116, long after the Chinese had ceased to bother about such compartmentalisation, the Koreans added "elegant music" (*aak*) to their two categories. . . . (1987:32)

Howard, Pares, and English indicate that by the time of the *Koryŏsa* (1451),

> court music was by now divided into three types: *aak* (Chinese ritual music played in what was considered an authentic style), *tangak* (other music of Song Chinese origin) and *hyangak* (indigenous music; other texts refer to this as *sogak*). The most significant dates for music were 1114 and 1116, when the court received two gifts from the eighth Song emperor, Huizong. Korea was fast becoming a Confucian state, and kings had begun to observe Confucian rites to heaven, to agriculture, land and grain, and to royal ancestors. They needed suitable music and appealed to Huizong. The first gift, in 1114, of *dasheng xinyue*, music for banquets, consisted of 167 instruments, scores and illustrated instructions for performance. The second gift, in 1116, was what the Koreans wanted. This was *dasheng yayue*, music for rituals. It comprised a massive 428 instruments together with costumes and ritual dance objects. (1996:87)

These statements raise the issue referred to earlier of whether "music" automatically included "dance." (For further discussion of *tangak* and *hyangak* see Song Bang-song 1997:12–178.)

13. Although the term is taken from China's T'ang dynasty (618–907), the dances and their accompanying music are believed to have been imported beginning as early as the Sui dynasty (589–618). See, for example, Provine 1988 and Lee Byong-won 1992:192.

14. Chŏng Pyŏng-ho (Chung Byung-ho 1997b:146) suggests that both *tangak chŏngjae* and *hyang'ak chŏngjae* originated in China and were imported to Korea during the Unified Shilla period (668–935). He states that they were then modified by Korean dancers and musicians and called *hyangak chŏngjae*. Provine (1988:11) states this mixing occurred by 1368. For brief comments on the "Koreanization" of Chinese-derived music, which was likely paralleled in dance, see Song Bang-song 1997:176–177.

15. See especially Kealiinohomoku 1972 and Buckland 1983. For a discussion of related concepts in music see Chapter 2 of Howard 1990.

16. In English-speaking countries the terms "folkloric" and "theatricalized folk dance" are sometimes used to identify dances that are choreographed for theatrical performances as a *representation* of dances done in villages. Korean "theatrical folk dances," although derived from village folk dances, are intended to be dances in their own right, rather than representations of other dances.

17. Nagura (1996:284) indicates that "before World War II, new dance styles in Japan were called 'Neue Tanz' or "new dance,' after the German. The term, 'modern dance' came from the United States after World War II and was used for German-influenced dance as well as American modern dance."

18. The Chinese characters are *jin dai*. The *jin dai*, or "near era," is contrasted with the *dang dai*, "present era" or "contemporary era" and the *xian dai*, or "modern era." All three terms are vague and inconsistent in the specific periods to which they refer (Daniel Cole, personal communication 21 Jan. 1998).

19. Scholars differ on the dates of the *kŭndae* period. Korean history scholar Ch'oe Yŏng-ho suggests the time period from the 1876 Kanghwa-do choyak (treaty with Japan signed on Kanghwa island), when Korea opened its doors to

the outside world, through 1945, the liberation from Japanese annexation (personal communication 1995).

20. Korean dance critic Kim Ch'ae-hyŏn (in Choe Sang-cheul 1996:101) summarizes the various meanings *shinmuyong* has had as: a western-style dance, a new-style dance, a dance elaborated on in a creative way to make it relevant for the times and a new culture, traditional Korean dance modified for a stage in a theater and using a creative approach to a Korean aesthetic to convey a theme, and traditional dance creatively modified to suit modern times. Another term occasionally used beginning in the 1930s, but seldom, if ever, after the 1980s, was *kojŏn muyong*. *Kojŏn* is from Chinese, meaning "classical," and was based on Japanese terminology. In Korea, the term was used to refer to all types of dance prior to the development of creative dance (*ch'angjak muyong*). (See, for example, Ch'oe Sŭng-hŭi 1937.) Hence, it was broader than *kŭndae muyong* because it included court, religious, and what is described here as village folk dance.

21. For descriptions of several *ch'angjak muyong* dances see Chapter 1 and Choi Haeree 1995. For a discussion of creative music (*ch'angjak kugak*) see Killick 1992. Interestingly, the musical term includes "*kuk*," which implies "traditional." Hence, the musical term literally means "creative traditional music."

22. *Mŏt* and *hŭng*, described more fully in Chapter 1, refer, respectively, to an inner spiritual quality of charm or grace and a feeling of lively animation or interest.

23. For a discussion of Ch'angmuhoe and the development of *ch'angjak muyong* see Choi Haeree 1995.

24. Yuk's first modern dance teacher was Pak Oe-sŏn. Pak started dance studies at age fifteen, inspired by performances of Korean dancer Ch'oe Sŭng-hŭi, who had been a student of Ishii Baku. (See Chapter 8 for a discussion of Ch'oe Sŭng-hŭi.)

25. "Ballet" is a French term that originated in the Italian *bal*, *ballo*, and *balletto*, all referring to dances done in the ballrooms of the Italian court. Italian dancing masters were responsible for entertainment in the French courts and beginning in the sixteenth century wove together song, verse, dance, and music. This type of entertainment was known as "*ballet de cour*," "court ballet" (Sandra Hammond, personal communication 29 Jan. 1998). Over time, *ballet de cour* evolved into the highly codified technique performed by professional dancers in formal theater settings identified today as ballet.

26. Among the Korean style ballets is one based on the traditional Korean folktale, Shim Ch'ŏng. (See Chapter 1.)

27. Although Chŏng's formal training was in folklore, he did study some dance. As a child, he tried to follow along with the *nongak* performance of family servants, and shortly after high school he briefly studied western-style modern dance with a Japanese-trained Korean teacher. His research on Korean dance began in the early 1970s (personal communication 13 June 1998).

28. This does not in any way devalue the significance of the work of these individuals. Dance is inherently interdisciplinary, and to truly understand it and its relationship to culture as a whole many perspectives are needed. The point here is simply to underscore the impact of diverse disciplinary approaches on the development of dance terminology. The influence of dance critics is explicitly described by performing arts writer Chang Kwang-yŏl when he states that in the 1970s critics placed great emphasis on "the creation of creative dance works, in order to encourage dancers to take new dance roads," and that shortly thereafter they "focused narrowly upon the work of certain well-respected choreographers and helped diminish diversity and experimentation" (Chang Kwang-yŏl 1998:52).

29. American scholar Leonard Pronko describes a similar ambiguity as "typical of much terminology pertaining to the arts in Japan. . . . The fretful question of defining Japanese [dance] terminology cannot be simply resolved because the terms have been used for centuries in differing ways" (1985:118).

30. In recent times, dance critic Kim T'ae-wŏn has begun using *hyŏndae muyong* to refer specifically to western-style modern dance, and *hyŏndae ch'um* as a broad term to refer to all dance created in contemporary times, including *changjak muyong*, *hyŏndae muyong*, and ballet, a usage that parallels the current

meaning of *kŭndae muyong*—both are used to identify dance forms developed in a particular time period (Choe Haeree, personal communication 17 June 1998). In addition, at a January 1998 seminar held in Pusan and sponsored by the Han'guk Ch'um Pyŏngnon'gahoe (Korean Dance Critics Association), major discussions revolved around attempts to sort out terminology. However, diverse views continue to prevail.

31. Interestingly, three of the most commonly performed "new dances," all of which are derived from older dances, are a fan dance (Puch'aech'um), a drum dance (Changgoch'um), and a dance with some similarities to court dances (Hwagwanmu, or Flower-Crown Dance), and all three are frequently performed today as "trademarks" of Korean dance at official government events, at tourist venues, and by dancers visiting other countries. Because many *shinmuyong* pieces, particularly these three, use costumes, properties, and music that appear (at least to outsiders' eyes) to be traditional, they are easily misunderstood as being older, traditional (*chŏnt'ong*) dances.

32. Dance developments in Japan reflected a similar concern. However, according to dance critic Ichikawa Miyabi (in Nagura 1996:284) there was an equal emphasis on abandoning traditional dance forms rather than simply transforming them: "[I]t was mandatory that everyone abandon nonsensical dances as seen in Kabuki, and . . . make dances which had rational plots based on modern consciousness."

33. It is possible this policy was a legacy of Japan. In the late 1960s Hanayagi Tokubei, an important contributor to creative dance (*sosakubuyō*) in Japan, stressed the importance of using dances of the past to contribute to the development of a new kind of dance more relevant to contemporary times and with greater international appeal (in Pronko 1985:114).

34. In commenting on the fact that much early twentieth century scholarly writing on art was done by the Japanese, Ahn Hwi-joon states that the work is problematic because the Japanese

> aimed at planting a colonial historical view. Since their apparent objective was to justify Japanese colonial rule and its policy, they deliberately underestimated the cultural capability of the Korean people by exaggerating the Chinese influence on Korean art and by distorting the achievements of Koreans. Their endeavors succeeded in misleading the Japanese themselves, Korean intellectuals and the Westerners into having the prejudice that Korean art and culture developed merely under the strong influence of China and thus had no originality. (1986:139)

3. Dance and Korea's National Treasure System (pp. 51–62)

1. For a history of dance notation systems see Guest 1984.

2. Even prior to Japan's nineteenth-century laws, its very old *iemoto* system established a formalized procedure for passing on arts traditions (see Hsu 1975). For a discussion of the power and authority held by high ranking individuals in the *iemoto* system of Japan see Keene 1993.

3. Howard states this term was coined by journalist Ye Yong-hae, who first published it in a *Han'guk Ilbo* (Korean Daily News) newspaper series (1996:94).

4. For a full explanation of procedures involved in implementing the Law on the Protection of Cultural Properties see Yang Jong-sung 1994:Chapter 3.

5. Chongmyo cheryeak and *t'alch'um* are discussed in Chapter 1. Kanggang-sullae is considered a folk dance. According to legend, in the sixteenth century, during one of Japan's many invasions of Korea, young women along the southwest coast of Chŏlla province danced around bonfires on a hilltop to create the illusion of a large Korean military contingent awaiting the foreign invaders. The circle dance performed today (often in theatrical concert settings) is considered to have evolved from the subsequent repetition of the dance on the hilltop to commemorate the women's role in averting the enemy.

6. This classification dilemma is also evident in what is usually identified as *t'alch'um*. Although the term literally means "masked dance," it is often translated in English as "masked dance-drama," and other Korean terms for this genre include *kamyŏn mugŭk* ("masked dance-drama"), *kamyŏn gŭk* ("masked drama"), *t'al-nori* ("masked play"), and *t'alch'um nori* ("masked dance-play") (Yang Jong-sung 1988:12). Howard says that by 1991 seventeen music genres, seven dances, fourteen dramas, twenty-two plays and rituals, thirty "manufactures," and three additional assets concerned with food preparation and martial arts had been identified (1996:94). Items in the "dance" category are Ch'ŏyongmu and Chinju Kŏmmu (described here in Chapters 4 and 5), Hak Yŏnhwadae Ch'ŏyongmu Hapsŏl (described in Chapter 4), salp'uri (described in Chapters 1 and 6), sŭngmu (described in Chapter 1), and Sŭngjŏnmu and T'aepyŏngmu.

7. The institution primarily responsible for perpetuating court dances is the National Center for Korean Traditional Performing Arts (Kungnip Kugagwŏn). Muhyŏng Munhwajae Chŏnsu Hoegwan, transmission centers for Intangible Cultural Properties, are responsible for perpetuating group folk dances. There is a large Chŏnsu Hoegwan in Seoul, and many smaller ones in other cities where regional Intangible Cultural Assets are taught and performed.

8. The average salary range for a university dance professor in 1998 was 2–3 million *wŏn* per month (Choi Haeree, personal communication 15 June 1998). In 1994, the monthly government stipend for National Living Treasures was 550,000 *wŏn*, approximately $700 U.S. (Byun 1994:30), slightly more than half the urban wage at that time (Howard 1995:94). In November of 1997 the Korean economy took a radical downward turn, with the value of the Korean *wŏn* declining by as much as half its former value against the U.S. dollar. Job layoffs and budget cuts became common, as is reflected in the lower value of the stipend for National Living Treasures in 1998 as compared to 1994.

9. That the term *in'gan munhwajae*, "*national* living treasure," became more common than the official term *poyuja* (holder) (Yang Jong-sung 1994:102) is also an indicator of the esteem with which such individuals are regarded.

10. The National Living Treasure was Yi Mae-bang and the dance was sŭngmu. Yi charged a slightly lower fee, 3,000,000 *wŏn* ($3,000 U.S.) for salp'uri. The higher fee for sŭngmu was supposedly because of the extra time needed to learn complex drumming included in this dance (Yang Jong-sung 1994:107).

11. Howard uses similar terminology when he refers to obtaining rewards "through climbing rungs in the asset ladder" (1989:211).

12. Guthrie's definition is similar to that of anthropologist Roy Rappaport, who describes ritual as "the PERFORMANCE of more or less invariant sequences of formal acts and utterances not encoded by the performers" (emphasis in original) (1989:467). Repetition is an important component of theater scholar Richard Schechner's definition of ritual (1993). For a related discussion regarding ritual and Hawaiian hula see Kaeppler 1994:23–25.

13. For discussions of monetary exchange in the perpetuation of Japanese performing arts see Keene 1993 and Robert Smith 1993. Ethnomusicologist Keith Howard (personal communication 1994) suggests that the issue of money may not be as important in relation to Intangible Cultural Assets that are taught at the government-supported National Center for Korean Traditional Performing Arts as it is to music and dance that are taught outside the Center; in many instances, as individuals move up the ranks at the Center, National Treasure status may come almost automatically.

14. It is not surprising to find corruption in the National Treasure System, given the widespread and publicly acknowledged corruption in many arenas of contemporary Korean culture.

15. For comments on how formalized preservation systems have contributed to the "stifling of spontaneity and creativity" in traditional Japanese arts see Robert Smith 1993:43.

16. See Yang Jong-sung 1994:5 and his Chapters 3, 4, and 5 for discussions of the importance of adhering to this original version.

17. Ethnomusicologist Keith Howard describes the addition of songs to

Namdo *tŭl-norae* (field songs of Namdo) for its "improvement" during the process of designating it an Intangible Cultural Property (1989).

18. For an intriguing account of how one shaman ritual came to be designated an Intangible Cultural Asset, and creativity involved in the process, see Howard 1988:939ff. For discussions of the invention of tradition see Hobsbawm and Ranger 1983. For comments on the traditional as invented see Bharucha 1993.

19. See, for example, Fouser 1994 and Van Zile 1993. Similar circumstances occurred in Japan. According to Thornbury (1997:101), following World War II there was a strong inclination in Japan to reject the past. But since so much had been destroyed, there was also a desire to revive things from the past "as a way to rediscover or even build for the first time a foundation for local, as well as national, identity." Increased interest in "traditional" music was reported in Korea since the opening and closing ceremonies of the 1988 Seoul Olympics, which included extremely elaborate presentations of Korean dance and music. The growing interest in music is said to be, at least in part, the result, once again, of increasing "government efforts to promote traditional arts and culture as an important policy," and to be related to "special courses offered by civic groups on how to appreciate traditional music" that are increasingly attended by young people (Anonymous 1994). These circumstances are undoubtedly paralleled in dance.

20. Ethnomusicologist Andrew Killick (personal communication 30 Dec. 1997) suggests that reasons for firmly establishing Korea's system might have been more purely politically motivated: It was a way for Park Chung Hee, the president who implemented the system, to show "his military regime as a patron of Korean national culture (for which he had previously shown nothing but contempt) . . . a way for him to erase the Japanese military background of himself [as a former officer in the Japanese imperial army] and many of his confederates." See also Killick 1998:248–250, Kim Kwang-ok 1997:7, and Sorensen 1995:343. A less pessimistic view is that during the Japanese occupation Korean folklorists/scholars were trained in Japan, worked with Japanese ethnographers, and many spoke and read Japanese. Thus, they would have been familiar with the cultural property preservation system in Japan (Howard 1989:204–205). Howard also describes differences between the Japanese and Korean systems (ibid.). Yet another view is that Park Chung Hee was more concerned with supporting his economic plans and providing Koreans with the idea of a shared heritage as the basis for ideological support (Maliangkay 1997).

21. Yang Jong-sung suggests that it was both an interest in the past and a reaction against the bureaucracy established by the whole National Treasure System that, indeed, drove the development of creative dance, or *ch'angjak muyong* (1994:169–170). For discussions of this last type of dance see Chapters 1 and 2 here and Choi Hae-ree 1995.

22. Yang Jong-sung describes this phenomenon as "institutionalizing" and "reshaping" tradition (1994:13).

23. For an account of the reritualization of a Korean folk music genre see Howard 1989.

24. For discussions of ritual as involving repetition and rhythmic behavior see Schechner 1993:228.

4. *Ch'ŏyongmu (pp. 65–109)*

1. Although the Narye became a prominent government-sponsored event, it is possible the P'algwanhoe and Yŏndŭnghoe continued to be celebrated. Pihl states that *all* were celebrated during the Koryŏ period, and likens them to "national religious rites, replete with song and dance," that were meant to assure national peace and prevent disaster (1991:3). Kim Jong-myung indicates that the lighting of lanterns is done "in contemporary Korea, though not on a national scale, but in the monastic circles" (1995:255). For a discussion of the history of the P'algwanhoe and Yŏndŭnghoe see Kim Jong-myung 1995.

2. Kim Ch'ŏn-hŭng was among the individuals who learned dances at this

time, although he did not perform Ch'ŏyongmu—he was too short and small in stature. Later, he coauthored the official report that was instrumental in having Ch'ŏyongmu designated an Intangible Cultural Asset, was one of the five people designated by the government to perpetuate the dance, and has since performed it frequently and become the major teacher of the dance.

3. The *poyuja* were Kim Ch'ŏn-hŭng, Pong Hae-ryong, Kim Ki-su, Kim T'ae-sŏp, and Kim Yong. The *isuja* were Kim Chong-shik, Kim Chung-sŏp, and Kim Yong-man. Kim Chung-sŏp, originally an *isuja*, was subsequently designated *poyuja hubo* (*poyuja* candidate); he is in line to become a *poyuja* when he is sufficiently mature and his abilities are considered appropriate. Four additional *isuja* were subsequently appointed: Kim Chae-un, Pak Sŏng-gi, Ch'oe Sŏng-un, and Pae Yang-hyŏn.

4. The songs each contain four lines of seven syllables, and only the general nature of their subject matter is known. Mit'a Ch'an sings praises of Amita, the Buddha of the Western Paradise; Kwanum Ch'an praises the goddess Kwan Yin; and Ponsa Ch'an praises the location at which the chant is performed. The first two songs are still sung as part of the Buddhist Yŏngsanjae festival (Pak Song-am, personal communication 25 Nov. 1990).

5. Pratt states Ch'ŏyongmu may have originated in conjunction with the Obang Shinjangmu, "Dance of the gods of the five directions," and with the Ogwangdae masked play (1987:209).

6. See Chapter 3 for comments relating to basing a contemporary identity on that of the past.

7. The colors coordinate as follows.

tunic color	white	black	yellow	red	blue
symbolism	west	north	center	south	east
pants color	black	red	blue	black	red

8. The instrumental ensemble is comprised of two stringed instruments (*ajaeng* —a long, bowed, seven-stringed zither; and *haegŭm*—a bowed, two-stringed fiddle); two wind instruments (*p'iri*—a double-reed pipe; and *taegŭm*—a long, transverse, bamboo flute); and two drums (*changgo*—a double-headed, hourglass-shaped drum; and either *puk*—a small, barrel-shaped drum, or *chwago*—a medium-sized, barrel-shaped drum hung from a square wooden frame).

9. The Korean text, as recorded be Kim Ch'ŏn-hŭng and Sŏng Kyŏng-nin (1986:5, 6), reads as follows.

Ŏllak

Shilla sŏngdae sosŏngdae
Ch'ŏnha t'aep'yŏng nahudŏk
Ch'ŏyong abi, ishi insaengae,
Sangburŏ hashirandae,
Ishi insaeng ae sangburŏ hashirandae,
Samjae p'allan i ilshi somyŏl hashyatta.

Up'yŏn

Sanha ch'ŏlliguge kagiulch'ongch'ong hashyatta.
Kŭmjŏn'gujunge myŏngirwŏl hashini
Kunshinch'ŏnjaee hoeunyongishyatta.
Hŭihŭisŏsogŭn ch'undaesangiŏnŭl
Chejegunsaengŭn suyŏkchungishyatta.

For an English translation of Ŏllak see Prologue of Song of Ch'ŏyong: A Choral Dance for Exorcising Demons in Peter H. Lee 1974:52–53. I know of no full English translation of Up'yŏn.

10. For a western music transcription of the melody see Kim Ch'ŏn-hŭng and Sŏng Kyŏng-nin 1986:119.

11. Movement analysis presented here is rooted in theories of Rudolf Von Laban, as contained in such references as Hutchinson 1970 and Dell 1970. In this

system, movement planes are two-dimensional and are extensions of axes, which are one-dimensional. Dell states:

> When an individual is upright, the longitudinal axis of his body, the body midline, coincides with the plumb-line of the pull of gravity through his body toward the center of the earth. This line we call the vertical dimension, or axis, which is composed of the two directions, up, away from the pull of gravity, and down, toward the pull of gravity. Two other axes intersect the vertical axis at right angles, so that all three axes are equidistant— the horizontal axis going from side to side, and the sagittal axis going forward and backward. . . .
>
> . . . when we speak of planes or cycles, we speak of only three; the vertical [or lateral] cycle (door plane, cartwheel cycle) which combines the dimensions up-down and side-side and has as its axis the forward-backward dimension; the horizontal cycle (table plane, turning cycle) which combines the dimensions side-side and forward-backward and has as its axis the upward-downward or vertical dimension; the sagittal cycle (wheel plane, somersault cycle) which combines the dimensions forward-backward and up-down and has as its axis the sideward-sideward (right-left) or horizontal dimension. (1970:69, 73)

12. Elsewhere I have described movement density as "the number of body segments moving simultaneously and the number of separate movements occurring within a given time span. ([E.g.,] if the whole arm moves together, from shoulder to finger-tips, it is considered one movement; if the upper arm moves into a new direction at the same time the lower arm and hand move into different directions and a new finger position is assumed, four movements are occurring simultaneously)" (Van Zile 1983:66).

13. Starting from a position in which the feet are together the knees bend, then the left knee extends as weight is taken onto the left foot and the right knee lifts until the thigh is parallel to the floor, ankle flexed so the foot is also parallel to the floor. The right foot then steps forward, the left foot slides to meet the right, and the bending, lifting, stepping, and closing repeat on the opposite side.

14. Labanotation is a system for recording three-dimensional movement through two-dimensional symbols. For information on the system see Hutchinson 1970. Also see Note 11.

15. According to the printed program distributed to audience members, this version was based on the personal notes of Sŏng Kyŏng-nin, a musician who had performed other dances at the 1923 birthday festivities.

16. Because dance exists in both space and time, relying on information in iconographical form (either two-dimensional paintings and drawings or three-dimensional sculptures) is not unproblematic. As will be seen, however, the point here is not to attempt to reconstruct the past from iconographical representations, but rather to show the potential impact of iconographical representations on the present. For a discussion of issues relating to dance and iconography see, for example, Seebass 1991.

17. Pratt (1987:207) indicates the painting is dated 1730; An Hwi-jon (1989: 24) indicates 1720; Park Jeong-hye (1997:131) states 1719–1720. Given the supporting information provided in An Hwi-jon, the 1730 date appears to be in error. An (1989:207) states this is one of a series of fifty paintings done by a team of five painters (Kim Chin-yŏ and Chang T'ae-hŭng, who were in charge, and Pak Tong-bo, Chang Tŭng-man, and Hŏ Suk). According to Pratt (1987:208), in 1394 King T'aejo founded the Office of the Venerable Aged, Kirosa (Kisa for short), to honor high-ranking officials who were at least seventy years old. Kings were allowed to join at age sixty, but three joined when younger. Twice a year the Board of Rites arranged entertainment for members of the Kisa. The king provided a banquet on the first night and members held a private party the next day. In 1719, at the age of fifty-nine, King Sukchong became a member of the society. Ch'ŏyongmu was performed at the king's banquet on April 17 as well as at the members' party the next day. It is the banquet and party that are depicted in Plates 22–26.

18. According to An Hwi-jon (1989:207), the king gave silver goblets to the ministers at the party and ordered each to take five drinks before departing. That, together with drinking during the banquet, contributed to an inebriated exit by all. In this scene, the ministers, seated on the palanquins and sporting flowers in their hats, are escorted to their homes by musicians and Ch'ŏyong dancers.

19. The other dances represented, all of which are performed today, are Sŭngjŏnmu (a drum dance) at the bottom of the illustration; Kŏmmu (a sword dance performed today in several different versions—see Chapter 5), represented at the sides of the performing space just above Sŭngjŏnmu; and P'ogurak (a ball-playing dance), the dance represented in the center of the performing space. Except for Ch'ŏyongmu, the number of dancers shown for each dance does not coincide with the number of dancers indicated in various other documents nor in contemporary performances. And although Ch'ŏyongmu is depicted here with other dances, none of these is part of the suite in which Ch'ŏyongmu was originally performed.

20. This is a simplification of complex terminology that has changed over time. For a discussion of this see Park Jeong-hye 1997.

21. Pratt states there are discrepancies between text and pictorial representations and between different pictorial representations of the same event in the number of musicians participating. He indicates there were more musicians than pictorially represented, which he attributes to the difficulty of showing the large number of participants in a single image (1987:202). It is possible the same is true of dancers.

5. *Chinju Kŏmmu (pp. 110–147)*

1. See Rutt 1961 for a discussion of the *hwarang* tradition.

2. Rutt indicates the name is sometimes given as Kwanjang (1961:38).

3. The story is told in a slightly different manner in Rutt 1961:38. In this version the young boy returned to battle on his own (after only drinking "some water from his cupped hands"), and there is no mention of a sword dance.

4. "Kisaeng" is a "Chinese compound that can be translated loosely as 'students of the arts performed by females.'" *Kisaeng*

> participated in the full panoply of social events that comprised the cultural lives of Korea's governing elite. In the capital, as members of the Court Entertainment Bureau, *kisaeng* presented elaborately choreographed music and dance pieces on festival days and occasions of state, twirling long crimson sashes and carrying a dazzling array of banners emblazoned with pairs of phoenixes and peacocks; when court officials required "willow waists" and mouth organs to foster a party mood at private banquets they were summoned out as well. At government offices throughout the provinces rosters of *kisaeng* were kept so that "glistening eyebrows" and "crimson skirts" would be on hand to greet visiting dignitaries and newly appointed administrators. At the end of a long night of banqueting, they might also be called upon to "provide a pillow" and ease the loneliness of the hours remaining until dawn. (McCarthy 1994:6)

For discussions of *kisaeng* see, for example, Kim Yung-chung 1982: 54–55 and Lee Byong-won 1979.

5. In the context of other comments relating to the 1920s, Ch'oe Wan-ja is quoted as saying that the workshops "disappeared" (*Chinjushisa* 1979:1180).

6. According to Yi Yul-lye (personal communication 15 June 1983) the four were Yi Yul-lye, Kang Kwi-rye, Kim Cha-jin, and Kim Chŏng-ja.

7. Pak was born to a wealthy family in Chinju. Although not an artist himself, he was an avid supporter of folk traditions and strove to preserve Korean folk culture during the Japanese occupation. He is attributed with such activities as transcribing the text of the folk dance-drama, Chinju Ogwangdae; guiding Hwang Il-baek in the development of farmers' band music (*nongak*); building and serving as principal of the National High School for the Arts (Kungnip Yesul Kodŭng

Hakkyo) in Seoul when he later moved there; and having Chinju Kŏmmu reconstructed after a period of inactivity during the Japanese occupation (*Chinjushisa* 1979:1174–1175).

8. The four original members of the entertainers' union designated *poyuja* were Yi Yul-lye, Kang Kwi-rye, Kim Cha-jin, and Kim Chŏng-ja. The four "second generation" dancers designated *poyuja* were Ch'oe Ye-bun, Yi Ŭm-jŭn, Kang Sun-kŭm, and Kim Su-ak. The eight individuals designated *isuja* were Ch'oe Kŭm-sun, Chŏng Haeng-gŭm, Chŏng Kŭm-sun, Chŏng P'il-sun, Yi U-sŏn, Kim Sŏng-in, Kim Yŏn-i, and Sŏng Kye-ok. Although Kang Sun-kŭm was originally appointed one of the "second generation" *poyuja*, she resigned from her position (apparently due to personality problems in the group), and in 1977 was replaced by Sŏng Kye-ok. Upon her resignation as *poyuja* Kang Sun-kŭm began to play in the instrumental ensemble that accompanies Chinju Kŏmmu, performing on the *kayagŭm*, *changgo*, or *puk*. In September 1982, because of the advanced age of the *poyuja*, Chŏng P'il-sun, originally an *isuja*, was designated *poyuja hubo*—assistant *poyuja*, or *poyuja*-designate, and at the end of the twentieth century she was the senior teacher and performer.

9. The building presently used was built in 1982 with funds from the Cosa Libermann Company of Switzerland. The company had done business in Korea for about thirty years and wanted to make a material contribution to Korean culture. The building contains a comfortable-sized stage and audience facility that also serves as a dance studio, a smaller room used for music classes, a very small office space, and a costume storage and dressing room. In addition to Chinju Kŏmmu, other forms of traditional dance and music are also taught.

10. Part of Yŏngsan Hoesang also formed the accompaniment for Ch'ŏyongmu, described in Chapter 4. Because the earliest identifiable accompaniment is from the court repertoire, and because an adapted version of that is what is used today, it is tempting to infer that Chinju Kŏmmu was originally a court dance. This would be purely conjectural, however, since we do not know how long the dance had been performed to this music.

11. The sequence of patterns (some named with terms considered to be folk terms that are not used by scholars and performers of court music) in order is: *yŏmbul*, *t'aryŏng*, *chajin maji todŭri* (fast-tempo *todŭri*), *t'aryŏng*, *chajin maji todŭri*, *tŏtpaegi* (another name for *chajin mori* and also the name of a dance movement, but not a movement used in Chinju Kŏmmu), *pparŭn todŭri* (a still faster *todŭri*), and *todŭri*. *Yŏmbul* contains 6 beats per measure, and all the other patterns contain 4 beats per measure.

12. Other versions of knife dances performed today are most often danced by an even number of women (usually two to eight dancers) and occasionally by a female soloist.

13. In former times it was considered inappropriate for a woman to show the palms of her hands. Some Korean scholars believe the desire to conceal the palms contributed to female court dancers covering their hands with long sleeves.

14. During *sŭngmu* (monk's drum dance) the front surface of the torso becomes prominent when the dancer thrusts the long sleeves of the costume's jacket upward. But the opening of the torso area in this instance is the result of supporting the upward thrust of the sleeves. Also, in some shaman dancing the shaman will lean back with arms spread wide when his or her body is taken over by the powers of the spirits. In these instances the opening out of the torso area is the result of another movement or of a "supernatural" cause. In Chinju Kŏmmu the opening of the torso area is an independent movement.

15. In a conventional barrel turn, the dancer steps to the right side and tilts her torso forward to somewhere between a forty-five and ninety-degree angle off the vertical; pushes off and does a full counterclockwise turn while in the air, keeping the torso at approximately its same angle by tilting to the right side, backward, and left side while doing the air turn; and lands on the left foot with the torso in the same position as at the beginning of the sequence. This may be performed to the left side as well.

16. I use the category "male-female" (or "man-woman") here in relation to

aspects identified on the basis of physiological traits; "masculine-feminine" is used in reference to characteristics associated with nonphysiological traits. For example, some dances are performed only by men and some only by women, the labels referring to physiological traits of the performers. Movements identified as "masculine" may be those most usually performed by men and hence given the appellation "masculine," but they may also be performed by women.

17. Unfortunately documentation does not allow us to know precisely how appropriate feminine decorum of the period was translated into movement quality. Descriptions do, however, suggest softness, gentility, and humbleness: Women were considered inferior to men; an unmarried woman followed the dictum's of her father, a married woman those of her husband, and a widowed woman those of her son; a woman was responsible for maintaining purity in customs; women were to be strong and responsible but modest and submissive; and, above all, a woman had to be virtuous (Deuchler 1977:3–4). A wife was to be "loyal and pure, self-controlled, flexible and obedient, and serving others. She minds exclusively the domestic realm and does not concern herself with public affairs" (Deuchler 1993:574). For further comments on desirable characteristics of women during the Chosŏn period see, for example, Deuchler 1977 and 1993, Koh 1987, Janice C.H. Kim 1998, and Young Hee Lee 1994.

18. The report describes a number of specific movement differences between the version of the dance performed in Chinju and those performed elsewhere. It is unclear, however, in describing the specific rationale for considering the Chinju version the most authentic, authenticity being an important criterion for designating dances Intangible Cultural Assets. The report refers to documentation contained in several important historical works at the same time it comments on difficulties in knowing precisely how the Chinju movements relate to those described in only general ways in some of the sources. The age and memories of dancers alive at the time the report was written seem to be the primary rationale for establishing authenticity, which is equated with closeness to some original performance.

19. In both cases the dance was done by two performers (Kim Ch'ŏn-hŭng et al. 1966).

20. Views of *kisaeng* varied. According to Kim Yung-chung,

> [t]heir social status, as members of the *ch'ŏnmin* [lower class] along with female shamans, was confused by the close association they had with royalty and the *yangban* [male aristocrats]. . . . Glorified, admired, and at times raised to national glory, they were nevertheless illegitimate in either class or kin terms. Thus, their social status must be considered exactly as it was—a contradiction within the class structure. . . . their role as retainers and transmitters of traditional arts and music helped create a Korean cultural tradition. (1982:54–55)

While some looked down on them with great scorn and considered them a "threat to Confucian propriety" (see, for example, McCarthy 1994:6), the nature of the dances they performed in the court appears to have epitomized the stereotypic notion of female Confucian propriety. They symbolically depicted the ideal while, in reality, were often accorded a far-from-ideal status.

21. According to Deuchler (1977:4), "The Confucian image of woman was . . . a double one: she had to be modest and submissive, but also strong and responsible. On the level of Confucian idealism, the image was considered virtuous; on the level of daily life, it often meant bondage." This notion of women having a dual image could provide an interesting explanation for taking an essentially masculine movement and modifying it for a more feminine execution.

22. For an indication of gender issues in relation to music see Howard:1995.

6. Movement in Shamanic Contexts (pp. 148–166)

1. For discussions of Korean shamanism see, for example, Kim T'ae-gŏn 1972, Yu Choi-shin and Guisso 1988, Hyun-key Kim Hogarth 1994, Kendall 1985, Howard, editor, 1998, and Covell 1986.

2. See Kealiinohomoku 1972 for a discussion, applied to dance, of Felix Hoerburger's concept of first and second existence events.

3. Despite inherent problems in using videotape for detailed movement analysis, this medium is adequate as the basis for information of the sort discussed here. In addition, I have observed a number of *kut* in Korea, and activities in these events corroborate much of the discussion here.

4. Folklore scholar Choi Chungmoo (1989) states that Korean shamans "delicately balance ritual efficacy and aesthetic felicity to come up with convincing dramatic performances" (p. 236), and that aesthetic skill contributes to efficacy of performance (p. 240). Examples of these issues in settings from other geographic areas are discussed in Armstrong 1981; Schechner 1981; and Schieffelin 1985. Rhie Sang-il (1975) specifically discusses the notion of *kut* as both ritual and festive (theatrical) event.

5. Defining "dance," as opposed to movement systems that are structured but not considered dance, is a task that goes beyond the scope of this volume. For discussions of the topic see, for example, Hanna 1979, Kaeppler 1989, and Kealiinohomoku 1983. Kendall (1991–1992:60) hints at some of these differences when she uses the term "playful dancing" in an effort to distinguish between structured movement that occurs in various contexts in Korea. For listings of stereotypic Korean dance movements see Loken 1978; Van Zile 1991 and 1992; Kim Joungwon 1997:136–193, and Chapter 1 here.

6. I am grateful to Mary Jo Freshley for making videotapes available to me.

7. Those involved with the program no longer recall the accompanying instruments used. The musicians are not shown clearly on the videotape, but based on sound contained in it, the instruments were most probably *kayagŭm* (zither), *haegŭm* (fiddle), *tanso* (possibly *taegŭm* and/or *p'iri*—oboes), cymbals, *changgo* (double-headed hourglass drum), and *puk* (drum).

8. For a description of typical sections (*kŏri*) of *kut* see Sorensen 1988.

9. In some forms of fortune-telling a client pulls a flag from a bundle of five differently colored ones and the shaman tells the fortune based on the flag's color.

10. The videotape was provided by Chŏng Chae-man.

11. For a discussion of paper streamers used in one form of *kut* see Howard 1991–1992.

12. A sequence seen in *kut* from Seoul and North Korea, this represents the passage of the soul of the departed to paradise.

13. I am grateful to Mary Jo Freshley for making the videotape available to me.

14. The musicians played *ajaeng* (bowed and plucked half-tube zither), *p'iri* (oboe), *puk* (barrel drum), *changgo* (double-headed hourglass drum), *ching* (gong), and a small bell.

15. For a description of the sections of an actual *kut* from Chindo see Howard 1990:173–189.

16. For an explanation of paper implements used in Chindo Sshikkim Kut and the manner in which they are manipulated see Howard 1991–1992.

17. I am grateful to Mary Jo Freshley for providing me with a copy of the videotape of Tunggi Kut (Taedong Kut) performed at an outdoor location in Seoul primarily by Kim Kŭm-hwa.

18. Alexandre Guillemoz (1998) describes formal classes for shamans that began in Seoul in 1989, and that include the teaching of dance.

19. I am grateful to Alexandre Guillemoz for informing me about this publication and for providing a copy of excerpts from it. The book is a product of the Association for the Preservation of Shamanism (Musok Pojonhoe) of the Korean Federation of Associations for Victory over Communism and Respect of Beliefs (Taehan Sŭnggong Kyŏngshin Yŏnhaphoe). (See Guillemoz 1998 for a discussion of these organizations.) The excerpts examined contain numbered footprints that describe particular floor patterns traced by the feet and very general movement indications, such as "raise the left hand" and "stretch both hands out and then bring them together." Photographs of isolated movements are also included.

20. In discussing *kut* as both ritual and theatre, Rhie Sang-il states that it is "an activity conducted according to rules recognized and prescribed by the par-

ticipants" (1975:24). Loken-Kim indicates that a shaman from the north who becomes possessed during *kut* "learns ritual movement, but she does not learn dance in a technical sense" (1989:45). Loken-Kim also refers to Kim On-gyŏng in stating that shaman dances "have no standard dance steps" and that their dances "are not choreographed presentations" (ibid.:46–47). These seemingly contradictory indications further reflect my idea that while movements are taught, detailed accuracy in the ritual performance of learned patterns is not the key issue.

21. The manuals to which I refer are that written by Halla Huhm and that of the Association for the Preservation of Shamanism, described in Note 19 above. Ku Hee-seo suggests other possibilities for the teaching of movements used in *kut*. According to her, dancer Kim Suk-cha was "the daughter of a family of hereditary shamans . . . [who] form[ed] the Korean Shamanic Arts Association (Han'guk Musok Yesul Hyŏphoe), a group that brought many *kut* to the stage" (1997:164). The extent of the organization's activities, however, remains unclear. Did Kim Suk-cha, or others affiliated with the organization, teach "shaman movements" to dancers, and/or did they teach "dance-like" movements to shamans? In addition to these items relating to the teaching of dancing, Choi Chungmoo describes an interaction between a shaman and an initiate that she considers to be a lesson in acting (1989:241).

8. Ch'oe Sŭng-hui (pp. 185–219)

1. The number of passengers is based on information in a January 13, 1938, article in the *New World-Sun Daily* (Anonymous). *Hanto no Maihimei, The Dancing Princess of the Peninsula*, is the title of a film in which Ch'oe performed.

2. Apart from performance reviews, many articles about Ch'oe were published in Japan and discussion of her was included in books about her primary dance teacher, Ishii Baku (see, for example, Ikeda Ringi 1953; Hirabayashi Hisae 1977 and 1978; and Takashima Yusaburo 1982). In 1959 Japanese author Takashima Yusaburo published the first book about her, titled simply *Sai Shoki*. In 1994 the Japanese-language *Seiki no bijin buyōka Sai Shoki* (*One of the Most Beautiful Dancers of the Century Sai Shoki*), jointly authored by Takashima and South Korean writer Chŏng Pyŏng-ho, was published. Ch'oe also penned an autobiography when she was only twenty-five years old. This was first published in 1936 in Japanese (*Watakushi no jijoden*), and then in 1937 in Korean (*Naŭi chasŏjŏn*). Studies in South Korea about Ch'oe were prohibited for many years. This prohibition was lifted in the 1990s, and in 1995 Chŏng Pyŏng-ho published *Ch'um chunun Ch'oe Sŭng-hŭi—Segyerŭl hwiŏ chabŭn Chosŏn yŏja* [*The Dancing Ch'oe Sŭng-hŭi—The Korean Woman Who Captivated the World*]. Since then several masters theses about Ch'oe were written in Korea, and in 1996 Choe Sang-cheul authored a doctoral dissertation on her. Choe's dissertation is one of the most analytical studies. None of these works, however, deals extensively with Ch'oe's U.S. tour, and information is sometimes contradictory. Biographical information given here is based primarily on Chŏng, Yusaburo and Chŏng, and Choe Sang-cheul, unless otherwise indicated. When conflicting dates were provided in sources and verification was not possible, those given here are ones that seem most logical in light of the interrelationship between various activities. I am particularly grateful to Maeshibi Naoko for translating (with funding provided by a grant from the University of Hawai'i Office of Research Services) Japanese texts referred to in this chapter.

3. With Japanese colonization, in August of 1911 a school system was established that focused on mass education in the Japanese language.

4. Traditional Korean law prohibited foreign ownership of land. Japanese occupation policies legalized foreign ownership.

5. It is unclear who this contract was with. See Appendix 7 for indications of known managing groups. Political problems (described in the analysis section here) are said to have contributed to terminating Sai's contract with Metropolitan Music Company, the sponsor of her initial New York performances. Hurok At-

tractions assumed management of at least some of her performances when she returned from Europe.

6. Official lists of participants were published on various occasions, and individuals conducting research on North Korea often consult these lists as an indication of who is in political favor (Hugh Kang, personal communication 13 Apr. 1998).

7. Information on Ishii's training and philosophy is based on Hirabayashi Hisae 1977, Chŏng Pyŏng-ho 1995, and Takashima Yusaburo and Chŏng Pyŏng-ho 1994. It is not clear whether Ishii actually studied with such people as Duncan and Wigman, or was only greatly influenced by works of theirs that he saw. M. S. Park states that he actually studied with Wigman (in Choe Sang-cheul 1996:5), but Chŏng Pyŏng-ho states that he only saw performances of Duncan and Wigman during an extended visit to Europe (personal communication 13 June 1998).

8. In the 1990s, a number of television shows about Ch'oe were produced, and many included dancing attributed to Ch'oe. One of these (produced by MBC in 1995) is a docu-drama containing excerpts of many dances from Ch'oe's early career, but it does not indicate the basis for the choreography displayed. Another (produced by Arirang TV in 1998) contains documentary footage of Ch'oe herself, with brief excerpts from her early career and lengthier excerpts from her later career. A third (also produced by Arirang TV) documents 1998 performances by Paek Hyang-ju, a Japan-based Korean who claims to be a disciple of one of Ch'oe's students. Thus, the majority of information about dances in Ch'oe's early repertoire is contained in writings about her and photographs.

9. According to Chŏng Pyŏng-ho (1995:151), while in Paris Ch'oe began to use her Korean name and began to identify herself as Korean, despite what her passport said.

10. The discussion here is based on approximately 150 U.S. newspaper articles and advertisements, advertising brochures and flyers, printed programs from six performances, photographs in private collections and newspaper morgues, several documents from the 92nd Street Y in New York City and the U.S. National Archives, several newspaper articles from Japan and Korea, and the Japanese- and Korean-language sources referred to in this chapter. Most materials were located at the following libraries and archives: Dorathi Bock Pierre Dance Collection of the Beverly Hills Public Library (California); Viola Hegyi Swisher Collection of the California Institute of the Arts (Santa Clarita); photo and newspaper collections of the History and Genealogy Department and the Carolyn Cole Photo Collection of the Los Angeles Public Library; the private collection of Susan Ahn Cuddy (California); the morgues of the *Los Angeles Daily News* and *Los Angeles Times* in the Special Collections of the University of California, Los Angeles; the morgue of the *Los Angeles Examiner*, in the University of Southern California's Regional History Center of the Department of Special Collections; the *Shinsokai Asahi* and *New World-Sun Daily* collections of the Japanese American History Archives (San Francisco); San Francisco Performing Arts Library and Museum; the Music Scrapbooks (Art and Music Department) and San Francisco History Collection of the San Francisco Public Library; the Dance Collection of the New York Public Library; and the Archives of the New York YMHA (92nd Street Y). I am grateful to librarians at all of these places for assistance in locating materials.

11. "*Kisaeng*" is romanized in various ways in the sources used for this chapter. Except for direct quotes, the term is standardized here to conform to the McCune-Reischauer system used throughout this volume.

12. In one brochure a picture of Sai in a court dance costume is identified as Ancient Spring (Figure 41). However, a dance with this title was never performed during Sai's U.S. tour. A brief film excerpt (see Note 6 below) of Sai that is titled "Sleeve Dance" shows her in a quite different costume, but manipulating long sleeves.

13. Despite the fact that cherry trees are found in both countries, there is not the same level of adoration for them in Korea as in Japan. Many dances referring to cherry blossoms are performed in Japan, but there is no tradition of such dances

in Korea. It is possible Sai learned one or more of them or choreographed her own version, and performed such a dance in Japan. There is no record of her performing a cherry blossom dance in the United States.

14. In this review, Fisher describes both Sai's performance and that of Spanish dancer José Cancino, which occurred on the same weekend. She states the performances were "only about 50 per cent 'authentic,' " and clarifies that the lack of authenticity relates to Sai's musical accompaniment and some of Cancino's female dancers, and that the Spanish program had more variety.

15. Mei Lan-fang, a noted Chinese opera performer, and Anna Pavlova, a renowned Russian ballerina, had both performed in the United States.

16. A notable exception is San Francisco music editor Marjory Fisher, whose review contains substantive dance comments.

17. Use of "Miss Shoki" (Shoki was Sai's given name) may relate to common references to American modern dancer Ruth St. Denis as "Miss Ruth," or to the common lack of knowledge relating to which Japanese, Chinese, or Korean name was the family name and which the given name: Sai was the Japanese pronunciation of Ch'oe's family name, and Shoki the Japanese pronunciation of Sŭng-hŭi, her personal name.

18. The 92nd Street Y was the sponsor of countless dance performances, many by new, as yet unknown, dancers. Many performances at the Y received extensive press coverage.

19. Sai surely would have seen performances by many kinds of dancers in the United States as well. An article in the August 8, 1938, *Bennington Banner*, a newsletter of Bennington College, Vermont, noted Sai's presence at their August-November festival series and described her as "the Korean Pavlova . . . on tour in the U.S. . . . The first woman to raise the dance in Korea to the station of an independent stage art" (in Kriegsman 1981:79–80). It is likely she saw works there by such modern dance choreographers as Doris Humphrey, Hanya Holm, and Martha Graham, but there is no indication that she performed as part of the festival.

20. There are several references to Sai negotiating with an American film producer, but this project never came to fruition.

21. Angna Enters, to whom several writers compared Sai, was a dancer and mime. She toured a solo mime program in the United States and Europe for more than thirty years, beginning in the late 1920s.

22. For discussions of the dance of Uday Shankar see, for example, Erdman 1996.

23. The Buddhist Monk (undoubtedly related to the dance performed in the United States under the title Buddhist Temptress) and Sword Dance are reported to have been performed in 1934 in one of Sai's earliest performances in Japan (Kim Ch'ŏng-uk 1999:77); a printed program from a 1930 performance in Seoul includes Music of the Jade Flute, Three Traditional Rhythms, and Fortune Teller's Dance (Sŏng Kyŏng-nin, personal communication 9 June 1998), all similar to titles in Sai's U.S. programs; and titles of other dances performed in the United States are similar to some dances mentioned in Sai's 1937 autobiography.

24. A brochure authored by Denishawn dancer Jane Sherman states:

> This devotional work was conceived by Ruth St. Denis when she stood at Beijing's Temple of Heaven and asked herself, "What is the most precious thing in China?" From the answer, "White jade," she created her vision of the Goddess of Mercy, Kuan Yin, as carved in luminescent stone. This became the most popular solo of those St. Denis brought back in 1926 from the Denishawn Far Eastern Tour. (Sherman 2000:4)

25. One member of the Denishawn company says that St. Denis's Indian Nautch, an Indian-inspired dance, was among the favorites of the Japanese (Doris Humphrey in Wentink 1977:26).

26. I am grateful to Kim Mae-ja and Choe Sang-cheul for showing me this excerpt. It is believed it was taken by an amateur photographer during Sai's American tour.

27. In an August 1936 London article unrelated to her U.S. performance, the caption of a photograph of Sai read "a Japanese dancer who has started a new

dance movement in an attempt to modernize the traditional dances" (Sawatake, p. 493).

285

Notes

9. *Korean Dance in Hawai'i (pp. 220–234)*

1. Warren Kim describes the Nam-Pung-Sa, an organization he says was established in 1922 by the Korean National Association of Hawaii

> to teach the unique Korean arts. The majority of its promoters were old immigrants who had training in the classical music and court dances of Korea. The organization brought musical instruments and other paraphernalia from Korea, taught young people the heritage of Korean arts, and made efforts to introduce them to the American public during its five-year existence. (1971:45)

See also Nishiguchi 1982:24.

2. The name of the woman known in Hawai'i at various times as Halla Huhm, Halla Pai Huhm, and Pai Halla, is not entirely clear. She, herself, gave different explanations to different people at different times. The most consistent explanation appears to be that she was born Pae Yong-ja, Pae being her family name and Yong-ja her personal name. At some time she took Halla as her personal name, from Mount Halla in Korea. (According to Joann Kealiinohomoku, personal communication February 2000, the name Halla, from Mount Halla on Korea's Cheju Island, was given to Huhm by her father.) Huhm was the family name of John Huhm, the Korean-American she eventually married but then divorced. (Yong Cha Huhm is the name on her permanent resident visa application.) From the time she lived in Hawai'i, she consistently romanized Pae as Pai. Because her mentor, Pae Ku-ja, recognized her as an official carrier of the Pae Ku-ja dance style, possibly actually bestowing the name Pae Ku-ja II on her (Mary Jo Freshley, personal communication 14 Feb. 1999), Halla Huhm may have decided to sustain this recognition by keeping Pae, romanized Pai, as part of her name. The romanization Huhm used, Pai, is retained here.

3. Information on Halla Huhm and the history of the Halla Huhm Korean Dance Studio is based on Nishiguchi 1982, materials in the Halla Huhm Dance Collection owned by Mary Jo Freshley, and personal interviews.

4. Most people say she came to Hawai'i in 1949. Nemethy (1956) indicates she came in 1950, following her husband's discharge from the service, and a 1952 newspaper article (Anonymous) states she arrived in the islands in August of 1950. A fellow immigrant from around the same time says she was in the islands in 1948.

5. For a history of the studio see Nishiguchi 1982.

6. Choy and Sutton (1991) refer to a "few traditional musicians" in the Hawai'i community, including an elderly drummer who lived in Hilo, in the 1920s or 1930s. In 1974, Sŏng Kŭm-yŭn, a well-known *kayagŭm* player, and her husband, a drummer, came to Hawai'i. However, there were never a sufficient number of different kinds of musicians residing in Hawai'i to provide a full ensemble of the sort that would have been most appropriate to accompany the kinds of dances Huhm did.

7. Certification of qualified students is common practice among Japanese and Okinawan dance and music studios in Hawai'i.

8. These events were sponsored by the Committee on the 90th Anniversary Celebration of Korean Immigration to Hawai'i in cooperation with the University of Hawai'i at Mānoa's Department of Theatre and Dance, Music Department, and Center for Korean Studies; the University of Hawai'i at Hilo; and the Big Island Korean Club.

9. This dance bears interesting similarities to descriptions of Dream of Youth, a dance performed by Ch'oe Sŭng-hŭi in the United States during her 1938–1940 tour (see Chapter 8).

10. *Hwanggap*, the sixtieth birthday, is a particularly important event in Korean culture, and is generally celebrated with elaborate parties.

11. In a discussion of Okinawan music in Hawai'i Sutton states, "Gaining recognition from the larger Hawaiian community is valued by performers of all ethnic groups in Hawai'i. . . . Participation in multicultural shows . . . has long served as a sign of cultural legitimacy in Hawai'i" (1983:62). For a discussion of dance and its role in Hawai'i's multicultural community see Van Zile 1996.

12. The number of students fluctuates greatly, generally decreasing in the summer months and increasing before a major studio recital. In the spring of 1997 there were approximately fifty students, ranging in age from six to sixty-eight years old. Although most students were female, there were several older male students. Only three students were of ethnicities other than Korean: one of European ancestry, one of European and Hawaiian ancestry, and one of Chinese ancestry. Many students, particularly younger ones, were of mixed ethnicity.

13. Chang's embarrassment at publicly displaying her Korean heritage and similar concerns of students today are echoed among members of other ethnic groups in Hawai'i. Sutton reports feelings of shame expressed by young Okinawan-Americans over acknowledging their participation in traditional Okinawan music, which they describe as "old folks type music" (1983:68). He also indicates that this negative attitude can be outweighed by positive reinforcement from adult members of the Okinawan community (ibid.).

14. Yu states that "all Korean churches and community organizations are defined on the basis of the language they use, for the Korean-speaking adults and their English-speaking children lead separate lives and socialize in separate orbits" (Yu Eui-young 1993:147). Lee Kwang-kyu states, "For many Koreans, the church is the only place outside the home where they can speak the Korean language" (1993:28). Language ability of students at the Halla Huhm Studio ranges from those whose first language is Korean and who speak minimal English to those whose first and only language is English. In addition, the first and primary language of the studio's current major teacher is English, while that of her assistant is Korean. Together with the fact that students range in age from six to sixty-eight years old, these factors indicate that only some students at the Halla Huhm Studio follow the model described by Yu, and that the studio provides an alternative to churches where Korean is spoken outside the home.

15. See, for example, Choy Bong-youn 1979; Hurh Won-moo and Kim Kwang Chung 1984; Kim Byong-suh and Lee Sang Hyun 1980; Kim Hyung-chan and Patterson 1974; and Yu Eui-young 1988.

16. Shortly after Halla Huhm died the Halla Huhm Foundation was established to support Korean cultural activities in the community. The parent of one studio student became actively involved as a board member, and continued her support even after the student left the islands to attend college on the U.S. mainland.

17. In a 1988 publication Barbara B. Smith commented on "a recent conversation with a distinguished Korean of long-term residence in Hawai'i about . . . recent [Korean] immigrants" in which the Korean indicated "the majority of the adults are too busy catching up economically and the children too busy catching up educationally to have the time for the arts" (p. 142). I suggest that parents could vicariously participate in the arts by having the studio take on this task for their children.

18. Yu Eui-young says:

> During a discussion session at the Korean-Canadian youth conference, students were asked what aspects of Korean tradition they would like to preserve. After lengthy deliberation, they came up with two elements of Korean culture they would like to keep. One was "kimch'i" [spicy pickled vegetables] and the other was the custom of respecting elders. . . . Regarding "kimch'i," all said they would like to retain it, but complained that their mothers were not teaching them how to make it.
>
> These conversations highlight the fact that the first-generation parents are even neglecting to teach their children very simple aspects of Korean traditional culture . . . (1994:271–272)

19. The repertoire taught at the studio has always emphasized traditional

court and village dance and occasionally new choreography solidly based on these older forms. It is interesting to note that in a study of Korean music in Los Angeles, Riddle points out "overwhelming interest" and solid financial support (in the form of "good attendance at concerts" and "dues-payments and various donations") among the Korean-American community are given to training and participation in western music rather than Korean music (1985:194). He points out differences between the Korean immigrant community and those of other ethnic groups by saying

> [t]hey have never been forced to live in ghetto-like isolation from the larger society, as the Chinese once were: the musical heritage they bring from their homeland is *already* Western. And, as with first-generation immigrant groups in general, wherever their origin, the search for financial and emotional security has to be uppermost, taking clear precedence over artistic pursuits in general, though music has a respected role in religious worship and for the cultural edification of the younger generation. (ibid.:195)

Some students at the Halla Huhm Studio also study such western forms as piano and ballet, giving precedence to activities in these forms when there are choices to be made.

20. In describing Korean music in Los Angeles in the 1980s, Riddle refers to

> the lingering vestiges of traditional Korean social stratification, in which professional musicians, together with their counterparts in drama and dance, are ranked at the bottom of the social ladder. And to the urban Korean—whether in Seoul or Los Angeles—traditional music and dance is associated with rural naiveté. (1985:193)

K. Connie Kang, a Korean-American journalist raised in Japan and Okinawa who first came to the United States to attend college, says that in her teens she "kept dreaming of becoming a writer, singer, and actress, although I knew full well that no Korean from a decent family could aspire to sing or act" (1995:146). I am certain that "dance" would also be included in this list. Nora Okja Kim, Korean-American author of *Comfort Woman* who grew up in Hawai'i, says that her parents' attitude toward all arts was that they were "wasteful, suspect, and unstable" (1998). It is intriguing to note that in a 1982 article describing the contributions of Koreans to America, Choy identifies writers, political scientists, medical and chemical researchers, judges, politicians, painters, pianists, violinists, cellists, Hollywood actors, athletes, and physicians, but no dancers—of either Korean dance or any other kind of dance (Choy Bong-youn).

21. Because there is a good deal of Korean spoken at the studio, one student said she felt sorry Freshley could not understand all of the discussions, and often wanted to translate conversations for her.

22. In 1992 Freshley obtained a grant from the Hawai'i State Foundation on Culture and the Arts to work with Halla Huhm, on a mentor-apprentice basis, to document the costumes used by Huhm. Freshley's report, now part of the Halla Huhm Dance Collection, contains a large number of photographs and detailed explanations of costume components, including Korean terminology for them.

23. Halla Huhm lived many of her formative years in Japan and spoke Japanese fluently. When she first came to Hawai'i she associated a great deal with the Japanese community, and the travel agency she eventually worked for was owned by a Japanese man. Some people believe she was much more comfortable with Japanese people during her early days in Hawai'i, and that is why some of her early students were Japanese.

24. Despite Freshley's commitment and Huhm's support of her, her relationship with Halla Huhm was not always smooth. Tensions arising with the pressures of performances and juggling artistic desires with financial reality and community relationships contributed to some trying times. But Freshley's devotion to Korean dance, the studio, and Halla Huhm never flagged, and she has been the only person with long-standing and complete dedication—to the studio, her own ongoing study of Korean dance, and the furtherance of Korean culture, through dance, in the Hawai'i community.

GLOSSARY

Terms

aak	雅樂	아악	"elegant" music; court ritual music
Aiya, Chŏ San Nŏmŏe Muŏshi?	—	아이야 저 산 너머에무엇이?	Hey, Children, What's Beyond the Mountain? (dance name)
ajaeng	牙箏	아쟁	long, bowed, seven-string zither
Akhak kwebŏm	樂學軌範	악학궤범	*Guide to the Study of Music* (1493)
akkong	樂工	악공	musician
aksaeng	樂生	악생	musician
Arirang	—	아리랑	title of song and dance
Bunkazai Hogohō	文化財保護法	—	Cultural Properties Protection Law (Japanese)
buyō	舞踊	—	Japanese term for dance
chaeinch'ŏng	才人廳	재인청	school for traditional artists
chajin maji todŭri	—	자진맞이도드리	a rhythm pattern
chajin mori	—	자진모리	a rhythm pattern
chakpŏp	作法	작법	Buddhist ritual dance
Chaktu kŏri	斫頭거리	작두거리	section of a *kut*
changagwŏn'gi	掌樂院妓	장악원기	highest rank of *kisaeng* (also *sŏnsanggi*)
changga	長歌	장가	long poem
changgo	杖鼓	장고	hourglass-shaped drum
changgoch'um	杖鼓춤	장고춤	hourglass-shaped drum dance

Ch'anggyŏngwŏn	昌慶苑	창경원	name used for Ch'anggyŏng-gung during Japanese occupation when this palace was used as a park
ch'angjak	創作	창작	creative
ch'angjak ch'um	創作춤	창작 춤	creative dance
ch'angjak Han'guk muyong	創作韓國舞踊	창작한국무용	creative Korean dance
ch'angjak kugak	創作國樂	창작 국악	creative music
ch'angjak muyong	創作舞踊	창작 무용	creative dance
ch'angjak muyong palp'yohoe	創作舞踊發表會	창작무용발표회	creative dance concert
ch'angjaksŏng	創作性	창작성	creativity
Ch'angmuhoe	創舞會	창무회	name of dance company
cheŭi muyong	祭儀舞踊	제의무용	ritual/religious dance
cheung	—	제웅	straw effigy used at New Year time
ch'ima	—	치마	traditional Korean skirt
chinch'an ŭigwe	進饌儀軌	진찬의궤	record of large court banquet
Chindo Sshikkim Kut	珍島씻김굿	진도씻김굿	type of *kut* from Chindo
ching	鉦	징	gong
chinjak ŭigwe	進爵儀軌	진작의궤	record of small court banquet
Chinju Kisaeng Chohap	晋州妓生組合	진주 기생 조합	Chinju Female Entertainers' Union
Chinju Kŏmmu	晋州劍舞	진주 검무	Chinju Sword Dance
Chinju Muhyŏng Munhwajae Chŏnsu Hoegwan	晋州無形文化財傳修會館	진주무형문화재전수회관	Chinju Intangible Cultural Properties Teaching Center
Chinju Ogwangdae	晋州五廣大	진주오광대	dance-drama genre from Chinju
Chinju P'al Kŏmmu	晋州八劍舞	진주 팔 검무	Chinju Sword Dance for Eight
Chinjushisa	晋州市史	진주시사	*History of the City of Chinju*

Chinogwi Kut	眞오귀굿	진오귀굿	a type of *kut*
chinyŏn ŭigwe	進宴儀軌	진연의궤	record of medium court banquet
chŏgori	—	저고리	traditional Korean blouse
Ch'oip paeyŏlto	初入排列圖	초입배열도	Diagram of the Arrangement upon Entering
Ch'oksŏngnu	矗石樓	촉석루	pavilion in Chinju
chŏllip	戰笠	전립	military hat
Ch'ŏnan kŏri	天安거리	천안거리	section of a *kut*
chŏnbok	戰服	전복	military jacket
Chŏndo Ch'ŏ-yongmu	前度處容舞	전도처용무	The "Former" Dance of Ch'ŏyong
chŏngak	正樂	정악	"orthodox" music; music played by literati
Chŏngak yanggŭmbo	正樂洋琴譜	정악양금보	book of scores for *yanggŭm*
chŏngjae	呈才	정재	court entertain-ment dance
chŏng-jung-dong	靜中動	정중동	motion-in-stillness
Chongmyo cheryeak	宗廟祭禮樂	종묘 제례악	Royal Ancestors' Shrine Dance and Music
ch'ŏnmin	賤民	천민	lower-class people, during Chosŏn dynasty
chŏnsu chang-haksaeng	傳修獎學生	전수 장학생	scholarship student
chŏnsuja	傳修者	전수자	one who is instructed or initiated into something traditional
chŏnt'ong	傳統	전통	traditional
chŏnt'ong muyong	傳統舞踊	전통 무용	traditional dance
Chosŏn Aktae	朝鮮樂隊	조선악대	folk dance and music perform-ing group
Chosŏn Kwŏnbŏn Kisaeng Yŏnsŭpso	朝鮮券番妓生演習所	조선 권번 기생 연습소	name of female entertainers' institute
Chosŏn wangjo shillok	朝鮮王朝實錄	조선왕조실록	annals of the Chosŏn dynasty
Ch'ŏyongga	處容歌	처용가	Song of Ch'ŏyong
Ch'ŏyongmu	處容舞	처용무	Dance of Ch'ŏ-yong

Ch'ŏyongnang	處容郎	처용랑	title of dance-drama
chukkanja	竹竿子	죽간자	ceremonial attendants
ch'um	—	춤	dance
Ch'um	—	춤 매거진	*Dance* (magazine title)
ch'umkkun	—	춤꾼	dancer
ch'ump'ae	—	춤패	dance group
ch'ump'an	—	춤판	dance performance
ch'umt'ŏ	—	춤터	dance theater
Ch'unaengjŏn	春鶯	춘앵전	Nightingale in Springtime (dance name)
Chungyo Muhyŏng Munhwajae	重要無形文化財	중요 무형 문화재	Important Intangible Cultural Asset
Chungyo Yuhyŏng Munhwajae	重要有形文化財	중요 유형 문화재	Important Tangible Cultural Asset
chwago	座鼓	좌고	medium size barrel-shaped drum
dang dai	當代	—	present era (Chinese)
dasheng xinyue	大晟新樂	—	banquet music (Chinese)
dasheng yayue	大晟雅樂	—	ritual music (Chinese)
geisha	妓生	—	female entertainer (Japanese)
haegŭm	奚琴	해금	single-course, bowed, two-string fiddle
Hakch'um	鶴춤	학춤	Crane Dance
Hak Yŏnhwadae Ch'ŏyongmu Hapsŏl	鶴蓮花臺處容舞合設	학 연화대 처용무 합설	Crane, Lotus Pavilion, Ch'ŏyong Dance Suite
han	恨	한	frustration, bitterness, unsatisfied desire
hanbok	韓服	한복	traditional Korean attire
Hangmu	鶴舞	학무	Crane Dance

Han'guk	韓國	한국	Korea
Han'guk Chŏng-shin Munhwa Yŏn'guwŏn	韓國精神文化研究院	한국정신문화 연구원	Academy for Korean Studies
Han'guk ch'um	韓國춤	한국 춤	Korean Dance
Han'guk Ch'um P'yŏngnon'ga-hoe	韓國춤 評論家會	한국춤평론가회	Korean Dance Critics Association
Han'guk hyŏndae muyong	韓國現代舞踊	한국현대무용	Korean-style modern dance
Han'guk Kukche Munhwa Hyŏphoe	韓國國際文化協會	한국국제문화 협회	International Cultural Society of Korea
Han'guk Munhwa Yesul Chin-hŭngwŏn	韓國文化藝術進興院	한국문화예술 진흥원	Korean Culture and Arts Foundation
Han'guk Musok Yesul Hyŏphoe	韓國巫俗藝術協會	한국무속예술협회	Korean Shamanic Arts Association
Han'guk muyong	韓國舞踊	한국무용	Korean dance
Han'guk pulgyo t'ongsa	韓國佛敎通史	한국불교통사	*Treatise on Korean Buddhism*
Han'guk Yesul Chonghap Hakkyo	韓國藝術綜合學校	한국예술종합 학교	Korean National University of the Arts
han'gŭl	—	한글	Korean alphabet and script
hansam	汗衫	한삼	long sleeves used in court dances
harabŏji	—	할아버지	grandfather
Hogu kŏri	戶口 (別星) 거리	호구거리	section of a *kut*
Honam Sshikkim Kut	湖南씻김굿	호남 씻김굿	type of *kut* from Honam
Hŏnch'ŏnsu	獻天壽	헌천수	title of court music composition
hongsaek chŏndae	紅色戰帶	홍색전대	red sash
hongtti	紅띠	홍띠	red sash
Hŏnjong mushin chinch'an ŭigwe	憲宗戊申進饌儀軌	헌종 무신 진찬 의궤	name of an 1848 *ŭigwe*
hŏt'ŭnch'um	—	허튼 춤	spontaneous dance done at drinking parties
Hudo Ch'ŏyongmu	後度處容舞	후도처용무	The "Latter" Dance of Ch'ŏyong
Hŭidae	戲臺	희대	original name of theater now known as Wŏn'gaksa

hŭng	—	흥	lively animation or enthusiasm
huyue	胡樂	—	Chinese term for foreign music
Hwagwanmu	花冠舞	화관무	Flower-crown Dance
hwagwŏn	畫卷	화권	scroll painting
hwanggap	還甲	환갑	60th birthday
hwarang	花郎	화랑	"flower boys," warrior elite during Shilla dynasty
hyangak chŏngjae	鄉樂呈才	향악정재	court entertainment dance of Korean origin
Hyangdang Kyoju	鄉唐交奏	향당교주	title of court music composition
Hyŏmnyulsa	協律社	협률사	former name of Wŏn'gaksa Theater
hyŏndae	現代	현대	modern, contemporary
hyŏndae ch'um	現代춤	현대춤	modern/contemporary dance
hyŏndae Han'guk muyong	現代韓國舞踊	현대 한국 무용	contemporary Korean dance
hyŏndae muyong	現代舞踊	현대무용	modern/contemporary dance
iemoto	家元	—	system for passing on traditional arts (Japanese)
ilmu	佾舞	일무	Confucian shrine dances
imatpaji	—	이맛받이	thickly padded headband
In'gan Munhwajae	人間文化財	인간문화재	Human Cultural Asset
ipch'um	—	입춤	name of dance movement
isuja	履修者	이수자	one who has completed a course of study; successor to *poyuja*
jin dai	近代	—	near era (Chinese)
kabuki	歌舞伎	—	a Japanese dance-theater genre

Kain Chŏnmoktan	佳人剪牧丹	가인 전목단	Beautiful Women Picking Peonies (dance name)
k'al	—	칼	knife
K'alch'um	—	칼춤	Knife Dance
kamyŏn'gŭk	假面劇	가면극	masked drama
kamyŏn mugŭk	假面舞劇	가면무극	masked dance-drama
Kanggangsullae (or Kanggang-suwŏllae)	—	강강술래 (강강수월래)	dance name
Kanghwa-do choyak	江華島條約	강화도조약	treaty with Japan (signed on Kanghwa Island)
Kangnyŏng T'alch'um	康翎탈춤	강령탈춤	masked dance-drama genre from Kangnyŏng
Karak Tŏri	—	가락덜이	section of Yŏngsan Hoesang, a court music composition
kat	—	갓	Korean man's hat
kayagŭm	伽倻琴	가야금	plucked, twelve-string, long zither
kimch'i	—	김치	pickled vegetables
Kin Yŏngsan Hoesang	긴 靈山會上	긴 영산회상	section of Yŏngsan Hoesang, a court music composition
Kirosa	耆老社	기로사	Office of the Venerable Aged
Kisa	耆社	기사	short name for Kirosa
kisaeng	妓生	기생	female entertainer
kkwaenggwari	—	꽹과리	small gong
kojŏn	古典	고전	classical
kojŏnmu	古典舞	고전무	classical dance
kojŏn muyong	古典舞踊	고전무용	classical dance
kŏm	劍	검	sword
kŏmmu	劍舞	검무	sword dance
kŏmun'go	—	거문고	plucked, six-string zither
kŏri	—	거리	sections of a *kut*
Koryŏsa akchi	高麗史樂志	고려사 악지	music volume of 1451 treatise, *Koryŏsa*

Kosŏng Ogwangdae	固城五廣大	고성오광대	dance-drama genre from Ogwangdae
koyu	固有	고유	"traditional things"
ku kunbok	具軍服	구 군복	uniform of high-ranking officers of Chosŏn dynasty
kŭndae	近代	근대	new, modern
kŭndae muyong	近代舞踊	근대무용	new/modern dance
kungjung muyong	宮中舞踊	궁중무용	court dance
Kungnip Kugagwŏn	國立國樂院	국립국악원	National Center for Korean Traditional Performing Arts (originally known in English as National Classical Music Institute, and then Korean Traditional Performing Arts Center)
Kungnip Kugak Kodŭng Hakkyo	國立國樂高等學校	국립 국악 고등학교	National High School of the Performing Arts
Kungnip Palledan	國立 발레團	국립 발레단	National Ballet Troupe
Kungnip Yesul Kodŭng Hakkyo	國立藝術高等學校	국립예술고등학교	National High School for the Arts
kut	—	굿	shaman ceremony
Kutkŏrich'um	—	굿거리춤	dance name
Kwanŭm Ch'an	觀音讚	관음찬	Buddhist chant title
kwŏnbŏn	券番	권번	training school for female entertainers
kyobang	敎坊	교방	training school for female entertainers
Kyobang kayo	敎坊歌謠	교방가요	*Text Collection of Court Entertainers' Training Institute* (1872)

Kyŏngguk taejŏn	經國大典	경국대전	Chosŏn dynasty code of law, compiled 1460–1484	297 *Glossary*
madanggŭk	마당劇	마당극	"field theater"	
Mannam	—	만남	Meeting (dance name)	
manshin	萬神	만신	shaman	
minjung	民衆	민중	"the people," the masses	
minsok ch'um	民俗춤	민속춤	folk dance	
minsok muyong	民俗舞踊	민속무용	folk dance	
Mit'a Ch'an	彌陀讚	미타찬	Buddhist chant title	
mŏt	—	멋	inner spiritual quality of charm and grace	
mu	舞	무	dance	
mu	巫	무	shaman	
Mudang Ch'um	巫堂춤	무당춤	Shaman Dance (dance name)	
Mudang Kibon Tongjak Ch'um	巫堂基本動作춤	무당기본동작춤	Basic Shaman Dance Movements (dance name)	
mudo	舞蹈	무도	dance (western-style ballroom dance and dancelike fitness exercises)	
mudong	舞童	무동	young male court dancer	
mugam	巫感	무감	portion of a *kut*	
muhyŏng munhwajae	無形文化財	무형문화재	intangible cultural asset	
Muhyŏng Mun-hwajae Chŏnsu Hoegwan	無形文化財傳修會館	무형문화재전수회관	Transmission Center for Intangible Cultural Properties	
muhyŏng mun-hwajae poyuja	無形文化財保有者	무형문화재보유자	carrier of intan-gible cultural asset	
mumu	武舞	무무	Confucian "mili-tary" dance	
mumu	巫舞	무무	shaman dance	

Munhwajae Kwalliguk	文化財管理局	문화재 관리국	Cultural Property Preservation Bureau
Munhwajae Pohopŏp	文化財保護法	문화재 보호법	Law on the Protection of Cultural Properties
Munhwajae Wiwŏnhoe	文化財委員會	문화재 위원회	Committee on Cultural Properties
Munhwa Kongbobu	文化公報部	문화공보부	Ministry of Culture and Information
munmu	文舞	문무	Confucian "civil" dance
munmyo cheryak	文廟祭禮樂	문묘제례악	Confucian shrine dance and music
Musanhyang	舞山香	무산향	dance name
musok ch'um	巫俗춤	무속춤	shaman dance
Musok Pojonhoe	巫俗保存會	무속보존회	Association for the Preservation of Shamanism
muyong	舞踊	무용	dance
muyongkwa	舞踊科	무용과	dance department
Nabich'um	—	나비춤	Butterfly Dance
naengmyŏn	冷麵	냉면	cold noodles
naeyŏn	內演	내연	"inner" formal banquet
Namdo tŭl-norae	南都들노래	남도들노래	field songs of Namdo
Narye	儺禮	나례	New Year celebration
nihon buyō	日本舞踊		Japanese dance
Noin Ch'um	老人춤	노인춤	Old Man's Dance
Non'gae Pyŏlche	論介別祭	논개별제	festival honoring Non'gae
nongak	農樂	농악	farmers' band dance and music
Obang Chaktae	五方作隊	오방작대	Dance of the Five Directions
Obang Chaktaedo	五方作隊圖	오방작대도	Diagram of Dance of the Five Directions
Obang Shinjangmu	五方神將舞	오방신장무	Dance of the Gods of the Five Directions

oeguk hyŏndae muyong	外國現代舞踊	외국 현대무용	Western-style modern dance	299
oeguk muyong	外國舞踊	외국무용	foreign dance	*Glossary*
oeyŏn	外演	외연	"outer" formal banquet	
ŏkkae ch'um	—	어깨춤	"shoulder dance"	
Ŏllak	言樂	언락	song title	
paekt'ong	白통	백통	alloy of copper and nickel	
Paektusan Shin'gok	白頭山神曲	백두산 신곡	Myth of Mount Paektu (dance name)	
pak	拍	박	wooden clapper musical instrument	
p'al	八	팔	eight	
P'algwanbo	八關寶	팔관보	government office for managing P'algwanhoe	
P'algwanhoe	八關會	팔관회	Festival of the Eight Vows	
P'algwansa	八關寺	팔관사	government office for managing P'algwanhoe	
palle	—	발레	ballet (Korean pronunciation)	
p'ansori	—	판소리	storytelling vocal genre	
Parach'um	婆囉춤	바라춤	Cymbal Dance	
Pidan Kil	—	비단길	The Silk Road (dance name)	
Pihaeng	飛行	비행	Flying (dance name)	
p'iri	—	피리	double reed pipe	
P'ogurak	抛毬樂	포구락	Ball Playing Dance	
pŏmmu	法舞	법무	court dance	
pŏmp'ae	梵唄	범패	Buddhist chant	
Ponsa Ch'an	本師讚	본사찬	Buddhist chant title	
Pon Yŏngsan Hoesang	本靈山會相	본영산회상	section of Yŏngsan Hoesang, a court music composition	
Pŏpkoch'um	法鼓춤	법고춤	Monk's Drum Dance	
pŏsŏn	—	버선	Korean-style socks	

poyuja	保有者	보유자	"one who possesses knowledge"; carrier of a tradition; national living treasure
poyuja hubo	保有者候補	보유자후보	*poyuja* designate
pparŭn todŭri	—	빠른 도드리	a rhythm pattern
Puch'aech'um	—	부채춤	Fan Dance
puk	—	북	small barrel-shaped drum
Pukch'um	—	북춤	Drum Dance
Pulsa kŏri	佛師거리	불사거리	section of a *kut*
p'ungsokhwa	風俗畵	풍속화	folk painting
Pyŏ	—	벼	Rice Plant (dance name)
Pyŏltang Asshi	別堂 아씨	별당 아씨	Woman of the Separate Cottage (dance name)
p'yŏngsang	平床	평상	small wooden platform
p'yŏn'gyŏng	編磬	편경	set of large jade chimes
p'yŏnjong	編鍾	편종	set of large metal bells
sach'an	賜饌	사찬	foods for royalty
saektong	色動	색동	multicolored long sleeves used in court dances
Saengsaronan Ye Ishyamae	生死路는 예 이샤매	생사로는 예 이샤매	The Road of Birth and Death Is Right Here (dance name)
salp'uri	煞풀이	살풀이	"dance to expel evil spirits"
Salp'uri Kut	煞풀이굿	살풀이굿	dance name
Samguk yusa	三國遺史	삼국유사	*Memorabilia of the Three Kingdoms*
Sandae Togam	山臺都監	산대도감	Office of Masked Dance-Drama
sangmo	象毛	상모	small, flexible rod in hat used in *nongak*

Sang Yŏngsan Hoesang	上靈山會相	상영산회상	section of Yŏng-san Hoesang, a court music composition
sasŭp	私習	사습	workshop
Seoul Nori Madang		서울놀이마당	name of outdoor performing area
Shim Ch'ŏng	沈淸	심청	traditional Korean story about a young girl, Shim Ch'ŏng
shin	新	신	new
shin buyō	新舞踊	—	Japanese term for new dance
shin-chŏnt'ong muyong	新傳統舞踊	신 전통무용	new traditional dance
Shin'gosan T'aryŏng	新高山打令	신고산타령	name of a folk song
shin'gŭk	新劇	신극	new theater
shin'gyoyuk	新教育	신교육	new education
Shinjang kŏri	神將거리	신장거리	section of a *kut*
shinmuyong	新舞踊	신무용	new dance
shinnyŏsŏng	新女性	신여성	new woman
shinshi	新詩	신시	new poetry
shin-shinmuyong	新-新舞踊	신 신무용	new-new dance
Shiyong Hoemudo	時用回舞圖	시용회무도	Diagram of Beginning and Ending Turning Dance
Shiyong hyangakpo	時用鄉樂譜	시용향악보	*Lyrics of Native Korean Songs*
sogo	小鼓	소고	small handheld frame drum
sŏgu muyong	西歐舞踊	서구무용	Western dance
sŏnsanggi	選上妓	선상기	highest rank of *kisaeng* (also *changagwŏn'gi*)
Sŏnyurak	船遊樂	선유락	dance name
sosakubuyō	創作舞踊		Japanese term for "creative dance"
Sshikkim kut	—	씻김굿	shaman ritual for the dead
sugŏn	手巾	수건	handkerchief
sugŏnch'um	手巾춤	수건춤	possible early name for *salp'uri*
Sujech'ŏn	壽齊天	수제천	title of a court music composition

Sŭngjŏnmu	勝戰舞	승전무	dance name
sŭngmu	僧舞	승무	monk's dance
Sunjo kich'uk chinch'an ŭigwe	純祖己丑進饌儀軌	순조기축진찬의궤	name of an 1829 *ŭigwe*
Sunjo muja chinjak ŭigwe	純祖戊子進爵儀軌	순조무자진작의궤	name of an 1828 *ŭigwe*
Suyŏnjang Chigok	壽延長之曲	수연장지곡	title of a court music composition
suyue	俗樂	—	Chinese term for popular music
Tae	竹	대	Bamboo (dance name)
Taedong Kut	—	대동굿	name of a particular *kut*
Taegam kŏri	大監거리	대감거리	section of a *kut*
taegŭm	大笒	대금	long, bamboo, transverse flute
Taehan Sŭnggong Kyŏngshin Yŏnhaphoe	大韓勝共敬信聯合會	대한승공경신연합회	Korean Federation of Associations for Victory over Communism and Respect of Beliefs
T'aju	打柱	타주	Dance of the Eightfold Path
t'alch'um	—	탈춤	masked dance-drama
t'alch'um nori	—	탈춤놀이	masked dance-play
t'al-nori	—	탈놀이	masked-play
tangak chŏngjae	唐樂呈才	당악정재	Chinese-derived court entertainment dance
tanso	短簫	단소	small notched bamboo vertical flute
t'aryŏng	打令	타령	a drum rhythm
Todang Kut	都堂 굿	도당굿	name of a particular *kut*
Tongguk seshigi	東國歲時記	동국세시기	*Account of Korean Seasonal Customs*
Tonggyŏng chapki	東京雜記	동경잡기	*Capital Miscellany*
To Salp'uri	都 煞풀이	도 살풀이	dance name
tŏtpaegi	—	덧배기	a rhythm pattern

ttaensŭ	—	댄스	dance (Korean pronunciation of "dance")
Tunggi Kut	—	둥기굿	name of a particular *kut*
Ŭiam	義岩	의암	Righteous Rock
Ŭiam Pyŏlche	義岩別祭	의암별제	name of festival honoring Non'gae
ŭigwe	儀軌	의궤	record of royal ceremonies
ŭishik muyong	儀式舞踊	의식무용	ritual dance
Up'yŏn	羽編	우편	song title
wŏn	圓	원	Korean currency
Wŏn'gaksa	圓覺社	원각사	name of a theater
wŏnhyŏng	元刑	원형	original form or version
xian dai	現代	—	modern era (Chinese)
yangban	兩班	양반	aristocratic class
yanggŭm	洋琴	양금	wire-string, struck dulcimer
Yedo	藝道	예도	The Way of Art (dance name)
yenŭng muyong	藝能舞踊	예능무용	classical dance
Yiwangjik Aakpu	李王職雅樂部	이왕직 아악부	Court Music and Dance Academy
yŏmbul	念佛	염불	a rhythm pattern
Yŏmbul Todŭri	念佛 도드리	염불 도드리	section of Yŏngsan Hoesang, a court music composition
Yŏndŭnghoe	燃燈會	연등회	Buddhist lantern festival
Yongjae ch'onghwa	慵齋叢話	용재총화	*Collected Writings of Yongjae*
Yŏngsan Hoesang	靈山會相	영산회상	court music composition title
Yŏngsanjae	靈山齋	영산재	Buddhist ceremony
Yŏnhwadaemu	蓮花臺舞	연화대무	Lotus Pavilion Dance
yŏnp'ungdae	燕風臺	연풍대	name of a dance movement

An Ae-sun	安愛順	안애순
An Che-sung	安濟承	안제승
An Hwi-jun	安輝濬	안휘준
An Mak	安漠	안막
Ch'ae Hŭi-wan	蔡熙完	채희완
Chang Sa-hun	張師勛	장사훈
Chang T'ae-hŭng	張泰興	장태흥
Chang Tŭng-man	張得萬	장득만
Ch'oe Kŭm-sun	崔今順	최금순
Ch'oe Sŏng-un	崔性云	최성운
Ch'oe Sun-i (professional name, Wan-ja)	崔順伊 (完子)	최순이 (완자)
Ch'oe Sŭng-hŭi	崔承喜	최승희
Ch'oe Ye-bun	崔禮分	최예분
Chŏng Chae-man (Jung Jae-man)	鄭在晩	정재만
Chŏng Haeng-gŭm	鄭幸今	정행금
Chŏng Kŭm-sun	鄭今順	정금순
Chŏng P'il-sun	鄭畢順	정필순
Chŏng Pyŏng-ho	鄭昞浩	정병호
Ch'ŏyong	處容	처용
Chu Ong-nyŏ	朱玉女	주옥녀
Ha Kyu-il	河圭一	하규일
Ham Hwa-jin	咸和鎭	함화진
Han Sang-gŭn	韓相根	한상근
Han Sŏng-jun	韓成俊	한성준
Hŏ Suk	許俶	허숙
Hong Kyŏng-hŭi	洪敬姬	홍경희
Huizong	徽宗	
Hwang Ch'ang-nang	黃昌郎	황창랑
Hwang Il-baek	黃日白	황일백
Hwang Pyŏng-gi	黃秉翼	황병기
Hyomyŏng (Prince) (posthumously, Ikchong)	孝明世子 (翼宗)	효명세자 (익종)
Im Sŏng-nam	林聖男	임성남
Iryŏn	一然	일연
Ishii Baku	石井漠	──
Kang Kwi-rye	姜貴禮	강귀례
Kang Su-jin	姜秀珍	강수진
Kang Sun-kŭm	姜順今	강순금
Kang Ye-na	姜藝那	강예나
Kim Cha-jin	金子眞	김자진
Kim Ch'ae-hyŏn	金采賢	김채현
Kim Chae-un	金在運	김재운

Kim Ch'ang-ha	金昌河	김창하
Kim Chi-a	—	김지아
Kim Chin-yŏ	金振汝	김진여
Kim Ch'ŏn-hŭng	金千興	김천흥
Kim Chŏng-ae	金貞愛	김정애
Kim Chŏng-ja	金貞子	김정자
Kim Chong-shik	金鍾植	김종식
Kim Chŏng-wŏn	金貞媛	김정원
Kim Chung-sŏp	金重燮	김중섭
Kim Hong-do	金弘道	김홍도
Kim Hye-shik	金惠植	김혜식
Kim Ki-su	金琪洙	김기수
Kim Kŭm-hwa	金錦花	김금화
Kim Mae-ja	金梅子	김매자
Kim Mok-hwa	金木花	김목화
Kim Pyŏng-sŏp	金炳燮	김병섭
Kim Sŏng-in	金性仁	김성인
Kim Suk-cha	金淑子	김숙자
Kim Sun-nyŏ (professional name, Su-ak)	金順女 (壽岳)	김순녀 (수악)
Kim T'ae-sŏp	金泰燮	김태섭
Kim T'ae-wŏn	金泰源	김태원
Kim Tŏg-yong	金德龍	김덕용
Kim Yŏn-i	金蓮伊	김연이
Kim Yong	金龍	김용
Kim Yŏng-je	金寧濟	김영제
Kim Yong-man	金容萬	김용만
Kim Yong-ok	金容沃	김용옥
Kim Yŏng-wŏl	金暎月	김영월
King Chinhŭng (r. 540–576)	眞興王	진흥왕
King Chŏngjong (r. 1035–1046)	靖宗	정종
King Hŏn'gang (r. 875–886)	憲康王	헌강왕
King Kojong (r. 1863–1907)	高宗	고종
King Sejong (r. 1418–1450)	世宗大王	세종대왕
King Sŏngjong (r. 981–997)	成宗	성종
King Sŏngjong (r. 1470–1494)	成宗	성종
King Sukchong (r. 1674–1720)	蕭宗	숙종
King Sunjo (posthumously, Ikchong; r. 1800–1834)	純祖(翼宗)	순조 (익종)
King Sunjong (r. 1907–1910)	純宗	순종
King T'aejo (r. 1392–1398)	太祖	태조
King U (King Shinu; r. 1374–1388)	禑 (辛禑) 王	우왕 (신우왕)
Kuk Su-ho	鞠守鎬	국수호
Kwanch'ang	官昌	관창
Kyebaek	階伯	계백
Mei Lan-fang	梅蘭芳	—
Min (Queen)	閔妃	민비

Min Chun-gi	閔俊基	민준기
Mun Hun-suk (Julia H. Moon)	文薫淑	문훈숙
Mun Il-chi (Moon Il-ji)	文一枝	문일지
Nam Chŏng-ho	南貞鎬	남정호
Non'gae	論介	논개
Pae Ku-ja	裵龜子	배구자
Pae Yang-hyŏn	裵良鉉	배양현
Pae Yong-ja (name, at birth, of Halla Pai Huhm)	裵龍子	배용자
Paek Hyang-ju	白香珠	백향주
Pak Chun-ju	朴俊珠	박준주
Pak Hŏn-bong (sobriquet, Kisan)	朴憲鳳（岐山）	박헌봉 (기산)
Pak In-o	朴仁伍	박인오
Pak Oe-sŏn	朴外仙	박외선
Pak Song-am	朴松岩	박송암
Pak Sŏng-gi	朴性起	박성기
Pak Tong-bo	朴東普	박동보
Pak Yong-gu	朴容九	박용구
Park Chung Hee (Pak Chŏng-hŭi)	朴正熙	박정희
Pong Hae-ryong	奉海龍	봉해룡
Pu Yi	溥儀	
P'umil	品日	품일
Rokusuke Ketanimura	六助毛谷村	—
Sai Shoki (Japanese pronunciation of Ch'oe Sŏng-hŭi)	崔承喜	최승희
Shim Ch'ŏng	沈清	심청
Shin Sŏn-hŭi	辛仙姫	신선희
Sŏng Kŭm-yŏn	成錦鳶	성금연
Sŏng Kye-ok	成季玉	성계옥
Sŏng Kyŏng-nin	成慶麟	성경린
Tan'gun	檀君	단군
To Chŏng-nim	都貞任	도정님
Tsubouchi Shōyō		
Yang Chong-sŭng (Yang Jong-sung)	梁鍾承	양종승
Ye Yong-hae	芮庸海	예용해
Yi Ae-ju	李愛珠	이애주
Yi Chi-san (Lee Ji-san)	李芝山	이지산
Yi Chi-yŏng	李知瑛	이지영
Yi Ch'ŏm	李詹	이첨
Yi Han-yŏl	李韓烈	이한열
Yi Hang-gu	李恒九	이항구
Yi Hye-gu	李惠求	이혜구

Yi Mae-bang	李梅芳	이매방
Yi Sang-il	李相日	이상일
Yi Sŏng-bu	李盛夫	이성부
Yi Su-gyŏng	李壽卿	이수경
Yi Tu-hyŏn (Lee Du-hyon)	李杜鉉	이두현
Yi U-sŏn	李又仙	이우선
Yi Ŭm-jŏn	李音全	이음전
Yi Wan-yong	李完用	이완용
Yi Yul-lye	李潤禮	이윤례
Yu Ki-ryong	劉起龍	유기룡
Yuk Wan-sun (Yook Wan-soon)	陸完順	육완순

REFERENCES CITED

Ahn, Hwi-joon (An Hwi-jun; see also An Hwi-jon)

1986   "History of Korean Art: A Review of Studies," in *Introduction to Korean Studies*. Republic of Korea: The National Academy of Sciences, pp. 137–162.

Allen, Horace N.

1896   "Some Korean Customs. Dancing Girls," *The Korean Repository*. Vol. III, no. 10 (October), pp. 383–386.

An, Hwi-jon (An Hwi-jun; see also Ahn Hwi-joon), editor

1989   *P'ungsokhwa* (Folk Painting). Seoul: Chungang Ilbosa.

Anderson, Jack

1997   *Art Without Boundaries*. Iowa City: University of Iowa Press.

Anonymous

1937a   "Sai Shoki Makes Good," *Seoul Press*, February 23.
1937b   "They All Dance," *Chicago Tribune*, December 12. Graphic section, p. 11.
1938a   Captioned photograph. *Los Angeles Morning News*. January 27.
1938b   "A Korean artist designs costumes for a dancer," *Los Angeles Evening News*. January 27.
1938c   "Korean Pavlowa [*sic*] to Dance Here," *San Francisco Chronicle*. January 12, p. 15.
1938d   "Hantō no minyo odori wo sekaiteki buyō ni . . . : Bijin maihime, Sai Shōki san Chaku Sō" (Making Folk Dance of Peninsula into a Universal Dance: Beautiful Dancing Princess Sai Shoki Arrives in San Francisco), *Shinsokai Asahi*. February?/January? 13.
1938e   "Sai Shoki, Exotic Korean Dancer, Thrills at Ebell," *Los Angeles Examiner*. February 3.
1938f   "Sai Shoki Is Truly Beautiful," *New World-Sun*. January 13.
1938g   "Sai Shōki—Ikkō nanka e" (Sai Shoki Troupe Goes South), *Shinsokai Asahi*, January 25.
1939   "Review" and captioned photograph. *The Dancing Times* (London). January, pp. 510–511.
1940a   "Current Music News," *Chicago Sunday Tribune*. February 18, part 7, p. 5.
1940b   "Dancer Arrives," *Chicago Daily Tribune*. February 21, section G.
1940c   "Here from Korea," *Chicago Daily News*, February 22, p. 9.
1940d   "Asia Dancer to Present Recital," *Hollywood Citizen News*. March 30, p. 4.
1940e   "Sai Shōki san buyōkai subarashii zenkeiki beijin hōmen no kitai wa ōkii" (Expectations for Sai Shoki's Dance Concert Run High: American Audience Expectations Are Big), *Shinsokai Asahi*. April 3.
1940f   "Japanese Dancer at Curran Sunday," *San Francisco News*. April 3, p. 6.
1940g   "Sai Shoki, Premier Korean Dancer to Give Concert Today at Curran," *New World-Sun Daily*. April 7.

1940h   "Sai Shoki Returns to Score Another Triumph in Engagement at Curran; South America Next on Her Tour," *New World-Sun Daily*. April 9.

1940i   "Hantō no reijin Sai Shōki san no buyō senyo no kanshū wo miryō" (The Beauty from the Peninsula. Sai Shoki's Dance Charms More Than a Thousand Audience Members: Satisfying Program Receives a storm of Applause), *Shinsokai Asahi*. April 9.

1952   "War Bride Exponent of Korean Classical Dance," *Honolulu Advertiser*, section 3, p. 13.

1959   *Topics from Korean History*. Korea: Ministry of Education.

1961   "The Romanization of Korean According to the McCune-Reischauer System," *Transactions of the Korea Branch of the Royal Asiatic Society*, Vol. XXXVIII, pp. 121–128.

1979a   *A Handbook of Korea*. Seoul: Korean Overseas Information Service, 3rd edition.

1979b   "Outstanding Korean Picked by Council," *Honolulu Star-Bulletin*. February 17.

1990   "Traditional Dance *Pyŏ* to Be Staged," *Korea Herald* (October 20), p. 10.

1992   "Metropolitan Troupe Performs 'Social-Problem' Dance," *Korea Times*, November 24, p. 5.

1994   "Popularity for Traditional Music," *Newsreview* (July 2), p. 34.

Armstrong, Robert

1981   *The Powers of Presence: Consciousness, Myth and Affecting Presence*. Philadelphia: University of Pennsylvania Press.

Asia Society

1978   *Shaman Ritual from Korea*. New York: Asia Society. Videocassette.

Bausinger, Herman

1990   *Folk Culture in a World of Technology*. Bloomington: Indiana University Press. Translated by Elke Dettmer.

Bharucha, Rustom

1993   "Notes on the Invention of Tradition," in Bharucha. *Theatre and the World*. London: Routledge, pp. 192–200, 208–210.

Buckland, Theresa

1983   "Definitions of Folk Dance: Some Explorations," *Folk Music Journal*. Vol. 4, no. 3, pp. 315–332.

Byun, Eun-mi (Pyŏn ŭn-mi)

1994   "'Human Cultural Asset System' Struck by Corruption, Scandal, Stagnation. Efforts to preserve tradition may be killing it off." *Newsreview* (March 5), pp. 30–31.

Chang, Connie

1991   Letter, in *Funeral of the Late Halla Pai Huhm*. Hawai'i: Hosoi Garden Mortuary, 1994, p. 16.

Chang, Kwang-yeol (Chang Kwang-yŏl)

1998   "Korean Modern Dance's Pathway to International Recognition," *DanceForum*, Vol. 1, no. 1 (Winter), pp. 50–52.

Chang, Sa-hun

1978   "Korean and Chinese Chongjae," *Korea Journal*, Vol. XVIII, no. 2 (February), pp. 14–25.

1984   *Han'guk muyong kaeron* (Introduction to Korean Dance). Seoul: Daekwang munhwasa.

Chinjushisa (History of the City of Chinju)
1979   Chinju, Korea: Chinju Shimin Hŏnjang, pp. 1174–1182.

Choe, Sang-cheul (Ch'oe Sang-ch'ŏl)
1996   Seung-hee Choi [*sic*], Pioneer of Korean Modern Dance: Her Life and Art Under Japanese Occupation 1910–1945. Ph.D. dissertation, New York University.

Ch'oe, Sŭng-hŭi
1936   *Watakushi no jijoden* (My Autobiograpahy). Tokyo: Nihon Shoso.
1937   *Naŭi chasŏjŏn* (My Autobiography). Kyŏngsŏng: Imundang.
1990   "Toraon Ch'oe Sŭng-hŭi" (Return of Ch'oe Sŭng-hŭi), in Kim, Paek-pong, Hyŏn-ch'ŏn Yu, Min-ho Chang, and Pŏm-sŏp Ch'a, editors. *Han'guk yesul ch'ongjip Yŏn'gŭkp'yŏn. II* (Collection of Korean Arts. Theatre. II). Seoul: Taehan Minguk Yesurwŏn, pp. 547–549. (Republication of article originally published in the January, 1941 issue of *Shinshidae*.)
1999   "Muyong Oshimnyŏn" [Fifteen Years of Dance], *Ch'um* (February), pp. 82–98. (Reprinted from *Chogwang*, Vol. 51 (January).
(1940)

Choi, Chungmoo (Ch'oe Chŏng-mu)
1989   "The Artistry and Ritual Aesthetics of Urban Korean Shamans," *Journal of Ritual Studies*. Vol. 3, no. 2 (Summer), pp. 235–249.
1995   "The Minjung Culture Movement and the Construction of Popular Culture in Korea," in Kenneth M. Wells, editor. *South Korea's Minjung Movement. The Culture and Politics of Dissidence*. Honolulu: University of Hawai'i Press, pp. 105–117.

Choi, Haeree (Ch'oe Hae-ri)
1995   "*Ch'angjak Ch'um*: History and Nature of a Contemporary Korean Dance Genre. M.A. thesis, University of Hawai'i.

Chŏng Byŏng-ho (Chŏng Pyŏng-ho; see also Chŏng Pyŏng-ho and Chung Byung-ho)
1997   "I. Ancient–1945: From Ancient Beginning[s] to 1945," in Yang Hye-suk, editor. *Korean Performing Arts. Drama, Dance & Music Theater*. Korean Studies Series No. 6. Seoul: Jipmoondang Publishing Company, pp. 79–102.

Chŏng, Pyŏng-ho (see also Chŏng Byong-ho, Chung Byung Ho, and Chung Byung-ho)
1992   *Han'gukŭi minsok ch'um* (Korean Folk Dance). Seoul: Samsŏng Ch'ulp'ansa.
1995   *Ch'umch'unŭn Ch'oe Sŭng-hŭi—Segyerŭl hwiachabŭn Chosŏn yŏja* (The Dancing Ch'oe Sŭng-hŭi—The Korean Woman Who Captivated the World). Seoul: The Deep-Rooted Tree Publishing House.

Choy, Bong-youn (Ch'oe Pong-yun)
1979   *Koreans in America*. Chicago: Nelson-Hall.
1982   "The History of Koreans in America. Part II. The Korean Contribution to America," *Korean Culture*, Vol. 3, no. 3 (September), pp. 12–19.

Choy, Peggy and Andy Sutton

1991   "Ha Soo Whang: Woman pioneer of Hawai'i (1892–1984), *Korea Times* (Los Angeles edition), October 16, p. 4.

Chung, Byung Ho (Chŏng Pyŏng-ho: see also Chŏng Pyŏng-ho, and Chung Byung-ho)

1997a   "The Characteristics of Korean Traditional Dance," *Korea Journal*. Vol. 37, no. 3 (Autumn), pp. 93–109.

1997b   "An Overview of Traditional Dance," in Joungwon Kim, editor. *Korean Cultural Heritage. Volume III. Performing Arts*. Korea: Korea Foundation, pp. 136–155.

Chung, Hyun-kyung (Chŏng Hyŏn-gyŏng)

1990   *Struggle to be the Sun Again. Introducing Asian Women's Theology*. New York: Orbis Books.

Chung, Hyung-min (Chŏng Hyŏng-min)

1997   "Korean Aesthetics Seen in an Exhibit of Early Choson Dynasty Treasures," *Korean Culture*, Vol. 11, no. 1 (Spring), pp. 60–67.

Chung, Ki-young (Chŏng Ki-yŏng)

1996   "Institutions and Policies on Intangible Cultural Properties," in *Methodologies for the Preservation of Intangible Heritage*. Korean National Commission for UNESCO & The Office of the Cultural Properties of the Republic of Korea, pp. 123–130.

Costello, John

1938   "Music Notes. Sibelius and Sai Shoki," *San Francisco News Letter and Wasp*, January 28, p. 22.

Covell, Alan Carter

1986   *Folk Art and Magic. Shamanism in Korea*. New Jersey: Hollym Corp.

Dell, Cecily

1970   *A Primer for Movement Description Using Effort-Shape and Supplementary Concepts*. New York: Dance Notation Bureau.

Deuchler, Martina

1977   "The Tradition: Women during the Yi Dynasty," in *Virtues in Conflict. Tradition and the Korean Woman Today*, Sandra Mattieli, editor. Korea: Royal Asiatic Society, Korea Branch, pp. 1–48.

1993   "Sin Sukchu: 'House Rules,'" in Peter H. Lee, editor. *Sourcebook of Korean Civilization. Vol. I. From Early Times to the Sixteenth Century*. New York: Columbia University Press, pp. 571–574.

Erdman, Joan L.

1996   "Dance Discourses. Rethinking the History of the 'Oriental Dance,'" in Gay Morris, editor. *Moving Words. Re-writing Dance*. London: Routledge, pp. 288–305.

Fisher, Marjory

1938   "Sai Shoki Is Acclaimed in Debut," *San Francisco News*, January 24.

1940   "Sai Shoki Proves Fine Artist: Soloists Featured at Y.P. 'Sym.'" *San Francisco News*. April 8, p. 15.

Fouser, Robert J.

1994   "Kim Young-dong (Kim Yŏng-dong) and the Dilemma of 'Kore-
            anesque,'" *Korean Culture* (Vol. 15, no. 1, Spring), pp. 4–11.

Frankenstein, Alexander (A.F.)

1938   "Korean Dancer Makes Debut," *San Francisco Chronicle*. Janu-
            ary 23.

1940   "Sai Shoki, Korea Dance Specialist, Is Good as Ever," *San Fran-
            cisco Chronicle*. April 8, p. 7.

Fried, Alexander

1938   "Korean Dances of Sai Shoki Lack Variety," *San Francisco Exam-
            iner*. January 23.

Gilfond, Henry

1938   "Review of the Month," *The Dance Observer*. Vol. V, no. 4
            (April), p. 55.

G.N.B.

1940   "Sai Shoki," *The Dance Observer*. Vol. VII, no. 1 (January), p. 18.

Guest, Ann Hutchinson

1984   *Dance Notation. The Process of Recording Movement on Paper*.
            New York: Dance Horizons.

Guillemoz, Alexandre

1998   "What do the *Naerim Mudang* from Seoul Learn?" in Keith
            Howard, editor. *Korean Shamanism. Revivals, Survivals, and
            Change*. Korea: Royal Asiatic Society, Korea Branch, pp. 73–89.

Guthrie Stewart

1976   "Ritual," in David E. Hunter and Phillip Whitten, editors. *Ency-
            clopedia of Anthropology*. New York: Harper and Rowe, Publish-
            ers, pp. 336–337.

Hanna, Judith Lynn

1979   *To Dance Is Human. A Theory of Nonverbal Communication*.
            Austin and London: University of Texas Press.

Hannas, Wm. C.

1997   *Asia's Orthographic Dilemma*. Honolulu: University of Hawai'i
            Press.

Henthorn, William E.

1971   *A History of Korea*. New York: The Free Press.

Heyman, Alan

1964   *Dances of the Three-Thousand League Land*. New York: Dance
            Perspectives, Inc. (Republished in 1966 by Dong-A, Seoul; in 1970
            by Johnson Reprint Corp.; and in 1981 by Seoul Computer Press,
            Korea.)

Hirabayashi, Hisae

1977   "Sai Shoki to Ishii Baku" (Sai Shoki and Ishii Baku), *Zainishi
            Chosenjin jinno genjo* (The Present State of Korean Residents in
            Japan), special issue no. 12 (November 1), pp. 186–192.

1978   "Sai Shoki to An Baku" (Sai Shoki and An Mak), *Sanzenri*. No. 14 (May 1), pp. 166–173.

Hobsbawm, Eric, and Terence Ranger, editors.
1983   *The Invention of Tradition*. Cambridge: Cambridge University Press.

Hogarth, Hyun-key Kim (Kim Hyŏn-gi)
1994   "Korean Shamanism and Cultural Nationalism," *Transactions of the Royal Asiatic Society, Korea Branch*, Vol. 69, pp. 1–22.

Howard, Keith
1988   "Preservation or Change?, the Sponsorship of Folk Music in Chindo within the Intangible Cultural Asset System," in *Papers of the 5th International Conference on Korean Studies: Korean Studies, Its Tasks and Perspectives. II*. Korea: Academy of Korean Studies, pp. 935–958.
1989   "Namdo Tul Norae: Ritual and the Korean Intangible Cultural Asset System," *Journal of Ritual Studies*. Vol. 3, no. 2 (Summer), pp. 203–216.
1990   *Bands, Songs, and Shamanistic Rituals: Folk Music in Korean Society*. Seoul: Royal Asiatic Society, Korea Branch, second edition.
1991–1992   "Paper Symbols in Chindo Ssikkim kut," *Cahiers d'Extrême-Asie*, Vol. 6, pp. 65–86.
1995   "Gender Issues in the Conservation of Korean Music: Some Presumptive Assumptions," in Klaus Wolfgang Niemoller, Uwe Patzold, and Kyo-chul Chung, editors. *Lux Oriente—Begegnungen der Kulturen in der Musikforschung: Festschrift for Robert Günther zum 65 Geburstag*. Köln: Gustav Bosse Verlag, pp. 181–195.
1996   "Preservation and Presentation of Korean Intangible Cultural Assets," in *Methodologies for the Preservation of Intangible Heritage*. Korean National Commission for UNESCO & The Office of the Cultural Properties of the Republic of Korea, pp. 85–114.

Howard, Keith, editor
1998   *Korean Shamanism. Revivals, Survivals, and Change*. Korea: Royal Asiatic Society, Korea Branch.

Howard, Keith, editor, with Susan Pares and Tessa English
1996   *Korea. People, Country and Culture*. London: School of Oriental and African Studies.

Hsu, Francis
1975   *Iemoto: The Heart of Japan*. Cambridge, Massachusetts: Schenkman Pub. Co.

Huhm, Halla Pai
1980   *Kut. Korean Shamanist Rituals*. New Jersey and Seoul: Hollym International Corp.

Hulbert, Homer Bezaleel
1902   "Korean Products," *The Korea Review*. Vol. 2, no. 8 (August), pp. 341–345.
1962   *History of Korea*, volume II. Edited by Clarence Norwood Weems. New York: Hillary House Pub. Ltd. (Originally published in Seoul in 1905.)

Hurh, Won Moo and Kwang Chung Kim (Hŏ Wŏn-mu and Kim Kwang-jung)
1984   *Korean Immigrants in America. A Structural Analysis of Ethnic*

Confinement and Adhesive Adaptation. England: Associated University Presses.

Hurok Attractions
1938(?)   *Sai Shoki*. New York: Hurok Attractions. (Publicity brochure, New York Public Library Dance Collection Clipping File—Sai Shoki.)

Hutchinson, Ann
1970   *Labanotation. The System of Analyzing and Recording Movement.* Third edition, revised. New York: Theatre Arts Books

Ikeda, Ringi
1953   *Ishii Baku to Sasara Odori* (Ishii Baku and Sasara Odori). Japan: Seikatsu Kiroku Kenkyujo.

Ito, Sachiyo
1979   "Some Characteristics of Japanese Expression as They Appear in Dance," in *Dance Research Annual X: Dance Research Collage.* Edited by Patricia A. Rowe and Ernestine Stodelle. New York: CORD, pp. 267–281.

Jackson, George
1999   "Modern Dance Birthing," *Dance Magazine* (June), p. 18.

J.D.B. (J.D. Bohm)
1938   "Sai Shoki and Huapala Appear in Exotic Dances. Corean [*sic*] and Hawaiian women at Guild Theater," *New York Herald Tribune.* February 21, p. 9.

JVC
1990   *JVC Video Anthology of World Music and Dance.* Cambridge, Massachusetts: Victor Company of Japan in Collaboration with Smithsonian/Folkways Records. Tape 2, section 9, "Mudang kut."

K.T.
1938   "Two Dancers Seen in Exotic Programs," *Musical America.* November 25, p. 23.

Kaeppler, Adrienne
1989   "Dance." *International Encyclopedia of Communications.* New York: Oxford University Press, pp. 450–454.
1994   "Ritual, Theater, and Spectacle for Gods and Mortals: A Personal View of Classical Hawaiian and Japanese Dance," in *Island Creativity and Tradition—Japan and Hawaii.* Unpublished manuscript distributed at a July 12, 1994, symposium at the University of Hawai'i at Mānoa presented by the Onoe Kikunobu Dance Company.

Kang, K. Connie
1995   *Home Was the Land of Morning Calm. A Saga of a Korean-American Family.* Massachusetts: Addison-Wesley Publishing Company.

Kaye, Joseph Arnold
1938   "Dance in Review," *Dance.* Vol. 4, no. 1 (April), pp. 29–30, 33–40.
1939   "Dance in Review. Sai Shoki, Guild Theatre," *Dance.* Vol. 5, no. 3 (January), p. 13.
1940   "Dance in Review," *Dance.* Vol. 7, no. 2 (January), p. 12.

Kealiinohomoku, Joann

1972   "Folk Dance," in Richard Dorson, editor. *Folklore and Folklife. An Introduction*. Chicago: University of Chicago Press, pp. 381–404.

1983   "An Anthropologist Looks at Ballet as a Form of Ethnic Dance." *Impulse; the Annual of Contemporary Dance*. pp. 24–33.

Keene, Donald

1993   "The *Iemoto* System (No and Kyogen)," in *Fenway Court* (periodical publication of the Isabella Stewart Gardner Museum, Boston, Massachusetts). 1992 volume, pp. 30–36.

Kendall, Laurel

1977   "Mugam: The Dance in Shaman's Clothing," *Korea Journal*. Vol. 17, no. 12 (December), pp. 38–44.

1985   *Shamans, Housewives, and Other Restless Spirits. Women in Korean Ritual Life*. Honolulu: University of Hawai'i Press.

1991–1992   "Of Gods and Men: Performance, Possession, and Flirtation in Korean Shaman Ritual," *Cahiers d'Extrême-Asie*, Vol. 6, pp. 45–63.

Kendall, Laurel and Diana Lee

1991   *An Initiation "Kut" for a Korean Shaman*. Hawai'i: University of Hawai'i Press. Videocassette.

Killick, Andrew P.

1992   "Musical Composition in Twentieth-Century Korea," *Korean Studies*, Vol. 16, pp. 43–60.

1998   The Invention of Traditional Korean Opera and the Problem of the Traditionesque: *Ch'anggŭk* and Its Relation to *P'ansori* Narratives. Ph.D. dissertation, University of Washington.

Kim, Byong-suh and Sang Hyun Lee, editors (Kim Pyŏng-sŏ and Yi Sang-hyŏn)

1980   *The Korean Immigrant in America*. New Jersey: The Association of Korean Christian Scholars in North America.

Kim, Ch'ŏn-hŭng

1995   *Shimso Kim Ch'ŏn-hŭng. Muak ch'ilshimnyŏn* (Simso (professional name) Kim Ch'ŏn-hŭng. Seventy Years of Dance and Music). Seoul: Tosŏ Ch'ulp'an Minsogwŏn.

Kim, Ch'ŏn-hŭng and Kyŏng-nin Sŏng, verifiers

1986   *Kungjung muyong mubo* (Court Dance Notation), Volume 1, *Ch'oyongmŭ*. Seoul: Kungnip Kugagwŏn.

Kim, Ch'ŏn-hŭng, Hŏn-bong Pak, and Ki-yŏng Yi

1966   *Ch'inju kŏmmu. Muhyŏng munhwajae chosa pogosŏ* (Chinju Kŏmmu. Intangible Cultural Asset Research Report). Seoul: Munhwajae kwalliguk.

Kim, Ch'ŏng-uk, editor

1999   "Tonggŏng e itssŏso ŭi Ch'oe Sŭng-hŭi che il-hoe palp'yohoe Insanggi" (Written Impressions of Ch'oe Sŭng-hŭi's First Performance in Tokyo), *Ch'um*. April, pp. 76–81.

Kim, Donald

1993   Public comments at the January performance of the Halla Huhm Dance Studio, Kennedy Theatre, University of Hawai'i at Mānoa.

Kim, Elaine
1989   "War Story," in Asian Women United of California, editor. *Making Waves. An Anthology of Writings by and About Asian American Women*. Boston: Beacon Press, pp. 80–92.

Kim, Hyung-chan (Kim Hyŏng-ch'an) and Wayne Patterson, editors and compilers
1974   *The Koreans in America. 1882–1974. A Chronology & Fact Book*. New York: Oceania Publications, Inc.

Kim, Janice C.H.
1998   "Processes of Feminine Power: Shamans in Central Korea," in Keith Howard, editor. *Korean Shamanism. Revivals, Survivals, and Change*. Korea: Royal Asiatic Society, Korea Branch, pp. 114–122.

Kim, Jong-myung (Kim Chong-myŏng)
1995   "Buddhist Rituals in the Koryo Dynasty (918–1392)—Focusing on the P'algwanhoe, Yondunghoe, and Inwanghoe," in *A Collection of Theses on Korean Studies*. Seoul: Korea Foundation, pp. 233–279.

Kim, Joungwon (Kim Chŏng-wŏn), editor
1997   *Korean Cultural Heritage. Volume III. Performing Arts*. Seoul: Korea Foundation.

Kim, Kwang-ok
1997   "The Role of *Madanggŭk* in Contemporary Korea's Popular Culture Movement," *Korea Journal*, Vol. 37, no. 3 (Autumn), pp. 5–21.

Kim, Kyoung-ae (Kim Kyŏng-ae)
1997   "Dance Since 1945," in Joungwon Kim, editor. *Korean Cultural Heritage. Volume III. Performing Arts*. Seoul: Korea Foundation, pp. 178–185.
1998   "To Join with the World of Dance," *DanceForum*, Vol. 1, no. 1 (Winter), p. 4.

Kim, Kyunghee (Kim Kyŏng-hŭi)
1993   "The Status of Dance in Korean Higher Education." Ph.D. dissertation, Texas Woman's University.

Kim, Moon-hwan (Kim Mun-hwan)
1996   "Koreans Abroad and the New Generation," *Koreana*, Vol. 10, no. 3 (Autumn), pp. 80–82.

Kim, Nora Okja
1997   *Comfort Woman*. New York: Viking.
1998   Panel presentation at University of Hawai'i Center for Korean Studies and Korean American History Society of Hawai'i workshop, Korean American Writers in Hawai'i: Their Stories, January 24.

Kim, Seong-kon (Kim Sŏng-gon)
1991   "On Native Grounds: Revolution and Renaissance in Art and Culture," in Chong-Sik Lee, editor. *Korea Briefing, 1990*, Boulder: Westview Press, pp. 97–117.

Kim, T'ae-gŏn
1972   "Components of Korean Shamanism," *Korea Journal*, Vol. 12, no. 12 (December), pp. 17–25.

Kim, T'ae-wŏn

1992   "Han'guk ch'angjak ch'umŭi michŏk t'ŭksŏnggwa hyŏn tan'ge"
(The Aesthetic Characteristics and Present Status of *Ch'angjak Ch'um*), *Chum*, December, pp. 62–71.

1997   "III. 1981–1997: The Rapid Growth of Creative Activity and the Appearance of New Dance Genres and Generations," in Yang, Hye-suk, editor. *Korean Performing Arts. Drama, Dance & Music Theater.* Korean Studies Series no. 6. Seoul: Jipmoondang Publishing Company, pp. 123–152.

Kim, Warren Y.

1971   *Koreans in America.* Seoul: Po Chin Chai.

Kim, Yersu (Kim Yŏl-su)

1976   *Cultural Policy in the Republic of Korea.* France: UNESCO.

Kim, Youngna (Kim Yŏng-na)

2000   "Korean Arts and Culture at the End of the Twentieth Century," in Kongdan Oh (Kong-dan O), editor. *Korea Briefing 1997–1999. Challenges and Change at the Turn of the Century.* New York: M.E. Sharpe, in cooperation with the Asia Society, pp. 101–122.

Kim, Yung-chung, editor and translator

1982   *Women of Korea. A History from Ancient Times to 1945.* (An abridged and translated edition of *Han'guk yŏsŏng-sa*, written under the direction of the Committee for the compilation of the History of Korean Women.) Seoul: Ewha Womans University Press.

Kim, Yung-hee (Kim Yŏng-hŭi)

1994   "Women's Issues in 1920s Korea," *Korean Culture.* Vol. 15, no. 2, pp. 26–33.

Koh, Hesung Chun

1987   "Womens' Roles and Achievements in the Yi Dynasty," in *Korean Women in Transition. At Home and Abroad.* Eui-Young Yu and Earl H. Phillips, editors. California: Center for Korean-American and Korean Studies, California State University, Los Angeles, pp. 29–45.

Kolodin, Irving (I.K.)

1938   "Sai Shoki Dances. Korean Artist reappears in Guild Theatre," *The Sun* (New York). November 7, p. 39.

1939   "Ballet Caravan Gives Loring Work. Sai Shoki Also Dances at St. James," *The Sun* (New York). December 29, p. 9.

Korea Annual 1990

1990   Seoul: Yonhap News Agency, p. 280

Korea Annual 1991

1991   Seoul: Yonhap News Agency, p. 296.

Korean National Commission for UNESCO

1975   *Traditional Performing Arts of Korea.* Seoul, Korea: Korean National Commission for UNESCO.

1983   *Korean Dance, Theatre, and Cinema.* Korea: Si-sa-yong-o-sa and Oregon: Pace International Research.

Kozo, Yamaji (translated by Frank Hoff)

1983   "Early Kabuki Dance," in Betty True Jones, editor. *Dance as Cul-*

tural Heritage. Volume One. Dance Research Annual XIV. New York: Congress on Research in Dance, pp. 105–112.

Kriegsman, Sali Ann
1981   *Modern Dance in America. The Bennington Years.* Massachusetts: G.K. Hall, 1981.

Ku, Hee-seo (Ku Hŭi-sŏ)
1997   "Masters of Traditional Dance, in Joungwon Kim, editor. *Korean Cultural Heritage. Volume III. Performing Arts.* Seoul: Korea Foundation, pp. 156–169.

Lanes, Doreen A.
1979   "The History of the Ninety Second Street YM-YWHA: 1934–1954," in Rowe, Patricia A. and Ernestine Stodelle, editors. *Dance Research Collage. A Variety of Subjects Embracing the Abstract and the Practical. Dance Research Annual X.* New York: Congress on Research in Dance, pp. 251–265.

Lee, Byong-won (Yi Pyŏng-wŏn)
1979   "Evolution of the Role and Status of Korean Professional Female Entertainers (*Kisaeng*)," *The World of Music*, Vol. XVI, no. 2, pp. 75–81.
1992   "Korea," in Stanley Sadie, editor. *The New Grove Dictionary of Music and Musicians*, Vol. 10. London: Macmillan Publishers, pp. 192–208.

Lee, Du-hyon (Yi Tu-hyŏn)
1968   "Korean Masks and Mask-Dance Dramas," *Korea Journal.* Vol. VIII, no. 3 (March), pp. 4–10.
1970   "Dramatic Arts," in *Korean Studies Today. Development and State of the Field.* Seoul: Institute of Asian Studies, Seoul National University, pp. 183–197.

Lee, Hye-ku (Yi Hye-gu)
1981   *Essays on Korean Traditional Music.* Translated and edited by Robert C. Provine. Seoul: Royal Asiatic Society.

Lee, Ki-baik (Yi Ki-baek)
1984   *A New History of Korea.* Translated by Edward W. Wagner with Edward J. Shultz. Seoul: Ilchokak Publishers.

Lee, Kwang-kyu (Yi Kwang-gyu)
1993   "Overseas Koreans in the Global Context," in Lee, Kwang-kyu and Walter H. Slate, editors. *Overseas Koreans in the Global Context.* Seoul: Association for Studies of Koreans Abroad. Seoul National University, pp. 7–34.

Lee, Peter
1974 (1964) *Poems from Korea. A Historical Anthology.* Honolulu: University Press of Hawai'i.

Lee, Peter H., editor
1969   *Lives of Eminent Korean Monks. The Haedong Kosung Chon.* Massachusetts: Harvard University Press.
1981   *Anthology of Korean Literature from Early Times to the Nineteenth Century.* Honolulu: University of Hawai'i Press.

Lee, Young Hee (Yi Yŏng-hŭi)

1994   "Women's Literature in the Traditional and Early Modern Periods," *Korean Culture*. Vol. 15, no. 2, pp. 14–25.

Livingston, Tamara E.

1999   "Music Revivals: Towards a General Theory," *Ethnomusicology*, Vol. 43, no. 1 (Winter), pp. 66–85.

Loken, Christine

1978   "Moving in the Korean Way: Movement Characteristics of the Korean People as Expressed in Their Dance," *Korea Journal*, Vol. 18, no. 2 (February), pp. 42–46.

Loken-Kim, Christine

1989   *Release from Bitterness: Korean Dancer as Korean Woman.* Michigan: University Microfilms International.

Loken-Kim, Christine and Juliette T. Crump

1993   "Qualitative Change in Performances of Two Generations of Korean Dancers," *Dance Research Journal*, Vol. 25, no. 2 (Fall), pp. 13–20.

Maliangkay, Roald

1997   Post to Korean Studies listserve <korean-studies@mailbase.ac.uk>, September 25.

Manning, Susan

1993   *Ecstasy and the Demon. Feminism and Nationalism in the Dance of Mary Wigman.* Berkeley: University of California Press.

Marsh, O. Gaylord

1937   Unpublished letter to American Consulate, Washington, D.C. February 23. (U.S. National Archives Document 123 M 351/452)

Martin, John

1938a   "Dances of Regions Far Apart Shown," *New York Times*. February 21, p. 14.

1938b   "Sai Shoki Is Seen in Korean Dances," *New York Times*, November 7, p. 6.

1939   "The Dance. The Holiday Festival," *New York Times*. December 29, p. 10.

McCarthy, Kathleen

1994   "*Kisaeng* and Poetry in the Koryo Period," *Korean Culture*. Vol. 15, no. 2, pp. 4–13.

Military Attaché Report

1942   "Japanese activities in Columbia," unpublished classified report, Military Intelligence Division. May 25. Declassified May 3, 1972. (U.S. National Archives Document 894.20221/49 PS/TL)

Nagura, Miwa

1996   "Cross-Cultural Differences in the Interpretation of Merce Cunningham's Choreography," in Gay Morris, editor. *Moving Words. Re-writing Dance*. London: Routledge, pp. 270–287.

Nemethy, Emery

1956   "Dancing Diplomat Halla Huhm," *Paradise of the Pacific*. Vol. 68, no. 2, p. 27.

Ness, Sally A.
1997   "Originality in the Postcolony: Choreographing the Neoethnic
            Body of Philippine Ballet," *Cultural Anthropology*, Vol. 12, no. 1
            (February), pp. 64–108.

Nishiguchi, Ann Kikuyo
1982   "Korean Dance in Hawaii: A Study of the Halla Pai Huhm Korean
            Dance Studio." M.A. thesis, University of California, Los Angeles.

Ogawa, Masataka
1968   *The Enduring Crafts of Japan. 33 Living National Treasures.* New
            York: Walker/Weatherhill.

Ohtani, Kimiko
1991   "Japanese Approaches to the Study of Dance," *1991 Yearbook for
            Traditional Music.* Vol. 23, pp. 23–32.

Park, Jeong-hye (Pak Chŏng-hye)
1997   "The Court Music and Dance in the Royal Banquet Paintings of
            the Chosŏn Dynasty," *Korea Journal.* Vol. 37, no. 3 (Autumn), pp.
            123–144.

Partsch-Bergsohn, Isa
1994   *Modern Dance in Germany and the United States: Cross Currents
            and Influences.* Philadelphia: Harwood Academic Publishers.

Pihl, Marshall
1991   "*P'ansori* Origins Within Shaman Culture," *Newsletter of the
            International Cultural Society of Korea*, Vol. II, no. 1 (March),
            pp. 2–5.

Pratt, Keith
1987   *Korean Music. Its History and Its Performance.* London: Faber
            Music Ltd.

Pronko, Leonard C.
1985   "*Shin Buyō* and *Sōsaku Buyō*: Tradition and Change in Japanese
            Dance," in *Dance as Cultural Heritage, Volume Two: Selected
            Papers from the ADG-CORD Conference 1978.* Edited by Betty
            True Jones. New York: CORD, pp. 111–121.

Provine, Robert C.
1983   "'Chinese' Ritual Music in Korea: The Origins, Codification, and
            Cultural Role of A-ak," in Korean National Commission for
            UNESCO, editor. *Traditional Korean Music.* Korea: Si-sa-yong-
            o-sa Publishers, Inc., pp. 60–79.
1988   *Essays on Sino-Korean Musicology. Early Sources for Korean Rit-
            ual Music.* Seoul: Il Ji Sa.

Raher, David
1986   "Dance in Korea: Contemporary Forms Getting Recognition,"
            Korean Culture, June, pp. 15–25.

Rappaport, Roy A.
1989   "Ritual," in Erik Barnouw et al., editors. *International Encyclope-
            dia of Communications.* New York: Oxford University Press. Vol.
            3, pp. 467–473.

R.C.B.

1938   "Korean Dances Given at Guild Theater," *New York World-Telegram*. March 7, p. 27.

Rhie, Sang-il (Yi Sang-il; see also Yi Sang-il)

1975   "Dramatic Aspect of Shamanistic Rituals," *Korea Journal*. Vol. 15, no. 7 (July), pp. 23–28.

Rialtan

1940   "Sai Shoki Charms Dance Fans," *Los Angeles Evening Herald and Express*. April 1, p. A-11.

Riddle, Ronald

1985   "Korean Musical Culture in Los Angeles," *Ethnomusicology*. Vol. VII, pp. 189–196.

Robertson, Michael

1979   *The Origins and Development of Korean Nationalist Ideology, 1920–1926: Culture, Identity, National Development and Political Schism*. Ph.D. dissertation, University of Washington.

Rutt, Richard.

1961   "The Flower Boys of Silla (Hwarang). Notes on the Sources," *Transactions of the Korea Branch of the Royal Asiatic Society*, Vol. XXXVIII (October), pp. 1–66.

1964   *Korean Works and Days*. Korea: Korea Branch, Royal Asiatic Society.

Sabin, Robert.

1940   "Holiday Festival Brings New Dancers and Works," *Musical America*. January 10, p. 16.

Sanborn, Pitts

1938   "Hawaii and Korea on Dance Programs," section in "Toscanini Program and 'Faust' in Week-end Music," *New York World-Telegram*. February 21, p. 11.

Sawatake, Mune Y.

1936   "Japanese Dance," *The Dancing Times* (London). (August), pp. 492–494.

Schechner, Richard

1981   "Performers and Spectators Transported and Transformed," *The Kenyon Review. New Series*. No. 4 (Fall), pp. 83–113.

1993   *The Future of Ritual: Writings on Culture and Performance*. London and New York: Routledge

Schieffelin, Edward L.

1985   "Performance and the Cultural Construction of Reality," *American Ethnologist*. Vol. 12, no. 4 (November), pp. 707–724.

Schlundt, Christena L.

1962   *The Professional Appearances of Ruth St. Denis and Ted Shawn. A Chronology and an Index of Dances 1906–1932*. New York: New York Public Library.

Seebass, Tilman

1991   "Iconography and Dance Research," *Yearbook for Traditional Music*, Vol. XXIII, pp. 33–51.

Shawn, Ted, with Gray Poole
1960   *One Thousand and One Night Stands*. New York: Doubleday and
             Company.

Sherman, Jane
1976   *Soaring. The Diary and Letters of a Denishawn Dancer in the Far
             East 1925–1926*. Connecticut: Wesleyan University Press.
1979   "Denishawn Oriental Dances," *Dance Scope*. Vol. 13, nos. 2 and
             3, pp. 33–43.
2000   *Denishawn Dances On! A Guide to the Videotaped Program of
             Selected Choreography by Ruth St. Denis and Ted Shawn*. New
             Jersey: Five Corners Publications.

Smith, Barbara B.
1988   "Music in Hawai'i in Historical Perspective with Special Refer-
             ence to Contacts with Korea, Korean Music and Dance, and Ko-
             rean Scholars and Performers," in *Korean Studies. Its Tasks &
             Perspectives. Papers of the 5th International Conference on Ko-
             rean Studies. II*. Seoul: Academy of Korean Studies, pp. 133–146.

Smith, Cecil
1940   "Sai Shoki Has a Light Touch for Her Dances," *Chicago Tribune*.
             February 23, p. 20.

Smith, Robert J.
1993   "Transmitting Tradition by the Rules: An Anthropological Inter-
             pretation of the *iemoto* System," in *Fenway Court* (periodical
             publication of the Isabella Stewart Gardner Museum, Boston,
             Massachusetts). 1992 volume, pp. 37–45.

Sohn, Ho-min (Son Ho-min)
1993   "Features of the Korean Language," in *A Festival of Korea: Hu-
             manities Guide*. Hawai'i: University of Hawai'i at Mānoa Summer
             Session, p. 11.

Song, Bang-song (Song Pang-song)
1974   "Korean Kwangdae Musicians and Their Musical Traditions,"
             Korea Journal. Vol. 14, no. 9 (September), pp. 12–18.
1997   "I. Ancient—1945: A Short History of Korean Traditional Music,"
             in Yang, Hye-suk, editor. *Korean Performing Arts. Drama, Dance
             & Music Theater*. Korean Studies Series No. 6. Seoul: Jipmoon-
             dang Publishing Company, pp. 156–189.

Song, Kyong-rin (Sŏng Kyŏng-nin)
1963   "Korean Classic Dance," *Korea Journal*. Vol. III, no. 2 (February),
             pp. 6–10.

Sorensen, Clark
1988   "The Myth of Princess Pari and the Self Image of Korean Women,"
             Anthropos, no. 83, pp. 403–419.
1989   "Introduction," *Journal of Ritual Studies*. Vol. 3, No. 2 (Summer),
             pp. 155–165.
1995   "Folk Religion and Political Commitment in South Korea in the
             1980s," in Sabrina Petra Ramet and Donald W. Treadgold, edi-
             tors. *Render Unto Caesar. The Religious Sphere in World Politics*.
             Washington, D.C.: The American University Press, pp. 325–353.

Sutton, R. Anderson
1983   "Okinawan Music Overseas: A Hawaiian Home," *Asian Music*.
             Vol. XV-1, pp. 54–80.

1987   "Korean Music in Hawaii," *Asian Music*, Vol. XIX, No. 1 (Fall/
                Winter), pp. 99–121.

Swisher, Viola Hegyi
1938   "Korea Dance Star Lauded," *Hollywood Citizen News*, February 3.
1940   "Korea Dance Program Applauded," *Hollywood Citizen News*.
                April 1, p. 4.

Takashima, Yusaburo
1959   *Sai Shoki*. Japan: Sekai Gakuhu Shoin.
1982   "Sai Shoki and Me," *Sanzenri*. No. 30 (May 1), pp. 118–124.

Takashima, Yusaburo and Chŏng Pyŏng-ho, authors and editors
1994   *Seiki no bijin buyōka Sai Shoki* (One of the Most Beautiful Danc-
                ers of the Century, Sai Shoki). Japan: MT Publishing Company.

Terry, Walter
1939   "Bach Variations Are Danced by Ballet Caravan," *New York Her-
                ald Tribune*, December 29, p. 9.

Thornbury, Barbara E.
1997   *The Folk Performing Arts. Traditional Culture in Contemporary
                Japan*. New York: State University of New York Press.

Tomoaki, Fujii
1996   "The Significance of Conserving Intangible Cultural Properties
                and Intangible Folk-Cultural Properties and the Transition of the
                Japanese Government's Protection Policies," in Korean National
                Commission for UNESCO. *Methodologies for the Preservation of
                Intangible Heritage*. Korea: Korean National Commission for
                UNESCO and the Office of the Cultural Properties of the Republic
                of Korea, pp. 9–14.

Van Zile, Judy
1983   "Balasaraswati's 'Tisram Alarippu': A Choreographic Analysis,"
                in Wade, Bonnie C., editor. *Performing Arts in India. Essays of
                Music, Dance, and Drama*. Maryland: University Press of Amer-
                ica. (Monograph Series no. 21, Center for South and Southeast
                Asia Studies, University of California, Berkeley), pp. 47–104.
                (Reprinted in Vol. XVIII, no. 2 [Spring/Summer 1987] issue of
                Asian Music, pp. 45–102.)
1984   "How Much Does a Score Say?" in *Proceedings of the Thirteenth
                Biennial Conference 2–14 August 1983*. Ohio: International
                Council of Kinetography Laban, pp. 104–106.
1987a   "*Ch'oyongmu*: An Ancient Dance Survives," *Korean Culture* (Vol.
                8, no. 2, summer), pp. 4–19.
1987b   "How the Korean Government Preserves Its Cultural Heritage,"
                Korean Culture (vol. 8, no. 2, summer), pp. 18–19.
1991a   "Dance in Contemporary Korea," *Korea Journal*, Vol. 12, no. 3
                (Fall), pp. 10–21.
1991b   "Chinju's Dance Treasure," *Asiana*. Vol. 3, no. 10 (October), pp.
                8–14, 16–17.
1991c   "*Chinju Kommu*: An Implement Dance of Korea," *Studia Musico-
                logica Academiae Scientiarum Hungaricae*, vol. 33, nos. 1–4 , pp.
                359–366.
1992   "Korean Dance, an Introduction," *A Festival of Korea Humani-
                ties Guide*, University of Hawai'i, pp. 13, 18.

1993   "The Many Faces of Korean Dance," in Donald N. Clark, editor.
        Korea Briefing, 1993. Festival of Korea. Boulder: Westview Press
        in cooperation with the Asia Society, pp. 99–119.
1995   "From Ritual to Entertainment and Back Again: The Case of
        Ch'oyongmu, a Korean Dance," *Dance, Ritual and Music. Pro-
        ceedings of the 18th Symposium of the Study Group on Ethno-
        choreology, the International Council for Traditional Music.* War-
        saw, Poland: Polish Society for Ethnochoreology Institute of Art—
        Polish Academy of Sciences, pp. 133–140.
1996   "Non-Polynesian Dance in Hawai'i: Issues of Identity in a Multi-
        cultural Community," *Dance Research Journal,* Vol. 28, no. 1
        (Spring), pp. 28–50.

Venable, Lucy
1984   "Korean Project, The OSU Perspective," in *Proceedings of the
        Thirteenth Biennial Conference 2–14 August 1983.* Ohio: Interna-
        tional Council of Kinetography Laban, pp. 107–109.

Vitak, Albertina
1940a   "Sai Shoki, December 28," section in "Dance Events Reviewed,"
        The American Dancer. Vol. XIII, no. 4 (February), p. 17.
1940b   "Dance Events Reviewed," *The American Observer.* Vol. XIII, no.
        8 (June), pp. 20–21, 36, 38.

Wakamatsu, Miki
1995   "Some Scholarly Reflections on Dance in Japan," in Solomon,
        Ruth and John, editors. *East Meets West in Dance. Voices in the
        Cross-Cultural Dialogue.* Switzerland: Harwood Academic Pub-
        lishers, pp. 209–213.

Wentink, Andrew Mark
1977   " 'From the Orient . . . Oceans of Love, Doris': The Denishawn
        Tour of the Orient as seen through the Letters of Doris Hum-
        phrey," *Dance Chronicle.* Vol. 1, no. 1, pp. 22–45.

Yang, Jong-sung
1988   *Madangguk*: The Rejuvenation of Mask Dance Drama Festivals as
        Sources of Social Criticism. Unpublished M.A. thesis, Indiana Uni-
        versity (Folklore).
1994   Folklore and Cultural Politics in Korea: Intangible Cultural Prop-
        erties and Living National Treasures. Ph.D. dissertation, Indiana
        University (Folklore).

Yi, Sang-il (see also Rhie Sang-il)
1993   "Korean Dance: Finding Modern Status," *Koreana.* Vol. 7, no. 4,
        pp. 24–29.

Yi, Un-yong (Yi ŭn-yŏng)
1989   "Han'guk ch'um-e itsŏsŏ chŏnt'ong mit minjoksŏng ŭi munje"
        (The Problems of Tradition and Nationalism in Korean Dance),
        M.A. thesis, Ewha Woman's University.

Yim, Dawn-hee (Im Ton-hŭi) and Jang-hyuk Im (Im Chang-hyŏk)
1996   "Preservation and Transmission of Korean Intangible Cultural
        Properties (ICP)," in *Methodologies for the Preservation of Intan-
        gible Heritage.* Korean National Commission for UNESCO & the
        Office of the Cultural Properties of the Republic of Korea, pp.
        207–222.

Yŏ, Sŏk-ki

1997   "II. 1946–1970: Korean Drama," in Yang, Hye-suk, editor. *Korean Performing Arts. Drama, Dance & Music Theater.* Seoul: Jip-moondang Publishing Company, pp. 37–54.

Yu, Choi-shin (Yi Ch'oe-shin) and Richard W. I. Guisso

1988   *Shamanism. The Spirit World of Korea.* Berkeley, California: Asia Humanities Press.

Yu, Eui-young (Yu Ŭi-yŏng)

1981   "Koreans in America: Struggling for Cultural Adjustment," *Korean Culture*, Vol. 1, no. 4 (Winter), pp. 18–23.

1988   "Korean American Communities and Their Institutions: An Overview," *Korean Culture*, Vol. 9, no. 4 (Winter), pp. 33–45.

1993   "The Korean American Community," in Donald N. Clark, editor. *Korea Briefing, 1993. Festival of Korea.* Boulder: Westview Press, in cooperation with the Asia Society, pp. 139–162.

1994   "Ethnic Identity and Community Involvement of Younger-generation Korean Americans," in Dae-Sook Suh, editor, *Korean Studies: New Pacific Currents.* Honolulu: Pacific Association of Korean Studies, pp. 263–282.

Zong, In-sob (Chŏng, In-sŏp)

1956   "The Music and Dance of Korea," *Occasional Papers, Kansai Asiatic Society (Kyoto, Japan).* No. IV (November), pp. 27–56.

Numbers in bold italic refer to figures and plates.

About the Author

Judy Van Zile is Professor of Dance at the University of Hawaiʻi at Mānoa. She is author of *Dance in India: An Annotated Guide to Source Materials* (Asian Music Publications, 1973) and *The Japanese Bon Dance in Hawaiʻi* (Press Pacifica, 1982). Her essays have appeared in numerous books, including "Capturing the Dancing: Why and How?" in *Dance in the Field: Theory, Methods and Issues in Dance Ethnography*, edited by Theresa Buckland (London: Macmillan, 1999; New York: St. Martins Press, 1999). Her articles on dance have appeared in such journals as *Asian Music*, *Dance Research Journal*, and *Yearbook of Traditional Music*.